PENGUIN BOOKS

THE SUNDAY

Dr Philip Beresford
He was born in Egyp
career on *Engineering*
city desk of the *Sund*
Sunday Times Business News where he was, successively,
industry and transport correspondent and associate
editor. He lives in Ealing, loves trains, and is married to
a *Financial Times* correspondent.

THE SUNDAY TIMES
Book of the Rich

PHILIP BERESFORD

PENGUIN BOOKS

PENGUIN BOOKS

Published by the Penguin Group
27 Wrights Lane, London W8 5TZ, England
Penguin Books USA Inc., 375 Hudson Street, New York, New York 10014, USA
Penguin Books Australia Ltd, Ringwood, Victoria, Australia
Penguin Books Canada Ltd, 10 Alcorn Avenue, Toronto, Ontario, Canada M4V 3B2
Penguin Books (NZ) Ltd, 182–190 Wairau Road, Auckland 10, New Zealand
Penguin Books Ltd, Registered Offices: Harmondsworth, Middlesex, England

First published by Weidenfeld and Nicolson 1990
Published in Penguin Books 1991
1 3 5 7 9 10 8 6 4 2

Copyright © Philip Beresford, 1990
All rights reserved

The moral right of the author has been asserted

Filmset in Monophoto Times New Roman
Printed in England by Clays Ltd, St Ives plc

Except in the United States of America, this book is sold subject to
the condition that it shall not, by way of trade or otherwise, be lent,
re-sold, hired out, or otherwise circulated without the publisher's
prior consent in any form of binding or cover other than that in
which it is published and without a similar condition including this
condition being imposed on the subsequent purchaser

Contents

Acknowledgements

This book would not have been possible without the support of all my colleagues at the *Sunday Times* who have suggested names to me and helped with facts and figures. I should also like to express my appreciation of the time I was given free from the trials of journalism to concentrate on this project by Andrew Neil, the *Sunday Times* editor. Ivan Fallon, the deputy editor, inspired me to look into wealth in Britain many years ago when he was City editor on the *Sunday Telegraph*. His encouragement over the years has been crucial. Roger Eglin, the editor of the *Sunday Times* business section, was particularly kind and patient during my long absence from the ranks. Steve Boyd at the *Sunday Times* magazine has been a wonderful inspiration, editing the two issues of the magazine devoted to the rich in 1989 and 1990.

A special word of thanks to Eugene Weber and his staff at the Press Association Library, and to Brian Arrowsmith and the staff at the News International Library, who never lost their sense of humour no matter how late the hour or how difficult the request.

I have also had invaluable support from Kevin Cahill and Paddy Masters, who have toiled for many hours on my behalf, often well into the night, searching for a fact or checking entries. I cannot express my appreciation for their efforts too highly. My thanks to Kay Cahill, who did the indexing and checked the arithmetic.

Of course, nothing would have been accomplished without the encouragement of Della, to whom I dedicate the book.

Picture acknowledgements

The publishers wish to thank the following for their help and for the use of photographs:

Camera Press
Press Association
Pressens Bild, Stockholm
Sun
Times Newspapers Ltd

Picture research by Deborah Keeping

Introduction: Britain's Richest 400

IVAN FALLON, deputy editor, the *Sunday Times*

PAUL Getty used to say, 'No one is really rich if he can count his money.' In Getty's day, anyone with £1 million (or even $1 million) rated as 'rich' and anyone with more than £5 million was 'very rich'. Above *that* and you were in the 'super-rich' category, and when you got above the £50 million level, you rated as a 'can't count'. Nelson Bunker Hunt, who with his brother inherited a fortune even greater than Getty's, was a 'can't count' man before he tried to corner the silver market. Asked by a Senate committee how much he was worth, he snapped, 'Hell, if I knew that, I wouldn't be worth very much.'

In the United States for many years *Forbes Magazine* and *Fortune*, among others, have published lists of the very wealthy which have been eagerly awaited events in a society where wealth is a macho symbol, to be boasted about rather than hidden. In Britain, however, wealth is something best not talked about, and it has never been easy to establish authoritatively just who owns what, and what they are worth.

In 1989 the *Sunday Times* broke with tradition by publishing the first real guide to Britain's wealthy, causing a considerable amount of unease among those who hated being on it, but remarkably few criticisms of our calculations. In 1990 we repeated the exercise, adding a further 70 names to the list and raising the minimum stake to £50 million. Both the 1989 and 1990 lists occupied most of one entire colour magazine, well-thumbed copies of which have become collectors' items. In 1991, when the minimum figure was still £50 million, a further 44 new names were added. The list took up the entire magazine. The lists have since been widely discussed and copied by the rest of Fleet Street. They have also been used as ammunition by both sides of the Old Britain versus New Britain debate, quoted on the one hand to show how even in the Thatcher years old money has reinforced its power, and on the other hand to record the rise and rise of the new rich at the expense of the old.

Much work has gone into updating and refining the list, which in this book runs to 400 people and families who are worth between them £53.2 billion, over 42% of it concentrated into the hands of the top ten. These 400 own 4.4 million acres of land, nearly 10% of the total land area of the United Kingdom and equivalent in size to 6 average counties.

The list includes 1 sovereign, 13 dukes (out of 24), 21 earls and 2 countesses (out of 156), 12 viscounts (out of 27), 26 lords, 8 marquesses and 1 baroness. There are 103 aristocrats in the 400, just over a quarter of our total. We also have 27 knights, but some of them represent the wealth of the New Britain. The total number of inheritors is 207, most of whom have added to their wealth, which accounts for 50% of the total.

The public schools are well represented. There are 79 Old Etonians, 12 Harrovians and 3 Wykehamists. And if you want to know how clubbable the wealthy are, we have 42 members of White's, 29 members of the Turf or Jockey Club, 11 members of Boodles and 3 members of the Garrick.

When the *Sunday Times* published the first list in 1989, the paper commented editorially on its own study, mourning the fact that, after a decade of Thatcherism, old money still dominated and paternalism appeared to be making a comeback. Others of course took an entirely different view of the list, expressing astonishment at the amount of new money, at the relative *decline* of old wealth, and the degree of egalitarianism which had crept in. It started a debate which still goes on, and will be further fuelled by the extra material in this book, which contains twice the number of names published in the newspaper.

Some who were on the 1989 list took pleasure from it, one for instance phoning from the Bahamas to announce himself to a competitor: 'This is number 48 ringing 64.' Others wrote or rang to request they be removed because their presence in such a list made their previously anonymous lives uncomfortable. Others still (not many, it should be admitted) rang to wonder why they had been excluded, and sent personal balance sheets to prove their worthiness. There were those who regarded the list as a significant contribution to understanding Britain's changing (or unchanging, depending on your point of view) social order; others who felt it was a gross invasion of privacy that the *Sunday Times* should reveal details which only account-ants and taxmen (and preferably not even the latter) should know about.

However the list itself is interpreted, there is a consensus view, even among some of the wealthy themselves, that accurate and detailed information on Britain's very wealthy is much overdue. There is a positive correlation between great wealth and influence, and therefore a need to know who actually owns Britain, on the grounds that it may tell us something more about who really runs it. The list in this book is a contribution to the discussion, raw material for the social economists who will find in it a wealth of information to make of what they will.

We can however give them some nudges. In the year between compiling our first list and this book there were events which confirmed the relative fragility of the new wealth and the stab-ility of the old. Most of the new money has been made through owning shareholdings in companies quoted on a booming stock market. 1989 was another excellent year for stock markets, which around the world rose an average of 96% from the bottom of the crash of October 1987 to their peak in January 1990, yet in that time there were spectacular dips in our table. Arundbhai Patel, millionaire newsagent in early 1989, and in 116th place with a fortune of £50 million, put his company into liquidation. Sophie Mirman, founder of Sock Shop and one of the brightest of the new generation of female entrepreneurs, also lost much of her fortune. Asil Nadir, the most spectacular casualty in 1990, saw his £213 million fortune vanish in a matter of days. Alan Sugar, the man behind the extraordinary rise of Amstrad in the mid-1980s, saw his wealth decline in a single year by £314 million, or £1 million a day. By contrast, the Earl of Cadogan, roughly equal to Sugar in 1989, was still, a year later, worth £400 million. As Sophie Tucker might say, 'I've been rich and I've been poor; rich is better.'

The list of 400 features only 23 women, including the Queen – worth £7.4 billion between them. There are also 2 MPs, Michael Heseltine and Bill Benyon; we could probably have included Peter Walker. In the list as a whole we have identified 215 who have declared a political allegiance, of which 206 are Tory: we have 2 declared Labour supporters (Robert Maxwell and Paul

Hamlyn), and 7 Liberals. These political allegiances are of course not fixed; the rich are probably as fickle as anyone else in their voting intentions, although it would be no surprise to anyone to find a strong Tory bias. But it is no secret that Tiny Rowland, for instance, is actively opposed to Mrs Thatcher, or that David Sainsbury, the richest of the grocery family, has backed David Owen. Not everyone would agree with Voltaire's dictum that 'when it is a question of money, everybody is of the same religion'.

'What have you changed?' Mrs Thatcher was asked in 1979 when she became prime minister. 'I have changed everything,' she replied. By that she meant that, 100 years after Disraeli talked about Britain's Two Nations, she was reversing a century of decline by reviving the enterprise spirit. At the Tory Party conference in October 1985 Norman Fowler, the social services secretary, drew cheers when he reaffirmed, 'We could take no pride in the rebuilding of a prosperity that remained the privilege of the few.' A few months later, the Archbishop of Canterbury's Commission *Faith in the City* report pronounced, to Thatcher's fury, that rich and poor, privileged and deprived, 'have become more sharply separate from each other'. This table shows only the top end of that gap, and to support or disprove the commission's report one would have to take it much deeper down the wealth ladder; but it does leave an impression that despite the new arrivals on the list, nothing much *has* changed this past decade. Eleven years after Mrs Thatcher entered Downing Street, Peter Morgan, the head of the Institute of Directors, could get a standing ovation at a packed gathering in the Albert Hall with precisely that message. 'It is obvious that responsibility for the 100 years of decline of UK plc must be laid at the door of the Establishment.' Like all his generation at school, Morgan had learned of how Britain had once been the 'workshop of the world . . . cotton, coal and iron, canals and railways . . . and the heroes, Arkwright and Watt, Stephenson and Brunel', their legacy all now gone, killed, he said, by 'intellectual opposition from an establishment that espouses a different culture'. One view of this list is that the same Establishment is still guiding the affairs of the nation, more entrenched and richer than ever.

It contains very few families one might associate with the Victorian and Edwardian might of Britain, or even of the industrial companies which came later; we have a single Lever, Lord Leverhulme, but not Geddes or Slazenger (of Dunlop), no Armstrongs, Siddeleys, Sopwiths, de Havillands, Fergusons, Lyons, Morrises or Rootes; none of the great shipbuilding families who controlled Vickers, John Browns, Cammells, Lairds, Thorneycrofts, Vospers, Yarrows, Swans or Hunters. No Colvilles, Redmans, Dormans or Longs; no Courtaulds, Carringtons, Coats, Patons or Baldwins; no Hepworths or Wedgwoods. Gone, too, from the ranks of the very wealthy are the big shipping families, the Cunards, Ellermans, Andersons, Greens and Mackenzies, although we do still have the Inchcapes (Mackays) and Cayzers, neither of them now in shipping. The Swires and the Keswicks, who made their money in Hong Kong, still thrive, but the only old industrial family on our list is the Pilkingtons.

The nearest we have to a new self-made industrialist of the old school is Lord Weinstock, son of a Jewish tailor who arrived from Poland in 1906. Evan Cornish, whose packaging company is worth £97 million, also possibly qualifies as an industrialist, but scarcely of the kind that once made Britain great.

Yet for those who prefer a more mobile social order, and welcome the injection of the new rich, there is hope too. Britain has more millionaires – 20,000 at the latest count in comparison with over a million in the US – than it has aristocrats, and 193 of the 400 started with nothing (or next to nothing) to build their fortunes in a single generation. There are even 22 Asian immigrants, several of them among the Ugandans so abruptly rejected by Idi Amin. There is a considerable smattering of other immigrants too, some of whom came to Britain as children: Robert Maxwell (born poor in Czechoslovakia), Sir James Goldsmith (born rich in Paris), Tiny Rowland (born in a British internment camp in India of a German father), Lord Forte (born poor in Italy), the Saatchis (born well-off in Baghdad), Sir Mark Weinberg (born in South Africa), and Sir David Alliance (born in Iran). Some of the billionaires were also born abroad; John Paul Getty II, the Goulandris family and the Swedish Rausing brothers. Many others are second-generation British:

who for instance knew that the Wham! pop star George Michael (worth £65 million) is the son of Jack Panayiotou, a millionaire restaurant owner who arrived in London penniless from Greece?

The list therefore, despite the fixtures of the landed aristocrats, reveals a considerable amount of movement and something which has probably been true of Britain for centuries: a continual state of renewal, with some of the new rich adding titles and land and becoming the Establishment several generations on, but a high proportion of them losing their fortunes before they have had time to consolidate them. By a curious trick of statistics, the balance in the top 200 is an almost equal one between establishment and self-made money: 102 Old Rich play 98 New Rich.

This is however at the end of a period which has almost uniquely – at least this century – favoured the new. A financial crash on a mid-1970s scale would almost certainly shift the balance back. It is all too easily forgotten that some of the most successful New Rich were almost wiped out 15 years ago; Jimmy Goldsmith, Robert Maxwell, Gerald Ronson and many others had a huge struggle through the property and fringe banking crisis. The Beckwith brothers, in the list at £60 million, once had losses of £1.5 million. The Old Rich on the other hand came through it all relatively undented, having had generations to learn to cope with adversity.

We do not pretend the list is either complete or perfect: it cannot be when works of art, and even land and property, are so difficult to value accurately even by full-time experts with access to all the details of the assets they are selling. Many of Britain's richest families have no idea of their true wealth, and there is no reason why they should have. Even five years ago, works of art were still regarded as ancillary furnishings, worth something certainly, but not enough to qualify as real wealth. Now impressionist paintings sell for tens of millions of dollars, and a good collection of modern art, such as that built up by Charles and Doris Saatchi, can be worth far more. Even vintage cars, until recently an eccentric rich man's hobby, now represent serious money.

*

Putting a value on the wealth of the Royal family is not only difficult but to some extent pointless: there are art treasures and jewels in the Queen's collection which are priceless and will never be sold. Queen Elizabeth II is the 63rd monarch in a line going back 1,000 years, each one of whom has added to the collection. By contrast, for instance, the Saudi Royal family – which features ahead of her in the international *Fortune* list – has not ruled even for a century. In 1971 the Royal Chamberlain told a parliamentary committee set up to look into her finances that Her Majesty was concerned by 'the astronomical figures bandied about in some quarters' suggesting that the value of her personal fortune 'may now run into £50m to £100m or more'. The Queen assured the committee that these estimates were 'wildly exaggerated' – the royal collections, she pointed out, were not at her private disposal. She has not, as far as we are aware, objected to the far higher estimates which have lately been put on her wealth. It should however be remembered that when Edward VIII abdicated, he was able to take only a modest fortune and worried about money for the rest of his life. The Queen cannot take it with her, not even if she were to retire abroad.

Nevertheless, because she pays no tax, the Queen's fortune accumulates faster than a private individual's in the same circumstances. On *Fortune*'s list she ranks fourth, well ahead of the Sultan of Brunei.

This list is essentially the work of Philip Beresford, formerly Associate Business Editor of the *Sunday Times* and now editor of *Management Today*, who has spent much of the last decade compiling information on Britain's wealth, and now has on his computer files more information on the subject than anyone in the land, probably including the Inland Revenue. He has been assisted by Patrick Masters, who has combed through hundreds of unpublished accounts in Companies House, checking and cross-checking details. They have been backed up by a team of researchers led by Kevin Cahill, who has managed a network of *Sunday Times* local correspondents to provide details of land-owners and private millionaires, which have then been checked with estate agents, chartered surveyors and, in the case of works of art, with the leading auction houses. The list is as accurate as we can make it, although it will obviously soon be out of date as stock market conditions change and as individual company fortunes wax and wane.

Lady Astor said that 'the only thing I like about rich people is their money'. On this list there are people of all sorts, some nice, some not so nice, some mean, some generous – in fact probably a typical cross-section of the population, except that they all have a great deal of money. Does that by itself make them different? As Oscar Wilde might say: 'When I was young I thought that money was the most important thing in life; now that I am old I know it is.'

The Rules of Engagement

1. The book is based on our estimates of the minimum wealth of the 400 richest people or families in Britain. The actual size of their fortunes could well be – and probably is – much bigger than the figure we have given.

2. We measure identifiable wealth, whether land, property, race-horses, art treasures or significant shares in publicly quoted companies. We do not include cash in the bank (we have no access to such records) or small shareholdings in a private equity portfolio.

3. Many of the people on our list – particularly the landowners – could rightly claim that their wealth does not provide them with large amounts to spend; it is tied up in the land. They cannot easily dispose of it; there may be legal or tax problems; and, indeed, they are loath to do so. Their families have not remained rich over the centuries by squandering their holdings. We also regard those landowners whose lands and art treasures have been put into family trusts for tax purposes as the owners of those assets. They may not be able to sell them, but they enjoy the use of the assets for their life and can pass them on to their heirs.

4. Similarly, many business people with large shareholdings in their own companies are unwilling to sell to raise cash. By doing so, they could lose control or the sale could be interpreted as a sign of trouble which would lower the share price. Paper fortunes based on shares can also disappear quickly if a company runs into problems. The most notable casualty in 1990 was Asil Nadir, Polly Peck's former chairman.

5. Where an individual or family has sold the stake in a company (whether through an agreed or forced takeover) we have made an estimate of the likely tax bill they will have faced and adjusted their wealth accordingly. If they have gone into tax exile, the tax bill will be much less and we have taken that into account. We have also assumed that people who make such large capital gains are also astute investors with their cash. We assume that after the tax has been paid, the recipient is able to make it grow by 10% a year, which is a very conservative figure given the stock market performance of the last decade and profits to be made from being a member of a Lloyd's underwriting syndicate.

6. We have stuck to some broad rules:
- All share stakes in publicly quoted companies are valued at the price quoted in the *Financial Times* on 2 January 1991, which corresponds with last year's date.
- Private companies (and therefore share stakes in them) are valued on their latest post-tax profit figures multiplied by the prevailing price/earnings rations in their respective sectors as published in the *Financial Times* on 31 December 1990:

Construction	7.90
Electronics	12.63
Engineering	7.54
Brewing	12.03
Food Manufacturing	11.02
Food Retailing	13.23
Hotels	9.87
Media	12.04
Packaging	10.35
Stores	11.98
Textiles	9.50
Chemicals	9.01
Oil and Gas	10.70
Insurance Brokers	24.32
Merchants Banks	18.54
Property	11.64

If a private company does not fit one of these categories, we have valued it at a multiple of 10 on its post-tax profits.
- Family shareholdings are agglomerated where it is obvious that the family acts together to defend the company's interests,

in terms of what the Stock Exchange calls a 'concert party'. We usually name and picture the leading member of the family to represent the whole family interests, though in one or two cases, where there are very low-profile families, we have not highlighted a member of the family but just called the entry the Thomson or Clark family, for example.

7. Family trusts are also aggregated and included in our total.

8. Land is valued on what and where it is. Most valuable is London land with planning permission, then other urban land, then good farming, forestry, poor farming and finally desolate land. We took account of valuable shooting and fishing rights. We spoke to local agents and to four of Britain's major chartered surveyors/land managers, who did not want to be identified. They gave us their estimates of land values per acre for agricultural land. They differ considerably for various regions. As a result, land values per acre range from:

Scottish Highlands	Poor – up to £300 (Last year £300)
	Good – up to £1,200 (£1,000)
Scottish Lowlands	Poor – up to £300 (£600)
	Good – up to £1,500 (£2,000)
North of England	Poor – £800–£1,200 (£1,600)
	Good – £1,600–£3,000 (£2,000)
Wales	Poor – up to £100 (£200)
	Good – up to £1,200 (£1,700)
West Midlands	Poor – up to £1,000 (£1,400)
	Good – up to £1,600 (£3,200)
East Midlands	Poor – up to £1,000 (£1,600)
	Good – up to £1,800 (£3,125)
East Anglia	Poor – up to £500 (£1,500)
	Good – up to £1,000 (£4,000)
South-East	Poor – up to £800 (£1,500)
	Good – up to £1,600 (£2,200)
South-West	Poor – up to £800 (£750)
	Good – up to £1,400 (£2,750)

The current agricultural land prices series produced by the Agricultural Mortgage Corporation and MAFF had the following

average prices per acre for farms sold in 1990. We caution that
the market was falling from historically high prices and that
confidence has been severely dented by the uncertainty about
international trade as well as high interest rates.

Mainly dairy £3,201 (£3,401)
Mainly arable £2,270 (£2,335)
Mainly beef, sheep £2,124 (£2,390)
All commercial farms £2,171 (£2,445)
Mainly residential £1,282 (£4,635)
All farms sold £1,282 (£2,695)

9. Fishing and shooting rights: this market has been remarkably
resilient in 1990. There was little change from the 1989 prices
for rivers of around £10,000 for each salmon caught, and about
£150 a yard for good trout water. The very high prices obtained
in Scotland, up to £18,000 per salmon caught in one case, did
not hold, but such prices were exceptional. Grouse shooting
actually exceeded 1989's prices of £1,500 per brace shot, but
this part of the market is proving vulnerable to an influx of
cheap shooting in Eastern Europe. The reason for the resilience
of the market is simple: scarcity. Very little good water, or
shooting, came on the market, and a sample of how prices held
firm was shown by the £6 million price-tag on the 850-acre
Longparish Estate in Hants, and the £5.5 million price on the
1,200-acre Watergate Estate in Sussex at the end of 1990.

10. The 400 include people who may not be British citizens,
such as the Rausing brothers from Sweden. But in an increasingly cosmopolitan world they live and work in Britain, so they
are included. British citizens abroad such as Sir James Goldsmith or Malcolm Healey are also included, but we have not
included Rupert Murdoch, proprietor of the *Sunday Times*, as
he is an American citizen and is based in America. *Forbes*
magazine last year estimated his wealth at $1.2 billion. By the
same token, we do not include Alfred Taubman, the American
billionaire, despite his owning 56% of that very British institution, Sotheby's, because he is based in America.

11. Reference sources we have used include newspapers, company annual reports, Extel's financial information, Datastream's City prices and information, McCarthy's press cutting cards, *Jordan's Top 10,000 Privately Owned Companies, Who's Who, Debrett's Distinguished People of Today, Who's Who in the City, Crawford's Directory of City Connections, The Directory of Directors, Acquisitions Monthly, Strategic Holdings for Takeovers, The Hambro Corporate Register, Vacher's Parliamentary Companion, Who's Really Who, Nigel Dempster's Address Book* and *Debrett's Peerage & Baronetage*. We have also used a large network of local correspondents and the libraries of News International and the Press Association, where the staff have been extremely helpful.

Faces of the Future

WEALTH is a constantly moving feast. As stock markets and the price of art treasures and land fluctuate quite sharply at times, so a list of rich people will vary accordingly.

A slump in retail sales in 1990, for example, hammered the fortunes of several well-known figures who had prospered for most of the 1980s, including Sir Bernard Ashley, head of the Laura Ashley group, and Sir Terence Conran, the Storehouse chairman. Fortunes have been won or lost when millionaires sell their firms or, in their quest for growth, over-extend themselves.

But there will always be new blood coming along, whether rising business stars, sportsmen and women at the peak of their careers, or pop and film stars.

Who are some of the people to look out for as potential candidates for the next edition of *The Sunday Times Book of the Rich*? Michael Buckley, chairman of SelecTV, a television production company, is tipped as a future multi-millionaire. With several television hits, a link with 20th Century Fox, and Robert Maxwell as a major shareholder, SelecTV could go the way of Michael Green's Carlton Communications. In January 1990, it was still a minnow, worth just £10 million on the stock market.

Martin Sorrell, the former finance director of the Saatchi & Saatchi advertising agency, left in May 1985 to buy a stake in a small Kent engineering company which he has turned into the world's largest advertising agency. His stake in WPP (which originally stood for Wire and Plastic Products) is now worth some £6 million. Though the advertising market is suffering a sharp downturn now, Sorrell's management skills and his ability to keep a tight control on costs should enable him to emerge unscathed and, indeed, in a stronger position.

Shami Ahmad, one of the newest Asian millionaires, has built a £20 million fashion chain in Manchester called 'Joe Bloggs'. His toughest decision today is whether to take his

£200,000 Ferrari Testarossa or the more mundane £100,000 Bentley Turbo to work.

Nigel Rudd, chairman of the Williams Holdings industrial group, is tipped to be the next Lord Hanson. Based in Derby, Rudd has already built Williams from a loss-making foundry business which he took over in 1982 to a £1 billion company seven years later. He is currently worth some £7.5 million.

Michael Slade, the chairman of the Helical Bar property group, made the headlines in 1987 when his pay shot up to over £1 million a year. Though it is back to a more modest £330,000 today, he owns some £12 million worth of the high-flying property group and a yacht in the Caribbean.

From the field of sports, Stephen Hendry, the young Scottish snooker star, looks set to join the multi-millionaire class. Hendry managed to take his prize money past £1 million in February 1990, when he was just 21. He is now the world champion.

1

THE BILLIONAIRES

£1,000m and more

The Queen   £7,000m as head of state
£1,000m personally

dob 21 April 1926

ONE of the richest women in the world, the Queen's wealth stems from three areas. There are the Crown Estates, which contain some 267,000 acres of land, including 350 valuable acres in central London. Virtually all the land round the coast of Britain between the high- and low-water marks also forms part of the Crown Estates. This gives the Estates the rights to land when it is reclaimed and any mineral rights, giving an annual income of £2 million a year.

In 1987, the Crown Estates were valued at £1,200 million, but the Queen is really custodian rather than direct beneficiary. She pays all the revenues to the Treasury (£29.4 million in 1987) in return for an annual payment from the Civil List. In 1990, the Queen received £5.09 million.

Similarly, the royal art treasures are simply under the Queen's stewardship and not freely traded on the world market. The art collection includes works by Dutch and Italian masters, and several hundred drawings by Leonardo da Vinci. The royal antiques require a 75-volume catalogue to list them all, while the royal stamp collection, started by George V, runs to over 330 albums. The Queen's jewel collection contains some 20 priceless tiaras. The value of this treasure trove has never been documented but art experts believe it would run into several billion pounds.

The Queen's personal fortune, which she can more readily dispose of, consists of an equity portfolio managed by blue chip banks and brokers with utter discretion. American researchers valued this at around £1.9 billion after the 1987 stock market crash, but this figure is reckoned to be far too high. In 1971, the portfolio was estimated to be worth some £30 million. A sustained bull market for much of the last 20 years will have pushed the value of this portfolio up to around £500 million. Its tax-free status helps enormously. Even a modest 10% growth in values will result in a further £50 million added to the portfolio in one year.

In addition, the Queen does have some property in Britain (50,000 acres at Balmoral and 20,000 acres at Sandringham) which she owns personally. Her extensive racing and stud farm interests also fall into this category. She has 36 thoroughbreds in training, but is cutting back to around 25 in two years' time. In 1990, she finished 22nd in the owners' list with £148,000 in prize-money.

A long-term plan for the Queen's Civil List was unveiled in 1990. Her income from the Treasury will rise to £7.9 million a year for ten years. A built-in efficiency factor has been added to allow £5 million of savings over the period, and a senior City accountant appointed to oversee the efficiency drive. In all, the Royal family cost various government departments such as the Department of Transport and the Ministry of Defence some £56 million in the 1990–91 financial year.

Despite her wealth, both as head of state and personally, the Queen leads a modest and restrained lifestyle, hating unnecessary waste and spending. Now 65, she is universally loved and admired for her dignity and decorum.

Duke of Westminster £3,700m

LANDOWNER   dob 22 December 1951

IN his speech at the Farmers' Club annual dinner at the end of 1989, held appropriately at the Grosvenor Hotel, Gerald Grosvenor, the 6th Duke of Westminster, made a passionate plea for help for the emerging democracies in the eastern bloc. A fellow peer, sitting nearby, was heard to remark: 'I suppose this means that Gerald has just bought Prague.'

If any man in England has the wealth to buy whole cities, it is the Duke of Westminster, easily Britain's wealthiest man with a fortune of £3.7 billion. The Duke is descended from the Earl of Chester, chief huntsman to William the Conqueror and also his nephew. The dukedom itself is one of the last created in the UK. It was conferred by Victoria on the 23rd Earl of Chester in 1874.

The present Duke's fortune is traced to the marriage to Sir

Thomas Grosvenor in 1677 of Mary Davies, aged 12 and heiress to the Manor of Ebury and a small acreage of undrained marsh and bog on the edge of 17th-century London. Most of those acres, with the exception of Pimlico, which was sold after World War II, are still in the hands of the Grosvenors.

Even in Victorian times, however, John Bateman, a chronicler of the great estates and landowners, said of the newly created 1st Duke: 'He owns what is commonly supposed to be the most valuable London estate held by any of Her Majesty's subjects.' Bateman added that an uncle of his had shot snipe within half a mile of Belgrave Square in 1822. Today, the London estate includes 300 acres of Mayfair, some of the most valuable real estate in the world. The details of the estate, according to a brochure produced for the 300th anniversary of the wedding, read like an exaggerated version of Monopoly. Belgravia, Mayfair, Chester Square, Park Lane, Eaton Square, Oxford Street and Bond Street all figure in the portfolio.

The first Duke did not own anything approaching the same landholdings outside London as the 6th Duke does today. Nowadays, the Grosvenor estates run to around 150,000 acres, making Gerald Grosvenor the sixth largest landowner in modern Britain. In the 1880s the estates ran to a mere 19,000 acres. Outside London, the estate comprises 100,000 acres of Scottish forest, a large tract of Co. Fermanagh, and 13,000 acres around the Duke's home, Eaton Hall, in prime Cheshire countryside.

His international investments are made via Grosvenor International Holdings, based in Vancouver, Canada, where it owns over 12,000 acres. In real estate, it owns over 70 prime commercial properties in the English-speaking world. The estate built and owns the Wailea Beach Hotel, the Davies Pacific Center and other properties in Hawaii. In Australia, there are buildings and property in Sydney and Melbourne and a 10,000-acre sheep farm at Wagga Wagga. Since 1977 the Grosvenor estate has added real estate in Spain, Florida and other places to its holdings.

The present Duke lives in Eaton Hall, which is universally acknowledged to be an awful example of 1960s housebuilding. He is said to be planning to rebuild in a more tasteful style in keeping with the Prince of Wales' thoughts on modern architecture. He is also heading the Prince's new drive to help the rural poor.

The Duke was educated at Harrow, left with two O levels and is now a governor of the school. He wanted to be a footballer and had a trial for first division club Fulham. He has a shrewd business brain and commutes to his office in London by helicopter. He is patron or president, with his wife Natalia, of over 150 charities. His older sister, Lady Leonora Grosvenor, was formerly married to the photographer Patrick, Earl of Lichfield; his younger sister, Lady Jane, was formerly married to the Duke of Roxburghe (q.v.).

The Duke hit the headlines in 1990 in the unlikely guise of champion of the working class. A legal battle with the redoubtable Lady Porter (q.v.), the Tory chairman of Westminster Council, showed the Duke in his new colours. Westminster Council, which has seven blocks of flats belonging to the Duke on a long lease, wanted to sell the flats to anyone, while the Grosvenor Estate wanted them reserved as 'dwellings for the working class'. In the event, the High Court found in the Duke's favour. With two daughters, the Duke and Duchess were rewarded in January when a son and heir, Hugh Richard Louis, was born.

Gad and Hans Rausing £1,940m

INDUSTRIALISTS   dob HR 25 March 1926

FEW millionaires flee to Britain to escape higher tax rates elsewhere, but that is what Gad and Hans Rausing did in 1962. The two brothers live in London and Sussex respectively after leaving their native Sweden. Their wealth stems from Tetra Pak, one of the world's biggest food packaging groups. Founded by their father, Ruben, in 1951, Tetra Pak really grew after he developed a box-shaped drinks container, which he patented in 1969. By 1990 some 60 billion cartons were sold by the company, raising some $5 billion revenue. The two brothers turned over control of the business to outside managers in 1985, though they still maintain ultimate control through a Liechtenstein foundation and a Dutch holding company. The low-key group came into the news in January 1991 by making a £1.5 billion takeover offer for Alfa-Laval, a Swedish group making dairy and food-processing equipment.

Gad returns occasionally to Sweden to lecture at the university of Lund on archaeology, while Hans remains chairman of the company. He has degrees in economics and technology. Both are married and they each have three children. Gad's daughter, Kirsten, is a prominent racehorse owner in Newmarket, where she runs the Lanwades stud. In 1989 Hans Rausing's Sussex home was given the accolade Country House of the Year.

Lord Sainsbury and family   £1,850m

GROCER
dob JS 2 November 1927, DS 24 October 1940

BRITAIN's biggest and most successful supermarket chain began in 1869, when John Sainsbury opened a shop in Drury Lane, selling milk, butter and eggs. The first supermarket was opened in Lewisham in 1955 when rationing, introduced during World War II, ended.

By the end of the 1980s, 6.5 million customers were using the 250 Sainsbury supermarkets every week. Recession was an unknown word at Sainsbury, which produced £518 million pre-tax profits in the year to March 1991, a 15% increase on the previous year. The 300th store was opened at Crawley in Sussex in March 1991. At 80,000 square feet, it is the biggest store opened by the group and cost around £25 million.

Lord Sainsbury, great-grandson of the founder, is chairman while his cousin David Sainsbury is deputy chairman. The family control around 39% of Sainsbury shares, which were floated on the stock market in 1973.

His other great passion is supporting the arts. He is chairman of the Royal Opera House, and is married to Anya Linden, a former dancer with the Royal Ballet. The family has funded the £50 million extension to the National Gallery.

David is a founder member of the Social Democratic Party, and remained loyal to David Owen after the split over merging with the Liberals. The continuing existence of the SDP depends largely on David Sainsbury's willingness to fund its operation, and that in turn appears to depend on David Owen's willingness to stay in politics. Tim Sainsbury, Sir John's younger brother, is Conservative MP for Hove and serves as a junior minister in the Major government.

Garfield Weston   £1,750m

INDUSTRIALIST   dob 28 April 1927

GARFIELD Weston is chairman of Associated British Foods, which makes such household names as Sunblest bread and Twinings tea. The company is quoted on the Stock Exchange and the Weston family control 63% of the shares.

In 1882, Weston's grandfather, who had moved from New York to Toronto, started a door-to-door bread delivery service from a cart. Thirteen years later, he sold out for $1 million and went into biscuits. The business never looked back.

In the 1930s, a British business was established and the family went back into bread. About a third of all British bread now comes from ABF. At the beginning of World War II Weston's father wrote out a cheque for £100,000 to replace the first 15 Spitfires downed in the Battle of Britain.

The present chairman is renowned for his caution. In 1989 the company was sitting on a cash mountain worth £800 million. In the wake of the 1987 stock market crash, Weston pulled out of a takeover bid for S & W Berisford, owner of British Sugar. At the end of 1990, he made a successful £880 million takeover bid for the British Sugar group.

An intensely private man who shuns the limelight, Weston lists his hobbies as gardening, tennis and walking. In 1989,

Business magazine described him as one of the ten industrialists closest to Mrs Thatcher. He publicly urged her not to resign in 1990.

Younger brother Galen Weston (29/10/40) runs George Weston Ltd, based in Toronto, though he is active on the British social scene, playing polo with the Royal family.

John Paul Getty II   £1,450m

PHILANTHROPIST HEIR TO OIL INDUSTRY
FORTUNE   dob 9 July 1932

MORE English than the English themselves, American-born John Paul Getty II is best known for his charitable work. In recent years, he has given away around £100 million to various causes, including the National Gallery (£50 million) and the British Film Institute (£20 million). He loves watching cricket videos and his passion for the game is reflected in his donations to cricket grounds such as Lords and Trent Bridge, to help with ground improvements. He has a box at Lords and can boast membership of the Middlesex Cricket Club (MCC).

Mick Jagger, the pop star, introduced Getty to the game when they were neighbours in Chelsea's exclusive Cheyne Walk. Today, cricket stars like Alan Knott, Colin Cowdrey, Peter May and Derek Randall are frequent visitors at his 1,700-acre estate in Buckinghamshire.

Mrs Thatcher recognized his charitable work by awarding him an honorary knighthood in 1986. He would have taken up British citizenship had his accountants not advised against it for tax reasons.

Getty, eldest son of the legendary oil magnate of the same name, was born in California. He fought in the Korean War as an infantry corporal but later turned to drugs and was a heroin addict. In 1973, he came to Britain and has lived here ever since, gradually mellowing with age. He even enjoys a good English roast beef and Yorkshire pudding washed down with beer.

His fortune really prospered in 1984 when Texaco, the giant

American oil company, bought Getty Oil, the company founded by his father, for over $10 billion. Getty's share was worth nearly £900 million in cash. Invested, this generates an income of over £100 million a year. Not even his huge charitable contributions can stop his wealth simply piling up, and he is now worth around £1,450 million. A recluse for many years, he is gradually coming out into the limelight and has started giving press interviews. Apart from cricket, his main hobbies are watching films and collecting rare books.

Lord Vestey and Edmund Vestey   £1,300m

FOOD PRODUCERS   dob LV 19 March 1941

THE Vestey family fortune derived from mass-producing food for the burgeoning British population in the late 19th century. The Liverpool-based Vestey brothers built up vast cattle ranches and cold storage facilities round the world. They then acquired their own shipping lines to transport the food and, in Dewhursts, their own butcher's shops in which to sell it. Dewhursts' 1,400 shops are doing well with new investment and aggressive management. The family business, Union International, is now looking to expand behind the old Iron Curtain.

The two cousins, great-grandson and grandson of the founders, live in style. Twice married, Lord Vestey has a 4,500-acre estate, Stowell Park, in Gloucestershire. He is a keen player and patron of the game of polo, belonging to a select band of enthusiasts which includes Prince Charles. Edmund has three homes, including a 100,000-acre estate in Sutherland, which once belonged to the Duke of Westminster. He is joint master of the Puckeridge and Thurlow Foxhounds, and a keen huntsman.

The Vesteys caused considerable controversy in 1980 when a *Sunday Times* investigation revealed that they had paid virtually no tax for 60 years. In 1981 the Inland Revenue took steps to plug the loophole but a leading firm of tax specialists say that it is still possible to remit unlimited sums of money to UK residents, tax free and without breaking any laws, if proper provisions are made. As in the Vestey case, overseas trusts form the basis of the provision they would recommend.

Robert Maxwell   £1,200m

PUBLISHER· dob 10 June 1923

SON of a poor Czech labourer murdered by the Gestapo, Jan Ludwick Hoch escaped to Britain in the war. He joined the army, changed his name and, promoted to captain, won the Military Cross for gallantry. In 1948, he set up the Pergamon Press and later became a Labour MP.

Despite losing his Parliamentary seat in 1970 and once being branded by a government report as 'not a person who can be relied on to exercise proper stewardship of a publicly quoted company', Maxwell has thrived on an 18-hour day of tireless wheeling and dealing. Pergamon's scientific journals provided the basis for his fortune, but he is now building Maxwell Communications into one of the largest media conglomerates in the world, embracing everything from printing to newspapers and satellite television.

Home is Headington Hill Hall near Oxford, rented from Oxfordshire County Council; hence Maxwell's boast that he is a council tenant. He lists his hobbies as football and chess, but many suspect that it is the oxygen of publicity that keeps him going.

This was clearly demonstrated early in 1991 when he rescued the New York *Daily News*, taking the Big Apple by storm in typical Maxwell style. Soon after, he sold his Pergamon group to a Dutch publisher for £440 million, reducing his hefty debt burden. It was a wrench for Maxwell, selling a business he had built from scratch. But some compensation came in May 1991, when he floated the Mirror group on the stock market for £500 million. He had purchased the group when it was in a sorry state seven years previously for some £113 million. He has retained a 50% stake in the business worth £250 million.

Maxwell is a huge donor to charities in the UK, Israel, Africa and the former eastern bloc. Significantly, he appears to be trying to hand over more responsibility to his family and executives. In mid-1991, he announced he would give up his role in Maxwell Communications, his master company, appointing his 32-year-old son, Kevin, as chief executive. Peter Walker, the former Tory wet and cabinet minister, was to have been chairman but declined the job.

The Moores family   £1,200m

POOLS AND RETAILING   dob JM 25 January 1896

SIR John Moores founded Littlewoods Pools in 1923. Today, the business is the largest private company in Britain, making profits of £71.2 million in 1988, a small decline on 1987. It has branched out into 175 stores and mail order, but the pools, played by 12 million people every week, remains the base of the fortune. At the end of the 1980s the stores side of the business suffered severely from the Tory government's attempt to squeeze inflation out of the economy by increasing interest rates. In 1989, over 1,700 staff were made redundant. 1990 has proved a much better year with profits up 46% to £94.8 million. This sharp improvement was a rare feat for a retailer in the worst recession for years.

Moores left school at 14 to work as a post-office messenger, later showing interest in telegraphy. In World War I, he served as a wireless operator. The pools venture was started with two partners and paid out a £2.12s od dividend initially (against today's £1.5 million top prize). It was not an immediate success and Moores bought out his two colleagues. That was in 1923. By 1932 he had made his first million.

The Moores family of four sons and nineteen grandchildren live in Merseyside. Sir John, a keen Everton Football Club supporter all his life, used to watch virtually every match. His brother Cecil, the driving force behind the pools side of the business, died in 1989. The second and third generation of the family are believed to be keen on floating the company on the stock market to realize some of their enormous wealth. The mail order business is up for sale, with a price tag of £400 million.

Gopi and Sri Hinduja   £1,100m

INTERNATIONAL TRADERS   dob (unknown)

FOUR reclusive brothers control one of the largest trading empires in the world, stretching from India via the Middle East to Switzerland and Britain. The Hindujas – two of whom live and work in London – inherited the business from their father, Parmanand Deepchand Hinduja. Born in 1901, he started as a trader in Bombay, India's trading centre, and developed strong links with Iran, where he thrived under the Shah, supplying many of the country's import requirements and handling Iranian exports. Parmanand lost his eldest son at the early age of 32, but the other four came into the business. When he died in 1971, they expanded it into new industries and other parts of Asia. Among their Indian interests are telecommunications and Ashok Leyland, the Indian bus and truck maker, which they acquired in 1989. At the time, the Hindujas believed that the Ashok purchase would act as a cornerstone for future investment they planned in the transport field, including cars, hovercraft, shipping and airlines. They are also important players in power generation in India, signing an agreement with Bechtel, the giant American construction company, for joint venture projects in electricity supply. The brothers developed close links with the late Rajiv Gandhi, the former Indian prime minister. In India, influence at ministerial level in Government is vital in winning contracts. They also have access to the foreign exchange which they believed would be vital in re-equipping Ashok's factories. In March 1989, the Hindujas also gained full control of the Gulf Oil Trading Company, when they acquired a stake previously held by Sheikh Yamani, the former Saudi oil minister.

The two brothers in Britain, Gopi and Sri, live in a large house in exclusive Carlton Gardens in London. They also have large homes in New York and Tehran. They have been photographed meeting Mrs Thatcher and the Prince of Wales in recognition of their substantial work for charities through their Hinduja Foundation. Another brother is based in Bombay and the fourth is in Geneva. All the brothers are dedicated to business and hard work. Gopi's daughter was married over Christmas in Bombay. There were some 3,000 guests at the week-long celebrations, which one observer said were conducted 'like money was going out of fashion'.

2

THE
SUPER-RICH

£100m and more

Charles Feeney   £940m

RETAILER   dob (unknown)

CHARLES Feeney, who moved to London in the 1970s, began his life as an entrepreneur while he was a student at Cornell University in New York studying at the school of hotel administration. He supplemented his GI Bill (a Pentagon bursary for ex-army veterans) by selling sandwiches to fellow students in their halls of residence. In the late 1950s he joined a former classmate, Robert Miller, to start a business in Europe selling duty-free alcohol and European cars to American servicemen returning home. Later they expanded the same operation into the Far East. In 1961 and 1962, they made their most significant move by opening two duty-free shops at Hong Kong and Honolulu international airports.

When the US government changed the regulations on duty-free sales for servicemen, the pair came close to going out of business. But the two airport shops saved them, particularly after the 1964 Tokyo Olympics, which resulted in a huge surge in Japanese tourism. Today, Duty Free Shoppers is the largest duty-free retailer in the world and its several Hong Kong shops make it the biggest retailer in the colony. Sales of Duty Free Shoppers are thought to have passed the $2 billion mark, making it four times larger than any other group in the business.

By paying generous commission to Japanese tour guides to take their parties to his stores, Feeney has made a fortune from the growing purchasing power of the yen. By concentrating on well-known high-quality brands, they are able to achieve high profit margins and also wrest generous credit terms from their suppliers. The brands they market – Hermes ties, Gucci shoes, Fendi bags, Dunhill lighters, Wedgwood china and Chivas Regal whisky – are world renowned.

Since the early 1970s, Feeney and Miller have handed over day-to-day management of the Duty Free operation to professional managers, to concentrate their own efforts on investing their enormous profits in other ventures. Feeney's vehicle is a Bermuda-based company, General Atlantic Holdings, which has invested in dozens of businesses in Europe and Asia. He is considered a long-term investor and has recently targeted computer software companies. He shuns glamour stocks, preferring a company with steady sales and which he considers is undervalued. Recently, Feeney took a near 10% stake in Management Science America, an Atlanta-based group.

Sir James Goldsmith   £870m

FINANCIER   dob 26 February 1933

GAMBLING, whether in a fashionable London club or on the world's stock markets, has been the metier of Sir James Goldsmith. The son of a wealthy Tory MP and a French mother, he left Eton at 17, having already made a small £8,000 fortune from betting on horses.

His first brush with the gossip columns came at age 20, when he eloped to Scotland to marry Maria Isabel Patino, daughter of a Bolivian tin magnate and heiress to a £75 million fortune. She died four months later, giving birth to a daughter.

In the 1960s and 1970s, he was active building up a food empire, but kept his fascination for the gossips with his gambling exploits at the Clermont Club. He ranked Jim Slater (q.v.), John Aspinall (q.v.) and Jacob Rothschild (q.v.) among his close circle of friends.

In the 1980s he became one of the stars on Wall Street, buying and selling large companies with the same energy he had spent on gaming tables, but far more profitably. In 1982, he bought Diamond Corporation for £246 million and sold it for three times as much two years later. Even when he failed to take over companies, he made a handsome profit on the deals.

Goldsmith shrewdly anticipated the October 1987 stock market crash by selling all his major holdings two months previously when the market had reached an all-time high. In the year 1989 Sir James made his mark on the British financial scene. Through his Hoylake consortium, he launched Britain's biggest takeover bid – the £13 billion assault on BAT. Though the bid lapsed at the end of that year, it demonstrated that Goldsmith's appetite for buying and selling companies had not diminished after a decade in America.

Goldsmith is also busy developing a hugh complex on the western coast of Mexico. The estate, which includes tropical rain forests, unspoilt lagoons and a volcano, was the setting for the council of war early in 1989 at which Goldsmith and his two fellow BAT stalkers, Jacob Rothschild and Kerry Packer, planned the takeover bid. In 1990 Goldsmith retired from business to concentrate on ecology and the environment. His move was underscored by the formal abandonment of his £13 billion bid for the giant BAT group, followed by his decision to swap his large forestry interests in America for a 49% stake in a mining company owned by Lord Hanson (q.v.). The $1.3 billion stake requires little active management, and should earn Goldsmith a comfortable $100 million a year in dividends, which he can use to finance his ecological crusade from his vast Mexican estate.

His private life is colourful, with a former wife (he says his relationship with her has not altered 'one iota' since divorce) in Paris, a wife, Lady Annabel (formerly Birley, whose previous husband named a famous nightclub, Annabels, after her), and a mistress in New York. He has had seven children by four women.

Sir John and Sir Adrian Swire   £672m

SHIPPING
dob JS 28 February 1927, AS 15 February 1932

IN 1816, John Swire, a Yorkshireman, established his own company in Liverpool to take advantage of its growing world trade. By 1867, the company was established in the Far East and China. Despite extensive damage to their shipping, refining and dockyard interests in World War II, the Swires rebuilt and reinvested.

Today the Swire business includes ships, the Cathay Pacific airline, insurance, property and hotels and it is one of the largest companies in Hong Kong.

In 1988, the still privately run John Swire group produced after-tax profits of nearly £91 million, a sharp increase on the figure for 1987. The two Swire brothers sit on the board and control nearly 65% of the shares between them directly or in trusts.

The Swire Pacific group, the quoted arm of the Swire Empire, unveiled a 16.6 per cent drop in its first half profits in 1990.

Sir John, the elder brother, is honorary president of the company. Both brothers were educated at Eton and University College, Oxford. Sir John served in the Irish Guards in Palestine and, in 1950, joined the family business, working his way up to become chairman in 1966. He is married and has three children.

Sir Adrian served in the Coldstream Guards from 1950 to 1952 and later with the RAF Volunteer Reserves and the Royal Hong Kong AAF. He married Lady Judith Compton, eldest daughter of the 6th Marquess of Northampton, in 1970.

Richard Branson   £600m

MUSIC AND ENTERTAINMENT
ENTREPRENEUR   dob 18 July 1950

THE sweaters, jeans, flowing hair and beard, along with an office on a houseboat on the Regent's Canal, suggest a hippie locked in a 1960s timewarp. But Richard Branson – the man charged by Mrs Thatcher with cleaning up Britain – has a shrewd and tough business brain, despite not being able to work a calculator.

After a private school education at Stowe, which he left at 16 with just three O-levels, he founded *Student* magazine. Business followed quickly: Virgin Mail Order in 1969, Virgin record shop in 1971 and the Virgin label in 1973. His first signing of a recording contract was Mike Oldfield's album *Tubular Bells*.

This LP sold 5 million copies. In 1984, he started the cut-price Virgin Atlantic airline. He also owns nightclubs. In 1986, he took the Virgin group public, but, disenchanted with the City, has since made it a private company again.

Branson's unbusinesslike appearance did not prevent him making a deal in 1989 with the inscrutable and utterly conventional Japanese group Fujisankei, which enormously increased his personal wealth. For a sum of £96 million the Japanese took a 25% stake in Branson's Virgin group, valuing the rest of the company at nearly £300 million. A Japanese hotel group also paid £36 million for a 10% stake in Virgin Atlantic, Branson's airline, valuing the whole business at £360 million. The airline recently won landing rights at Heathrow.

Branson lives in fashionable Ladbroke Grove, London, and has an Oxfordshire mansion complete with recording studio for the weekends. He even owns a Virgin Island in the Caribbean, which he will rent out for $3,500 a day.

He is a great practical joker and has tried a series of hair-raising stunts including ballooning across the Atlantic and a power boat crossing competing for the coveted Blue Riband. In November 1989, he planned to cross the Pacific by balloon but his dreams were shattered when the £3 million balloon ripped and caught fire. In December, he finally married his long-time girlfriend Joan Templeman on their Caribbean island. Whether she can persuade him to settle down to the conventional life is unclear. He recently managed to carry out his Pacific balloon flight.

Leonidas Goulandris and family £550m

SHIPPING AND FINANCE   dob (unknown)

BASED in the heart of the City of London, the Goulandris group is run by the third generation of a Greek shipping family originally from the island of Andros. Leonidas Goulandris, the present head of the family, was educated at Cambridge.

Now in his mid-60s, he married a Greek tobacco heiress in 1958. They lived a low-key life, largely out of the gossip columns, though Goulandris's purchase of homes in Mayfair and the Glympton park estate in Oxfordshire were duly noted. In 1975, Goulandris showed some innovation in his business dealings by unveiling Britain's first electric car, the Enfield, priced at the princely sum of £2,808, and built by Enfield Auto-motive, one of his companies. The Mini look-alike did not prove a great success because of the weight of its batteries.

The Brenninkmeyer family £500m

RETAILING dob (unknown)

CLEMENS and August Brenninkmeyer opened their first store exactly 150 years ago in the small Dutch town of Sneek. Today, that stores chain – well known as C & A – is one of the most successful retailing operations in the world. It has spread from its original Dutch base to West Germany, Britain, France, Belgium, America and Brazil.

But while the stores are well known for their smart and good-quality fashions, very little is known about the Brenninkmeyer family, who still control the business with an almost obsessive secrecy. The family, said to number around 2,000, adheres to a strict Catholic code, and a well-developed hierarchy runs through the family. Everybody knows their place, while em-ployees, particularly senior staff, are well rewarded and taken care of, provided they are discreet about the family's business.

Though the family is still based in Holland, they have an important British branch, which runs operations here. Though only the sketchiest details of the business are apparent, there are at least nine British-based Brenninkmeyers based in the London area. *Forbes* magazine recently estimated the total wealth of the Brenninkmeyers at around £2.7 billion. As the British arm is actually one of the most important parts of the C & A empire, we have estimated their share of the total fortune at some £500 million.

Despite the family control, there is nothing slow or paternalistic in C & A's British operations, run from headquarters at the back of the C & A store in Marble Arch. Its executives are noted for making decisions in record time and getting the latest fashions into their stores quickly. They also enjoy excellent relations with their suppliers. Last year, C & A launched its new City collection of fashions. But even then the family did not make any real fuss. Their motto remains: 'Openness is a sign of weakness.'

Earl of Iveagh and family £500m

BREWERS AND LANDOWNERS
dob BI 20 May 1937

ARTHUR Guinness, the Dublin brewer, created the famous stout on the banks of the River Liffey in the 18th century. Today, the family still have links with the company, though its management is now in professional hands.

Lord Iveagh ('Benjie') presides over the Guinness family, which has had a run of bad luck in recent years, with the untimely death of several family members in unhappy circumstances. Benjie Iveagh lives as a tax exile in the Phoenix Park area of Dublin. In 1984 he was divorced from his wife Miranda.

He has a 23,000-acre estate at Elveden in Suffolk, worth an estimated £50 million. His grandfather, whom he succeeded, had revitalized the estate, which in Edwardian days was regarded as the best shoot in the country. In 1984, the contents of Elveden Hall were auctioned by Christie's for £5.7 million in a four-day sale. The house has not been occupied since the war.

Members of the Guinness family went to court in 1988 to challenge the interpretation of the 1st Earl of Iveagh's will. The High Court decided that several million pounds left in a trust by the Earl, who died in 1927, could be inherited by his great-great-grandchildren, Dorian and Garech Browne, whose father, Tara Browne, died in a car crash in Chelsea in 1966.

Ernest Saunders, the former Guinness chairman, once recounted how Lord Iveagh, the then head of the brewing firm, had said that he wanted the Guinness family to be as rich as the Rothschilds again. But in fact the family, whose wealth stems from the rich dark drink brewed in Dublin since the 18th century, were already as wealthy as the Rothschilds, if not more so. This wealth, largely based in Canada, can be traced back to a £15 million investment in Western Canada before World War I by Sir Arthur Guinness. Most of the funds were used to buy the North Shore of Vancouver and to found a company called British Pacific. Known locally as the Guinness company, it is difficult to value as it is an unlimited company. British Pacific is actually wholly owned by a Swiss company called Sofisa Sa. The only indication of a Guinness link comes in the Register of Members' interests by Paul Channon MP, a prominent member of the Guinness family, who is the biggest individual shareholder in a family trust, Iveagh Trustees. Channon declared an interest in Sofisa Sa and the link was established. Inquiries in Vancouver financial circles put a value on British Pacific of between $2 billion and $4 billion. Since it is difficult to know the profit record and exact stake held by the Guinness family in British Pacific, we have been conservative in our valuation of £500 million for the family.

David and Frederick Barclay   £450m

HOTEL AND PROPERTY OWNERS
dob 27 October 1934 (twins)

KNOWN as Britain's most secretive businessmen, the Barclay twins were born in London of Scottish parents. They began as estate agents and later moved into property and hotels in the early 1960s. They specialized in converting Bayswater boarding houses and hotels. The small, dapper twins survived the 1973-4 property crash and prospered in the 1980s. A series of quick-fire deals culminated in the takeover of the famous Ellerman shipping and property empire in 1983. They transformed the business and sold the shipping line back to its management.

In 1982, they bought a chain of temperance hotels. Within a year they sold it, apart from a large tract of land for housing, making a substantial profit on the deal. In 1983, they bought three railway hotels in London from British Rail for £17 million and sold two of them in 1985 for £37 million.

Today they employ over 4,000 people and own luxury hotels in London, New York and Monte Carlo, as well as breweries and a travel agency. They made a £12 million profit from the sale of a stake in the IC Gas business in 1987 when they abandoned plans to bid £750 million for the whole group.

David became chairman of the family business as he was born ten minutes before Frederick. They are identical twins, distinguishable only by having their hair parted on different sides. David is regarded as the dominant one and works in the business with his son Aidan.

In 1990 they offered to buy Canova's sculpture *The Three Graces* for £7.6 million to save it from being sold to a foreign buyer and shipped abroad.

Viscount Cowdray   £420m

FINANCIER   dob 10 February 1927

UNDER heavy fire in the retreat to Dunkirk, Lord Cowdray took over from his wounded driver and, with a mangled arm, drove to the beaches. This was an early display of the dogged determination that characterizes so many of the Pearson family.

The Cowdray fortune had been built up by his grandfather, Weetman Pearson, in the late 19th-century construction boom. Pearson built tunnels in New York and London, Dover harbour, and railways in Spain and China. He drained swamps round Mexico City and dredged channels in Egypt and the West Indies. Banking and newspaper interests soon followed.

The present Lord Cowdray took over the reins after the war and the family still controls over 20% of the Pearson Group, which is worth around £1.7 billion.

Lord Cowdray, formerly an expert shot and a keen polo player despite his wartime injury, lives modestly in Cowdray Park, his 17,000-acre estate in Sussex. He prefers beer to whisky and once said he hated fancy food, preferring 'cottage pie and meat and potatoes'. He also has a 60,000-acre estate in Aberdeenshire.

His sons and daughters have proved colourful. His heir, the Hon. Michael Pearson, was an active member of the London social and gaming scene, often betting for high stakes against the likes of James Goldsmith. His elder daughter Lucy was briefly married to the Argentine socialite Hector Basualdo while his younger daughter Rosanna, formerly the *Independent*'s inner cities correspondent, married a Jamaican reggae performer. Lord and Lady Cowdray did not attend the wedding.

The family business, which had been regarded as a prime candidate for takeover, has been described as a collection of priceless jewels. These range from the *Financial Times* to the merchant bank Lazards, the Château Latour vineyard, and Royal Doulton, the china group.

In its 1991 interim results, Pearson unveiled a 58% fall in pre-tax profits to £40.7 million. A recent decision to merge the British Satellite Broadcasting system, 22% owned by Pearson, with rival Sky will stem a heavy drain on Pearson resources. Cowdray has little direct involvement with the business today, which is run by his nephew, Lord Blakenham. He prefers to enjoy life on his large Cowdray Park estate in Sussex.

Earl Cadogan   £400m

LANDOWNER   dob 13 February 1914

THE Cadogan family owns 90 acres of fashionable Chelsea in London. The holdings came as a result of the marriages of three families in the 18th century, families whose names will be familiar to Chelsea residents today: the Cadogans, the Cheynes and the Sloanes. But it was the 5th Earl, one of Queen Victoria's ministers, who turned Chelsea from a slum into a top residential area.

The present Earl has a distinguished war record, having won the Military Cross in the Western Desert in 1943. He fought single-handed in his tank until it was disabled and caught fire, then he helped evacuate wounded crew members under heavy German gunfire.

Today, the Earl, who was a Jockey Club steward and owns some of the finest grouse moors in Scotland, is semi-retired. He lives in Chelsea and on the Scottish estates in Perthshire. The Cadogan estates are run by his son, Viscount Chelsea, formerly a merchant banker. He has homes in London and Oxfordshire.

Lord Cayzer   £400m

FINANCE AND SHIPPING MAGNATE
dob 21 January 1910

IN 1878, the Clan shipping line was launched by a one-time shipping clerk, Charles Cayzer. The line grew to take over Union Castle and diversified into finance in the 1950s and 1960s.

Lord Cayzer, grandson of the founder, heads the family, which until recently had a 31% stake in the group (now called British & Commonwealth Shipping). This was reduced to 4.9% in June 1987, raising £427 million. Though British & Commonwealth collapsed in 1990, the Cayzers were guaranteed money owing to them by the banks. Their remaining investment vehicle, Caledonia Investment, continues to prosper, raising its profits for the first half of 1990 by 15%.

Cayzer is an ardent supporter of the Conservative Party, and lavishes thousands of pounds on party funds every year.

He has homes in Mayfair and Suffolk, and lists golf and shooting as his hobbies. In recent years, Cayzer has been in the news over plans to redevelop his Redhill airfield into an executive jet base. The move infuriated the local Tiger flying club, whose membership includes Princes Charles, Philip and Andrew.

Paul McCartney   £380m

MUSICIAN   dob 18 June 1942

THE golden touch which has made Paul McCartney allegedly the highest-earning pop musician of all time has, apparently, deserted him – if only temporarily. It is six years since he was last at the top of the pop charts, with 'Pipes of Peace'; almost three years since the release of his last album of new material. Yet McCartney can afford to rest comfortably on his laurels and on the revenue from the extraordinary string of successes he enjoyed with the Beatles and as a solo performer.

The key to McCartney's wealth lies not simply in the sales of his records, but in his activities as a songwriter and owner of music copyrights. He has always been mindful of the value of his songwriting. Until 1969, the rights to Beatles songs composed by Lennon and McCartney were owned by Northern Songs, in which both writers were substantial shareholders. In 1969, prior to ATV taking control of the company for £10 million, John Lennon was surprised to find that while his holding in Northern was still the original 644,000 shares, McCartney had quietly built up his stock to 751,000 shares. 'It was a matter of investing in something you believed in instead of supermarkets and furniture stores,' McCartney explained at the time.

The ownership of Northern Songs subsequently passed to Robert Holmes à Court, and eventually, in 1985, to Michael Jackson for £47 million. Even without owning the catalogue, however, McCartney still collects composer's royalties amounting to some 3% of the retail price of every Beatles record sold, as well as Performing Rights Society royalties for radio plays of the songs. This, of course, also includes the countless 'cover' versions of Beatle hits; 'Yesterday', for example, is said to be the most recorded song ever, with 1,600 different versions made between 1965 and 1986.

McCartney continues, of course, to own the rights to all songs written by him since his Beatles days, and over the years he has invested in a portfolio of other publishing catalogues. Perhaps the most lucrative among these is the Buddy Holly song-publishing catalogue. But he also owns the copyrights to such

Broadway musicals as *Grease, A Chorus Line, Hello Dolly* and *Mame*, as well as more obscure titles like *Lily of Laguna* and *Meet Me at the Cowshed*.

For all his wealth, McCartney leads a steadfastly modest and unostentatious life. He has a five-bedroom farmhouse in Sussex, known locally as Paulditz because of its security arrangements – and his three children, Mary, Stella and James, have been educated at state schools. His wife Linda places great store on the unassuming values of 'a good breakfast, and nice neighbours'. The family also own an estate on Mull of Kintyre, which inspired his hit record of the same name.

He commutes to London by train. He rarely goes out, preferring to eat home-cooked vegetarian stews and drink mineral water. He drives a battered Range Rover. The local hunt is banned from his 160-acre estate.

He is chairman of his own company, MPL Communications Ltd, which embraces 17 different companies responsible for song-publishing, films and video. MPL showed a profit of £234.444 for activities in the year ending December 1987, showing a retained profit of £3.8 million.

While his career has suffered setbacks in recent years, not least in the failure of the self-financed film *Give My Regards to Broad Street*, a report published in 1987 alleged that McCartney was continuing to accrue royalties at the rate of £3,750 an hour – £62.50 a minute – for an average 30-hour working week.

In the 1960s McCartney was a frequent supporter of 'underground' causes such as the advice centre BIT and the newspaper *International Times*, as well as lavishing hundreds of thousands of pounds on ill-fated ventures through the Apple foundation. He continues to give away large sums of money each year to charity, but always with the condition of anonymity. The offer is withdrawn if there is the slightest hint of publicity – a fact, perhaps, which has contributed to a reputation for parsimoniousness.

His 1990 world tour, McCartney's first for 13 years, is estimated to have earned him £12 million profit. In 1990, he was expected to make £43 million, all told. But the richer he becomes, the bigger social conscience McCartney has developed. A pop song recorded for Christmas, entitled 'All My

Trials', generated a storm of protest in the tabloid press after McCartney wrote a press release for the record stating: 'There are millions of people in Britain who are suffering and this song's for them.' He also offered to pay the wages for the nurses at his local hospital threatened by spending cuts and announced plans to set up a pop school in his native Liverpool. It's a long way from his early days 30 years ago playing in Hamburg and Liverpool's Cavern Club.

David Thompson   £380m

FOOD PROCESSING INDUSTRIALIST
dob 4 March 1936

UNTIL 1985, few people outside Smithfield meat market had heard of Hillsdown Holdings. But when it was floated on the stock market in 1985, 100,000 people wanted to buy the shares. The stampede made David Thompson, a shy north London businessman, a multi-millionaire.

Hillsdown, which produces everything from Buxted chickens to Smedley peas, was founded in the mid-1970s, when Thompson merged the meat business he inherited from his father with some property interests of a solicitor, Harry Solomon. The business was named after Thompson's luxury north London home.

In April 1987 Thompson sold half his stake in Hillsdown for £145 million. Since then, he has sold his entire stake and moved into property companies. He is currently chairman of Glentree, a north London estate agency.

Outside work, his great passion is the turf and he owns two Newmarket studs, Cheveley Park and Sandwich. The best price Thompson achieved for a yearling was 42,000 guineas. He also owns a controlling stake in the Royal Windsor racecourse, the Queen's favourite. The value of his racing interests alone is over £30 million.

His son Richard handles the family's finances when he is not chairing Queen's Park Rangers Football Club. The family are now the biggest shareholder in Quinta da Largo, a luxury holiday centre and golf course in the Algarve.

Viscount Portman £360m

LANDOWNER   dob 22 April 1934

THE Portman fortune stems from 100 acres of London around Portman Square and Oxford Street. The estate was granted by Henry VIII to Lord Chief Justice Portman in 1533. It was further extended in Queen Mary's reign.

The 9th Viscount, who inherited the title from his uncle in 1967, is a Herefordshire farmer with over 3,000 acres of farmland. He also enjoys music, and plays five instruments with considerable virtuosity.

Over the years the family estates have been gradually diminished by death duties. In the 1940s, some £7.5 million had to be raised on the death of the 7th Viscount. This led to the sale of a 3,800-acre Dorset estate and 26 acres in London, including 221b Baker Street, the 'home' of Sherlock Holmes. In 1955, the Portman family trust was created with an initial value of around £4 million.

Jack and Fred Walker £360m

EX-INDUSTRIALISTS   dob (unknown)

JACK Walker's father started a small sheet metal business in Blackburn in 1945. When he died in 1951, Jack took over the company at the age of 21, having left school at 14. In the late 1950s, he took the business, C. Walker, out of sheet metal and into steel stockholding. He never looked back. In 1956 sales stood at £46,000. In 1988, they were £623 million with £48 million profits. By then, the company had 3,400 employees, spread around 50 British sites. In October 1989 the business was sold for £330 million to British Steel – the largest price ever paid for a private British company. The money goes to Jack, now aged 60, who lives in Jersey, and his elder brother Fred, aged 64, who still lives in Lancashire.

The Walker success was built on establishing a nationwide chain of offices, in the 1960s. They also acquired the steel stockholding interests of GKN, which doubled the size of C. Walker. Before the sale to British Steel, the two groups had built up a close working relationship.

British Steel was said to give Walker special rates, and is believed to have helped in the purchase of the GKN operation after the government restricted its own steel stockholding plans.

The two brothers were very hard-working and made some shrewd moves. Jack had no inhibitions and got to big-name customers early. He got the taste to be biggest and he employed good people. He is very straightforward and down to earth, one rival told the *Financial Times* just after the sale to British Steel.

Jack had already retired by this stage, and was simply a consultant to the group. Fred, the chairman, had indicated his intention of following his brother into retirement in the near future. The two will concentrate on building up Jack's airline, which flies out of Jersey to the continent. The 50 Walker offices also remain with the brothers. Despite his wealth, Jack lives modestly and drives an old Renault around the island. He has invested some £30m in Jersey European Airways and is determined to build it as a major regional carrier. In five years, the number of passengers carried has climbed from 160,000 to 460,000, while turnover has risen from £9 million to £26 million.

As chairman of Blackburn Rovers, Jack Walker is also financing the Club's efforts to return to the First Division after a 25-year absence.

Robin Fleming and the Fleming family

£320m

BANKING AND LAND   dob (unknown)

ROBIN Fleming is the chairman of Robert Fleming, one of the last independent merchant banks in the City of London. Founded in 1873 as an investment trust in Dundee, Robert Fleming later became a merchant bank, and finally arrived in 1980 when it became an accepting house, joining the top tier of merchant banks in the process.

Although the Fleming family no longer completely controls the bank, its stake is around 40%, according to an authoritative report in the *Financial Times*. With its most recent after-tax profits for the year to the end of March 1990 showing a 34% advance to £36.5 million, the stock market would have valued the whole bank at around 18 times that sum at the beginning of 1991, giving a price tag of £676 million. The family's 40% stake would be worth £270 million.

But the family also has substantial estates in Scotland including the 51,000-acre Blackmount Estate and the 41,000-acre Glenkinglass Estate, both in Argyllshire. The family also has land in Gloucestershire. These estates push up the wealth of the Flemings to around £320 million.

A close friend of the Duke of Kent, Robin Fleming was an usher at the Duke's wedding, while four members of the Royal family attended his wedding to the daughter of a Yorkshire industrialist in 1962.

Harry Hyams

£305m

PROPERTY OWNER   dob 2 January 1928

CONTROVERSY has always dogged Harry Hyams, son of an East End bookmaker. Owner of Ramsbury, a 600-acre estate in Wiltshire (bought from Lord Rootes, the motor magnate) complete with art treasures and some of the finest shooting in the country, Hyams is best remembered for one urban building, Centre Point in London. This remained unoccupied for 13 years and Hyams regularly sued – and won – if any paper dared to allege that it was being kept empty deliberately. The Centre Point saga fuelled Hyams' obsessive desire for secrecy. He used to hold annual meetings on New Year's Day and refused entry to the press. As a result, several financial journalists held shares in the company simply to be able to question him. But he does not always have his own way. Ex-employees have won cases of unfair dismissal against Hyams.

His yacht, *Shemara*, has also hit legal minefields. First Hyams tried to cancel the purchase from Sir Bernard Docker, the industrialist. That failed and later Hyams was locked in dispute over repairs carried out by the Vosper Thorneycroft yard. In 14 years, the yacht did not leave the yard.

Hyams' major stake in Oldham Estates (bought in 1959 for £50,000) was taken over for £150 million in 1988.

Jack Dellal   £300m

PROPERTY AND GENERAL TRADER
dob 2 October 1923

IN 1972, Jack Dellal was paid £58 million by the City banking group Keyser Ullman for his secondary banking group, Dalton Barton, based in Manchester. 'Black Jack', as he is called by his friends, joined the Keyser board as deputy chairman but resigned in 1974. Dellal had been active in the property finance field, backing such well-known figures as William Stern.

Known as a brilliant wheeler-dealer since his days in Manchester (where he was raised), Dellal has often emerged as a key stock market player, building stakes in groups which he then sells for a profit.

He married an Israeli air hostess in 1952, and they had a son and four daughters. Tragedy struck in 1981, when one daughter, Suzy, died of a drugs overdose. Another daughter, Gabrielle, is making a name for herself as an actress. Jack Dellal sent her to drama school in Los Angeles for four years.

Parted from his wife, Dellal has been spotted by the gossip columnists with attractive younger women on his arm. 'Black Jack' lives in London, and has a farm in Hampshire and a luxury yacht on the Mediterranean. He lists tennis, squash, music and art as his hobbies.

His money-making skills were again revealed in November 1989 when he sold Bush House, home of the BBC World Service, to the Japanese Kato Kagaku company for £130 million. Two years previously he paid £55 million for the building. Dellal has recently turned his formidable money-making talents to Poland, looking for investment opportunities in the newly capitalist economy.

Gerald Ronson £300m

PROPERTY AND PETROL STATION OWNER
dob 26 May 1939

RONSON's Heron group is Britain's second largest private company, embracing self-service filling stations, house-building and the HR Owen car dealership.

Ronson left school at 15 to work in a furniture business with his father Henry, the son of Russian Jewish refugees who fled tsarist pogroms. In 1956, they moved into property and later into petrol.

Ronson works a six-day week from his Marylebone head-quarters, and has built Heron into a £1 billion per annum turnover business. In the year to the end of March 1989, the group made after-tax profits of £54.8 million, then valuing Ronson at some £548 million. But City success has eluded him. In 1982 and again in 1983 he lost two bid battles by refusing to pay what he considered over the odds for companies.

He lives a quiet private life in a luxury north London home with his wife Gail, a former model, and four daughters. His only indulgence is a penchant for luxury cigars and Bentleys from HR Owen. He has a £10 million yacht called *MY Gail III*, complete with an enormous 7-foot jacuzzi. It is based in the Mediterranean. In 1989 Ronson held his 50th birthday party on board surrounded by his close friends and trying to forget the problems of his trial over his role in the Guinness affair.

Convicted for his role in the Guinness scandal, Ronson was sentenced to a year's imprisonment but served just 6 months in Ford Open Prison. He emerged having lost weight and 'exceedingly fit' in his own words. Heron produced a loss of £145 million in 1990, reducing the value of Ronson's fortune to £300 million.

Ronson is a well-known supporter of charities such as the National Society for the Prevention of Cruelty to Children. He is no lover of publicity and is said to have shunned a stock market quotation for his company in order to avoid unwelcome media attention.

Lord Howard de Walden   £280m

LANDOWNER   dob 27 November 1912

LONDON's Harley Street and many of the consulting rooms around it are owned by Lord Howard de Walden through his private company, Howard de Walden Estates. The company owns 110 acres of prime London land and some 1,200 houses, which are mainly used as smart offices.

The London estate was acquired in 1710 and Lord Howard de Walden inherited in 1946. He is a member of the Jockey Club, and has been senior steward three times. The three studs he owns – in Yorkshire, Newmarket and Berkshire – reflect his passion for racing.

He lives on a Berkshire estate and also has a Mayfair flat.

With no male heir, his four daughters are all named as co-heiresses. He married Countess Irene Harrach in 1934. She died in 1975. Three years later, he married his second wife Gillian, Viscountess Mountgarret.

Educated at Eton and Magdalene College, Cambridge, Lord

Howard de Walden has a splendid country mansion set in its own estate at Avington, on the edge of Hungerford Common in Berkshire. He is a friend of Lord Carnarvon, the Queen's racing manager, who looks after her equine interests from his estate at Highclere Castle about eight miles away on the north side of Newbury.

Lord Howard de Walden's estate stretches over 3,000 acres of some of the best arable farming land in the Thames Valley.

A multi-millionaire, he bought the estate in the 1950s. When he took over, he ordered the bulldozing of all the historic and picturesque farm buildings and some cottages to streamline the farm and provide more land for crops. He pulled down the Manor House, which had a ballroom, and moved into one of the big farmhouses of the estate called Avington Manor, which became his country seat.

He keeps cattle and sheep but mainly concentrates on corn and other crops. The estate is one of the most famous in the area for top-class pheasant and partridge shoots during the November to January season. He employs his own gamekeepers and also controls a stretch of the River Kennet through the estate, one of the most sought-after trout-fishing rivers in Britain, where a rod can cost £1,000 a session. But he reserves most of the shooting and fishing for his wealthy friends.

He is described by locals as 'aloof' but they also say he can be charming.

Duke of Buccleuch £270m

LANDOWNER dob 28 September 1923

OWNING 247,000 acres of Scotland and Northamptonshire would on its own make the fortune of the Duke of Buccleuch, Britain's largest private landowner. But it is the art treasures in his four homes that make him super-rich. They include a Titian which is too valuable to insure, so the Duke takes it with him when he moves between houses every three months.

In his Northampton home, Boughton House, there is a set of 37 oil sketches by Van Dyck, as well as works by El Greco and Gainsborough. At Bowhill, near Selkirk, the Duke has more works by Van Dyck, Reynolds, Gainsborough and Canaletto. At the main family seat, Drumlanrig Castle, the single most valuable work is Rembrandt's *Old Woman Reading*. The art treasures are complemented by a superb array of French porcelain and furniture.

The Buccleuch land goes back to the days of Robert Bruce. The Douglas clan, which the Duke heads, was given its land by Bruce as a reward for their support. The present Duke was Conservative MP for North Edinburgh until he succeeded to the title in 1973.

In October 1990, a small advert appeared in the weekend section of the *Financial Times* offering 'an exceptional opportunity to secure a 21-year lease of a specified week on the exclusive private water at Drumlanrig'.

Joe Bamford   £250m

CONSTRUCTION EQUIPMENT
MANUFACTURER   dob 21 June 1916

THE bright yellow JCB diggers seen on construction sites around the world owe their existence to a down-to-earth Staffordshire businessman, Joe Bamford. The Bamfords were a long-established farming family, but Joe branched out on his own after the war.

He first tried to develop a rival to Brylcreem but the problem with his Smartfix was that it turned hair green, 40 years too early for punks. But in 1945, he broke away from the family agricultural business and built odd bits of farm machinery until he hit on the idea of the backhoe loader, with its distinctive arm on the back and bulldozer-style excavator at the front. From then he never looked back.

Today the firm, still entirely controlled by the Bamfords, operates from a modern factory in Staffordshire. It is one of the few British industries to beat its Japanese and American competitors. The firm has never had to borrow a penny and regularly updates its model range. In 1988, it made profits of £25 million. It runs an impressive display team which performs amazing feats of simulated combat and the like with JCBs.

The business is now run by Anthony Bamford, Joe's son. Joe lives in comfortable retirement in Switzerland, though he still comes to England to keep an eye on the business. The first digger he ever built is now on proud display at the new factory.

Anthony recently bought Daylesford in Gloucestershire, one of Britain's finest stately homes, from Baron Henry Thyssen for £12 million. He also owns a 2,500-acre farm in the Midlands and a Barbados property that cost him £1 million in 1979. He beat Alan Bond, the Australian magnate, in the bidding for Daylesford.

Joe educated Anthony at Ampleforth and then at 16 put him to work as an apprentice on the shop floor at Massey-Ferguson. When he was 22 Anthony survived a 100 m.p.h. crash in his racing car.

Despite its high productivity and huge development programme, the business is not immune from the recession, and in December 1990, it was reported that the staff would get no Christmas bonus from the profit-sharing scheme following the halving of production levels.

Viscount Hambleden and family   £230m

NEWSAGENTS   dob VH Smith 2 April 1930

WILLIAM Henry Smith was only a month old when his father died in 1792, leaving his mother to struggle with a small newspaper delivery business. But he went on to lay the foundations for the present W. H. Smith empire. He designed light horse-drawn vehicles to send papers over a wider area and took advantage of the railway boom in Victorian Britain.

Today, with profits surging from £70 million in 1988 to nearly £88 million in 1990, the core of the business remains the same:

newspaper distribution and sales. There are 379 high-street branches and 68 at airports or railway stations. The company has also diversified into record shops via the purchase of the Our Price chain and DIY with its Do-It-All shops.

The family has around a third of the voting shares and two Smiths, one a peer, sit on the board. The Smith peer is Viscount Hambleden, who lives in the Manor House at Hambleden, near Henley-on-Thames.

The Hambleden family are close friends of the Royal family and the Viscount's mother, the Dowager Viscountess, has been a lady in waiting to the Queen Mother since 1937. Viscount Hambleden himself is a close friend of Princess Margaret, and in the 1960s was part of what was known as the Annabels set, centred on Annabels club in Mayfair. He now farms extensively at Hambleden. He married the daughter of an Italian count in 1955, and they have five sons. He and his wife were finally divorced in 1988. Viscount Hambleden has since been romantically linked with Lesley Watson, a model.

Edwin and Malcolm Healey   £220m

PROPERTY DEVELOPERS   dob EH April 1938

EDWIN and Malcolm Healey's roots are in the home-decorating business in Hull. Their father Stanley started the business in 1931, pushing a handcart loaded with ladders, paint and decorator's tools and knocking on doors for work. During the war, while Stanley was in the army, his wife Sarah carried on the business. Back home Stanley concluded that selling the materials was better than decorating. Healey Brothers, as the business was called, opened its first shop in Hull, paying a rent of just £1 a week.

In the 1970s Stanley Healey moved into the former Dance De Luxe ballroom and, trading as Status Discount, sold paint and wallpaper. His eldest son John joined him in 1954. A year later, Edwin joined at the age of 16. Eventually Malcolm, the youngest son, also joined.

While working for Status Malcolm became increasingly disenchanted with late deliveries, poor workmanship and price rises from British manufacturers. In 1976, he decided to make his own kitchens and bought a 40,000-square-foot factory and second-hand machinery. Humber Kitchens was born. Experts said the machines would break down but Healey kept them in top working order. In 1981 he acquired the Hygena name and built it up to the point where it made £20 million pre-tax profits in 1987.

He then sold the company to the MFI group, netting £200 million in cash and shares. A private man, Malcolm Healey has now emigrated to America, where he is planning to 'take the American furniture industry apart'.

Edwin, his elder brother, was the driving force in Status. In 1972 he floated Status on the stock market and spent the next eight years building it up before agreeing a £30 million takeover by MFI. He stayed for three years and then branched out on his own, shunning the limelight and building up his property group, Stadium Developments, which he intends to keep as a private company. He became a leading force in building retail warehouses and in 1987 built 1 million square feet. Currently, he is developing the huge Meadowhall site in Sheffield with fellow Yorkshire property man, Paul Sykes (q.v.). The latest accounts for Stadium Developments, where Healey and his wife Carol own all the shares, show after-tax profits of over £15 million.

Today Edwin lives in Hull's exclusive executive belt west of the city, an easy drive from his business base at Melton. In April 1988, he had a party at the Hall to celebrate the 21st birthday of his daughter Anne and his own 50th birthday on the same day. The party for 400 guests cost an estimated £250,000. The band of the Royal Artillery played on a mock castle in the 20-acre grounds and there was a firework display which was seen five miles away.

Edwin Healey, like his father, is a very private person, devoted to family and the business. He plays no part in local or county politics, and is regarded as a nice quiet man with 'no side' – a Yorkshire expression meaning that he has not changed with success. He is occasionally seen in the village pub not far from his home and it is said that he has private invitations from royalty in recognition of the help he has given to various good causes.

Viscount Rothermere £210m

NEWSPAPER PUBLISHER   dob 27 September 1925

BRITAIN's most private press baron enjoys the good life but still keeps a very shrewd eye on the family business founded by his grandfather, Alfred Harmsworth, the legendary newspaper man. Rothermere may not have the ego of a Beaverbrook or of a Maxwell, but he has seen off both the *Express* and the *Mirror* publishers. The *Daily Mail* and latterly the *Mail on Sunday* (which Rothermere supported courageously through the years of heavy losses until it became immensely profitable) have carved out a dominant position in the middle market of the British press. Rothermere managed to sink Robert Maxwell's *London Daily News* by relaunching his own *Evening News* as a spoiler. Typically, this was a spur-of-the-moment Rothermere decision which he ordered to be put into effect instantly.

Rothermere's strong support for the Tory cause is reflected in the editorial columns of the *Daily Mail*. His coyness about publicity is in direct contrast to the high-profile party-going activities of his wife, known to gossip columnists as 'Bubbles'. Apart from his main Paris base, Rothermere also has homes in London. New York, Sussex, Jamaica and Los Angeles. He lists painting, sailing and reading as his hobbies.

In 1989 the *Mail* group moved into its smart new offices in Kensington, and a high-technology printing operation has also been commissioned. The benefits of a lower cost base are now making his newspapers highly profitable again. But recession gripped the Daily Mail & General Trust, Rothermere's controlling vehicle. In the year to the end of September 1990, pre-tax profits tumbled to £44.2 million, against £113 million in 1989. The threat of redundancy was in the air at its newspapers. But no one expects the shrewd Rothermere to be seriously damaged by the economic clouds.

William Brown   £200m

INSURANCE BROKING   dob (unknown)

BILL Brown holds the distinction of being Britain's highest paid director. The latest accounts of his family-owned insurance broker, Walsham Brothers, reveal that in 1989 he received an annual salary of £8,136,274 – or £22,250 a day. But then Brown can easily afford it as one of Lloyd's top brokers and undisputed king of high-risk insurance. In its 1989 accounts, Walsham showed its class by unveiling £20.4 million after-tax profits on a £36 million turnover. With insurance brokers selling for 24 times their after-tax profits at the start of the year, that would put a price tag of nearly £480 million on Walsham, but we have discounted the price as the business is so clearly dependent on William Brown and his three brothers, Henry, James and Ronald. A more realistic price would probably be around £200 million.

A low-profile character, Brown came from the East End of London and entered Lloyd's, working his way up to become a member in 1960 at the age of 23. His two daughters by his first wife, Angela, are international showjumpers. He and Angela were divorced in 1987. He has homes in Hove, Chelsea harbour and in Jersey, and a pick of cars ranging from a Rolls-Royce to a Ferrari, a Porsche and a Mercedes, complete with number-plate, BILLY.

Rothschild family: £200m
Evelyn de Rothschild

BANKER   dob 29 March 1931

and Jacob Rothschild   £150m

dob 29 April 1936

IN 1804 Nathan Rothschild arrived in Manchester with £20,000 to start a textile business. By the time of the Battle of Waterloo in 1815, he had built his company into a commanding position in the banking heart of London. He learned, even before the British Prime Minister, of Wellington's famous victory. The bank that still bears his name, NM Rothschild, is run by his great-great-grandson Evelyn.

Evelyn's tenure at the bank has been marked by controversy, wholly at odds with the traditional Rothschild family unity and discretion of the past two centuries. In the mid-1970s the customary positioning of the Rothschild heirs in relation to the heart of their inheritance – the bank – changed. The chairmanship, held by Baron Edmond de Rothschild, had been expected to go to his nephew, Jacob. It went instead to Jacob's father, Lord Victor Rothschild, then coming to the end of a long career as head of various Whitehall think-tanks and a spell as an intelligence officer. When the time came for Victor to step down, he nominated his nephew Evelyn, not his son, Jacob, to succeed him. Evelyn also controlled over 40% of Rothschild Continuity, the trust which controls the Rothschild bank. Jacob spoke for less than 10% of Rothschild Continuity.

In September 1980 Evelyn wrote to Jacob, then head of the corporate finance department at the bank, insisting that if he did not cease banking under his own name in any part of the world, steps would be taken to remove him from the board of NM Rothschild. Jacob left and took over the management of RIT, a small investment trust. He has parleyed this into a major financial institution and recently partnered Sir James Goldsmith in his ambitious bid to break up BAT. But with the abandonment of the BAT bid, Jacob's interest in business has waned and he is now more interested in the National Gallery, where he is chairman of the trustees.

Evelyn emerged from the cousinly confrontation with renewed energy and NM Rothschild Bank is once again a leading player in the City big league. Evelyn is a shy man, twice married, who avoids publicity at all costs, despite being chairman of the *Economist* magazine. He is also chairman of the key banking institution, the British Merchant Banking and Securities Houses Association. In 1988 their aunt Dolly, widow of James de Rothschild, died leaving £92 million in her will, the largest sum ever left in a will in Britain. Much of that sum was represented by Waddesdon, a French château in Buckinghamshire which she donated, with all its treasures, to the National Trust. It has been described as by far the finest and greatest bequest ever made to a body already well endowed with castles and palaces.

A racing fan all her life, she left her stable to Jacob, who it is said cares little for horses, while Evelyn, who is chairman of United Racecourses, received 'not a leg', as one racing critic put it. Evelyn was educated at Harrow and Trinity College, Cambridge, and is known in banking circles as a traditionalist.

Sir John Templeton £200m

FINANCIER   dob (unknown)

F EW people renounce their American citizenship, take British citizenship and are awarded a knighthood. But Sir John Templeton, born in Tennessee, and one of the most successful financiers in America, achieved this distinction. The son of a lawyer, he went to Yale in the Depression. After his father lost most of his money, Templeton could only stay on there by winning scholarships and working hard. A top student, he became a Rhodes Scholar at Oxford, which developed his love of Britain. His life on Wall Street started in 1937, and he eventually built up one of the top fund management groups, Templeton, Galbraith & Hansberger, where he has a large stake. Noted for his ability to spot undervalued shares, and one of the first investors in the Japanese market, Templeton is also known for his thrift, often travelling economy class. He lives in the Bahamas and was knighted in 1986 for his services to charity and education. For example, he funded Oxford's Templeton College.

Tiny Rowland £190m

INDUSTRIALIST dob 27 November 1917

BORN Roland Fuhrop in a British internment camp in India, the son of a German trader and a British mother, Tiny Rowland's life has been dogged by controversy. He was briefly interned as an enemy alien in the war. He went to Africa in the late 1940s to become a farmer and trader, and at the request of Angus Ogilvie took over the tiny London & Rhodesian Mining and Land Company (Lonrho), in 1961. Today it is Africa's largest food producer and publishes the *Observer* newspaper.

Rowland loves feuds and pursues his enemies remorselessly. When Edward Heath described him as 'the unacceptable face of capitalism' in 1971, Rowland retorted that 'it was the only notable thing he had ever said'.

Currently, he is embroiled in a battle with the Fayed brothers, owners of Harrods. Rowland is bitter about the manner in which they acquired the store and the House of Fraser chain, and he has put all his energy and the *Observer* columns into questioning the source of their wealth.

Over the last few years Tiny has stepped up the pace of his attacks against his enemies. A devastating onslaught on the Australian financier, Alan Bond, led eventually to the virtual collapse of the Bond empire, loaded down with debts. Bond had had the temerity to take an unwelcome stake in Lonrho.

Tiny's feud with the Fayeds continued to fascinate a bemused British financial establishment and Fleet Street into the 1990s.

In 1989 in an unprecedented midweek edition the *Observer* published extracts from the then unpublished report by the Department of Trade and Industry into the Fayed takeover of the House of Fraser stores group. The report, which branded the Fayeds as 'liars', was finally published in 1990 and appeared to vindicate Rowland's position. The Government refused to take any action against the Fayeds.

Despite his advancing years, Tiny shows no sign of abandoning business or ending the feuds, which he appears to relish. His burning interest outside the company is Africa and African politics.

One of his proud boasts is that he owes no bank money, he belongs to no clubs and he has no entry in *Who's Who*. He lives quietly with his wife Josie in Berkshire on the banks of the Thames. There were reports, later played down, that Lonrho was thinking of merging with the huge Gencor mining concern in South Africa. Such a move would provide a secure future for Lonrho after Tiny.

Ken Morrison and family   £185m

SUPERMARKET OWNER   dob 20 October 1931

THE Morrison family still controls over half the shares of the Wm Morrison northern supermarket chain. The business was started in Bradford at the turn of the century by Bill and Hilda Morrison, who sold eggs and butter to householders and then moved on to a market stall. The company opened its first supermarket in 1961. Today there are over 50 Wm Morrison stores and the business is run by Ken Morrison, son of the founder.

Enterprise Five is the Morrison flagship store in Bradford. It has its own mock Tudor half-timbered 'high street' and a Victorian arcade inside.

The group has been a perpetual takeover target but with the family controlling over 50% of the shares, no realistic takeover bid could be mounted until 1990 when their holding was ultimately reduced to around 44%.

The health of the group has not been affected by the recession and was underlined in September 1990 when Ken Morrison revealed a near 30% increase in profits and said: 'We appear to be enjoying a strange bequest from the economy . . . people are taking fewer holidays and taking fewer meals out.'

Marquess of Tavistock   £180m

LANDOWNER   dob 21 January 1940

FATE has dealt the Marquess of Tavistock a mixed hand. He was a reluctant inheritor of Woburn Abbey and its treasures, preferring that his father, the Duke of Bedford, tread the path of duty a little longer before fleeing to tax exile and freedom in Monte Carlo in 1974. Then, early in 1988, Tavistock suffered a devastating stroke, from which he is now fully recovered.

When his father transferred the family lands and property to his heir, Robin Tavistock was a contented 34-year-old City stockbroker. Educated at Harvard, he preferred the company of American friends and had little in common with the hereditary antediluvians of the House of Lords.

When the Marquess's wife, Henrietta, heard that the Duke was becoming a tax exile and that she and her husband would have to live at Woburn, she made her famous outburst: 'I never wanted to live there. It was extremely selfish of my father-in-law to go. My husband was enjoying his life. At 34, to be made a prisoner of an inheritance is very cruel.' She probably reflected her husband's view.

The Marquess is renowned for being a difficult, almost chilly, individual. 'I don't know why I'm so formal,' he once confessed. 'I just think some people are slightly more reserved than others. Some people are slightly shyer than others, too.'

Millions of visitors a year enter Woburn and its 13,000

sculpted acres. The Duke was practically the inventor of the stately home game as it is now played. In 1955 he opened his ancestral home to the charabanc trade largely to pay off the death duties with which his own father had saddled him. Since taking over, the Marquess has followed his father's example and Woburn is a top tourist attraction. Yet this is only the visible side of a two-pronged foray into modernizing the Bedford Assets. Twenty acres of Bloomsbury, one of inner London's most rapidly improving areas, came with the portfolio. The Bloomsbury acres have subsidized Woburn for many generations.

The first Earl of Bedford, a crony of Henry VIII, received a parcel of land just north of the Strand as his portion of the booty from the dissolution of the monasteries. In the 1680s, his grandson commissioned Inigo Jones to develop Covent Garden. A marriage to the Southamptons secured another 100 acres and Bloomsbury was born. Unfortunately, in the early years of the century, the 11th Duke decided to sell off such choice items as Covent Garden and the British Museum site, netting £2 million that no one in the family really needed at that time.

Lord Forte and family   £167m

HOTELIER   dob CF 26 November 1908

IN 1913, Charles Forte left a remote hilltop village in Italy to come to Edinburgh with his mother. He later served milkshakes in his father's Alloa café. Today, Lord Forte presides over the Trust House Forte empire employing over 70,000 people in 800 hotels.

A strict paternalist and ardent admirer of Mrs Thatcher, Forte built up THF in the 1960s and 1970s through a mixture of shrewdness and hard work. But one prize eluded him for many years: the Savoy group, where annual shareholders' meetings became a ritual battle. In 1989, a peace agreement was signed between the two sides and the war officially ended.

Rocco Forte, 46, his heir, is the only son among his six children. He worked in the business even while he was at school, washing dishes and making sandwiches. Once when he broke a tray of dishes, his father deducted the cost from his wages. He is now an able chief executive and led the assault on the Savoy. He still finds time to indulge in a passion for running and marathons.

Father and son are close, living on opposite sides of the same Mayfair street. Rocco's sister Olga is THF's design director, and holds shares worth over £80 million in the company. The company, which has changed its name to Forte, is being hit by the recession. In the year to the end of January 1991, pre-tax profits fell by 27% to £190 million.

Lord McAlpine and Bobby McAlpine   £165m

BUILDERS dob LM 14 May 1942

THE McAlpine family now run two separate and competing building companies, Newarthill and Alfred McAlpine, but they were once a united family.

Newarthill was the Lancashire town where, in 1847, a Robert McAlpine was born and started work as a miner at the age of seven, on the princely wage of one penny a week. Later he became a bricklayer and then started his own company at the age of 22. By the time he was 28, he had 1,000 staff and two brickyards, but he later went bankrupt when a Glasgow bank collapsed.

He rebuilt his fortune, however. When he died in 1934, his second son William took over the family business; then his third son Alfred branched out on his own, in 1935.

The two companies – Sir Robert McAlpine (now called Newarthill), run by William, and Alfred McAlpine, run by Alfred – used to divide the country up to avoid competition. But no more. In 1989, Newarthill went private and gave up its stock market listing. Confusingly, it still trades under the Sir Robert McAlpine name.

William died in 1951. His son Lord McAlpine of Moffat, who headed the Newarthill branch, died in 1990. Unusually, his son is also a life peer but is best known for once being treasurer of the Conservative Party and an impressive fund-raiser, who used his business connections to raise millions for party funds. His parties at Conservative annual conferences are always said to be most lavish.

He also collects modern art and gave 60 sculptures to the Tate Gallery in 1971. He once boasted he had had 500 lunches at the Dorchester (then owned by the family) in five years. Lord McAlpine had a narrow escape last year when an IRA unit exploded a bomb outside a house he had recently vacated. But for McAlpine the worst that happened last year was the resignation of Mrs Thatcher. McAlpine, like many prominent industrialists, was desolate at her going, and is financing her new private office.

On the other side of the family, Alfred McAlpine lives in Cheshire, where the company is now based. His son, Bobby, is vice-chairman of Alfred McAlpine.

John Clothier and family £160m

SHOE MANUFACTURER   dob (unknown)

JOHN Clothier is the great-great-grandson of James Clark, the J. of C. & J. Clark, now Britain's largest shoemakers. Clark was founded over 150 years ago by Cyrus and James Clark in the Somerset town of Street, which is still its headquarters. The company now employs over 23,000 people.

Oxford-educated Clothier has been with the business all his life. There are other Clarks on the board including Daniel, the great-grandson of James.

Recently the growth of imports has hit the business, and it has launched Project Thrift to cut out wasteful spending. But it still managed a healthy £29 million post-tax profit in 1989. It has recently built a new factory near Bath to make children's shoes.

The Clark family are well-known local Liberals, and exerted a strong Quaker influence on Street, which had no pubs until 1975.

John Clothier, who lives near Taunton, is a keen sailor and farmer. He was in the 1979 Fastnet race, which was hit by a severe storm that killed a number of the competitors. He is hoping to float the business on the stock market when the economic climate improves.

Samuel Whitbread and family £160m

BREWER   dob SW 22 February 1937

THE Whitbread brewing empire is run by a family member, some 250 years after the business was founded by Samuel Whitbread, a Bedfordshire farmer, who used a £2,000 inheritance to set it up.

Today, Samuel Whitbread, his great-great-great-great-grandson, is chairman of what is Britain's third largest brewer, turning out 13 million barrels of beer a year. The family owns over 10 million shares in the group, which was valued at around £1.9 billion in January 1991. In the year to the end of March 1991, the group unveiled a 10% increase in pre-tax profits to £292 million.

Before joining the Whitbread board in 1972 as one of the family directors, Sam was a farmer. He read farming and estate management at Cambridge and later worked for a year as a shepherd on the Duke of Buccleuch's estate. He managed the Whitbreads' 100,000-acre estates in Bedfordshire. But gradually his interest in the family business grew. He took over as chairman in 1984, the first Whitbread to run the business since 1970 when his uncle, Colonel William Whitbread, retired.

The family also owns a 32,000-acre estate in Ross and Cromarty, Scotland, and all the family members enjoy country pursuits such as shooting and fishing.

Alan Sugar   £157m

COMPUTER MANUFACTURER   dob 24 March 1947

A GENUINE East End barrow boy raised in a council flat, who left school at 15 to sell car aerials out of a car boot, Sugar now owns nearly 250 million shares in Amstrad, the company he founded in 1968.

Standing for Alan Michael Sugar Trading, Amstrad sells computers, televisions, hi-fis and now satellite dishes more cheaply than anyone else. Sugar has a high-powered marketing and technical team at his Brentwood headquarters looking for niches in the consumer electronics market. They dream up new products and new attractive designs, which are then built in the Far East at a cut-price rate. Thus far, the formula has worked perfectly, with the exception of the economic downturn in 1989.

Sugar has no time for the old school tie network or the City. He tried to sue one stockbroker for hostile comments about Amstrad, and says that he is 'proud' to be called a barrow boy. He is married and has two sons and a daughter, with homes in Essex and Florida.

The year 1989 proved disastrous for Sugar. Problems with his computers, a slow-down in retail sales and high interest rates have hammered the group and his own shareholding. At one stage, his wealth was bleeding away at over £1 million a week. But it is too early to write off the tenacious Sugar.

In 1990, he staged a recovery. Bank borrowings were slashed, and the inventory of unsold computers which had hit the company in 1988 was sharply reduced. Though he produced lower profits in the year to June 1990 – £43 million against £76 million in the previous year – the City was sufficiently impressed by his timely action to mark up his shares. In March 1991, Sugar stunned the City by selling a 7.5% stake in Amstrad, raising £34 million, which he planned to invest in commercial property. In the event, in June 1991 he became chairman and major rescuer of Tottenham Hotspur football club.

His one innovation in recent times has been to install himself in a proper office rather than directing operations from a large armchair in the middle of his sales floor.

Albert Gubay   £150m

SUPERMARKET OWNER AND BANKER
dob *c.* 1930

IN the late 1960s, a mud-spattered figure in a donkey jacket
would often be seen building new supermarkets in Wales.
This huge figure was no ordinary navvy. It was Albert Gubay,
the boss of the Kwik Save supermarket chain, and he would
quite literally muck in to build his new stores.

Born in the North Wales town of Prestatyn of an Armenian
father and Irish mother, Gubay went into business on his own
after doing his National Service in the navy. Spotting that a
British public, tired of rationing, would want some luxuries in
the drab postwar world, Gubay first went into business selling
cut-price sweets from the back of a lorry. Borrowing £100, he
bought an old cinema and converted it into a factory to make
sweets, but by the late 1950s, with derationing, the big sweet-
makers moved into the field and cut the ground from under
him.

He then went into retailing and set up a cut-price store. This
was the age of Resale Price Maintenance, when manufacturers
could dictate the price of their goods. But Gubay managed to
overcome this problem by buying his stock under different
names, so that the manufacturers could not identify him and
cut off his supplies.

Through the 1960s the Kwik Save group prospered as Gubay
introduced new selling techniques such as late-night opening,
car parking, out-of-town stores and and a philosophy of selling
cheap goods out of boxes, often without labels, 25% below the
cost of well-known brands. He flouted local by-laws in Prestatyn
to keep his store open until 9 p.m. and simply paid the fines
and kept on trading. 'Every week we were summoned until it
looked as though I was going to prison for contempt of court,'
he said later. But the public loved it and coach parties used to
come on shopping expeditions to his stores from all over Wales.

In 1972, Gubay sold all the shares in Kwik Save and moved
to New Zealand, where he had a 290-acre stud farm, to breed
trotting horses for harness racing, one of his hobbies.

The sale of the Kwik Save shares, which netted Gubay some £12.5 million, attracted considerable criticism in the City. But Gubay shrugged that off and went on to build up a large chain of modern supermarkets in New Zealand. In 1975, he returned to Britain to live on the Isle of Man, where he already owned a castle. Since then, he has led a quiet life on the island, turning to property development and the Celtic Bank, which he bought in 1984.

In 1985, he reckoned his master company Montrose Holdings would be worth £200 million if quoted on the stock market. He keeps in touch with his extensive business interests via his £2 million Gulfstream private jetplane.

David Wilson   £148m

HOUSEBUILDER   dob 5 December 1941

IN 1960, 18-year-old David Wilson joined his father in a housebuilding business in Ibstock, a gritty Leicestershire mining town. Twenty-seven years later, though the father had died, the fruits of that partnership were realized when their company, now called Wilson Bowden, was floated on the Stock Exchange. The share sale was oversubscribed four and a half times. In 1990 David Wilson's stake was worth £148 million.

Wilson Bowden specializes in building high-quality four-bedroom houses in the Midlands and the north of England, but not the south-east. It has also branched out into commercial development and has built an eleven-screen cinema complex in Nottingham.

Wilson himself has enjoyed the fruits of his success and bought a house costing £1 million in 1981. He has been married twice. Recession in the housebuilding sector appears to have left Wilson relatively unscathed. He saw his profits in 1990 fall by 25%. But the company has a long bank of cheap land which should see it through the recession. In March 1991, Wilson also tapped his shareholders for an extra £34 million to expand that land bank.

Ken Scowcroft and family £147m

INSURANCE   dob 8 August 1928

FROM modest beginnings in 1957, using the front room of his Manchester home as his office, Ken Scowcroft has built an insurance empire. At one time, only the Automobile Association insured more cars than his Swinton Insurance Services, named after the area of Manchester which was and still is his base. In 1989, Scowcroft sold a 30% stake in the group to the Sun Alliance insurance group for £30 million. In May 1990, Sun Alliance bought another 19% for £31.7 million and in January 1991, it bought yet another 26% for £43.3 million. This left the Scowcroft family with just 25% of the shares, but a great deal of cash.

The deal gave Sun Alliance 1 million customers, and enabled Scowcroft to indulge his hobby of breeding horses for carriage driving. Scowcroft pioneered television advertising of insurance. Of his first year's commission of £227, he spent £73 4s on advertising. In 1964, he followed this by opening the first high street insurance shop selling insurance over the counter. Today there are 320 branches and 200 staff employed at the head office. The budget for advertising has now risen to nearly £3 million a year. Scowcroft remains chairman, while his son, Brian, a chartered accountant, who joined the company in 1981 is chief executive. His daughter, Janet, a solicitor, is legal director.

Sir Donald Gosling £145m

CAR PARK OWNER   dob 2 March 1929

FOR a man obsessed with the sea, Sir Donald Gosling could hardly have chosen a more landlubbing job than running National Car Parks, which owns many of Britain's big city car parks.

He joined the navy as a boy signalman at 15, towards the end of the war, and, just after it, saw service in the Mediterranean on HMS *Leander*. He was seen as officer potential and promoted to leading seaman, but by 1949 the shrinking navy had no further need of his services. He loved the navy and described the day he left as 'the blackest of my life'.

There were compensations. Gosling, who had been born in Streatham, London, became a trainee surveyor with Westminster City Council and would have stayed there but for a chance encounter with Ronald Hobson (q.v.), an ex-soldier who wanted to clear one of the innumerable bomb sites in Holborn and set up a car park. He needed planning permission and Gosling told him how to get it. They became firm friends and partners. They are still together and the business has grown to become one of Britain's largest private companies with a turnover of around £100 million.

But Gosling has never lost his passion for the sea. He runs a £3 million yacht in the Mediterranean called *The Brave Goose*, the third vessel he has owned bearing that name. The original name came from an incident when Gosling was visiting his son, who was seriously ill in hospital, and called him a 'brave goose'; his son replied that that would be a good name for the boat Gosling was buying. The latest, in 1987, was the largest vessel ever to be built on the Thames, costing £3 million to build and around £300,000 a year to maintain. Equipped lavishly with gold thread carpet and a secure satellite communications system, *The Brave Goose* can be chartered for £34,000 a week. Gosling regularly holds board meetings on the yacht, which is berthed at Port Gallice on the Riviera. The largest boat in the port, it can only dock by occupying three berths rather than one.

Gosling was knighted in the Wilson resignation honours list in 1976. He was a close friend of Harold Wilson though he is a staunch Conservative. His knighthood was awarded for services to the Forces. He is a leading figure in the White Ensign Association, formed to advise ex-naval and marine personnel on finances after leaving the forces.

But super-patriot Sir Don has run into problems with the British establishment. In 1988, he quietly withdrew his proposed membership of the Royal Yacht Squadron, where Prince Philip is admiral, fearing he would be blackballed.

He married a doctor's daughter in 1959. She is an heiress in her own right, as her father was a principal shareholder in the

Palmer & Harvey confectionery business. Gosling is chairman of Palmer & Harvey and is credited with turning its fortunes around. In 1988, the couple parted.

NCP was in the news last year, when the *Sunday Times* Insight team reported that it had hired a secretary to infiltrate a rival company to find out useful commercial information in a classic case of industrial espionage.

Ronald Hobson £145m

CAR PARK OWNER   dob (unknown)

LONDON's frustrated motorists can thank Ronald Hobson for at least some relief from the chronic parking problems of Britain's capital city. It was his idea to start car parks in the late 1940s on old bomb sites that led to the chain of National Car Parks – complete with bright yellow signs – found off many city streets today.

Hobson, an ex-soldier, realized that postwar Britain would see a motoring explosion, and somewhere would be needed to park cars. He had a site in Holborn which he wanted to develop for a car park and went to see 20-year-old Donald Gosling (q.v.), a Westminster planner, about how to get planning permission. The two hit it off and went into business together with £200, offering a free car wash service to entice customers.

Today they remain firm friends. Hobson lives in Mill Hill in north London.

Paul Hamlyn £144m

PUBLISHER   dob 12 February 1926

NO one in the English-speaking world is ever likely to forget the *Spycatcher* affair. Between 1985 and 1988 the British government, in courts across the world, sought to suppress the memoirs of a tired and embittered secret service man, Peter Wright. At vast cost to the British taxpayer, and at equally vast profit to Wright and his publisher Paul Hamlyn, the government lost the case.

Hamlyn, the son of a Jewish paediatrician who fled to London to escape Hitler's tyranny in 1933, and one of the most successful publishers in Britain, was approached by various 'friends' of the government while the case was in progress. It was made politely clear to him that if he were to drop his attempt to publish the book, 'it would be viewed favourably by the government'. As the *Observer* tells the story, Hamlyn's reply was, 'Tell them that nothing less than a Dukedom will do.'

It was typical of the man who opted out of school and the intense middle-class respectability of St John's Wood, London, at the age of 16 to become an office boy at *Country Life* magazine. A lifelong Labour supporter, his form of national service sent him down a Welsh coal mine as a medical orderly. He combined this job with that of stringer for the *South Wales Argus* and driving a bus at weekends. His involuntary service to the nation complete, he rented a shop in Camden, then the Irish ghetto of London, and began the career as bookseller that was to see him earn two immense fortunes.

His first publishing venture, Paul Hamlyn Associates, specialized in cheap popular works: mostly hobbies, art, cooking and travel. He refused to join the Publishers Association, and expressed antipathy for the Net Book Agreement, the trade's monopoly arrangement, designed to protect the price of books. He was frowned upon as an iconoclast. Nobody in the business seemed to notice that his cheap popular Shakespeare had sold over a million copies and his pocketbook Kafka sold 73,000 copies.

In 1964 he sold out to IPC, then run by Cecil King, for the sum of £2.25 million, about £40 million in 1990 terms. For a while he dithered at News International as Rupert Murdoch's joint managing director, but soon left and later set up Octopus Publishing Group, based on the book options he extracted from Murdoch for £50,000. In 1987 he sold Octopus for £535 million, £214 million of that being his own stake in the company. He had always encouraged his staff to take up shares and his chauffeur made £200,000. Twice married, Hamlyn has homes in

London and France. He is the brother of the poet Michael Hamburger, who bears the original family name. One of Hamlyn's first acts on completion of the sale of Octopus was to give £50 million to charity. In 1990, he gave £100,000 to the Labour Party, an unusual move for an industrialist. Hamlyn has also recently bought an £8 million executive jet which he uses for world business trips, especially to India. He likes to gamble.

Marquess of Bath £140m

LANDOWNER   dob 26 January 1905

LONGLEAT – famous for its lions and other exotic creatures such as gorillas, white tigers and rhinos – is also the family home of the Marquess of Bath. Dating from the Elizabethan period, Longleat is also filled with priceless art treasures and has 10,000 acres of grounds.

The Marquess, who drives a small Japanese station wagon, is regarded as a modest man. He spends hours directing visitors around Longleat, weeds the garden and will pick up any litter he sees left around.

The family wealth is tied up in trust funds, which means it cannot be spent. But in 1987, the Marquess had a public row with his son and heir, the eccentric Viscount Weymouth, over the sale of paintings. Four paintings were sold by the Marquess and replaced by identical colour photos mounted in similar frames. The Marquess said he had every right to sell them. His son did not agree.

Bruno Schroder and family £135m

BANKER   dob 17 January 1933

DESPITE inheriting a German title conferred on his grandfather by the Kaiser, Baron Bruno Schroder has an impeccably English pedigree: Eton, Oxford and the Life Guards. He is the only Schroder on the board of one of the City's most prestigious and profitable merchant banks. His brother-in-law, George Mallinckrodt, is chairman.

The bank was started in 1804 when John Henry Schroder left Germany to set up the British arm of his brother's merchant bank. It merged with Herbert Wagg in 1962. It has survived and prospered in the cut-throat market since the City's Big Bang deregulation in 1987 by offering top-class advice and help to companies fighting big takeover battles. In 1988 it became embroiled in the £2.9 billion takeover bid by Minorco for Consolidated Goldfields, the mining group. In 1988 it was also involved in the battle for Rowntree, the confectionery group.

Bruno has a home in London and another in Scotland: his hobbies are flying and shooting. The family still have a controlling 44% interest in the bank.

After Eton and Oxford, Bruno attended the Harvard Business School and married in 1969. His wife, Piffa, won the Edge Challenge Cup, one of shooting's major trophies, at Bisley in 1974. It was the first time in 82 years that a woman had won the cup.

Sir Antony Pilkington and family   £132m

GLASS MAKER   dob AP 20 June 1935

FOUNDED in 1826, Pilks – as it is known in its St Helens base – is Britain's biggest glass maker. But it only became a world force in 1959 after the invention of the float glass technology used to make high-quality glass. This involves floating molten glass in a bath of hot metal. It took seven years and £7 million to perfect. Today, it is the world's top float glass company. The Pilkingtons still control over 10% of the company shares. Despite 10,000 redundancies in the recession of the early 1980s, the family has a paternalistic reputation in St Helens, one of the few company towns in Britain.

Chairman Sir Antony Pilkington, a fifth-generation family

member, was educated at Ampleforth and later went to Trinity College, Cambridge, gaining an MA in history. He did his two years' National Service with the Coldstream Guards, where he was commissioned with the rank of of lieutenant. He is married, lives at Frodsham in Cheshire and has three sons and a daughter. His hobbies are cars – he used to race saloon cars – reading, skiing, sailing and squash.

He really gained his spurs in 1987 when he fought off a £1.2 billion bid for the company from the BTR group. The whole of St Helens, led by the Labour-controlled town hall, united behind the company. But at the end of 1990, BTR, which had kept a small stake in Pilks, raised its holding from 3.75% to 4.04%, reviving speculation that it would bid again.

In 1987 he was awarded an honorary law degree from the University of Liverpool and in the same year was presented with the Liverpool Publicity Association's Gold Medal Award for promoting Merseyside. In 1989 he became Deputy Lieutenant of Merseyside.

Duke of Atholl   £130m

LANDOWNER   dob 19 June 1931

'WEE Iain', the 6ft 4in Duke of Atholl, is the only man in Britain allowed to have his own private army, although it is limited to 80 soldiers who perform strictly ceremonial duties.

A confirmed bachelor, the Duke inherited the title at the age of 25 when his third cousin died. Despite the determined efforts of society hostesses, he shows no sign of wanting to marry their daughters.

He has no need to do so for money. The Atholl estates in rich Perthshire run to 130,000 acres; and his mother was sister to Lord Cowdray, head of the Pearson empire. The decline of the family lands has been much less rapid than for many other Scottish aristocrats. One hundred years ago, the Atholl estates covered 194,500 acres.

The Duke lives in Blair Castle, and is an active supporter of the Scottish Landowners' Federation and the National Trust.

Henry and Simon Keswick   £130m

FINANCIERS AND TRADERS
dob HK 29 September 1938, SK 20 May 1942

NOBLE House, the recent television adaptation of James Clavell's famous novel, was supposedly based on the activities of Jardine Matheson, the Hong Kong trading group. Jardines was founded in 1832 by William Jardine, a Scottish doctor and sometime opium trader, along with his partner, James Matheson.

The Keswicks, a Dumfries family, married into the Jardines in the mid-19th century, and five have served as chairman.

The current *taipan* (Chinese for big boss) is Simon, who succeeded his brother Henry. The family has around 10% of the company shares, and also owns a substantial Gloucestershire estate.

Henry is now based in Britain. He is a keen follower of the turf (racing horses) and owned the *Spectator* magazine until 1981.

Last November, the Jardine Matheson group threatened to de-list its shares from the Hong Kong stock market, fearing uncertainties arising from the Chinese takeover of Hong Kong in 1997. This provoked a row with the Hong Kong Stock Exchange authorities, who feared that the colony's future as an international financial centre would be undermined if companies of Jardine's stature moved overseas. The row was settled in March when the Stock Exchange agreed to draw up plans for a special form of stock market listing for companies such as Jardine, allowing them to be regulated overseas.

Duke of Devonshire   £120m

LANDOWNER   dob 2 January 1920

THERE are some 3,000 drawings at Chatsworth, the 175-room Derbyshire seat of the Duke of Devonshire. These include works by Leonardo, Raphael, Veronese, Claude, Rubens, Van Dyck and Rembrandt. In 1984, a collection of surplus Old Masters raised £21 million for the Duke. Aside from his paintings, the Duke also owns 70,000 acres in Derbyshire, Yorkshire and Sussex, including most of Eastbourne's sea front.

Noted as a keen gardener and an SDP supporter who defected from the Tories, the Duke is married to one of the famous Mitford sisters. He is ever conscious of the need to preserve the Chatsworth inheritance. In 1985 he put Lismore, his 200-room castle in Eire, up for rental at £2,600 a week.

His pale yellow racing colours are the oldest registered in Britain, and he has been a member of the Tote board and Jockey Club.

Charles and Maurice Saatchi   £120m

ADVERTISING AGENCY OWNERS
dob CS 9 June 1943, MS 21 June 1946

'LABOUR isn't working' worked wonderfully for the Saatchi brothers. As the advertising agency employed by the Conservative Party in 1979, the Saatchis devised the controversial poster and slogan attacking Labour's record. It won Mrs Thatcher the election and the Saatchis national fame.

The middle sons of a north London textile merchant, the Saatchis started their own advertising agency in 1971. By the end of the decade, they were the biggest agency in Britain. Until recently they were the biggest in the world. They achieved this by a hectic takeover of rival agencies and by branching out into new markets such as management consultancy. They even considered bidding for the Midland Bank at one time.

The two brothers disdain personal publicity and being photographed. Maurice lives in a Sussex mansion and enjoys gardening, tennis and renovating cars. Charles and his ex-wife Doris have what is acknowledged as one of the finest and most valuable collections of modern paintings in the world.

A disappointing year at work (1989), leading to a 30% pay cut in 1990 for the two Saatchi brothers, has only been relieved by the valuation now put on the art treasures. The collection is conservatively valued at £120 million. But the art cannot hide the disappointing performance of the advertising group that bears the brothers' name. The explosive growth that propelled Saatchi & Saatchi into the largest advertising business in the world began to peter out in 1989 when painful retrenchment became the order of the day. The results for the year to the end of September 1989 revealed a pre-tax loss of over £58.5 million. Robert Louis Dreyfus, a brilliant French businessman, was appointed to revive the group's fortunes.

But it has been a tough battle for survival. In the year to the end of September 1990, losses rose to £98.2 million. The Saatchi share price fell sharply, hitting the paper fortune built by the brothers. Their one real asset is the art collection.

The Marquess of Cholmondeley   £118m

LANDOWNER   dob 27 June 1960

THE Lord Great Chamberlain of England, the 7th Marquess of Cholmondeley, has two fine houses in Cheshire and Norfolk. He also owns over 12,000 acres of prime land in those two fast-growing counties. He inherited the title from his father in 1990. Cholmondeley, educated at Eton and the Sorbonne, was a page boy to the Queen from 1974 to 1976. He was in trouble at school for smoking and drinking, and was regarded as a somewhat bohemian figure. With a deep interest in art, he mixed with artists in France and toured Europe, learning five languages. He then had a spell at a Paris merchant bank, picking up financial skills that will serve him well in running the estate.

Death duties were avoided as much of the estates were put into a private company, the Rocksavage Estate Company. This may explain the surprise when the will of the 6th Marquess was published in December. Few expected it to be £118 million, the biggest will ever published in Britain.

Houghton Hall, the Norfolk home, was built by Sir Robert Walpole. It is described as 'a magnificent Palladian mansion' by one expert. Another says that the house is a monument to Walpole's passion for art and architecture.

Family portraits by Reynolds, Kneller and Batoni are on display together with fine French furniture and porcelain. There are also 20,000 model soldiers on parade. Whenever the family has needed money, they have simply sold off an antique or a painting. In recent years, sales have included an ink-stand owned by Walpole, that went for £1 million, and a Zoffany portrait for £1.9 million. The title Lord Great Chamberlain is largely ceremonial, but there are specific duties on state occasions and he is responsible for the conduct of royal affairs in the Palace of Westminster. His symbol of office is a gold key.

Benzion Freshwater £117m

RESIDENTIAL PROPERTY OWNER
dob 24 April 1948

OSIAS Freshwater arrived as a Polish refugee in Britain three days before the start of World War II. He started out as a textile merchant during the conflict but turned to property. By the early 1970s he was London's biggest private landlord with 20,000 tenants.

Growth had been achieved with the help of his son-in-law, William Stern, who joined the business in 1960. They were neighbours in two luxury homes in Hampstead, London. Stern left in 1970 to start up his own business but that folded in the 1974 property crash with debts of over £200 million.

Osias Freshwater, who had been on the Angry Brigade hit list in 1971, died in July 1976 and was succeeded by his son Benzion.

Today, the family has a near 80% share stake in a public company, Daejan Holdings, through which they control their property empire. This stake is worth around £117 million. In 1978, Benzion, who controlled a network of 200 companies, bought a modest flat in Hampstead for his wife and three children.

Duke of Northumberland   £115m

LANDOWNER   dob 1 July 1953

HENRY Percy inherited the title of Duke of Northumberland from his father, the 10th Duke, who died in October 1988. The new Duke's inheritance covers 80,000 acres in Northumberland, Syon Park in Middlesex and an estate in Surrey.

The family seat, Alnwick, which is about 20 miles from the Scottish border, is filled with art treasures. There is a fine collection of Italian paintings including three Titians and works by Tintoretto, Palma Vecchio and Canaletto. There is also a collection of English and Dutch paintings by Reynolds, Gainsborough, Turner and Van Dyck. Alnwick has been the seat of the Percy family since 1309; the dukedom was created in 1766.

The Duke is nephew of the Duke of Buccleuch, who is the largest landowner in the United Kingdom. His mother, Lady Elizabeth, is the elder sister of the (late) 9th Duke of Buccleuch. He was educated at Eton and Oxford, where he read History and English. He is known to be a film buff and has expressed an interest in becoming a film producer.

He and his elder sister, Lady Caroline, live at Syon House overlooking the Thames and Kew Gardens. The Queen is one of his godparents. The Duke has been linked in society columns with Natasha Grenfell, the daughter of Lady St Just.

John Stuart Bloor   £112m

BUILDING   dob (unknown)

STAFFORDSHIRE businessman John Bloor started his
business career as a self-employed plasterer while still a
teenager in the 1950s. Today his building group, Bloor Holdings, is one of the most profitable private companies in Britain.
In the year to the end of March 1989, Bloor Holdings made
£19.7 million after-tax profits on a turnover of £86 million.
Bloor himself owns 95% of the shares in the group, which
specializes in medium-priced estates in the Midlands. Bloor, an
extremely private man who hates the term magnate or multi-
millionaire, is also making a name for himself as a saviour of
the British motorcycle industry.

In 1983, he bought the Triumph motorbike company from
the liquidator, and determined to revive one of the most famous
marques in British engineering. In 1984, he set engineers to
work on a new bike and has invested several million pounds in
the project, including building a new factory at Hinckley in
Leicestershire. The range of six new Triumphs was received
with critical acclaim by the motorbike press when it was unveiled
late in 1990. Bloor told the *Independent* that he was not 'interested in any rubbish about saving the industry. I'm interested in
whether the public likes the bike. We want to make a fine bit of
equipment that appeals to people.'

Bob Edmiston   £112m

CAR DEALER   dob (unknown)

AS a young married man in Dagenham, Bob Edmiston
found it difficult to make ends meet on his salary as a
bank clerk. So he did up old cars such as Morris Minors, and
sold them for £50. Hooked on cars and trained as a cost and
management accountant, he rose through the car industry to
become finance director of the glamorous Jensen sports car

company. But behind the glamour, Edmiston found a company that was on the verge of financial ruin. His first act was to lay off half the staff, and when the company eventually folded his last job was to pay himself a £6,000 redundancy cheque. He was then 29.

He used the money to launch International Motors in 1976, with the backing of a Californian businessman. Initially it dealt with Jensen parts and served the loyal band of Jensen Interceptor owners. Later it was to become the United Kingdom concessionaire for Hyundai, the South Korean car manufacturer, and two Japanese manufacturers, Subaru and Isuzu. The company has a plush headquarters in West Bromwich.

Edmiston initially had 15% of the company, which he increased to 25% in 1980; by 1987 he was up to 50%. That year he spent £9 million acquiring the remaining 50%. In its latest accounts, IM Holdings, as it is called, revealed profits of over £21.5 million and had cash reserves of some £30 million. That would put a stock market value on the company of around £120 million at least. Much of the success of IM Holdings has been based on the British public's appetite for the four-wheel drive vehicles from the Far Eastern manufacturers.

Edmiston is noted as a big supporter of charities and also has a profit-sharing scheme for his 150-strong workforce.

Hugh and Patrick Murphy   £110m

PROPERTY
dob HM 8 March 1909, PM 21 February 1912

THE Murphy brothers left their small farm in the Newry area of Northern Ireland before the war to settle in Leicester. Sinking £3,000 into their company, Murphy Brothers, they began by reconditioning and selling old vehicles. Within 20 years, they had diversified into haulage, plant hire, civil engineering, earth moving and concrete. In 1968, they sold the business for £8 million cash to the giant BET group. But the Murphys did not retire to enjoy their wealth. Today, they own a large property group in Leicester, Charles Street, which made some £13.2 million after-tax profits in the year to the end of November 1989. With healthy reserves and little debt, the group would be worth over £110 million if floated on the stock market, according to the prevailing prices for property companies at the start of 1991. The Murphy brothers still live in the Leicester area.

The Clark family   £109m

PROPERTY DEVELOPERS   dob (unknown)

IN 1938 Scottish businessman Robert Clark founded his own company, which was later to be called Equity Trust. In 1951 he teamed up with Joe Levy, a London bookie's son, to create one of the most successful post-war property companies, Stock Conversion. Clark died in 1984, and the family's stake in Stock Conversion was sold for some £58 million a year later.

The family still control Equity Trust (now renamed Taylor Trust) and have extensive interests in leisure, entertainment, forestry, farming, property and finance. Their shares are held either directly by the family or through family settlements set up over the years. A charity, the Underwood Trust, also has an 18% stake in the business.

Accountants who have examined the latest accounts of Taylor Clark estimate that the company is worth well over £100 million, with net assets of £126.5 million.

Sir Kirby and Sir Maurice Laing

£109m

BUILDERS
dob ML 1 December 1918, KL 21 July 1916

SOME 140 years after the first Laing house was built in the Carlisle area, the Laing construction business is now one of Britain's leading building companies.

The business started around 1800 when David Laing drove cattle from Scotland to England and settled in the village of Sebergham, near Carlisle, to take up a job repairing buildings. His son branched out into new work and the business never looked back. After the war, it went international and has carried out construction work in the Falklands.

Both Sir Kirby and Sir Maurice have been chairmen of John Laing plc, but Martin Laing, Sir Kirby's son, now runs the business, which once included a valuable property company. In January 1990, this was the subject of a successful £441 million takeover bid from Elliott Bernerd (q.v.) and Sir Jeffrey Sterling of the P & O group.

Sir Kirby's first wife died in 1981 and left £1.5 million in her will. He married a doctor in 1986. The Laing brothers both live in north London and have had honours heaped on them by the civil engineering fraternity.

The Thomson family

£107m

PUBLISHING   dob (unknown)

THE Thomson family publish the *Beano*, Britain's best-selling comic, with the legendary Bash Street Kids and Dennis the Menace, but they only entered publishing by chance. In the 1870s, William Thomson, a Dundee shipowner, took an interest in a firm which published the local paper, and in 1886 he took complete control, putting his son D. C. Thomson in charge.

The firm is now dominated by Thomsons. Five are on the

board and the family owns nearly two-thirds of the shares. In 1990, D. C. Thomson made profits of £19.3 million, after tax.

It has a reputation as a publisher of staid and conservative papers, and of magazines such as *My Weekly* and the *People's Friend*. It is a strategy that works. Both sell nearly 600,000 copies while the *Sunday Post* sells 1.4 million. The company is also looking to the future and has major television and cable interests.

Brian Thomson, the current chairman, who was educated at Charterhouse, joined the business in 1937. During World War II he served in the Fife and Forfar Yeomanry. He married in 1947 and has a son and four daughters. He lists his hobbies as golf and shooting.

Elliott Bernerd   £105m

PROPERTY DEALER   dob 23 May 1945

ONE of the major figures in the London property market today, Elliott Bernerd started young. He left school at 16 and joined the estate agent Michael Laurie & Co., becoming its youngest ever partner while still in his early twenties. By the age of 24, he had already built up a substantial personal property portfolio.

Today, he runs a private property company called Chelsfield, which at one time owned the old *Times* building in London's Gray's Inn Road. He sold shares in another property company called Stockley in May 1987 and picked up over £21 million. In its accounts for 1988, Chelsfield made after-tax profits of £22.6 million compared with just £568,000 in 1987. The company is controlled from Panama, and Bernerd owns 80% of its share capital. In January 1990, Bernerd joined forces with his old friend Sir Jeffrey Sterling, the boss of the P & O group, to mount a £441 million takeover bid for the Laing property group, which succeeded in April 1990.

Bernerd is a keen skier and regularly spends Christmas at St Moritz. He likes to go to the south of France during August.

He has powerful international contacts in New York, Hong Kong and Tokyo.

He works an 18-hour day. Though not a qualified chartered surveyor, his business is built on experience and an innate feel for markets.

He manages to include a wide variety of outside interests in his hectic life. He is chairman of the council of the London Philharmonic Orchestra, sits on the board of the National Trust and is an avid collector of modern and Chinese art. He lives in Belgravia, London, and has a selection of black luxury cars.

Anita and Gordon Roddick   £103m

RETAILERS
dob AR 23 October 1942, GR 27 April 1942

AS Britain sweltered in the 1976 heatwave, Anita Roddick opened her first Body Shop in Brighton with a £4,000 overdraft. The hot weather made people more aware of their bodies and on the first day the stocks virtually sold out, netting £130. Despite being next to a funeral parlour, which caused considerable confusion, she persevered. The Body Shop secret is to use natural products, no-nonsense packaging and refillable bottles. The Roddicks travelled the world looking for new products. It worked. By 1990, there were over 400 stores round the world, over half of them overseas. Anita Roddick had become the byword for British businesswomen's success.

Husband Gordon is not as well known but is crucial. He dreamt up the idea of franchising the Body Shop to spread the business faster. In 1984, the Body Shop was floated on the stock market and its share price doubled within a week, such was the demand for the shares and the excitement the company generated in the City. The Roddicks between them still own around a third of the shares.

The seal of royal approval came in 1986 when the Princess of Wales opened the company's new headquarters in Littlehampton in Sussex. The Roddicks live in the area. They are keen supporters of Third World projects. Anita used to work for the housing charity Shelter and supports CND. But her children went to private schools. The Roddicks and their Body Shop proved to be the great survivor of all those stars in the mid-1980s retailing revolution. While other retailers were hammered by the slow-down in consumer spending of the late 1980s the Body Shop went from strength to strength. Its shops were packed over the Christmas 1989 period, as an increasingly 'green' British population sought out Anita's natural environmentally friendly products.

Despite a healthy growth in sales and profits, the Body Shop group has not been immune to falling values of retailing shares in 1990–91. But Anita and Gordon Roddick have not been deterred by City sentiment and have embarked on a large overseas expansion of the environmentally friendly chain. Apart from eyeing Eastern Europe, the first Body Shop has opened in Tokyo. It seems to be working.

In 1990, pre-tax profits rose 38% to £20 million. There are plans to have 200 Body Shops in Japan by the end of the decade.

Sir Euan Anstruther-Gough-Calthorpe   £100m

LANDOWNER   dob 22 June 1966

HARROW-educated baronet, Sir Euan Anstruther-Gough-Calthorpe, stands to inherit a £100 million fortune, but he is having to fight for it. At stake are several square miles of leafy Birmingham around the Edgbaston cricket ground, American property, European interests and a Hampshire farm, where Sir Euan lives. But the inheritance is in trust, with his uncle and other aristocrats acting as trustees. Sir Euan, who inherited the title from his grandfather in 1985, wanted to replace these trustees with more professional advisers. The row, which was being heard in the High Court, caused some embarrassment to the normally low-profile family. But it was dropped in an out-of-court settlement when the trustees resigned. Sir Euan is married to the ex-wife of Dai Llewellyn, the former nightclub host.

Lady Glover   £100m

LANDOWNER   dob (unknown)

ELEANOR Glover, British born, was first married to the Swiss financier Edwin Hurlimann, who died in 1966. He left her his magnificent Schloss Freudenberg estate on Lake Zug near Geneva, complete with 2,000 acres of parkland. In 1976 she married Sir Douglas Glover, the former Conservative MP for Ormskirk, following the death of his wife of 42 years.

Sir Douglas, who was a prominent member of the Anti-Slavery Society and also an active supporter of the Commonwealth, died in 1982. But that was after he had introduced Margaret and Dennis Thatcher to the delights of holidaying in Switzerland. In 1978, the Thatchers spent five days at Schloss Freudenberg and came back again in 1980 for a further ten days. After Sir Douglas died, the Thatchers returned for further holidays, by which time Mrs Thatcher had struck up a firm friendship with Lady Glover. But in 1989, when Lady Glover was ill, Mrs Thatcher went elsewhere for her summer vacation. Now Mrs Thatcher has left Number 10 Downing Street, she will have more time to spend with Lady Glover in Switzerland.

Lady Glover herself has an apartment in Paris and a permanent suite at Claridge's hotel in London. She is famous for her houseparties at Schloss Freudenburg, considered to be one of Switzerland's most sumptuous houses, with a particularly fine cellar. A motor yacht is kept permanently on standby on Lake Zug to take guests to picnics and tours near by.

Charles Hambro and family   £100m

BANKERS   dob CH 24 July 1930

THE name Hambro conjures up the image of the charming, smooth and utterly British banker. And that is exactly what the various members of the family are.

Started in 1839 by the Danish Baron Hambro, the bank is now run by Charles Hambro (Eton and the Coldstream Guards). Cousin Jocelyn Hambro and his son Rupert are also well known in the City.

The Hambros used to own 49% of the bank through the Hambro Trust, but this was dissolved and the shares were bought by the bank, releasing the family wealth.

Charles lives on an 800-acre farm near Cheltenham, while Jocelyn has two homes, one in London's Mayfair and another on a Gloucestershire estate. His son Rupert lives a few doors away from him in London.

Trevor Hemmings   £100m

BUILDER AND LEISURE OPERATOR
dob (unknown)

TREVOR Hemmings started as a builders' apprentice in the Lancaster town of Leyland after World War II. He first set up in business on his own, building a pair of semi-detached homes. Today, he controls 15 companies, ranging from property companies to one of Britain's largest ice-cream makers.

But Hemmings' first break dates back to 1967 when he met Sir Fred Pontin, the holiday camp king. Hemmings was asked to build a Pontins camp in Southport, complete with 3,000 beds. Those were the days of the Hi-di-Hi style holiday camps. Hemmings did the job in nine months. The partnership prospered and he built another camp in Wales. Eventually he ended up as Sir Fred's right-hand man when Sir Fred took over his building firm.

But when Pontins was taken over, first by Coral and later by the brewing giant Bass when it acquired Coral, Hemmings saw his opportunity. He felt that Pontins was languishing as part of a large group, and he assembled his own management buy-out team, which bought the business early in 1987. Within two years, he had sold it to Scottish & Newcastle Breweries, netting nearly £100 million.

Hemmings stayed with Scottish & Newcastle. He runs their leisure division, as well as being their largest single individual shareholder, with over 5% of the shares, worth some £73 million.

He commutes regularly round his various operations, but his base is still firmly in Chorley in his native Lancashire, where Pontins provides employment for 150 people.

Elton John   £100m

MUSICIAN   dob 25 March 1947

REGINALD Dwight from Pinner started work as a tea boy in Denmark Street, in the heart of London's music industry. He became a pub pianist and changed his name to Elton John after two famous musicians he had played with.

Today he is a world superstar with hits including the classic 'Rocket Man'. He had five number one hits between 1973 and 1975. He lives in a Windsor mansion, complete with six Bentleys in the garage, a theatre with 100 seats and a chandelier over the swimming pool.

He counts royalty among his friends and played at Prince Andrew's stag night. He was chairman of Watford Football Club, and has seen it moved from the fourth to the first division. He spent £1 million on improving the ground and training facilities. He tried to sell the club in 1987 to Robert Maxwell (q.v.) but the Football League thwarted the deal. He has since sold it to a property developer. He has also won £1 million in damages off the *Sun* newspaper for a serious libel, which they eventually settled out of court.

Vijay Mallya   £100m

BREWING   dob (unknown)

IN 1948, Vittal Mallya made some money on the stock market in India. He invested the money to buy three British-owned breweries and a food company in the newly independent India. Eight years later he bought a drinks company which he turned into a distillery.

By the 1970s, he was running India's second largest distillery when disaster struck. The Indian government of Moraji Desai introduced prohibition. With everyone trying to abandon brewing, Mallya took a gamble and bought ten breweries and distilleries when prices were rock-bottom.

The government fell and prohibition was cancelled, leaving Mallya the largest brewer in India. Over the next few years, he expanded into telecommunications, electronics and chemicals. When he died in 1983, his son Vijay took over the group. In 1987, he decided to become a tax exile, and moved to a large Surrey mansion, from where he directs the group, which produced sales of nearly $700 million in 1989.

Well known in Indian business circles, Vijay Mallya pilots his own BAe 125 jet. He also owns a string of racehorses and a fine collection of vintage cars.

Ian Bentham McGlinn   £100m

INVESTOR   dob (unknown)

IN 1976, Ian McGlinn, a Sussex garage proprietor, made the wisest investment of his life. He put £5,000 into the Body Shop – the fledgling cosmetics business being started by Anita Roddick (q.v.).

Today, that investment represents nearly a third of the Body Shop's share capital and makes McGlinn a multi-millionaire. When the Body Shop was floated on the Stock Exchange with the usual razzmatazz in 1984, the modest McGlinn was typically

out of the limelight on holiday in Portugal. McGlinn himself
has nothing to do with the day-to-day operations, merely collecting a huge dividend from his shareholding, which nearly quadrupled in value in 1989 due to City excitement over prospects for
the Body Shop. The shares lost ground in 1990, but McGlinn
remains exceedingly rich.

Simon Miller   £100m

PROPERTY   dob (unknown)

SIMON Miller runs the Charter Group, one of London's
most profitable private development companies, which in
its accounts for 1989 made profits of £16.2 million after tax, on
a turnover of £104 million. With large cash reserves, the group
would really be valued at some £100 million. Miller's success
came from spotting the development potential of London's dockland at the right time. He undertook three major projects in the
Isle of Dogs Enterprise zone in the mid-1980s. Among his
schemes was a Business Efficiency Centre and the 1.25 million
square foot Harbour Exchange. The group also undertakes interior design work for offices and supplies office furniture. In
September 1989, Miller started work on the Exchange Quays
project in Manchester docks, a 600,000 square foot development. His aim is to repeat his London success, and his highly
professional approach in bringing in the right experts, together
with his architect's training, should help him. Miller, who, with
his family, owns all the shares in Charter, lives in a manor
house outside London.

David Rowland   £100m

PROPERTY DEVELOPER AND DEALER
dob 10 September 1933

WHEELER-DEALER and darling of the 1960's and
early 1970's stock market, Rowland was a millionaire at
23. The son of a London scrap merchant, he left school before
taking any O-levels and started work at 16 in a stockbroker's
office. He left because he couldn't see a way of making real
money. He then went into estate agency and after a year –
armed with a £9,000 inheritance from his father – set up on his
own using his mother's front room as his office. By the time he
was 21, he had bought his first public company for £200,000. In
1970, he sold up and went to live in tax exile in Paris. He has
made occasional forays into the London stock market – not all
successful. He lost £3 million on a deal to buy 25% of Vickers
in the mid Seventies and his main company collapsed in 1982
with losses of £25 million. In the 1970s he invested heavily in
the London casino business. He planned to become involved in
a lucrative casino in Tehran, but the fall of the Shah put paid to
those plans. In the early 1980s, he owned Maxim's, the West
End club. In 1990 he bought and then sold a 30% stake in
Edinburgh's Hibernian Football Club. He also paid $120 million
for a half share in a Rome property development. His former
wife, Sheila, was a member of the Hibs board. They have five
children.

Laxmi Shivdasani   £100m

BREWING AND ALUMINIUM   dob (unknown)

INDUR Kumar Shivdasani came to Britain from India in
the 1950s and built up a worldwide business empire. On his
death, his wife Laxmi took over the reins of the business, which
includes a brewery and other factories in Nigeria, vineyards in
France and a bank in Geneva. Laxmi's Oxford-educated son,

Azad, and her daughter, Bina, are both heavily involved in the business. Azad is based in Geneva, while her younger son, Sonashah, runs luxury hotels in the Far East. The family are generous contributors to charity.

David Sullivan   £100m

SOFT PORNOGRAPHIC MAGAZINE AND
NEWSPAPER OWNER   dob 5 February 1949

THE 'girlie magazines' found on the top shelves in news-agents have helped David Sullivan to a £100 million fortune. Britain's leading titillator certainly looks the part. Small, brash, with absolutely no taste for the finer things in life (apart from a huge appetite for chocolates and chips) and completely unemotional about the women he uses ('I'm not sure I could ever stop having lots of women,' he said in a recent interview), Sullivan lives in Essex.

Born of a father serving in the RAF, Sullivan led an itinerant life as a child, including a spell at boarding school, which he hated. After taking a degree in economics at Queen Mary College, London University, he went into advertising, working as an account executive on dog food. But soon the 'shy' Sullivan, who confessed to the *Mail on Sunday* that he lost his virginity only at age 21, was selling nude pictures by mail order through *Exchange & Mart*. 'I offered 20 nude lovelies for £1. I went from earning £88 a month to £800 a week and I only had to work three hours a day,' he recalled.

Thus was born one of Britain's biggest soft-porn empires, which in the 1970s embraced 125 sex shops and 25 magazines. In 1982, Sullivan was convicted of living off the immoral earnings of prostitutes and was jailed for nine months and fined £10,000. Before the conviction was quashed on appeal, he spent 71 days in prison, in Wormwood Scrubs and in an open prison. He claims that the experience 'mellowed' him.

He changed the direction of his business after that, though still retaining a stable of eight magazines. He became a newspaper publisher through *Sunday Sport* and the twice-weekly *Sport*, which hit a new low in sleaze with its fantasy stories and acres of semi-naked women. But it has proved to be a big hit, making Sullivan the most successful of the new breed of newspaper owners.

Sullivan, unmarried, lives in Chigwell, in a nine-bedroom house which is covered in pictures of nude women. He has recently bought Birch Hall in Epping Forest for £1 million, and he has a Marbella home and a stud farm near Bishop's Stortford. Despite his magazines and papers, Sullivan claims to 'have very established views deep down. I believe in tolerance and moderation. Believe me, I am very law abiding, anti-violence, anti-hooligan and anti-drugs. I've never taken a drug or smoked a cigarette in my life.'

In May 1990, the Monopolies and Mergers Commission blocked Sullivan's plans to take a controlling interest in the *Bristol Evening Post*.

3

THE VERY RICH

£50m and more

Stephen Rubin   £98m

SHOE MANUFACTURER   dob 3 December 1937

AMERICA's fitness fad has made the Reebok running shoe a best seller. And that has made Stephen Rubin a rich man, with a home in north London, a flat in Florida and a yacht in the south of France. Rubin, who trained as a lawyer, has always seemed to have an uncanny eye for good deals. He runs his father's old company, Pentland Industries, which started life as Liverpool Shoes in 1936. In 1981, it bought a 55% stake in the then struggling Reebok for $77,500.

Rubin's best investment, however, was made in 1974 when Pentland bought 51% of Unicam, a home-brewing business, for £51. In 1978, that stake was sold to Robertson Foods for £1 million.

In 1989 and 1990, so as to lessen Pentland's dependence on Reebok, which provides 75% of its profits, Rubin bought two greetings card companies. A restructuring of the group, in which Rubin holds 55% of the shares, also released some £50 million in funds to shareholders. Ten years after its Reebok purchase Pentland had sold most of its stake in various tranches, raising the huge total of $700 million all told. Rubin has now found another Reebok in which to invest his profits. In the summer of 1991 he bought a stake in the Adidas shoe company.

Being a one-time Liberal candidate did not prevent Rubin from asking Mrs Thatcher to open Pentland's new headquarters in her Finchley constituency.

Evan Cornish   £97m

PACKAGING MANUFACTURER   dob (unknown)

LINPAC makes much of the metal, plastic and paper packaging we take for granted today. It is a private company based in the Lincolnshire town of Louth. The managing director and chairman is Evan Cornish. He makes most of the business decisions for the firm himself. It has around 4,000 employees worldwide and is a diverse packaging group dealing with anything from plastic cups to fast-food packets.

Evan Cornish founded the company 26 years ago and runs it from a small, untidy office. In its first year turnover was in tens of thousands of pounds. By 1969 it had risen to £7 million, and in 1977 had jumped to £100 million. Cornish once said that 'We like to have small sites of no more than around 300 employees.' In its accounts for 1989, the group had sales of £530 million. The firm shuns publicity. Cornish lives in Woodhall Spa. His brother is a director of the company, at least one member of the next generation of Cornishes also works there, and the accounts show that the Cornish family have a sizeable stake of over 50%.

In the year to the end of 1989, the company made profits after tax of over £19.5 million and it has huge cash reserves of £141 million.

Evan Cornish, the founder, drives an old battered Renault – and runs the business with his sons – who prefer sports cars – from an office on the edge of the town. The company also owns racehorses which all have LinPac in their name. They are stabled with the trainer Charles Elsey at his North Yorkshire stables at Malton.

William and Frank Brake   £92m

FOOD DISTRIBUTORS   dob FB 21 November 1933

RAISED above a London pub, the three Brake brothers saw at first hand the British love of a pub lunch with a good pint of beer. All three developed their knowledge and skills at catering college in the late 1940s and early 1950s. When William, the eldest, married and moved to run the Bull Inn at Lenham in Kent, his two younger brothers Frank and Peter went with him.

As a sideline started in 1958 they rose at dawn to run a

business killing and plucking chickens for sale to local pubs, villages and restaurants.

Chickens awaiting delivery began to pile up at their premises, so they built a cold store to freeze them in 1963. As the store was so big, they filled it with other foods to freeze and sell. In 1969, the brothers opened a purpose-built factory in Lenham to produce frozen prepared meals.

By the early 1970s, the sale of frozen food was going so well that it supplanted the poultry business, which was discontinued in 1974. The Brakes were quick to spot the potential of computers in running their business and now boast of being able to supply customers within a few hours of receiving an order.

By 1986, the company was supplying 35,000 customers round the country from 16 cold store depots. The company was floated on the stock market that year. The two brothers, who are chairman and managing director, each kept 25% of the shares. Peter, the youngest brother, who was purchasing director, died in 1987, but the combined family shareholding is now worth £92 million. In 1990, the company's profits rose 27% to nearly £15 million.

Sir Bernard Ashley   £90m

RETAILER   dob 11 August 1926

THE kitchen table of a Pimlico house was the birthplace of the Laura Ashley legend in 1953. It was there that Bernard Ashley, newly demobbed from the army, and his wife Laura pioneered the flowery fashions with which the British – and latterly the American – middle classes fell in love.

A chain of shops named after Laura Ashley was formed. Bernard, a large ex-Gurkha, balked at having the flowery prints named after him.

Tragically Laura was killed in a fall in her Welsh home just weeks before the hugely successful flotation of the group on the Stock Exchange in 1985. Some £2 billion worth of money chased the £60 million of shares on offer. The family retain about 59% of the shares.

In 1989–90, the group was badly hit by the slump in consumer spending. Profits disappeared and the group made losses of £4.7 million in the year to January 1990. In September that year some 1,500 jobs were lost as many of the group's Welsh factories were closed, and the Japanese Aeon Group paid some £29 million for over 35 million new shares in Laura Ashley. The year 1991 proved to be even more difficult, with losses increasing to £6.7 million.

Sir Bernard, knighted in 1986, lists his hobbies as sailing, swimming and walking. He is impatient of bureaucrats and turns up unannounced in his executive jet at European airports without a passport, demanding entry to the country under the terms of the Treaty of Rome.

He has bought the derelict Llangoed Castle near Brecon for £150,000 and plans to spend £3 million on restoring it for opening in 1991 as the first of a chain of luxury £100-a-night country hotels. To add to Sir Bernard's problems, these plans have run foul of local conservationists. The £3 million conversion has been described by the National Forum, a Welsh conservation body, as 'Mammon masquerading as art'. One consolation for Sir Bernard was his marriage to Madame Regine Burnell from Brussels in May 1990.

He lives in a large Brussels town house and, apart from his executive jet (kitted out in Ashley prints), owns a French château, a 500-acre Welsh farm and a house in the Thames Valley. He also has the millionaire's obligatory plaything, a yacht.

Earl of Derby £90m

LANDOWNER dob 21 April 1918

THE famous Derby horse race is named after the 12th Earl of Derby, who instituted it at Epsom in 1780.

Today, the 18th Earl is just as interested in horses. He has 18 in training and he owned a £250,000 stake in Shergar, the Irish horse valued at £10 million which was kidnapped in 1983 and never found again.

He owns 30,000 acres in Merseyside and also has a Newmarket estate. Part of Knowsley House, an ancestral home, is let to the local police.

It was the 17th Earl who really made the Derby name in the 20th century. Known as the 'King of Lancashire', he was a formidable figure on the turf with his racing colours of black silks and white cap. He also spearheaded the army recruiting drive across Britain during World War I.

The present Earl has no children and his heir is a nephew, Edward Stanley, a godson of the late Duke of Windsor.

Lord Hanson   £90m

INDUSTRIALIST   dob 20th January 1922

IF any businessman represented the style of Thatcherite Britain, it is Lord James Hanson, head of the £9.3 billion empire that bears his name and straddles the Atlantic.

Hanson started out running his father's haulage business. In his youth, he was well known to gossip columnists and was once engaged to Audrey Hepburn. But from the moment he started the Hanson Trust in 1965 with his partner Lord White (q.v.), the accent has been on hard work, on making his assets sweat and on an ability to buy up companies cheaply and sell the bits off one by one for more than the cost of the whole. It is a strategy that came into its own in the 1980s – in America as well as Britain. Food, typewriter, battery, brick companies were swallowed up almost effortlessly. The City loves what Hanson has achieved.

He showed his superb timing in 1989 by taking over Consolidated Goldfields for £3.5 billion. With the skill and timing of a chess player, Hanson saw that ConsGold was vulnerable and struck quickly to sew up an agreed deal, which turned out to be the biggest and most successful takeover in British history so far.

In the summer of 1990, Hanson emerged as a potential suitor for Powergen, the generating company, but nothing came of it. One deal that did work was Hanson's swap of $1.3 billion worth of gold shares with Sir James Goldsmith's forestry interests. In May 1991, Hanson startled the stock market by taking a 2.8% stake in ICI Britain's largest manufacturer.

In his private life, he is now more subdued. He has homes in London, Berkshire and America. He is a passionate supporter of the Conservative Party and was created a life peer in 1983.

Earl of Inchcape   £90m

LANDOWNER AND INDUSTRIALIST
dob 27 December 1917

THE Inchcape family have had a long association with the sea. The grandfather of the present Earl created the modern P & O shipping group. The Earl, who no longer runs P & O, collects City directorships. At one stage, he had at least 30.

The family wealth came from both P & O and the Inchcape group, which is valued at over £700 million on the stock market. In the early 1970s, the family owned 40% of the Inchcape shares. The Earl, who was chairman from 1958 to 1982, is now life president of the company.

He is a keen follower of field sports. But he can no longer stalk the red deer at his 14,000-acre Scottish estate of Glen Isla as he has had to sell it. In 1968, he bought a 1,500-acre Essex estate for £500,000 and sold it in 1980 for £5 million.

He still has another home in Scotland and a manor house in Buckinghamshire.

Sir Kenneth Kleinwort and family   £90m

BANKER   dob 28 May 1935

KLEINWORT and Sons started as a merchant bank in 1830 and later merged with Robert Benson Lonsdale to form the present Kleinwort Benson group. It has been quoted on the stock market since 1961 and is valued at over £530 million in 1990.

The Kleinwort family, headed by Sir Kenneth, a tax exile in Switzerland, still have a 24% stake in the business. He remains a director of the bank.

He lists his hobbies as travel, photography, skiing, shooting and gardening. Despite his Swiss base, Sir Kenneth is also a committed supporter of the Slimbridge Wildfowl Trust and a council member of the World Wildlife Trust. His son, Richard, works as a banker in Germany.

Kleinwort Benson's 1990 results, showing a huge loss of £68 million, left the bank severely weakened and a prime candidate for a takeover. The bank had been hit by huge losses in its stockbroking arm and a downturn in the formerly lucrative corporate finance business.

Lord Laing and family   £90m

BISCUIT MANUFACTURER   dob 12 May 1923

BISCUITS have always been part of Lord Laing's life. His grandfather, the first chairman of McVitie and Price, concocted the famous 'Digestive' biscuit recipe at the end of the last century. Laing, recently retired as chairman of the giant £2 billion United Biscuits group, jealously guarded that recipe. In 1989, the company made 5 billion packets of various foods, including half the biscuits eaten in Britain.

A leading member of the Scottish establishment, Hector Laing was educated at Loretto and served in the war with the Scots Guards as a tank commander, winning the American Bronze star. In 1947, he started his business career at McVitie's Harlesden factory in west London, humping sacks of flour. A year later, McVitie merged with Macfarlane Laing to form United Biscuits, where he stayed, becoming a director in 1953, managing director in 1964 and chairman in 1972.

Laing's management style was modelled on Field Marshal

Montgomery. He tried to visit half his 46,000 workforce every year, and the company is obsessive about communicating and training its staff. He also insisted on being at work at 7.15 a.m. and did not take huge pay increases when his staff were being held down to modest ones. 'In army parlance, I am not an officer who sits back in headquarters while troops risk their lives and then decides I ought to double my salary,' he told the London *Standard*.

In 1986, Laing lost a bruising £2.8 billion takeover battle for control of the huge Imperial group to Lord Hanson. The defeat seemed to sour Laing's feelings towards the City of London, and though a strong supporter of Mrs Thatcher, he was critical of the City's short-term approach to British industry.

'If too many of our major companies are taken over by non-British owners,' he wrote in *The Times*, 'and free market forces make that more rather than less likely, then the UK will become increasingly a satellite economy ... We have fought wars to keep Britain independent. Are we going to sell that heritage for instant cash gratification?'

Laing, who was regularly invited to lunch and dinner by Mrs Thatcher, advised her on industry. In 1982, he lent a plane to help in the search for Mark Thatcher, missing in the Sahara. He has been a joint treasurer of the Conservative Party. He also helped establish a fund to support the legal expenses of miners fighting against the 1984 strike call by Arthur Scargill.

His links with government do not stop Laing having a finely developed social conscience. He is chairman of Business in the Community, an organization that helps small businesses and other job-creation schemes. He also started the Per Cent Club, which is busy persuading the top British companies to devote not less than 0.5% of their profits to the community.

Laing lists his hobbies as flying, gardening and walking. He enjoys piloting his company plane round Britain.

Eva Larsson   £90m

TAX EXILE   dob (unknown)

LIKE the Rausing brothers (q.v.), Eva Larsson finds the British tax regime much more congenial than that in Sweden. Most private, she lives with her husband, a doctor, on their Surrey estate. Her wealth stems from her father, Lars-Eric Lundberg, who built up a construction company in the Fifties, before moving into property development. Taking the precaution of handing over his wealth to his children in the early Eighties to escape the taxman, Lundberg paved the way for his daughter to head for England with a reputed sum of around £90 million.

Sir Peter Shepherd   £90m
and family

BUILDERS   dob 18 October 1916

IN 1890, Sir Peter Shepherd's grandfather started a building business in York. Today the Shepherd Building Group is one of the largest building firms in the north of England and, under Sir Peter's leadership, it has built hospitals in York, Leeds and Lincoln, and other buildings at York university, as well as extensions to Leeds and Durham universities. The group is also noted for its high-quality houses and it has built a garden village estate for 2,000 residents at Woodthorpe in York. But it was the restoration work on York Minster between 1967 and 1972 that won Shepherd worldwide acclaim.

Sir Peter, whose father was an alderman of York, became a director of the then Shepherd Construction Company in 1940 and chairman in 1958. He retired in May 1988 to become president of the group. Colin Shepherd, his younger brother, took over as chairman.

A lifelong passion for training and education led Sir Peter to head the Construction Industry Training Board and similar bodies for other industries. In 1982 he warned the CBI conference that regional pay bargaining should be introduced to reflect inequalities in local prosperity and labour demand. He also criticized educationalists who know little about industry's needs.

Sir Peter lives in retirement in York, and lists sailing as his hobby. His four sons, who are all connected with the company, also live in the city. With their relations, they own most of the equity in the group, which produced £16.2 million after-tax profits in the year to the end of June 1989. The group also had £14 million in cash at the bank and £25 million in investments.

Lynn Wilson and family £90m

BUILDER   dob 8 December 1939

FORTUNES are not always made in America, as Thomas Wilson, a Northampton shoemaker, found when he went out to Massachusetts in 1905. Although he met his wife there and had a son, times were hard and he returned to Northampton, but not to the shoe industry. He entered the building trade and made a house from a windmill. The house still stands as a testament to his workmanship.

His son, Connolly, succeeded him in the family business. His grandson, Lynn, became chairman in 1981 and has proved to be a rare breed – a construction man whose circumstances actually improved. In the first half of 1990, Wilson (Connolly) actually managed to sell some 1,087 homes, against 770 in the previous year. Wilson runs a tight management structure, reducing borrowings from 30% to 18% of its net assets. But in the second half of 1990, the company was badly hit by the recession and the full year profits showed a 42% fall to £31 million.

John Asprey   £86m

JEWELLER   dob 8 November 1937

THE Aspreys have been supplying jewels and expensive trinkets to the wealthy for 200 years, since they fled the persecution of the Huguenots in 18th-century France. Today, they are jewellers to the royal family and will supply individual diamonds costing over £1 million to anyone who cares to enter their shop in New Bond Street, London.

In the past they have supplied solid gold collar stiffeners, a collapsible gold toothbrush and even a model of a bacon and egg sandwich worked in precious metal.

The stock market crash in 1987 did not apparently affect the spending habits of the wealthy and the business is booming. The Asprey family have around 46% of the equity and have staved off takeover bids in the past. In 1980 a long-running feud between rival Aspreys was finally settled when disgruntled family members were bought out, so preventing a takeover by Dunhill. The family claims to be more motivated by respect for tradition than money.

John Asprey, the present chairman, is a tall blond ex-Scots Guards officer. He lives in London and has three sons. After the bitter family feud over Dunhill which pitted him and his father against his uncle and cousin, he said he 'simply would not allow' a similar feud in the next generation of the family. Aspreys largely escaped the 1980s recession in the retailing sector caused by high interest rates and a collapse in consumer confidence. In December 1989, it reported half-year profits up 51%. But in the first half of 1990, its profits slipped marginally from £12.3 million to £11.9 million. During the year, Asprey added two well-known Regent Street names to its portfolio, those of Mappin & Webb and Garrards. The two jewellers were acquired from Sears Holdings in a paper deal which increased Sears 25.5% holding in Aspreys by a further 18.5 million participating preferred shares.

Terry Curry and family   £85m

FORMER RETAILER   dob 5 March 1939

AS the great-grandson of the founder of the Curry's electrical chain, Terry Curry seemed in a safe job for life. The family controlled up to 35% of the company while it was well run and highly profitable. But they reckoned without Stanley Kalms, the boss of rival Dixons, and Roger Seelig, then a star merchant banker at Morgan Grenfell and Kalms's main adviser. In December 1984, they managed to wrest Curry's from the family in a bitterly fought £250 million takeover battle. One consolation was the £87 million payout for the family's stake. The victors' lot has not been particularly happy: Seelig was caught up in the Guinness affair and has left Morgan Grenfell, while Dixons' profits have suffered as the consumer boom of the Eighties came to an end. Since the takeover, Curry has kept a low profile. The family invests in the stock market, but Curry has no other known business interests. In the years before the takeover, he distanced himself from the City. His home is near Maidenhead; his children are now grown up.

George Moore   £85m

FURNITURE MANUFACTURER   dob (unknown)

HAVING left school at 14, George Moore later regretted that 'I missed my way educationally and felt I could not make the grade, but I loved creating things,' as he told the *Yorkshire Post*.

The lack of education proved no barrier to Moore, however. His first job was to rent a shop in the north Yorkshire town of Knaresborough, where he repaired toys. He then trained as a joiner and moved to Bingley, where at the age of 17 he bought an old henhouse for £45, which he converted into a joinery workshop.

A year later Moore was able to afford to hire a skilled tradesman, allowing him to finish his own apprenticeship.

The business prospered and in the mid-1960s he was able to buy up a huge old munitions factory site at Thorp Arch, outside Wetherby in Yorkshire, for £200,000. He converted it into a trading estate, building around the huge reinforced concrete ammunition bunkers where he couldn't afford to demolish them. He established a Moore's Furniture factory there and in the late 1970s sold off a large part of the site to a Greek shipping group based in Jersey called Kuliam Investments, netting some £8 million. But Moore kept the furniture factory and other choice sites on the estate. The business went from strength to strength and, with another factory in Co. Durham, it had 900 staff by the mid-1980s. It also claimed 15% of the market for kitchen furniture, selling to DIY stores, local authorities and private housebuilders.

While the business prospered, Moore's health did not, and in late 1986 he decided to sell the furniture company, a decision that was reinforced by a heart attack he suffered in January 1987. Neither his son nor his daughter wanted to carry on with the business.

Though Moore made a good recovery, he still determined to sell and bids were invited from potential purchasers. His managing director, Fred Davies, who had been at Moore's since 1974, led a management buy-out in October 1987. Originally this had been ruled out because of the price demanded, but the nine managers involved did not want to work with any of the four or five prospective purchasers. In the event a deal was arranged in ten days. Moore now lives in the smart commuter village of Linton, though he is rumoured to be interested in buying a large estate in Yorkshire. His daughter runs a local financial company.

Hon. Vincent Weir and family £84m

SHIPPING OWNER   dob 8 February 1935

ANDREW Weir, later the 1st Baron Inverforth, built up Andrew Weir and Co. into a powerful shipping and insurance company in the late 19th and early 20th centuries. The company controlled the Bank shipping line, Invertanker Ltd and the Inver Transport and Trading Company. Like other Scottish magnates such as Carnegie and Andrew Mellon, he had a passion for commerce, hard work and thrift.

Today the business is run by the Hon. Vincent Weir, son of the 2nd Baron, and it has branched out into investment, property, insurance, hotels and fine art dealing.

In the mid-1980s it was hit by the slump in shipping and moved into loss, but it has since recovered. In 1989 it achieved post-tax profits of nearly £5 million. The business has huge assets valued at around £128 million. It remains in the hands of the Weir family, who appear to be generous employers. During its 1985 centenary each member of staff received an extra month's wages. Vincent Weir lives in Mayfair, London; his interests are natural history and wildlife conservation.

The Bank line recently announced that it was going back into carrying passengers on its container ships at a cost of £50 per passenger a day for the five-month round trip to the South Pacific.

Gerald Carroll and family   £80m

BUILDING   dob (unknown)

THE Essex-based Carroll group was founded as a construction company before World War II. Today, it is one of Britain's largest and most successful property companies with a multi-million-pound building development. It built the 400,000-square-foot shopping complex on top of the A1 motorway in Hertfordshire. It also bought an enormous 48-acre site from the Central Electricity Generating Board at Croydon. The redundant power station site cost Carroll £65 million but, with new privately financed road connections to the nearby A23 road, it was turned into a £475 million retail, leisure and business park development.

Carroll has also showed a penchant for involvement in aerospace. In 1986, Carroll was selected to develop a civil airport at the Royal Aircraft Establishment in Farnborough, with a

726,000-square-foot business park attached. In a strange move for a property group, Carroll also offered to help fund Hotol, the revolutionary spacecraft designed by British Aerospace. Nothing came of the move.

Gerald Carroll, a third-generation family member, now runs the business as chairman, and is pushing it into further large-scale property development. In its last accounts, to the end of March 1989, Carroll Industries made £13.4 million after-tax profits on a £42 million turnover. But with high borrowings of £141 million, the group would probably only be worth £80 million today. The Carrolls are generous supporters of charities through the Carroll Foundation, which owns a large stake in the business. Its aim 'is to assist disadvantaged young people living within the United Kingdom'.

John James Fenwick and family £80m

DEPARTMENT STORE OWNER   dob 19 August 1932

IT may not be Harrods but the Fenwicks chain has built up a solid reputation and turnover. In 1989 it made profits of over £14 million.

John James Fenwick founded the first store in Newcastle in 1882, followed by another in London's exclusive Bond Street in 1891. Today the group has branches dotted round the country and is run by another John James Fenwick, great-grandson of the founder. The family still own most of the company's shares. But with the downturn in retail spending in 1989 and 1990, the value of the business, if floated on the stock market, could be clipped back to £80 million against £95 million in 1988.

John Fenwick was educated at Rugby and Pembroke College, Cambridge. In 1957 he married Gillian Hodnett, a physiotherapist at the Newcastle General Hospital. They have three sons. He is a member of the Marylebone Cricket Club and the Garrick Club and lists travel, theatre and shooting as his hobbies. Though he lives in a fashionable area of Chelsea, he has strong links with the North-east and is a governor of the

Royal Grammar School in Newcastle and a director of the Northern Rock Building Society.

Andrew Lloyd Webber   £80m

COMPOSER   dob 22 March 1948

THE man who almost single-handedly revived the British musical was born into an artistic family in South Kensington, London. Money might have been short – but not music. Andrew Lloyd Webber's father was director of the London College of Music, while his mother was a music teacher.

By the age of 9, his prodigious musical talent was apparent. He was composing his own songs and staging shows by himself. At 12, he went to Westminster School, where he was obsessed by musicals such as *South Pacific* and *The Sound of Music*. He won an exhibition to Magdalen College, Oxford, but left after one term to team up with Tim Rice, who had written to him hearing that he wanted a lyricist. Although *The Likes of Us*, their first musical, about a Dr Barnardo's children's home, was a flop, the second, *Joseph and the Amazing Technicolor Dreamcoat*, was a hit. That persuaded David Land, a West End estate agent, to pay them £30 a week to allow them to concentrate on writing. They came up with *Jesus Christ Superstar*, which brought them outstanding success. *Evita* followed in 1976. Then the partnership foundered.

But Andrew kept going with a string of bigger box-office hits, including *Cats*, which has grossed more than £50 million in nine years, making it the most successful musical in history. The latest, *Aspects of Love*, took £4 million in advance bookings.

The Midas touch has allowed Andrew to live in style, though he hates spending money on himself. His Berkshire estate, Sydmonton, complete with 1,200 acres, is next door to that of one of the Saatchis (q.v.) and the famous Watership Down. He hosts an annual Sydmonton festival to try out new musicals. He has a Belgravia flat, a house in the South of France and an apartment in New York's exclusive Trump Tower. He also owns one of the greatest collections of Pre-Raphaelite paintings in the country as well as a private publishing house, Aurum Press. His main source of wealth is his large stake in the Really Useful Group, which controls his theatrical management operations. It came to the stock market in 1986 valued at around £36 million.

His second wife, the singer Sarah Brightman, starred in *Phantom of the Opera*. He still maintains a cordial relationship with his first wife and their two children. He bought her a home to share with her second husband. He is also an active supporter of charities, and recently gave £400,000 to support research into diabetes. His first wife is a victim of the disease and he is haunted by the fear that their children may have inherited it.

In 1990, Lloyd Webber took Really Useful private, removing its stock market listing. He was initially blocked by the late Robert Holmes à Court, the Australian entrepreneur, who refused to sell his 6.7% stake, but after his death, his widow Janet sold the shares to Lloyd Webber. Early in 1991, he married for the third time. His new wife is Madeleine Gurdon.

James Miller and family £80m

BUILDERS   dob (unknown)

JAMES Miller, the son of an Edinburgh architect, was destined to enter the same profession as his father after some training with the family firm. But he elected to become a builder instead and started building homes and housing estates in the Pentland hills to the south of the city. The company prospered and branched out both into civil engineering and into England, with branches in Wakefield and London.

Knighted in 1953, Sir James retired in 1973 and handed over the running of the company to his son, also called James. Sir James died in 1977, but his group, now called the Miller Group, has prospered and is one of Britain's largest independent construction and property development companies. The shares are all held by 16 individual shareholders and 14 family trusts. In 1988 results showed a spectacular growth, with post-tax profits more than doubling to £18 million and turnover up by nearly a quarter to £234 million. But by 1990, the company had been hit by recession and profits fell to £10.8 million.

James Miller, the chairman, is assisted by his brother Roger, who runs the housebuilding division, and his cousin Keith (a keen sailor), who heads Miller Developments. The company is heavily involved in open-cast mining, as well as urban renewal projects in Scotland, a leisure complex at Perth, a section of the Edinburgh bypass and office building in the City of London. It recently won a contract to extract some 480,000 tonnes of open-cast coal from the former Patent Shaft steelwork site at Sandwell in the West Midlands. The group is now expanding into micro-tunnelling and environmental services.

James Miller, described as shy and private by *Scottish Business Insider* magazine, has no intention of taking his company to the stock market for a flotation.

Christopher Moran   £80m

FINANCIER   dob 16 January 1948

LEAVING school at 16 with a few O-levels proved no handicap to Christopher Moran, who then went to work in the Lloyds insurance market. In 1982, at the age of 32, he had been expelled, the first time in the 300-year history of Lloyds that the whole of its disciplinary machine had ever been used. The market stopped trading for four hours as members gathered to hear the evidence against Moran and a colleague. Their expulsion was later upheld by the Court of Appeal. But Moran was not to leave a poor man. He had built up a £3 million fortune.

Since then he has traded his way in and out of companies, buying them cheaply when he reckons they are undervalued and selling them on at a profit.

He anticipated the October 1987 crash and cut his exposure to the stock market. He lives in a Chelsea penthouse, owns the 45,000-acre Glenfiddich estate (of whisky fame) near Balmoral and has two personalized chauffeur-driven Rolls-Royce cars.

He is married to a former Miss Thames Television. He scored a notable coup in 1989 when the Court of Appeal decided that he had obtained squatter's rights over a £100,000 plot of council land near a Buckinghamshire home he owned.

David Murray £80m

INDUSTRIALIST   dob (unknown)

FIFTEEN years ago, David Murray's life seemed shattered. Returning from playing outside half for Dalkeith Rugby Club, his Lotus sports car crashed. 'I had a blowout at 70 miles an hour and struck a tree. Both legs were smashed below the knee,' he told the *Glasgow Herald*, adding, 'I don't consider myself disabled. I swim every day in the pool at home and I play snooker and get involved with the sports teams which the company sponsors. I'm very lucky really. I could be in the grave-yard.'

Murray, the son of an Ayr coal merchant, did not give up. 'You could say that the accident concentrated my mind on business from then on.' At the time he had just taken out a second mortgage on his home to set up Murray International, in which he owns 90% of the shares. Initially he bought and sold metal from a modest Edinburgh base.

In the first year, he made a £100,000 profit on a £2 million turnover. With the advent of North Sea oil, he moved to a bigger site near Livingston and became Scotland's biggest supplier to the newly developing industry. In the last thirteen years turnover in the business – covering property, metal and office equipment – has soared from £2 million to £110 million.

Sport has been a continuing passion and he is chairman of Glasgow Rangers, one of the country's richest football clubs. In 1988, he bought 75% of Rangers for £6.5 million. Earlier he had failed in a £450,000 takeover bid for Ayr United, a Scottish second division club. Murray also owns a sports complex near Livingston, where his top basketball, indoor hockey and volley-ball teams are based. He is planning to redevelop a large area of

Edinburgh near Princes Street. The £80 million Port Hamilton scheme aims to create a London docklands setting in the Scottish capital.

Murray's business acumen has been recognized. In 1984, he became Young Scottish Businessman of the Year, and he heads the government anti-litter campaign as chairman of UK 2000 in Scotland. He still drives and has four homes: in Edinburgh, Jersey, the Borders, and New Zealand. He has also launched Murray Media, with the aim of starting a popular Sunday newspaper for Scotland and buying other publishing titles. But the *Sunday Scot*, his new paper, had a rough ride in a highly competitive market. In July 1991 it closed at the cost of £3 million.

Lord Weinstock and family £80m

INDUSTRIALIST dob 29 July 1924

ARNOLD Weinstock has built up the General Electric Company from near bankruptcy to become Britain's biggest and most successful electronics combine, with profits of nearly £800 million and 145,000 employees. But to the young Arnold Weinstock, running a large business seemed unlikely. Born of a Polish tailor who emigrated to Britain in 1906, he grew up in the Jewish community of north-east London, where he was a shy and bookish child. His father died when he was five. Four years later, his mother Golda also died, leaving him to be raised by his elder brother, a hairdresser. Despite being evacuated to Warwickshire at 15 when war broke out, he was able to win a scholarship to the London School of Economics, where he took a degree in statistics.

At the end of the war, he was working as a £420-a-year clerk for the Admiralty in Bath, supplementing his income by lecturing for the local Workers' Educational Association.

In 1947, when he was demobbed, his brother persuaded a client, Louis Scott, a West End estate agent, to give Weinstock a job. He became Scott's personal assistant, and found he liked the cut and thrust of the commercial world.

Scott later introduced him to Netta Sobell, daughter of Sir Michael Sobell, founder of Radio & Allied Industries. They were married in 1949 and Sobell, with no son, saw in his young son-in-law the qualities needed to run the business, which thrived in the 1950s television boom.

In the early 1960s a successful Radio & Allied Holdings acquired the ailing and much larger GEC through a reverse takeover. Soon Weinstock was running the whole show. He instituted a ruthless pruning operation that was to be his hallmark. The head-office staff was cut from 2,000 to 200 and 35 regional offices were shut. This was typical of Weinstock, who had always loathed waste. Much more was to follow. In 1967, he took over the lumbering AEI group in a bitterly fought takeover. Among his first acts he cancelled one of the two copies of the *Financial Times* ordered by the AEI headquarters, asking 'Why do they need two copies?' Even today GEC staff religiously turn off the lights when a room is empty to save electricity.

Later he took over English Electric to create the basis for the modern GEC. He was, and remains, a tough manager. In the first two years after the AEI and English Electric mergers, 20,000 jobs were lost. Hugh Scanlon, then the leader of the Engineering Union, dubbed him 'Britain's largest unemployer'. But the City loved him, as did the Labour government in the early 1970s. Whole industries such as telecommunications and power generation were virtual monopoly preserves for GEC.

The onset of Thatcherism proved a blow to Weinstock. At first he was a close confidant of Mrs Thatcher and was part of a small group of senior industrialists advising on economic and industrial policy. But he found the increasing emphasis on competition applied to GEC's key defence and telecommunications markets hard to bear. He alienated the government by publicly condemning the privatization plan adopted for British Telecom. He also appeared to make GEC a haven for Tory wets by appointing a succession of them to the post of chairman.

In the 1980s GEC was criticized for its caution in not investing its profits in new equipment, preferring to leave them in the bank as a notorious cash mountain that reached £1.5 billion at one stage. Weinstock was also stung by the government's cancellation of the Nimrod early warning aircraft project in 1986 after £1 billion had been spent on developing its GEC radar. But subsequently Weinstock proved his critics wrong with a string of alliances and deals, the like of which had not been seen since he created GEC.

With Siemens, he finally took control of Plessey, run by Sir John Clark, his bitter rival for many years. He has steered GEC into a series of European alliances with French and German partners, not to mention a link-up with the American General Electric Group. He even saw off a half-hearted takeover attempt from a Plessey-led consortium.

In private, Weinstock is still a shy person but is charming and amusing, though he relishes heated debate where he can bring a powerful intellect and superb memory to bear. He has a wealth of anecdotes about people in power, and has many of them on his board as non-executive directors. He sits as an independent peer in the Lords.

Outside GEC his main passions are racing and opera. His spartan office at GEC is dominated by a portrait of Troy, his 1979 Derby winner, and he has been known to interrupt meetings to find out racing results. The family has a 300-acre racing stud in Ireland.

When he comes in to work from his London flat or Wiltshire estate, Weinstock spends the first few minutes listening to and even conducting his favourite Mozart operas before getting down to work. He frequently attends the Royal Opera House in Covent Garden.

Simon, his son, is as sharp as his father. He was educated at Winchester and Oxford and is a main board director of GEC. It is thought by some that he is being groomed as Weinstock's successor.

Captain Alwyn Farquharson   £79m

LANDOWNER   dob 1 May 1919

HEAD of Clan Farquharson, Captain Alwyn Farquharson inherited the Invercauld estate from an aunt in 1941 after her death in an air raid. He was on active service in the Royal Scots Greys at the time.

After the war, he took over running the land, which stretches over 100,000 acres in Aberdeenshire, Perth and Argyll. He became Clan chief in 1949. His American wife, a former fashion editor of *Vogue* and *Harper's Bazaar*, obviously enjoys life in the Highlands. She organizes theatre, film and music evenings in the local village and has established a craft gallery.

Balmoral is the neighbouring estate to Invercauld. Once the Queen Mother came to stay when her own house was being renovated.

The estate's best assets are the 24 miles of the River Dee, one of the finest salmon rivers in Scotland, and extensive grouse moors.

The family were given the estates in the 14th century by Robert Bruce after being ejected from the Speyside land-holdings by a rival clan.

Duke of Argyll £77m

LANDOWNER   dob 28 August 1937

IN 1877, the Argyll estates covered 175,000 acres. Today they are down to 81,000 acres. But the 12th Duke, Chief of the Campbell clan and Keeper of the Great Seal of Scotland, has done a lot to preserve and develop what is left.

The Duke sold the island of Iona to the Fraser Foundation for £1.5 million in 1979 to pay off duties owed since his father's death in 1973. Beginning in the mid-1980s, tourists were invited to spend up to £1,000 a week for the privilege of deer stalking with the Duchess of Argyll. The Duke also sells his own brand of 21-year-old Argyll single malt whisky to the Japanese for around £245 a bottle. There is a caravan park and a wildlife park on the family estate.

The Duke's home is Inverary Castle, which was nearly destroyed by a fire in 1975. It has now been restored and a magnificent Armoury Hall has a fine display of muskets, axes and Highland broadswords. The Duke married Iona, the daughter of a baronet, Capt Sir Ivan Colquhoun, in 1964. She is an expert shot and has competed at Bisley. His heir, the Marquess of Lorne, has been making his mark on the London social scene recently. He has been studying agriculture as preparation for running Inverary, a future he relishes: 'My heart is in the country. I'm not so much the city gent,' he once said.

Chris Blackwell   £77m

RECORD PRODUCER   dob (unknown)

HARROW-educated, Blackwell comes from an old-established Jamaica plantation family, the Delissers, who made their fortune in the 18th century. But Blackwell made his money more recently – and well away from the plantation business. After leaving school he went to New York in the late 1950s, where he developed a love of jazz. He went on to try his hand at watersports, real estate and accountancy, but boredom drove him out of those businesses. Combining his interest in jazz with the Jamaican music he had picked up in his childhood, he went on to found Island Records in 1962. He toured Britain's inner cities, selling his records from the back of an old Mini Clubman. At last he had found his true vocation.

In 1964, his first hit came with Millie's 'My Boy Lollipop', which reached number two in the pop charts. By the end of the 1960s, Island was Britain's leading independent record company and Blackwell branched out into the hippie market with groups like Traffic, Fairport Convention and Jethro Tull.

His biggest coup came in spotting and promoting an obscure Jamaican singer called Bob Marley in the early 1970s. Later, after some hesitation and an initial rejection, he signed the Irish super-group, U2.

Blackwell was offered £6 million for Island Records in 1969 by Warner Brothers, but he turned down the offer. It was not until 20 years later – and at a price that had risen to £200 million – that he finally sold out to Polygram, collecting some £70 million for his share stake.

Blackwell has homes and considerable real estate around the

world. These include Ian Fleming's old Caribbean house, Goldeneye, a Paris flat, two London homes and an Oxfordshire mansion. He also has a permanent suite in a New York hotel and a Los Angeles home. Intensely shy, he dresses informally in track suit bottoms and flip-flops, and prefers the company of musicians to sober businessmen.

Martin Deaner   £77m

OIL EXPLORATION   dob 1946

BORN in 1946 in Birmingham, Martin Deaner has made his fortune in the hard world of the North Sea oil industry. But in his early days, he worked as a trainee estimator and draughtsman with Stuart & Lloyd, a pipeline company. Bored with this work, Deaner wanted more adventure, and as the North Sea oil boom began, he took a diving course. Working in Borneo and Brunei for an Italian company to gain experience, he was then ready to tackle the gruelling North Sea. For four years, he worked as a saturation diver, living in a self-contained chamber up to 1,000 feet underwater. The work was highly paid and enabled Deaner to build up enough capital to go his own way. He started his own company, Offshore Marine Engineering, to design an even better saturation chamber, drawing on his own experience. He also had another company, Global Diving Services, which also boomed on the back of the North Sea work. Deaner then went to Holland to supervise the design and building of five specialist diving support vessels, which were quickly sold for £30 million each.

In 1986, when oil prices collapsed, Deaner decided to get into the exploration business himself and bought a 75% stake in the Jebsen drilling company for £8 million. Jebsen's main asset was a 44% stake in the Emerald oil field. Deaner then decided that a new style of semi-submersible platform would be needed to exploit the field. Jebsen was renamed Midland & Scottish Resources, and soon became one of the star performers on the stock market, making Deaner a multi-millionaire. But his one

remaining problem is a bitter legal row with the Davy Corporation, who are building the new rig. The rig has been hit by
delays and cost overruns, which Davy blames on alterations
demanded by Midland & Scottish, while Deaner has slapped in
a counter-claim. The lawyers will probably make millions out
of the case. Deaner, for all his love of the North Sea, remains a
committed fan of Birmingham City football club, where he has
a private box. He even tried to buy the club in 1990.

Len and Nigel Jagger   £77m

TRADER AND BUSINESSMAN   dob LJ 24 June 1925

CHANNEL Islands-based entrepreneur Len Jagger used to
deal in Ford cars in Essex but sold his business in 1972.
Since then he has built up a fortune by astutely investing in
fledgling companies which grow into multi-million-pound businesses.

He invested in UEI, a high-flying electronics company, where
he built up a sizeable stake. With his son Nigel, an American-
based financier, he made £64 million out of the sale of a stake
in Atlantic Computers, a computer leasing company run by the
late John Foulston. This racing car fanatic, who was killed in a
high-speed accident in 1987, had met Jagger on a beach in Barbados some years previously. Three months later, Jagger put £8
million into the business.

Duke of Beaufort   £75m

LANDOWNER   dob 23 March 1928

THE 11th Duke inherited the title in 1984 from his second
cousin, known to all as 'The Master', who was regarded as
the greatest foxhunter of his time and who started the Badminton Horse Trials in 1948. On his death all full-time employees

of the 52,000-acre Badminton estates in the West Country received £10 for each year of service.

The new Duke had to sell off some land to meet death duties. But this was not too much of a burden, as the Beaufort estates had actually grown, from the 19th to the 20th centuries, from 51,000 to 52,000 acres. Before moving into the 40-bedroom Badminton House, he insisted on installing lifts and central heating in what was a notoriously uncomfortable home. The Queen Mother, a frequent guest, once asked for carpet to be laid on the stairs.

By profession, the new Duke is a modern picture dealer in London and New York. Badminton itself is filled with art treasures bought mainly by the 3rd Duke in the 18th century. These include two famous paintings of Badminton by Canaletto, carvings by Grinling Gibbons, and portraits by Reynolds.

Beaufort came to prominence in 1988 in the course of Sir James Goldsmith's (q.v.) £13-billion takeover bid for BAT. Beaufort had been encouraged by his friend, Gianni Agnelli, the head of Fiat, to join a group of rich backers of the bid. With the prospects of huge rewards for splitting up BAT, the Duke was prepared to commit up to £10 million to the cause. In the event, the bid lapsed.

The Duke is selling the Badminton Cabinet, the most important piece of furniture in England, for £8.7 million. He told the *Sunday Times*: 'I have to find money to pay taxes. At the end of the day, it's really just a cupboard of which I was never very fond.'

Sir David Brown   £75m

EX-INDUSTRIALIST AND TAX EXILE
dob 10 May 1904

IN the middle of the last century, a certain David Brown started a pattern-making business in West Yorkshire. But it was his grandson, also called David, who really made the family name. Now Sir David Brown, he linked up with Harry Ferguson to produce a highly successful tractor and other farming equipment in the Thirties.

A brilliant industrialist, Brown went on to buy the Aston Martin car company and took a controlling stake in the Vosper Thornycroft shipyard. He also developed David Brown Gears to become one of the world's leading suppliers of specialist gears and transmissions for a wide range of heavy industry.

Sir David was effectively ousted from control of the group in the 1960s, and the group went through a traumatic period of losses through the early 1980s. Early in 1990, the company was finally sold by the Brown family to two professional managers for some £46 million. By then Sir David had long been a Monaco tax exile, quitting Britain in disgust at the nationalization of the Vosper yard by the last Labour government. There he enjoys the fruits of a considerable investment fund, and life with his third wife Paula, forty-eight years his junior. Currently, Sir David is working on a secret project – a 120-foot, water-jet-propelled catamaran, with a top speed of 44 knots.

Wilf Corrigan £75m

ELECTRONICS ENGINEER   dob 21 March 1938

WILF Corrigan is the most successful of the British high-tech boffins who went across to Silicon Valley in California to make their fortunes.

The son of a Liverpool docker, Corrigan was one of a large family. After taking a degree in electronics engineering from Imperial College, London, he headed for America on graduation. Later he justified his decision, saying, 'There was no future for enterprising people in the UK, even in the early 1960s.'

He worked for a number of the leading American electronics companies such as Motorola. By the early 1970s, he had been recruited to Fairchild, then a leading electronics group, which was going through a bad patch. Les Hogan, an ex-Motorola man, who was trying to rescue Fairchild, thought that his former protégé, Corrigan, was just the man needed to help him. They formed a team, nicknamed Hogan's Heroes by other Fairchild employees.

But it did not work out quite as Hogan wanted. Corrigan disagreed violently with him over the strategy and went above his head to the Fairchild family trustees, who largely owned the company. They supported him, and Hogan was ousted, with Corrigan taking his job. 'That guy has ice water in his veins,' said one American broking analyst at the time.

In 1980, Fairchild was sold to another large American group and Corrigan, who had built up a sizeable share stake during his tenure as chairman, received around $60 million and $4 million of bonuses.

He had developed a reputation as a tough hire-and-fire man, and was even reputed to sack people over the company tannoy. He also had close links with several leading venture capital funds. Out of one such link he set up LSI Logic, a specialized electronic chip maker, in 1981, with a personal stake of around 40%. That stake is now worth at least $170 million.

Married with three children, Corrigan lives in Silicon Valley's millionaire belt. He is a very keen family man, and his old image as a tough businessman has softened ever since he nursed his mother, who was dying of cancer. He is president of the Semiconductor Industry Association, the supreme accolade that can be given to a leading electronics engineer in America.

LSI Logic has two large subsidiary companies in Britain, and Corrigan serves as chairman of both, maintaining his links with his homeland.

Peter de Savary   £75m

FINANCIER   dob 11 July 1944

THE bearded face, the bald head and the large cigar are the familiar trade marks of Peter de Savary. But so is his penchant for hitting the headlines and gossip columns. One moment he is buying up yet another chunk of Cornwall, the next he is negotiating the British challenge in the America's Cup. His lifestyle is luxurious and ostentatious.

He owns a £7 million estate in Berkshire, a 'semi' in South Kensington (London), a West Indies home, and three yachts, including the 106-foot *Vagrant*, once owned by the Vanderbilt family. He has 26 cars, including one that used to belong to Hermann Goering, and travels round the world by private jet.

Yet it all began fairly modestly. Born in Essex, de Savary was educated at Charterhouse, where he managed only one O-level, in religious instruction. At 16, he went to Canada, working as a car and duplicator salesman. He returned home at 21 and joined his father's furniture firm, only to leave after three years as production manager when he was refused a pay rise.

He went to newly oil-rich Nigeria in the mid-1970s and established a successful business by being a link to the world markets for oil and bringing in vital imports such as cement and bricks. In 1977, he took on a similar role in the Middle East, particularly in Kuwait. Based out of Nassau in the Bahamas, de Savary was a millionaire at 32. In 1980 he established the St James's Club, which he sold for £22 million in October 1987. He boasts that he started the 1980s worth little but ended the decade worth £100 million.

In his private life, de Savary caused a stir by parting from his long-time girlfriend and fiancée, Linda Paton, to marry his secretary. In a matter of days he had returned to Linda, who became his wife.

He is busy increasing his fortune with a number of new deals, including a green skyscraper in New York, costing £200 million, which he claims will be the tallest in the city ever built by an Englishman. He is also building a floating methanol plant to be towed out to the Middle East, where it will convert natural gas into methanol.

Nearer home he is building a new hotel at John O'Groats to complement his work at Land's End. Some 4,000 houses are planned at a Canvey Island development and he is aiming to be the biggest ship repairer in Europe.

Mrs Pamela Harriman   £75m

INHERITANCE   dob (unknown)

PAMELA Digby, elder sister of Lord Digby, was a fully fledged member of the British aristocracy when she married Randolph Churchill, the son of Winston Churchill, in 1939. The first baron Digby had an Irish peerage created in 1620. In 1765, the 7th baron was created a British peer as Baron Digby of Sherborne. The 12th baron today still lives in Dorset near Dorchester.

Pamela gave birth to a son, called, appropriately, Winston. Today, he is Winston Churchill, the Tory MP for Stretford. His parents were divorced in 1946. Pamela then married a theatrical producer, Leland Heyward, who died in 1971. She soon married again, this time Averell Harriman, the American banker and friend of Franklin Roosevelt. In 1986, Harriman died and left his £75 million fortune to Pamela, who is now a prominent society hostess in Washington.

Mick Jagger   £75m

POP SINGER   dob 26 July 1943

A LITHE figure, pouting lips and gyrating hips were Mick Jagger's hallmarks on stage as he belted out hits like 'Jumping Jack Flash' or 'Honky Tonk Woman' to adoring female audiences for over 20 years. After a seven-year gap, the Rolling Stones – with Jagger at the helm – decided on a world tour in 1990.

Raised in the London dormitory town of Dartford by his father Joe, a PT instructor, Mick went to the London School of Economics but dropped out and turned to music. After a time in small clubs, the Rolling Stones finally achieved their first hit in 1963 and never looked back.

In the early days, Mick was a distinctly anti-establishment figure, swearing and, on tour, indulging in drugs and orgies at hotels with the inevitable groupies who followed the Stones.

But since the early 1980s Mick has mellowed and devoted himself to his family and Jerry Hall, the equally lithe American model who shares his life. She is wealthy in her own right, owning a Texas ranch.

There have been many women in his life and he has four children: a daughter by Marsha Hunt, the former star of *Hair*, another daughter by his former wife Bianca, and a son and daughter by Jerry Hall. In 1979, Bianca picked up an estimated £1 million in a British divorce settlement with Mick. He was considered lucky to have escaped so lightly. In America, she would have been awarded much more.

Today, Mick numbers Desmond Guinness and Jacob Rothschild (q.v.) among his friends. He collects paintings and houses. He owns a £2 million château in the Loire Valley, a £1.5 million Manhattan town house and a £5 million Caribbean retreat. Drugs and drink are out now as Mick pursues a punishing physical fitness regime to stay in trim and keep his weight at a constant 10 stone. 'It's horrible to be called the Grand Old Man of Rock,' he says.

Mick tried a solo career and earned £3 million for five concerts in Japan. But the magic was missing without the other Stones, so they agreed on the world tour, spending weeks in the Caribbean practising and recording.

He has had a stormy relationship with Keith Richard, the Rolling Stones guitarist, who resented Mick's assumption that he is leader of the group. They nearly split up permanently, but finally buried the hatchet at a meeting in Barbados in the summer of 1989.

Late in 1990, after the highly successful world tour, Mick finally married Jerry Hall in Bali.

Cameron Mackintosh £75m

IMPRESARIO   dob (unknown)

EVERY time a theatre-goer sees *Cats* or *Phantom of the Opera* or *Les Misérables*, Cameron Mackintosh gets that little bit richer. The youngest and most successful impresario in the history of the British theatre, he is the son of a businessman who ran a timber firm and a half-French, half-Italian mother. At 18 he became a stagehand at the Drury Lane Theatre, supporting himself by doing extra cleaning work in the mornings. By the age of 21 he had become a producer in his own right. He started out with a job in the musical *Camelot* and later toured with *Oliver* as an assistant stage manager. He once appeared nude on stage in Glasgow in the hippie musical *Hair*.

Though his first West End musical, *Anything Goes*, was a flop, his next two were minor successes. Finally his fourth, *Side by Side by Sondheim*, made money. But it was when he joined forces with Andrew Lloyd Webber (q.v.) in 1981 to produce *Cats* that the cash started rolling in. For a £450,000 initial investment, the show grossed over £500 million in 20 countries. Since then the money has kept coming in. In 1990 *Les Misérables* was running in 12 countries, and had grossed over £200 million, while *Phantom of the Opera* has made about £1 million in Britain and taken £106 million abroad. Mackintosh's next production, *Miss Saigon*, was voted best musical of 1989 by the London *Evening Standard*.

Though he now has a large London house, a cottage in Hampshire, a villa in the south of France and a small croft in Scotland, he has not always enjoyed such affluence. When describing his early days on the road, he said: 'There was a wonderful system called "putting a cheque on the road" whereby you had four or five bank accounts, at least one of which had to be in the Outer Hebrides, and one in Ireland, so your cheque would take two or three weeks to go through the system and by then you'd have put in another cheque to cover it. Hopefully, by the end of a 26-week tour, you'd be able to pay off all your bouncing cheques. I had no money at all. I used to get up very early on tour in order to draw my dole before the actors because it would upset them to meet their producer in a dole queue.'

Today, Mackintosh commutes by helicopter from London to Scotland and is a generous supporter of charities. He offered Oxford University £2 million in July 1989 to endow a professorship of drama. He also supports charities for children and for AIDS. He is renowned for dressing casually in jeans and T-shirt.

In 1990, Mackintosh put his name to a letter in the *Guardian* admitting he was gay.

Lord Rayne   £75m

PROPERTY OWNER   dob 8 February 1918

MAX, now Lord, Rayne has been a London property man since the 1940s. The son of an East End tailor who moved to Oxford Street, Lord Rayne worked for his father before the war. After wartime service with the RAF, he moved into property and found he could make more money letting his father's showroom than as a tailor.

He specialized in buying sites in areas that were unfashionable, developing them and watching as prices and rents soared. He was the first to spot the potential of the Angel, Islington (known to all Monopoly buffs), five minutes north of the Bank of England. His company, London Merchant Securities, is interested in oil and leisure industries as well as property.

He has been married twice and his second wife is the daughter of the 8th Marquess of Londonderry. His son, the Hon. Robert Rayne, is now also active in the family business.

Lord Rayne is a patron of the arts. For 16 years he was chairman of the National Theatre, retiring at the end of 1989. His office wall is dotted with valuable paintings; he gave £250,000 to the National Gallery to help it buy Cézanne's *Les Grandes Baigneuses*.

Taki Theodoracopoulos   £75m

JOURNALIST AND PLAYBOY   dob 11 August 1937

TAKI, a well-known figure on the London social scene, is possibly the richest journalist in the world. His £75 million fortune was inherited from his father, John, a Greek shipping magnate, who died in 1989. A correspondent for the *Spectator*, with his High Life column, Taki, as he is universally known, indulges in a savage crusade against his rich and aristocratic friends. He hit the headlines when he had to serve a three-month prison sentence in 1985 after being stopped at Heathrow attempting to smuggle 24.1 grammes of cocaine for his personal use. He once described wealth as 'digging your spoon into the caviar and it doesn't hit the bottom'. Educated at an American university, Taki is also a fine sportsman, representing Greece at tennis in the Davis Cup. He was also Greek karate champion for several years. He divides his life between London, New York and Gstaad. He has two yachts in the Mediterranean, where he spends the summer. A noted ladies' man and gambler, he has a particular eye for English upper-class women.

Maurice Wohl   £75m

FORMER PROPERTY DEALER   dob 4 January 1917

SO enraged was Maurice Wohl when corporation tax was introduced by the Labour government in 1965 that he suggested winding up his property company, United Real Property Trust. Instead, 11 years later he chose to become a tax exile and live in Geneva.

He owned over 51% of the shares of United Real, which had 14 prime West End and City properties. Other London property men continually sought to lay their hands on the business but Wohl would not sell until 1986.

By then he lacked the time or inclination to enter the wheeler-dealing world of redevelopment. So he sold the company to Tony Clegg (q.v.), a fast-moving Lancastrian, for £117 million.

Wohl nursed deep grievances over the British tax regime, even threatening to sue his auditor for negligence in advising on tax matters for a City office block. But he has a love of the arts and recently gave a discreet donation to the National Gallery to transform the dingy vestibule.

Sir David Alliance   £74m

TEXTILES INDUSTRIALIST   dob 15 March 1932

FROM running his first textile business in Iran at 16, Alliance has graduated to a business with 100,000 staff in 30 countries.

The son of a Jewish merchant, Alliance came to Britain in 1951 looking for supplies, and instead stayed on to move into the British textile industry. By 1953, he had bought his first mill for £8,000 and was on the way to a fortune. Today he runs Coats Viyella, and after a series of mergers in the 1970s and 1980s made it one of the world's largest textile companies. He is determined to make it bigger with a successful £252 million bid for rival Tootal.

But his luck has not always held up. Alliance was one of the biggest victims of the 1987 stock market crash. His shareholdings plunged in value by £73 million over 1988 – £200,000 a day. But they had slightly recovered by 1990 and, from a low point of £65 million, the Alliance fortune is now worth around £74 million.

Sir David Alliance lives in Manchester and London, and is an avid collector of L. S. Lowry paintings.

Leonard van Geest   £72m

FRUIT AND FOOD SELLER   dob 1 April 1950

LEONARD van Geest, a 6ft 7in multi-millionaire, had a textbook training to take over the family business, best known for its bananas and other exotic fruits. First he went into management consultancy, then worked for a top London accountancy firm before moving on to Marks & Spencer.

In 1976 he finally joined Geest and moved up the organization to succeed his father, also called Leonard, as chairman in 1980. His father was one of three Dutch brothers whose family were horticulturists. In the 1930s they started exporting bulbs to

Britain and in 1935 the three brothers came over to set up their own British company. With only £2,000 capital they began importing Dutch bulbs and selling them to commercial growers in Britain. The breakthrough came in 1952 when Geest negotiated a franchise to distribute the banana crops of the Windward Islands. Geest now handles half the bananas sold in Britain.

Today, the company that was responsible for introducing avocados, red peppers and kiwi fruit to this country is tempting British taste with new exotic fruits. It sells its products to major supermarkets and has moved into new areas such as prepared foods. It recently bought a manufacturer of chilled pizzas and it is spending heavily on new warehouses. Geest was floated on the stock market in 1986 and profits have been rising sharply. In 1990, the company made £24.8 million pre-tax profits, a 24% increase. The family sold half its 31.8% shareholding in the business in June 1991, raising £35 million.

Leonard van Geest lives in a Regency farmhouse near Spalding, Lincolnshire, surrounded by the firm's bulb fields. His wife, Gillian, is a physiotherapist and they have a young son, Ross.

He is a keen rugby and tennis player. The family are enthusiastic followers of horseracing, and have several horses at a Newmarket stable. In 1990, he also took over the role of non-executive chairman of Littlewoods.

Peter Greenall and family   £70m

BREWERS   dob 18 July 1953

THOUGH not yet into middle age, Old Etonian Peter Greenall has few heights left to conquer. As a Cambridge undergraduate he took a year off his studies to try to become a champion amateur jockey. He succeeded. Today he is busy making his way in the business world as chairman of the Aintree racecourse and in the brewing field, where he is being groomed to take over the helm of his family's Greenall Witley company.

Based in Warrington and famous for its Vladivar Vodka,

Greenall Witley, started by the Greenalls in the 18th century, is one of the largest independent brewers left in Britain. Peter Greenall is now the only family member on the board, though his younger brother John also works for the group.

Late last year, Greenall Witley announced that it was ending nearly 230 years of brewing on its site. The Campaign for Real Ale described the move as a cynical exercise. But this did not deter the company.

Peter Greenall's father, now Lord Daresbury, inherited the title last year from Peter's grandfather, a legendary sportsman. He was described in his obituary as the greatest foxhunter in the 20th century. He once fought a neighbour to a standstill in a bare knuckle fight.

Apart from his business interests, Peter is a keen skier and frequently entertains younger members of the Royal family such as the Prince and Princess of Wales and the Duke and Duchess of York at his luxury chalet at Klosters. John Greenall and his wife Gabrielle are also close friends of the Duke and Duchess of York, and Gabrielle is a godmother to Princess Beatrice.

John Hall   £70m

PROPERTY DEVELOPER   dob 21 March 1933

FOR a fourth-generation miner, John Hall is not doing badly for himself. He is the man who has turned 120 acres of derelict and muddy land in depressed Gateshead into the Metro Centre, described as Europe's most ambitious retail and leisure complex. People come miles to shop at the centre and others are planned in Edinburgh, Glasgow and Birmingham.

John Hall escaped from underground mining to work for the Coal Board's estate department. After qualifying as a fully-fledged chartered surveyor, he became a partner in a Sunderland firm of surveyors. He survived the 1974 property crash and then planned the Metro Centre.

Today, he is busy drawing up plans for Wynard Hall, the 4,500-acre estate and former ancestral home of the Marquess of

Londonderry, which he has just bought. Ironically, the Londonderry family used to be one of the largest mine owners in the country. John Hall plans to live in the house while creating a business centre, luxury hotel and three golf courses on the estate.

John Hall's family own the Cameron Hall development company, in which they all play an active role. In 1988, the company made £28 million profits.

David Kirch   £70m

PROPERTY DEALER   dob *c.* 1938

IN 1958, at the age of 20, David Kirch was left £5,000 by his father, a wholesale meat trader. Today, he is worth £70 million and lives in Jersey, home of tax exiles.

His money-making skills started at Tonbridge School, where he had a small business selling stamps. 'I wasn't clever enough to go to university. I went into Lloyds in insurance for a while,' he told the *Evening Standard* in 1970. He did not enjoy Lloyds and, when his father died, he joined the family meat business then run by his uncle. But Kirch could not get on with his uncle, and set up on his own, buying a cold store in Kingston and getting up at 5.30 every morning to choose meat at Smithfield market. The business was taken over after a year by a Dutch company who wanted the property, not the business.

That convinced Kirch that the future lay in property and he bought a half-share in a Hampshire estate agency. He gave that up to concentrate on property dealing, working out of his mother's house in Esher until 1962, when he went into partnership with his older brother, Peter. They formed a company, Crown Lodge Estates, and managed to borrow enough money from a bank and insurance company to buy up 23 houses near London's Gloucester Road. They expanded and, by 1970, had around 1,000 tenants. They also bought the Shaftesbury Theatre, which they threatened to demolish until a preservation order saved it.

The Kirch brothers survived the property crash in the 1974–6 period by turning their extensive interests private. David Kirch went to live in Jersey at the time and conducted his property dealings from there, taking control of the Channel Hotels and Properties group in the 1980s. In September 1988, he sold his last UK residential properties for £30 million.

Kirch lived a modest life in Britain until his Jersey exile. As the *Evening Standard* put it: 'Often at weekends, he takes his mother down to his cottage at Shoreham-on-Sea, otherwise he sits alone in his 15-room mansion in Hyde Park Gate and watches colour TV after eating his solitary dinner served by his Spanish butler.' In Jersey, Kirch is busy refurbishing his impressive mansion.

Alan Lewis £70m

TEXTILE INDUSTRIALIST   dob 2 March 1938

DISCIPLINE is all to Alan Lewis. A regime of karate in the morning and weight training in the evening, combined with no alcohol or smoking and a vegetarian diet, has helped him to the top in the British textile industry. But in 1975, he was bored and became a backgammon player in Barbados, where he got even richer buying shares at the bottom of the market.

He now runs Illingworth Morris. Pamela Mason, the former wife of the late James Mason, was a major shareholder. Lewis bought her shares in 1982 and launched one of the most bitter takeover battles in the City, culminating in his victory in 1983. In July 1989, Lewis took the company private, in a deal worth some £78 million. The move was not prompted through any hostility to the City, but Lewis wanted to take a long-term view, and felt that it would not be fair to outside shareholders to see profits depressed while he was busy investing for the future through moves into Europe and the like. Today, he reckons the group is worth 'at least' a net £70 million, as he told the *Evening Standard* recently.

Success was hard-fought. Lewis left school in Manchester at 15 and went to work in a printing company to pay his way through university. He built up his business interests through an Isle of Man-based company and came to prominence with the Illingworth bid.

Today he lives on the 640-acre Great Hundridge Manor estate in Buckinghamshire, and relaxes by reading poetry. He is a devout Christian.

Lord Lovat   £70m

LANDOWNER   dob 9 July 1911

THE actor Peter Lawford played Lord Lovat in *The Longest Day*, the film about D-Day, but the glamorous portrayal did not go down well with the original. One of Scotland's three top landowners, with 190,000 acres, he hates pomp and fuss. He boycotted the 40th anniversary celebration for D-Day in 1984, saying it was a jamboree.

Lovat's early years were relaxed: private school at Ampleforth, Magdalen College, Oxford, and the Scots Guards. In his autobiography *March Past*, he records: 'My youth positively reeked of privilege ... It will be no surprise to learn that my politics remain strictly feudal!' He sits in the Lords and takes the Tory whip.

Lovat raised a regiment of commando troops during the war and was decorated with the DSO, MC, the Croix de Guerre and Légion d'Honneur for his exploits during raids on Dieppe and Norway and later on D-Day, when he was badly wounded. The Soviet Union made him a member of the Order of Suvarov. David Stirling, knighted in the 1990 New Year's honours list, the man who founded the SAS, was a first cousin.

Lovat's war exploits were in line with family tradition. During the Boer War his father raised and commanded the Lovat Scouts, comprised of members of the Fraser Clan, of which he is the head. In the 18th century, a previous Lord Lovat was the last peer to be beheaded by the axe for treason on Tower Hill for supporting the 1745 Scottish revolt. His lands were confiscated, but his son distinguished himself as a British general and had the lands restored.

Lovat has made occasional forays into Parliament to speak on salmon fishing and deer stalking (and more often on the poaching thereof, a traditional obsession of Highland lairds). Today, he no longer lives at the family seat of Beaufort Castle outside Inverness, having passed occupancy to his eldest son and heir, Simon (also ex-Ampleforth and the Scots Guards). Simon, known as the Master of Lovat, sold one of the family salmon rivers for a record-breaking £11–15 million. Lovat's daughter, the Hon. Tessa Keswick (formerly married to Lord Reay), contested the Inverness-shire constituency for the Tories in the last General Election and came third. She was appointed special policy adviser and 'strategic thinker' to Health Minister Kenneth Clarke.

Peter Rigby £70m

COMPUTER DISTRIBUTOR   dob (unknown)

BORN in Liverpool, 46-year-old Peter Rigby has made his fortune in the computer industry, a rare feat for a Briton. Even rarer, he has managed to hold on to it and prosper in a highly competitive industry.

But there is little about the industry that Rigby does not know intimately. He started his career at the age of 18 working for the NCR group as an apprentice, where he stayed for 5 years. He then moved to Honeywell, the giant computer company. At 28 he was a branch manager. But by then he reckoned it was obvious that a British national's career path was blocked in the American computer giant, and 'I wasn't prepared to see my career path flattened,' he says.

Having raised £2,000 capital, he branched out on his own in the early 1970s. He chose the computer recruitment business as his field and, with the growing skills shortages in computing, he prospered. As the money poured in, he invested it in new areas of the computer industry, establishing his own computer bureau in the early 1980s.

Known as Specialist Computer Holdings, the business grew on the back of sales of IBM and Honeywell machines and Rigby's attention to detail. That was demonstrated when, in 1988 and 1989, SCH won what Rigby calls 'the badge that really matters' – the IBM dealer of the year award. The success was apparent in financial terms also. In the year to the end of March 1990, SCH's sales totalled £70 million, producing profits of £4.7 million. In 1990–91, Rigby is expecting sales of over £100 million.

With few borrowings and all the shares in his family hands, he says that he would not contemplate selling SCH for less than £75 million. Rigby lives in the smart West Midlands commuter belt with his wife, Patricia.

Raymond Slater   £70m

ENTREPRENEUR AND PROPERTY
DEVELOPER   dob 1934

BORN in Huddersfield just after the worst ravages of the Depression in 1934, Slater was brought up by his mother and grandmother after his father died. They ran a corner shop and young Raymond managed to get into the local grammar school before training as an estate agent in Bradford.

He showed early entrepreneurial talent by starting his own surveying and estate agency specializing in commercial property around Stockport. That was in 1959, a time when big property developers such as Jack Cotton and Charles Clore were doing deals in Manchester. Slater often acted for them and developed a taste for the business. He gave up his estate agency work and started dealing. Within a few years, he was director of 34 property companies.

In the 1970s he was in the news over his efforts to wrest the then sleepy Norwest Holt property company from its controlling Le Mare family. It took a bitter eight-year battle for Slater to win in 1980. After that, Slater bought out his former partner, John Lilly, sparking off another bitter row. But by the mid-1980s Slater had completely transformed Norwest Holt. A 1980 loss of nearly £2 million turned into a profit of £6 million in 1985. The group was planning a stock market floating, but the dispute between Lilly and Slater killed that off. Instead, a management buy-out took place and Slater received some £40 million for his shares.

He sold his Cheshire home and went into tax exile in Guernsey, where he still lives. He retains substantial property, oil and gas interests in America. Apart from a passion for music – he was a regular at the Hallé Orchestra and a Friend of Covent Garden – Slater's main interest is in sport. He supports Manchester United Football Club, is a good tennis player and also plays golf and skis.

Earl of Stockton   £70m

PUBLISHER   dob 10 October 1943

GRANDSON of Harold Macmillan, prime minister from 1957 to 1963, the Earl of Stockton is the major shareholder in the publishing firm Macmillan. The family own 95% of the shares in the company, one of the country's largest and most profitable publishers. Its accounts for 1989 give profits of over £8.35 million after tax on a turnover of £179.6 million. Although the publishing business is in a recession, Macmillan would be highly prized by large publishing houses and could command a price of over £70 million.

The present Earl inherited the title in 1986 on the death of his grandfather. A former journalist, the Earl moved into the family business in 1970. He lives in Chelsea, having sold the Macmillan family home, Birchgrove in Sussex, for over £5 million in 1989. He enjoys country pursuits such as shooting and fishing. He also lists motor racing and conversation among his hobbies.

John Thornton and family   £70m

CHOCOLATE MANUFACTURERS
dob 30 January 1944

IN 1911, Joseph William Thornton opened his first sweet shop in Sheffield. He aimed to have the best shop in 'Steel City' and he succeeded. Within two years, he had started making his own chocolates and the business has never looked back. Today, Thorntons, where the family still control some 70% of the shares directly, has expanded to over 330 stores round Britain. It also produces many of the upmarket chocolates to be found in Marks & Spencer.

The company owns three factories and, in 1988, moved production out of Sheffield to a new £9 million purpose-built site at Belper in Derbyshire. At the same time, the company came to the stock market, where its shares proved very popular. There were eight times as many applications as shares available.

It has used the proceeds from the sale of 25% of its shares to buy overseas companies and to fund expansion out of its northern and Midlands heartland into London and the southeast. Within weeks of its flotation, it had bought a Belgian confectioner for £2 million, followed a year later by the £7.6-million purchase of a French sweet and ice-cream retailer.

Lord White   £70m

INDUSTRIALIST   dob 11 May 1923

IN 1940, 17-year-old Gordon White left his job selling advertising space for his father's publishing business and went into the army, where he served in Force 136, a unit of the Special Operations Executive, the forerunner of the CIA and the SAS. It was there that he made friends with Bill Hanson, the younger brother of the future Lord Hanson (q.v.). After the war, the friendship continued when Bill went back to work for his family haulage business, Oswald Tillotson, while White became chairman of his family business, Welbecson, in 1947. In 1954 Bill Hanson died of stomach cancer, and White got to know James, the elder brother, who described him as a 'surrogate brother'.

They were to become partners when their respective businesses were taken over by the Hull-based Wiles Group. But later, Hanson and White bought out Wiles, which was later renamed the Hanson Trust. Today, Hanson is one of the largest and most successful British companies, with huge interests ranging from food to building materials, batteries and typewriters. It buys and sells businesses like any commodity, but always at a handsome profit. White never visits the companies owned by Hanson, preferring to leave their smooth running to top-class managers.

The 6ft 6in 'Gordy', as he is called, runs the American side of the operations (called Hanson Industries) from a Park Avenue address. He enjoyed a certain notoriety as a playboy, not marrying until he was 35. By then his name had been linked in gossip columns to Ava Gardner, Rita Hayworth and even Marilyn Monroe. Eventually Gordon settled down with a Swedish wife who produced two daughters; his second wife, a former starlet, Virginia North, produced a son.

He currently shares his life with Victoria Tucker, a model some 40 years younger than him. She has been pressing him to marry, but to no avail. One of his favourite phrases is: 'Never marry a young girl – they want babies.'

Apart from business, White finds time to relax aboard his 176-foot yacht, *Galu*. He has homes in New York, London and California. He also has extensive bloodstock interests and rescued the English Derby through sponsorship. He lists his other hobbies as skiing, riding, tennis and, as a qualified helicopter pilot, flying.

In the New Year 1991 Honours List, White received a peerage, allowing him to join Hanson in the Lords.

It was some consolation for White's disappointment over the failure of Hanson to acquire Power Gen, the electricity generator. Hanson had expressed interest in the company, but the Government decided to go ahead with a flotation.

Sir Phil Harris   £65m

CARPET MERCHANT   dob 15 September 1942

WHEN his father died, Phil Harris, a 15-year-old Streatham Grammar School boy, took over running the family's three lino and carpet shops in south London. Thirty-four years later, Sir Phil is worth a fortune, having sold his Harris Queensway company to James Gulliver (q.v.), the Scottish entrepreneur.

Until mid-1987 the Harris career had been a glittering success, with headlong expansion. New stores were opened, other companies acquired, and Harris was regarded as one of Britain's brightest young businessmen.

But then profits began to slide and eventually Harris sold the company, retaining only a soft furnishing business. Sir Phil seemed almost a beaten man.

But it is too early to write him off. While Harris Queensway (eventually renamed Lowndes Queensway) lurched from one crisis to another, leading to the resignation of Gulliver and its final collapse, Sir Phil has begun a new business called Carpetright. He competed directly with Lowndes and planned to have nearly 40 outlets in operation in 1990. He poached key executives from Lowndes.

Outside work, his great love is show jumping. He gives large amounts of his money to Guy's Hospital, the restoration fund for Westminster Abbey and charities such as Birthright.

Earl of Lonsdale   £65m

LANDOWNER   dob 3 November 1922

FOUR times married, Lord Lonsdale owns 80,000 acres of Cumbria. His family gave boxing the Lonsdale Belt. His grandfather was known as the 'Yellow' Earl both because of his extravagant lifestyle in Edwardian society and for his yellow carriages. His vast wealth came from rich undersea mines off

Whitehaven in Cumbria. This enabled him to keep two large yachts off Cowes and to entertain in style. He spent £3,000 a year on cigars alone and King Edward VII called him 'almost an emperor, not quite a gentleman'.

The present Earl has totally revitalized the estates, which were nearly bankrupt when he inherited in 1949. He is chairman and major shareholder in Lakeland Investments, which has extensive farming and forestry interests. Showing a practical turn of mind, he has installed an electronic sawmill on what was once the site of his own private railway station. Lowther Park, on his estate, is a mini-Alton Towers theme park.

In 1987, he made £400,000 by selling up to 30 Lords of Manor titles, which are in the original form in which English land and titles were expressed. In 1988, he sold a further 30 at an average price of over £13,000.

George Michael   £65m

POP STAR   dob 26 June 1963

HIS father gave him an ultimatum: 'You've got six months to make it or leave home.' That was enough to spur Georgias Kyriacos Panayiotou to take the plunge and enter the pop world with his school friend Andrew Ridgeley. The pair had first met as 12-year-olds at Bushey Meads comprehensive school. Thus was born Wham, with George changing his name to Michael and becoming the slickest pop star of the 1980s.

It is a classic rags-to-riches tale. George's father, Jack Panayiotou, arrived in London from Cyprus with little money and few prospects. But this Greek Cypriot moved into a cramped flat in Finchley and started work as a waiter, ending up as owner of a restaurant chain which made him a millionaire.

George left school in 1981 with two A-levels and orders from his father to find work. He was certainly not going to be spoiled. Three days on a building site and a spell in British Home Stores convinced George that this sort of work was not for him.

But pop music was. A £20 demonstration disc, 'Wham Rap',

led to a recording contract in 1982 for the unlikely pair. For the next four years, they toured the world and sold over 35 million records. Screaming fans pursued them and the Princess of Wales once described George as 'gorgeous'.

In 1986 the pair split, but George continued his solo career and was even more successful. His debut solo album, *Faith*, sold 15 million copies. In 1987 and 1988 his earnings totalled £24 million. Early in 1989, he earned £1 million for a day's work doing a Coca-Cola advertisement. In the past four years, his total earnings are estimated to have been $56 million.

He spends the money as fast as he earns it. His homes include a £1.4 million mansion near his parents' Hertfordshire house, a £500,000 Knightsbridge flat near Harrods, a £350,000 mews house in St John's Wood and an £80,000 Soho flat plus three more overseas. In total he has spent nearly £5 million on the homes and £3 million on a plane. He has also spent £10,000 on an indoor playroom for his labrador.

George started out as a socialist, appearing at a benefit concert during the 1984–5 miners' strike. But he came round to the view that Mrs Thatcher 'has given kids new drive'. He has not been happy with the fame and fortune, often appearing the worse for drink at awards ceremonies and lashing out at friends and photographers after the Wham breakup. He still remains good friends with Ridgeley.

Earl of Radnor   £65m

LANDOWNER   dob 10 November 1927

IN 1714, an eminent London merchant, William des Bouveries, was created a baronet by the Walpole government. Succeeding generations managed to rise in the ranks of the British aristocracy until one was created the 1st Earl of Radnor in 1765. The family name may be Welsh, but it is Salisbury in Wiltshire with which the family has long-standing links. William des Bouveries' son sat as MP for New Sarum, and a later Earl sat as MP for Salisbury and Wiltshire South in the 19th century.

Today Jacob Pleydell-Bouverie, the 8th Earl, lives in Longford Castle near Salisbury, where he has a 10,000-acre estate. His father, a noted expert on forestry and farming, died in 1968. His estate was then valued at £4.3 million. The present Earl was able to satisfy death duties on the estate in 1970 by selling a portrait by Velazquez which fetched £2.3 million. The loss of the picture barely dented one of the finest collections in Britain. This includes a Holbein portrait of Erasmus, a Claude landscape and two pictures by Franz Hals. One of the Hals and other paintings were stolen in 1969 but were recovered the following year. Even then, the stolen paintings were valued at £75,000.

Despite installing an elaborate alarm system, the Earl – family motto: 'My country is dear, my liberty is dearer' – refuses to open Longford to the public. He once said: 'The people who come around here might be very nice, but you wouldn't want to see and hear them all the time. I am told that you can even smell them, and eventually your house takes on an odour like a railway station.'

Apart from land and paintings, the Radnor family also has valuable London holdings. The Bouverie name gives the clue: this famous street – just off Fleet Street – contains two invaluable properties, Harmsworth House and Northcliffe House West, whose freehold is owned by Radnor's son, Viscount Folkestone. With former newspaper buildings in that area changing hands for up to £100 million the two properties are worth at least £40 million. The family also own substantial property in Folkestone, which is expected to appreciate considerably in value once the Channel Tunnel opens in 1993.

The Earl, who has been married twice and divorced twice, has two sons and four daughters. His heir Viscount Folkestone was educated – like his father – at Harrow. He then went to the Royal Agricultural College in Cirencester. He lives near Salisbury.

Duke of Roxburghe   £65m

LANDOWNER   dob 18 November 1954

IT was billed as the romance of the decade when Guy Innes-Ker, Duke of Roxburghe, married Lady Jane Grosvenor, the beautiful sister of the Duke of Westminster (q.v.). They met in 1975 at a party on the Duke of Westminster's Fermanagh estate (he owns much of the county) when Roxburghe was serving with the army in the élite Blues and Royals cavalry regiment. The gossip columnists had a field day, discussing the combined fortunes. That was in 1977.

In March 1990 the Duchess filed her divorce papers. She moved out of beautiful Floors Castle on the Scottish Borders and into a six-bedroom Georgian house a few miles away, taking her three children with her. It was said that the reason for the split was the Duke's 'roving eye'. The Duchess clearly hinted at such in an interview with the *Daily Express*: 'All I will say is that boys will be boys. And sometimes a busy mother with three children has to expect a little flirtation from her husband.'

Floors sits among 56,000 acres of good-quality farm and sporting land. It includes some priceless Tweed salmon-fishing rights. By selling a part of them off in 1974, the Duke was able to satisfy the death duties owing on the estate after his father's death. The Duke, educated at Eton and Sandhurst, where he took the Sword of Honour, the Academy's top award, later took a degree in land economy at Cambridge after he left the army. In 1988, he told *The Times* that he was planning to establish a number of executive homes and a small golf course at Floors.

Both the Duke and Duchess are close friends of the Royal family, who enjoy staying at Floors. The Duchess was godmother to the Duke and Duchess of York's first daughter.

The castle is filled with fine Brussels tapestries, many purchased by the wife of the 8th Duke, Mary Goelet, heiress to a 19th-century American magnate.

John Whittaker   £65m

PROPERTY DEVELOPER   dob 14 March 1942

IN 1986, John Whittaker burst into national prominence when his company, Peel Holdings, tried to take over the old Manchester Ship Canal Company. One of the most bitter take-over battles in recent times then ensued. While Whittaker was able to buy up a majority of shares, the voting structure of the company prevented him taking full control. Accusations and counter-charges flew from one side to another as the old manage-ment tried to resist Whittaker, who was attracted by the prop-erty potential alongside the canal. There were even reports of door-to-door canvassers out in Lancashire towns like Blackburn seeking to buy up small parcels of shares.

Whittaker never gave up, and nearly two and a half years later he finally obtained control of the canal. The deal is believed to have netted him a £20 million profit. It was typical of the opportunism that has made him one of the north's most success-ful property developers. With a farming background in the Rochdale area, the thrifty Lancastrian is a devout Catholic who once considered entering the priesthood but went into business instead. He started in quarrying when the trans-Pennine motor-way M62 was being built in 1962. The quarrying profits financed his expansion into demolition, knocking down redundant factor-ies and mills.

Whittaker soon saw that he could make more money by taking over the ailing companies, rationalizing them to develop their successful operations and then redeveloping their surplus factories. By the time the bid for the canal was launched, he employed 1,000 people in ten different companies around Liver-pool and Manchester. He also became one of the most successful out-of-town shopping and leisure park developers.

He saw the potential goldmine in the canal in the shape of 300 derelict acres at Barton Dock on the edge of Manchester. With access to four separate motorway junctions near by, it was an ideal site for a £100 million 'shopping city' able to draw on a customer base of 5 million people, all living within a 40-minute drive.

Whittaker is a secretive and elusive man. He bought up many

of the rundown companies via his parents' Isle of Man company, Largs Ltd. Largs owns half the shares in the quoted company, Peel Holdings, based in Rochdale.

Whittaker has surrounded himself with a young team of executives whom he allows to get on with the job, though he is said to pay low salaries. He is proud to be British and his favoured recreation is said to be going to the pub for a pint with the lads. He does not display any of the ostentation of a millionaire. He is known to turn up late to meetings with City analysts because he insists on travelling by tube. He has a home on the Isle of Man and a farmhouse near Rochdale.

The £410 million debt at John Whittaker's master company, Peel Holdings, looks like putting a brake on his ambitions for the immediate future. In the half year to the end of September 1990, profits collapsed from £9.5 million to £269,000, and the group withdrew from housebuilding in the North-West and East Anglia. In an effort to reduce the debt, Whittaker sold Peel's 10.8% stake in the Mersey Docks & Harbour company, making some £4.7 million profit on the sale.

Clarice Pears and family £64m

PROPERTY   dob (unknown)

ONE of London's largest and most low-key property groups, the William Pears Family Holdings is owned and run by members of the Pears family led by Clarice Pears. William Pears Holdings is also highly profitable, with its latest after-tax profits for the year ending 31 March 1989 showing an increase from £5.1 million to £9.6 million. With net assets of some £118 million, the group would be worth well over £60 million if floated on the stock market, even in the difficult climate today. The family live in a fashionable area of North London close to the company headquarters. In recent years, the group has been busy on the commercial property front all over Britain. For example, it is currently developing a £45 million office scheme near Edinburgh's Royal Mile.

Antony Crosthwaite-Eyre and family   £62m

FORMER PUBLISHER   dob 22 August 1940

THE Crosthwaite-Eyres have been connected with publishing since the days of Charles II through Eyre & Spottiswoode, their family firm.

This became part of Associated Book Publishers in the 1960s and the family took a 37% stake in the business. A few weeks before the October 1987 market crash, International Thomson took over ABP and bought the Eyre holdings for £77 million in cash, nearly three times their value a month later. Had either party waited until after the crash, the price could well have been reduced by around £14 million, as the value of many publishing company shares fell by nearly 20% in the débâcle.

The Eyres are a well-known New Forest family, and have owned a 1,000-acre estate near Lyndhurst for centuries. Antony's father, the late Sir Oliver Crosthwaite-Eyre, was MP for the area.

In the 18th century, one of the Eyre family paid £10,000 for the right to be the Queen's printer for 30 years. This royal patent was later extended and gave the family a virtual monopoly to print the Bible in England. Antony, the present head of the family, is a leading British Roman Catholic. He married a Belgian countess in 1960, but they later divorced. They have five children.

Michael Ashcroft   £60m

ENTREPRENEUR   dob 4 March 1946

AT first Michael Ashcroft had few advantages in his life besides a willingness to take risks and work very hard. Yet today, he runs a £2-billion business empire based in Bermuda. He left Norwich Grammar School and took a Higher

National Diploma in business studies. After a spell as a management trainee at Rothmans, which he described as 'the two most boring years of my life', he joined Pritchards, the office cleaning firm, before branching out on his own in 1972.

First he became a consultant advising companies and then, borrowing £20,000, he bought a struggling cleaning company with just 200 workers. Within four years it employed 4,000 and Ashcroft pocketed £1.3 million by selling it to the Reckitt & Colman group. This gave him the capital to build what was to become a huge business empire. He searched for a publicly quoted company that was near receivership and in 1977 alighted on the Hawley camping equipment manufacturer. He quickly acquired 25% of the company (a stake that has since been diluted to around 3%) and turned it round very quickly. Within a year, it had achieved profits of £22,000 and by 1984 it had made £31.4 million.

By 1987 Hawley was based in Bermuda, had made some 250 acquisitions and had 100,000 employees. Ashcroft had taken over Pritchard, the group where he cut his teeth cleaning. That year he also snapped up ADT, an American security group, for £440 million and renamed it Hawley-ADT.

For many years he ran a pub in Berkshire to relax from the pressure of business but now he lives in Bermuda with his second wife – formerly his secretary – and three children. He commutes regularly to London by Concorde from America and is a close friend of Denis Thatcher. ADT also sponsors the London marathon, though Ashcroft describes himself as only an occasional jogger. He enraged feminists early in 1989 when he remarked, 'You know what I always say ... the best place for a woman is either in the kitchen or the bedroom – and you shouldn't spend too much time in between the two.'

Of late, shares in ADT have been under pressure. The City has never really understood ADT's philosophy and harbours doubts about Ashcroft's management style.

Raj Bagri   £60m

METAL BROKER   dob 24 October 1930

ARRIVING in Britain from Calcutta in the late 1950s, Raj Bagri was initially drawn by the attractions of the world's top metals market. Starting as an apprentice, he worked his way up to become the owner of Minmetco, one of the largest metal and commodity dealing firms in the City. With a turnover of £353 million and after-tax profits of £4.3 million in the year to the end of September 1989, Minmetco would be worth at least £50 million if floated on the stock market.

Apart from his London business, Bagri also owns manufacturing companies in India, Canada and Malaysia. His son Apurv works closely with him in the business, while his daughter Amita is married to a member of the influential Birla business family in India. Today, Bagri is a director of the London Metal Exchange and one of its élite floor members. He lives in the fashionable St John's Wood area of London.

Peter and John Beckwith   £60m

PROPERTY DEVELOPERS
dob PB 20 January 1945, JB 19 March 1947

MANY of the stylish new buildings in the City are the work of the Beckwith brothers, John and Peter. Sons of an army colonel from Hong Kong, they had a conventional upper-middle-class education at Harrow and Cambridge. They set up their own property company, London & Edinburgh Trust, in 1971. But they were badly hit in the property crash of 1973–4, when they each suffered a £1.5 million loss.

The two brothers used their training as a solicitor and chartered accountant respectively to fight back. They paid off all their debts and today have the smooth, sleek look of the successful property developers they have become. They have branched out in recent years from building City offices to business parks. They are also very active in Europe and America.

Between them, the Beckwith brothers owned around 29% of the company. Both are fanatical sportsmen, enjoying tennis, football and skiing. They are both heavy supporters of charity; they both live in south-west London.

The brothers became increasingly disenchanted with the stock market and in April 1990 sold their joint stake to a Swedish company for £80 million. They are also coming up with new development plans all the time, their latest being a £350 million scheme to redevelop 25 acres of the former Bishopsgate Goods Yard on the edge of the City. They continue to run LET for the Swedish group. Currently, the Beckwiths are planning to enter the Italian property market.

Stephen Boler   £60m

ENTREPRENEUR   dob (unknown)

AT 16, Stephen Boler became a trainee with Unilever, but he left five years later to establish his own business in the tyre trade, inspired by his father, who had worked as a garage mechanic. Armed with £1,000 and an old Nissen hut, he rapidly built the business and four years later sold out to another company, Albany Tyre, netting some £400,000. That was in 1969, and Boler immediately started another similar business.

At the time, he was regarded as something of a playboy; as one paper reported in 1973: 'He is 29, divorced, good-looking and lives at the exclusive-sounding address of The Penthouse, Manchester.' By the time he was 35, Boler was living in a Cheshire thatched mansion with the former Miss Great Britain, Carole Redhead.

His biggest business coup came in 1980 when he bought 36 of the troubled Kitchen Queen retail outlets for £2 million. A few months later, he bought Wharf Mill, a furniture group. From these businesses he created Kitchens Direct, a group that specialized in selling fitted kitchens through an expensive advertising campaign in the national press. Within three years, he had built up a turnover of £22 million and in 1984 he sold the business to the then Hawley group for £22 million.

He diversified into different businesses, buying the exclusive Mere Golf and Country Club outside Manchester, a domestic and industrial security group and a £10 million-a-year conservatory business.

Together with Peter Swales, the chairman, Boler also controls 60% of the shares in Manchester City Football Club. In April 1989, he bought back a much bigger Kitchens Direct group, which also included the Moben company. In October, he reinforced his determination to become a major player in the fitted kitchens market by buying a subsidiary of the BET group, Farouche Cuisine.

Boler, a workaholic, travels to his various offices by his own helicopter. He has even had a pad installed at the MKD headquarters in Trafford Park. He has put the building on the market with an asking price of around £10 million.

Now single, he lives in considerable style, with a Warwickshire estate and a mansion in exclusive Knutsford. He keeps a very low profile today, and relies heavily on the advice of his right-hand man, Ashley Lewis, an accountant.

Peter and Ronald Goldstein   £60m

FORMER CHEMIST'S SHOP OWNERS
dob (unknown)

THE Goldstein brothers started working with a barrow for their father in London's East End, but eventually the business was taken over by Tesco. Ronnie and Peter Goldstein then branched out on their own, setting up their first chemist's shop in an old barber's premises in Putney High Street. That was in April 1966. The office was so small there that any conversations with sales reps had to take place standing up.

By 1983 they had established 143 of their cut-price Superdrug stores. The company was then floated on the stock market and the brothers became millionaires overnight. In 1987 they sold the chain – then 300 strong – to Woolworth and accepted 16 million Woolworth shares in payment. These are worth over £60 million today.

The brothers are part of a close-knit family. Neither smokes nor drinks, and they work 120 hours a week between them. Peter is a keen tennis player and Ronnie sings for relaxation. They live within walking distance of each other in Croydon. Today the brothers are building up a bookstore chain called Volume One.

Earl of Harewood   £60m

LANDOWNER   dob 7 February 1923

EVERYTHING about George Henry Hubert Lascelles, 7th Earl of Harewood, reeks of aristocratic grandeur. Tall and distinguished in appearance, he went to the traditional school, Eton, and from there to King's College, Cambridge. A cousin of the Queen, he was one of the most famous of the British prisoners held in the Colditz Castle prisoner of war camp during World War II. As he was 18th in line to the throne, the Germans considered him a unique prize. He was captured after being wounded while fighting as a Grenadier Guards captain in Italy in 1944.

After the war, he served in various appointments as an ADC to the Governor General of Canada and as Counsellor of State during the absence abroad of George VI and later Queen Elizabeth.

But he made his lasting mark on contemporary Britain as an arts patron and administrator. He was a director and executive of the Royal Opera House at Covent Garden and is chairman of Sadlers Wells Opera, now the English National Opera. He was also editor of the magazine *Opera*.

In 1967, he divorced his first wife Marion, and she later married the Rt Hon. Jeremy Thorpe, former leader of the old Liberal Party. He remarried the same year to Patricia Tuckwell, an Australian. He has four sons by the two marriages.

He owns Harewood House, one of England's finest historic buildings, which contains a genuinely priceless collection of the very best paintings by Hoppner, Gainsborough, Reynolds,

Titian, Tintoretto, Veronese, El Greco and Turner. In addition there is a valuable collection of Sèvres and Chinese porcelain and some of the finest furniture ever made in Britain. Most of the wealth came from the 2nd Earl's involvement in the slave trade at the end of the 18th century. In the late 19th century the estate ran to just under 30,000 acres, though this is thought to have slimmed down this century.

Wensley Haydon-Baillie   £60m

PHARMACEUTICALS   dob 7 November 1943

THE son of a Nottinghamshire surgeon, Wensley Haydon-Baillie read economics at Exeter University in the Sixties. After a brief spell in the City working for the Slater Walker group, he had amassed enough wealth to buy a controlling interest in a small, ailing engineering company called Watshams. Haydon-Baillie moved the company, renamed Optical & Medical, smartly into the newly emerging field of defence electronics, and achieved a spectacular turnround. By 1989, the group was producing profits of £7 million on sales of £55 million.

He so impressed the City with these moves that in 1985 he had little trouble in gaining backing for his most spectacular venture. He persuaded Kenneth Clarke, then health minister, to allow a new company, Porton International, to enter an exclusive marketing agreement with the Centre for Applied Microbiology & Research at Porton Down. Porton International attracted some £76 million in City backing. Haydon-Baillie, who initially owned over 2 million of the 4.8 million Porton shares, sold 294,000 of them in 1986, collecting some £24 million for them. At the time, that would have valued his remaining shares at over £142 million.

But Porton has yet to fulfil its early promise of exciting new drugs. While investors are content to wait for what they hope will be a big pay-off, its value as a business will have fallen sharply from its early heady days, and the £142 million belonging to Haydon-Baillie would fetch much less today.

In his personal life, Haydon-Baillie is described as extremely charming but very secretive. He owns two large country estates and a collection of vintage cars, planes and boats. They are housed in a private museum in Southampton. One of his estates is Wentworth Woodham, ancestral home of the Marquess of Rockingham. Haydon-Baillie is determined to restore the 300-room house, one of the largest stately homes in Britain.

Sir Julian Hodge   £60m

EX-FINANCIER   dob 15 October 1904

BORN in Camberwell but raised in Cardiff, Sir Julian Hodge was the son of a gas engineer. On his father's death, the young Julian had to leave school at 14 to help his mother raise the family. He went to work first in a chemist's shop and then for the Great Western Railway as a clerk, which enabled him to study accountancy at night school. In 1930, he became a certified accountant and started his own practice. He started to dabble in business, acquiring a chain of cinemas, a car dealership, and a hire purchase business. Gradually the Hodge Group, as it became, grew to become a major force, and in 1961 it went public, valuing Hodge's stake at £4.5 million.

In 1973, he sold the Hodge Group to the Standard and Chartered Bank for £55 million, receiving some £15 million for his family shares. At today's prices, that would be worth well over £60 million. Hodge was also a close friend of Welsh Labour politicians, principally the former premier, Lord Callaghan, who was a board member of Hodge's Bank of Wales from 1972 to 1974. Hodge has also been a prominent and generous supporter of many charities through the Jane Hodge Foundation, named after his mother, who died in 1946. He has now retired as a tax exile to Jersey.

Kenneth Horne and family   £60m

PAPER MERCHANT   dob 6 May 1913

IN the mid-1980s, the men who made their millions on the stock market were normally in their thirties and computer boffins to boot. But Kenneth Horne was the exception who proved the rule. His company, the Robert Horne Group, was a major paper merchant, and when it came to the Unlisted Securities Market in 1984, Horne was 71 years old.

But that did not stop eager City investors scrambling to invest in the business founded in 1925 by Horne's father, Robert, and based in Northampton. The share offer was over-subscribed by nine times, as pension funds sought to grab shares in the highly efficient group.

Horne, who was still active in the group six years later, though he had relinquished the post of chairman, controlled over half the shares. He also presided over a huge expansion in the business. In five years the tonnage of paper it handled rose by 60%, turnover trebled and profits quadrupled.

But early in 1990, Horne decided to sell to a Dutch group, and in March that year accepted a £154 million offer. This valued his family stake at £60 million.

Horne, educated at Haberdashers School and London University, lists his hobbies as his family and gardening. He has three sons and four daughters.

Lord Iliffe   £60m

PUBLISHER   dob 25 January 1908

THE Iliffe family founded and for many years owned the principal Birmingham and Coventry newspapers. The grandfather of the present Lord Iliffe started the *Coventry Evening Telegraph*; his father built up the publishing business with such journals as *Autocar*. One of the early employees of the firm was Alfred Harmsworth, later Lord Northcliffe, who edited a cycling paper for the Iliffes.

The present Lord Iliffe inherited the title in 1960. He also inherited a considerable estate and properties round the world. The Yattendon estate near Newbury in Berkshire, which was just 1,000 acres when his father bought it, had grown to 9,000 acres in 1960. His father had also bought a nearby 3,000-acre estate in 1929.

Lord Iliffe's first act was to rationalize his inheritance. In 1961, he sold his splendid Bahamas house to Jack Cotton, the legendary 1960s property dealer. Ten years later, he sold one of his two St James's Place flats which overlook Green Park. In 1978, he gave his 18th-century house, Basildon Park, to the National Trust, with a six-figure endowment for its upkeep. He had purchased this 30-room house overlooking the Thames in 1952, and it was agreed that he would retain one wing but the public would be allowed to visit the rest of the house. His other residence is the mock-Tudor Yattendon Court.

Lord Iliffe married in 1928 but has no children. His heir is his nephew Robert Iliffe (dob 22 November 1944), who lives in Kenilworth. He has been directing the family newspaper and publishing operations in recent years, through the family investment company, Yattendon Investment Trust, which produced £5 million post-tax profits in the year to June 1988.

In November 1987, Yattendon sold its Birmingham papers to the American publisher, Ralph Ingersoll II, for £60 million. Robert Iliffe recently bought a new £2.5 million motor yacht, an 80-foot craft called *Dalvina*. He is a member of the Royal Yacht Squadron.

John James   £60m

RETIRED BUSINESSMAN   dob 25 July 1906

'EASY come, easy go' could be John James's motto for money. The son of a miner, he showed early determination by picking enough blackberries to buy the coveted football boots his parents could not afford. Later he lied about his age to join the RAF, where he saved two-thirds of his wages and learnt as much about wireless development as possible. After leaving the RAF in 1934 he went to work in a radio shop in his native Bristol, drawing up plans to open his first shop in 1938.

But the war postponed those plans and he was called up to the RAF again, emerging as a squadron leader. He opened his first shop in 1946 and within a year had a chain of 10. At the end of 13 years, he had built the largest radio and television retailing group in the world, with 300 shops. In 1959 James, who still lived in the same modest suburban home as after the war, sold the business for £6 million. He agreed to stay on, though allowing himself the luxury of a new home and a Rolls-Royce. But by 1961 he had severed all ties and started out afresh.

He determined to make another fortune and started looking for business opportunities. He founded the John James Group of companies, which made furniture. He sold that business for £25 million in 1979. But perhaps his most remarkable coup was to be one of the first investors to spot the talents of Lord Weinstock (q.v.), the creator of the modern GEC. As an early television dealer, James often dealt with Radio & Allied holdings, run by Michael Sobell and his young son-in-law, Arnold Weinstock. Impressed by Weinstock's ability, James took a 10% stake in Radio & Allied. When Sobell and Weinstock made a reverse takeover of GEC, James ended up with 20.4% of the GEC shares and stayed as an investor for some years, adding considerably to his fortune.

James moved to Ascot in the mid-1960s. He has become a huge benefactor to charities. By the early 1980s, with his family trusts earning him some £250,000 a day, he was busy giving money away as fast as possible. He gave £4.5 million to Bristol schools, and over £1 million to major hospitals to help fund equipment or keep vital services running.

Earl of Jersey   £60m

LANDOWNER AND ART TREASURES
dob 15 February 1910

THE 9th Earl of Jersey is the first of his line to make a home on the island that bears his name. He moved to Jersey in 1947, shortly before his third marriage, to the daughter of an Italian industrialist.

The basis of Lord Jersey's wealth goes back to the late 18th century when the daughter of a prominent London landowner eloped with the Earl of Westmoreland. The enraged father, Robert Child, left a fine estate at Osterley in West London to their daughter to prevent them from benefiting. Their daughter eventually married the 5th Earl and the Jersey family acquired a valuable 1,000-acre estate. Before the war, the present 9th Earl had three estates, totalling some 9,000 acres.

In 1949, Jersey gave Osterley House and some 140 acres of surrounding parkland to the National Trust, leaving him with some 750 acres of valuable development land almost within shouting distance of Heathrow airport and the M4 motorway. In 1987, a scheme was drawn up by the Wates building group for a £250 million development on 180 acres of the Osterley site, which met with fierce opposition from the National Trust.

At the time, planning experts reckoned the land to be developed could be worth £1 million an acre. Though the scheme has yet to get off the ground, and the downturn in property prices will have affected the price of the Osterley land, it still remains a valuable asset to the Earl.

Sir Peter Michael   £60m

INDUSTRIALIST   dob 13 June 1938

SOME of the cleverest graphic illustrations seen on television news bulletins and the like come from a device called the Paintbox, designed by a high-tech company in Berkshire. UEI is the company responsible and its former chairman, Peter Michael, is the archetypal 1980s electronics entrepreneur. He worked from four half-timbered 18th-century cottages overlooking the Kennet and Avon canal, flew a helicopter, and relaxed by playing squash or tennis or listening to opera. He has recently bought a large farm in Wiltshire.

He was born in Croydon, the son of the 'Mick' Michael who built up the Stanley Gibbons stamp chain. He had a comfortable upbringing in the Croydon stockbroker belt, and went to private school followed by an electronics degree at London University.

After working in British industry and being depressed by its lack of vision, he branched out on his own to form a company called Quantel, which merged into UEI in 1982. He became chairman in 1982.

A former member of Mrs Thatcher's think-tank, Michael was knighted in the Queen's birthday honours list. Equally significant was his complete change of career from running UEI, a successful company, to becoming a company doctor, nursing an ailing company back to health.

In 1989 he agreed to merge UEI with Michael Green's Carlton Communications, in a £526 million deal which netted Sir Peter some £76 million personally. At the time he planned to stay on as joint chairman but he later decided to leave the group. He moved into the troubled Cray Electronics group, where he took a 5% stake along with two other ex-UEI colleagues. Their plan is to turn the company around in a move which could earn Michael another fortune of up to £15 million, according to City experts. In 1991 Cray launched a hostile takeover bid for rival computer company, SD-Scicon, worth £111 million.

Charlotte Morrison   £60m

LANDOWNER   dob 16 April 1955

WHEN Viscount Galway died, his 15-year-old daughter Charlotte Morrison became a millionairess. He left her 3,000 Nottinghamshire acres, and she also inherited 15,000 acres of Dorset and an area round exclusive Holland Park in London from her mother, Lady Teresa Agnew.

She lives in the 15th-century Melbury House near Dorchester, and also owns another country house near Doncaster.

Charlotte married Guy Morrison, an Old Etonian art dealer, in 1983. They met while out exercising their dogs in St James's Park one lunchtime. There were 1,200 people at the wedding service at Sherborne Abbey; Charlotte was 30 minutes late because her car broke down. She has a son, Simon, but is now divorced from her husband.

She spends most of her time now in Dorset and is keen on hunting, being joint master of the Cattistock Hunt. She is active in a number of charities.

In an interview with *The Times* on Chesil Beach, near the Dorset estate, she said she found it difficult being alone. 'The sadness is not being able to share it all.'

Sir Leslie and Lady Porter £60m

FOOD RETAILER   dob LP 10 July 1920

SIR Jack Cohen, the man who invented the 'pile 'em high, sell 'em cheap' slogan in his Tesco stores, started his business with a borrowed barrow in London's East End, using a £30 wartime gratuity. Later he went into self-service groceries and Tesco was born. He was known as Jack the Slasher or Jack the Nagger. He had two daughters and saw them married to two businessmen. Hyman Kreitman, who married one daughter, succeeded Cohen as chairman of Tesco. He retired in 1973.

The other daughter, Shirley, married Leslie Porter in 1949. Porter, who started as a car mechanic, went into car sales before the war. He was forced to drop this career to help his father out in his textiles business. After wartime service in the army, he came back to run the family firm, and expanded into new areas such as furnishings and fabrics. After his marriage to Shirley Cohen, he was under steady pressure to join the Tesco business but always refused. In 1958 he finally agreed to sell some of his textile goods in Tesco, and in 1959 he became a consultant to the business, advising on non-food sales. In 1960 he surrendered and joined Tesco full-time, working to get a new division selling clothes and other similar items off the ground. Within 12 years the Home 'n' Wear division had achieved sales of £75 million and Leslie Porter had become chairman.

In 1985 Porter retired as chairman, by which time his wife Shirley was commanding the headlines. Married at 18 and with two children at 22, she found herself with time on her hands and a great deal of energy after her children left home. In 1972 she became a magistrate and in 1974 she was elected a Conservative councillor in Westminster. In 1983, she became council leader, and immediately embarked on a radical Thatcherite approach to local government. Services were put out to tender and the council pay-roll was cut by 25%. She embarked on a number of crusades such as cleaning up Soho and waging war on litter louts in Westminster.

She was dogged by controversy over a council decision to sell off three council cemeteries for 5p each. Lady Porter has vigorously denied the resulting accusations of asset stripping. Her rule in Westminster has been controversial, with many council officials finding it difficult to accept her style. Within four years of her becoming leader, 48 senior officials had left.

A recent *Panorama* television programme made further allegations about Lady Porter's stewardship of Westminster. This has not deterred her from the goals defined in her entry in *Who's Who*, where she says her hobbies are 'waste hunting' and 'cleaning London'. In October 1989, Lady Porter and her sister were left over £9 million each by their late mother. Sir Leslie also had some 8.5 million Tesco shares worth around £16 million. In 1986, he sold some £5 million worth of Tesco shares from the Cohen family trust.

In 1991, Lady Porter announced that she was retiring as leader of Westminster Council.

Paul Raymond   £60m

PAUL Raymond, born Geoffrey Quinn in Liverpool, had a strong dose of religion and law and order in his youth. But it did not stop him developing one of the biggest soft-porn empires in Soho. His father was a haulage contractor and his mother a fierce Roman Catholic and daughter of a police superintendent. Up to the age of 13, he was all set to join the priesthood, but his mother stopped him entering a seminary. His interest found other outlets and he would often dress up as a priest, playing with holy statues and pretending to say Mass. On the outbreak of war, he was evacuated to Glossop in Derbyshire, where he remained until his early twenties.

During the war, he started work as an office boy with a Manchester estate agency by day, and at night he alternated between spells as a firewatcher and as a drummer in a local band. Eventually he went full-time as a drummer. He was called up by the RAF but managed to find a nice cushy billet there. He was able to spend his days buying and selling second-hand cars and organizing local dances at a big profit. 'I suppose you could say I was a spiv,' he said in the 1970s.

After the war, Raymond continued in show business. In 1947, he started work at Clacton-on-Sea funfair, where a palmist gave him a mind-reading code. He learnt this by heart and started doing a mind-reading act in Llandudno. In 1951 he left Glossop for good and came to London, where he played the drums again and started a revue show, which toured the country for six years. He started nude shows when a Manchester theatre owner would only give him a booking if he had nude dancers. Raymond paid two girl dancers 10 shillings a week extra to go topless. The show was exactly the same otherwise, but takings went up fivefold.

But as British theatres gradually closed down for financial reasons, Raymond realized that he would have to have his own place, and in 1958 he opened Raymond's Revuebar. It was an immediate success. He also invested in other theatres and ran two well-known soft-porn magazines, *Men Only* and *Club International*.

His wife – a former stage contortionist – divorced him in 1974 and received the then record British settlement of £250,000. She named Fiona Richmond, a star of the sex revues staged by Raymond, as co-respondent in the divorce action.

Today, Raymond has toned down his magazines and has tried hard to clean up Soho. He has branched out into lucrative property development. His daughter Debbie helps run his organization, which made £4.3 million profits in the year to the end of December 1988. He lives alone in a luxury flat in the St James area of London which was once the home of Lord Beaverbrook, a very different media magnate.

Roy and Donald Richardson £60m

PROPERTY DEVELOPERS dob 1930

IN the 1920s a couple called Richardson lived in a small house in the Black Country, paying 15 shillings a week rent. But it was too expensive so they moved next door, where they paid just 9 shillings a week for a two-up and two-down terraced house. That was where their twins – Don and Roy – were born in 1930 in the shadow of the Earl of Dudley's steelworks. The twins started their business career trading in ex-army vehicles after the war. They have worked all their lives together, cutting their property teeth in Stoke-on-Trent. Today, they are the leading West Midland property developers and are now busy developing the old Dudley steel site, bought in 1981, into the 2 million-square-foot Merry Hill shopping centre, which includes a ten-screen cinema. The site is the largest shopping centre in Europe, complete with its own £20 million monorail. The Richardsons plan to round off the development with what would be the world's biggest tower, 2,000 feet tall, costing some £100 million.

The brothers, who today live in Stourbridge and Halesowen, operate through their private Dudley company, which has large stakes in two publicly quoted companies. They also have another dozen significant private companies, with interests in financial services, engineering and transport.

Colin Sanders   £60m

COMPUTER ENGINEER   dob 23 February 1947

AS a 21-year-old, Colin Sanders deafened his parents with the sounds from his hi-fi. But what was then a hobby for the bright Oxford graduate who loved tinkering with electronics has turned into a multi-million-pound business.

It started in 1969, when Sanders – armed with £13 capital – invented an electronic device for use in organs to switch the air from the bellows down the right pipe. The device was snapped up by organ players and owners round the world. Some 12,000 were installed in places as far apart as Westminster Abbey and the Sydney Opera House, at a cost of £10,000 each.

Music-loving Sanders followed this up by inventing a computerized recording console in 1975, another of his favourite hobbies. In 1979, the BBC gave a boost to his company, Solid State Logic, by ordering £200,000 worth of equipment for its Manchester studios. In 1984, there followed a £250,000 order from the China Record Company for recording-studio systems.

By then, Solid State had an annual turnover of £20 million and 330 employees at its premises, a former convent school. By 1986, Solid State was able to boast some 50% of the world market for recording-studio equipment and was growing at around 25% a year. At this point, Sanders decided to join forces with UEI, a similar but much larger high-technology business. Sanders received UEI shares worth nearly £30 million at the time of the sale, which represented around 14.4% of the total share equity. Three years later, when UEI agreed a friendly £492 million merger with Michael Green's Carlton Communications group, Sanders's shares were worth over £60 million.

Jasminder Singh and family   £60m

HOTELIERS   dob (unknown)

JASMINDER Singh came to Britain from Nairobi in 1970. Four years later he had qualified as a chartered accountant. But after a spell working with a City firm and in his own practice, he sought the advice of an uncle on what career to pursue. His uncle, Satinder Vohra (q.v.), a well-known hotelier, gave him a thorough insight into all aspects of hotel operations.

The two went into partnership and bought the Edwardian Hotel in London's Harrington Gardens. After 18 months they sold it and bought another, the Vanderbilt. Soon after, Singh acquired the Savoy Court on his own and bought out his uncle's interest in the Vanderbilt. They are now friendly rivals.

Today Singh has nine hotels in central London, all part of the Edwardian Hotels group. They are four- or five-star, except for one three-star, and they aim to 'recapture some of the glamour of that more gracious age by the careful restoration and refurbishment of some of the best located hotels in central London', as one brochure recently put it.

The strategy appears to be working. In 1982 Singh bought three old properties from Grand Metropolitan. One of these was the old Stratford Court hotel. In 1987 it was closed and refurbished at a cost of £6 million, to reopen later that year as the Berkshire Hotel. In 1989 the Berkshire was named hotel of the year by *Caterer & Hotelkeeper* magazine.

Another Edwardian hotel, the Hampshire, was opened in April 1989 in what was the former Royal Dental Hospital building in Leicester Square. It was refurbished for a total cost of £25 million, bringing it to five-star status.

Singh's latest venture has taken him out of central London. Edwardian has bought the Skyway Hotel at Heathrow from Trusthouse Forte for £35 million. He has upgraded the three-star 450-bedroom Skyway to five-star status. That cost a further £25 million. More hotel purchases are in the pipeline.

Singh lives a very low-profile life. He was once apparently offered over £200 million for the group but he rejected the overture. Singh's family own around 64% of the shares in Edwardian Hotels.

Nat Somers   £60m

AIRPORT AND PROPERTY OWNER   dob 1908

JOHN Nathaniel Somers, now a Jersey-based tax exile, has made a fortune out of flying. Known simply as Nat, he has been involved with airports and aeroplanes almost all his adult life.

But his biggest financial coup came late in life. In 1988, at the age of 80, he sold Southampton airport for £50 million to Peter de Savary, the financier (q.v.). The deal was struck in secret via Somers's Jersey-based company, Saipur Investments, and Findhelp, an off-the-shelf de Savary company. Somers had originally bought Southampton airport from the city council in 1961 for a few thousand pounds. He built its present concrete runway in 1966. Saipur Investments made some £2 million after-tax profits in its accounts to the end of 1986. Certifying these, the accountants included a note to the effect that the properties were substantially undervalued.

Somers had a great love for the airport and said that selling it was 'a very great wrench'. He also once owned Halfpenny Green Airport near Wolverhampton, but sold out to Midlands businessman Maurice Collis in 1971. An expert pilot, he first flew in 1936, during a holiday in Bognor.

During the war he served as an instructor with the RAF, and won the Air Force Cross. He later won the King's Cup air race at Elmdon in 1949 with a Miles Gemini aircraft flying at an average speed of 164.25 m.p.h. Somers realized his 'lifelong ambition' to fly a Spitfire in 1988, at an age when he could almost draw a pension and a bus pass. He described it as 'a wonderful experience'.

Somers first visited Southampton when he ran away from home on a bike. He was 14 and keen to get a job on a ship. He arrived in Southampton after three days, only to find there was no work available. Hungry and dishevelled, he was questioned by police and spent the night in the cells before being sent home.

Willi Stern   £60m

PROPERTY   dob (unknown)

WILLI Stern was the toast of the 1960s London property market. As managing director of the Freshwater Group, he controlled some 20,000 flats on behalf of his father-in-law, Benzion Freshwater, still one of Britain's biggest landlords. By 1970, Stern wanted more and branched out on his own, setting up the Stern group. The Harvard-educated Hungarian refugee prospered mightily in the years of the Barber boom. Within two years its asset base had grown from £35 million to £200 million, mainly as a result of huge borrowings.

Stern lived in style in a luxury North London mansion and worked out of luxury offices in Kensington. But the first oil crisis in 1973, followed smartly by the steep decline of the London stock market, the collapse of the London property market, and the subsequent crisis facing the fringe banks, which were severely exposed to property, put paid to Stern's ambitions. In 1974, he became the most celebrated casualty of the crash, when the Stern Group collapsed. Stern himself was declared the world's biggest personal bankrupt with debts of £118 million, though he continued to enjoy a lavish lifestyle.

By the early 1980s, Stern had made a Lazarus-style recovery and in 1983, he received a suspended discharge from his bankruptcy. Stern, still living in a £1 million mansion, was able to resume his business career. Today, his private Dollar Land group is again active in the property field, with considerable success. In the year to December 1989, Dollar Land reported a 69% increase in pre-tax profits, mainly by concentrating on the Continent, rather than on the depressed British property sector.

Stanley and Peter Thomas   £60m

FOOD PRODUCERS   dob (unknown)

PIES and savoury snacks have always been in the Thomas blood. In 1952, Stanley Thomas senior decided to launch a pie business in Merthyr in the heart of the South Wales coalfields. He had taken over a local bakery in 1947 and concentrated on making bread and cakes until meat rationing was lifted in 1952. Stanley junior and Peter Thomas joined their father in the business aged 15 and 18 respectively.

The recipe for the pies had been concocted by their grandparents in their kitchen, years before. The business prospered mainly because of the hard work and the personal touch that the Thomas family put into it. Peter Thomas used to scrub pie tins until his hands bled and he also went out selling the pies: 'You might make as many as 23 calls in a single street. I remember travelling all over the valleys around Merthyr, starting at six in the morning and finishing at six at night. I might make 170 calls in one day,' he told the *Western Mail*. The business prospered so much that in 1965 it was sold to the Avana group.

In 1970, Stanley Thomas junior decided to launch his own business and he was joined by his brother Peter, with Stanley senior and sister Mary as directors. The company, called Peter's Savoury Products, gained a reputation for providing the solid fare needed by South Wales miners and their rugby clubs. Its pies were also sold in the Italian and Greek cafés in the valleys. In 1976, the company spent £1 million on building a modern pie factory in mid-Glamorgan and opened depots in Bristol and the Midlands. Later it took over other sausage and bacon manufacturers and built a £2 million sausage and beefburger factory.

In November 1988 the company was sold to Grand Metropolitan for £75 million, the largest sum ever paid for a private business in Wales.

Peter Thomas stayed on to run it under Grand Met. while Mary and Stan planned new careers. Peter lives in a five-bedroom Merthyr house with 16 acres of grounds and drives a Mercedes, while Mary, a Jaguar driver, lives in a similar Cardiff house with 2 acres. Stan, who also lives in Cardiff, said after the sale: 'I've just ordered a Bentley and I wouldn't mind a little sailing yacht.'

Nazmu Virani   £60m

PROPERTY OWNER   dob 2 March 1948

THE biggeset Asian-owned company in Britain is run by Nazmu Virani, a Ugandan Asian refugee, who set up his first supermarket in Dulwich 17 years ago.

Today he heads a business with a stock market value of nearly £94 million, embracing 16 hotels and 265 pubs. He deals as an equal with property magnates such as Gerald Ronson (q.v.).

An Ismaili Muslim, Nazmu professes a fanatical dedication to hard work and loyalty. He claims to be 'more married to my business than my wife'. He worked 18 hours a day for seven days a week at the Lordship Lane supermarket in London's smart Dulwich suburb, which he dubbed 'hardship lane'.

The move into hotels and pubs came by chance. His father had a heart attack while helping run the supermarket chain, that had grown to 19 by the mid-1970s. So Nazmu bought a hotel for him, hoping it would be less demanding. Within a year, his father had the hotel running smoothly and was bored. So more hotels followed.

Before the stock market crash in 1987, shares in his master company, Control Securities, were in huge demand, but they suffered a sharp downturn after Black Monday. Nazmu calls that day 'golden' Monday as he was able to buy up more shares in the business at a much lower price. His family now own 47% of the shares, which are also widely held by other members of the Asian community.

Peter Waterman   £60m

POP PRODUCER   dob (unknown)

BORN next to the Jaguar factory in Coventry, and later working as a coal miner, Peter Waterman had a tough early life. The rags-to-riches story really began when he became involved in the music industry in the early 1970s, when he ran a shop selling obscure imported American records. He also worked as a disc jockey in a club.

Real success came after he teamed up with two moderately successful pop stars – Mike Stock and Matt Aitken – in 1984 to start a record production company. With his marketing savvy and his own company, PWL, which now has a £60 million turnover a year, Waterman thrived in the partnership. Recording studios were established at a cost of £4 million in the scruffy Borough area of South London. In five years, a stream of hits followed, 95 in all, including 13 number ones. Their stars are household names to millions, led by Kylie Minogue, the teenage Australian singer, and her co-star from *Neighbours*, Jason Donovan. Other singers discovered by Stock, Aitken and Waterman include Sinitta and Rick Astley.

Waterman enjoys his wealth. As well as a large 1,500-foot warehouse attached to his studios, he has a house on Merseyside, a former British Rail diesel train, a Firestreak heat-seeking missile, a carp farm in Japan and 48 classic cars, including Ferraris and Jaguars, each worth at least £100,000.

Peter Wilson and family   £60m

PUBLISHERS   dob PW *c*. 1932

PETER Wilson ran what is probably one of the most profitable magazines in the world. *Estates Gazette* monopolizes the commercial property advertising market in Britain, and every week it is packed with glossy adverts, making it the 'bible' for the business. It has also made Wilson a multi-millionaire. With pre-tax profits of £7 million up to the end of 1989, no borrowings and huge reserves of £13.3 million, it was a prize for any large publishing empire. Wilson received £59.4 million for the business when he sold it to Reed International in 1990.

Wilson inherited the magazine some 20 years ago and he believes in a hands-on management style at its Wardour Street office, though eschewing all personal publicity.

He lives with his wife Audrey and daughters at a large Surrey mansion. He also has two other homes, one in Portugal and the other in the French Alps, where he is able to pursue his favourite outdoor hobby of skiing. He has now retired from the business.

A close estate agent friend, Clive Lewis, says Wilson is a friendly man who was dedicated to his business. 'It's a very impressive magazine and has had a monopoly market for some time. He is in the office all the time and involved in the day-to-day running of the business. As a surveyor, I can tell you that anyone who has a commercial property to sell will automatically expect an advert in the *Estates Gazette*. It has a lot of kudos and respect,' he added.

Esmond Bulmer and family   £59m

CIDER MAKER   dob 19 September 1935

THE serious business of cider making started in 1887 when Percy Bulmer, the son of a Hereford vicar, made 4,000 gallons with apples from his father's orchard. The first batch was sold for £157. By contrast, in its 100th year, H. P. Bulmer made £12.5 million profit. In 1990, Bulmer enjoyed a boom in sales buoyed by the fine summer weather. In the first half of 1990, interim profits rose by 6% to £8.07 million. The company even recruited some 60 extra staff for a sales push into pubs. Percy's brother Fred joined the business in 1888 after turning down the post of tutor to the King of Siam's children. The family are still heavily represented on the board, and own over half the shares.

Esmond Bulmer, the present chairman and Percy's grandson, was educated at Rugby and King's College, Cambridge. He was commissioned in the Scots Guards in 1954. He was the Conservative MP for Wyre Forest in Hereford from 1974 to 1983, but then stood down to concentrate on his business interests. He lives in an old rectory house and also owns a small private cider-apple farm. He and his wife Morella parted in June 1988 after nearly 30 years of marriage. They had met originally on a blind date when she needed an escort for a Conservative ball, and they married three years later.

His brother and cousin are also on the board. Esmond is a member of the National Trust's executive and enjoys gardening and fishing. He is also involved in local public and charitable work.

Paul Sykes   £59m

PROPERTY DEVELOPER   dob (unknown)

BARNSLEY, at the heart of the so-called socialist republic of South Yorkshire, does not produce many Thatcherite entrepreneurs – and even fewer who are miners' sons. But Paul Sykes is one. He left school at 16, and a year later had already had six jobs 'because I didn't agree with the way the businesses were managed – I was that arrogant,' he told *Business* magazine.

He then decided to enter the vehicle-breaking business and, armed with £170, he bought some cutting gear, a pick-up truck and a scrapped double-decker bus. Breaking the bus up and selling the scrap metal gave him a profit of £31, which was three times his previous weekly wage.

Six years later, he had made his first million. By then he was employing 17 men and breaking down 30 buses a week, selling the scrap metal locally and exporting the engines and other working parts to the Far East for use in powering fishing boats. He moved into all the ex-British colonies and also started sending truck parts over as well. At one stage, the operation involved moving two complete container loads of parts a day, and soon complete buses followed.

But the remorseless march of the Japanese eventually hit the business in the mid-1970s. The supply of sturdy old British buses also began to dry up. So Sykes diversified into coach distribution in Britain and supplying earth-moving equipment to the oil-rich Arab states, as well as some industrial property development. These various businesses were never as lucrative as the bus-breaking enterprise. In 1984 he sold them, only retaining a stake in the bus business, and moved whole-heartedly into property.

His most spectacular development has been the £200 million Meadowhall shopping centre in what was the devastated Lower Don Valley in Sheffield. He had to overcome ferocious resistance from the local Chamber of Commerce and also from a rival developer, Eddie Healey of Stadium Developments (q.v.), who was planning a rival centre in Rotherham. Eventually, after Sykes threatened to bring in London developers, Healey abandoned his Rotherham plans and joined Sykes in Sheffield. Sykes followed the Sheffield development up with a £50 million shopping mall near York.

He became embroiled in controversy in 1980 when, as chairman of the Barnsley Conservative Association, he claimed that local left-wingers were threatening him. He also sought to sponsor Roy Mason, the tough but independent-minded Barnsley Labour MP, when the local Labour Party was taken over by the left. Mason refused the offer. At the time, Sykes lived within 300 yards of the council house where he was born. He and his wife own all the shares in his company, which is based in Leeds.

He hit the headlines in 1989 when it was revealed in the *Sunday Times* that he was the highest-paid businessman in Britain, taking home a salary of £6 million in the previous year.

Today, Sykes has gone into semi-retirement, putting his energy into the National Trust and tree planting.

Stuart Lipton   £58m

PROPERTY DEVELOPER   dob 9 November 1942

LIPTON is one of the handful of property developers giving London its biggest facelift since Sir Christopher Wren. The huge Broadgate office complex around Liverpool Street Station is his most spectacular work to date. He started in the property market as an estate agent in the 1960s and had made his first million before he was 30. He sold his company, Sterling Land, for £28 million a month before the property crash in 1973. 'I was simply lucky,' he says of that time.

He was the first to realize that the 1960s City office buildings could not cope with the modern computer dealing rooms demanded by the post-Big Bang Stock Exchange. Broadgate's success helped Lipton's latest company, Stanhope Properties, raise profits from £12.5 million to £15.5 million in the year to the end of June 1989. Lipton owns a third of the equity in Stanhope and the Reichmann brothers, the Canadian developers of the huge Canary Wharf office project in London's docklands, own another third. Yet such is the City's disenchantment with property companies that the shares fell by nearly a third in value from 1988 to 1990, cutting Lipton's personal fortune from £150 million to £58 million. Despite this City view, Stanhope is pressing on with new developments, and recently announced plans for a new village near Cambridge with 3,000 homes.

Lipton, a very private married man, lives in north London. He drives a red Ferrari and has a luxury Mayfair office. He is a keen patron of the arts, recently joining the board of the National Theatre and becoming a Royal Fine Arts Commissioner.

John Apthorp and family

£57m

FORMER FROZEN FOOD ENTREPRENEURS
dob JA 25 April 1935

THE television dinner taken straight from the freezer owes its success in Britain to John Apthorp, a businessman noted for his distinctive bushy beard. In 1968, he started Bejam, a specialist retailer of both frozen foods and the freezers themselves, named after the initials of all his family members. The first store was in a Middlesex banana warehouse.

By 1975, there were 100 stores and, five years later, Bejam had sold 500,000 freezers.

Apthorp and his brother Brian, a Hong Kong doctor, were the principal shareholders in the group, and the family at one time owned 30% of Bejam. In late 1988 they lost control after a bitter takeover battle to the rival Iceland Frozen Foods chain, who paid £238 million for Bejam.

John Apthorp lives in Hertfordshire, enjoying shooting and fine wines.

Donald Bilton and family

£56m

PROPERTY   dob 28 July 1921

MAKING lubricating oil in his Ormskirk back garden and cycling round Lancashire selling it to farmers started Percy Bilton on the way to a fortune. In 1919, he went further and set up the Vizgol Oil company, which covered Britain, South Africa and America. Later, he moved into property and construction. By 1939, he pulled together his extensive house-building and industrial development operations under his own name. In 1962, the oil interests were sold to Standard Oil of Indiana, and in 1972 he took the company on to the stock market.

His designated successor, who had been deputy chairman, fell out with him in 1976 and left, amid bitter disputes over the company accounts. Percy was forced to soldier on until he was nearly 80 while he drafted his son Donald on to the board as his successor. In 1979, there was another problem when Percy's wife sold £840,000 worth of shares the day before the company announced disappointing results. Percy claimed he was as surprised by what she had done as everybody else.

Though he stayed on as chairman and was planning his retirement, he died early in 1983 in Cape Town, South Africa. His dream of being succeeded by Donald did not materialize. Though Donald continues to sit on the board he prefers instead to concentrate on his vineyard in South Africa. He is also a round-the-world sailor.

Shortly after Percy's death, a British property group launched an opportunistic takeover bid for the group but was defeated. New management was installed and the group's fortunes improved markedly. Pre-tax profits increased by 38% in 1988. But the later collapse in the property market and high interest rates hit the group's fortunes.

Bilton family trusts, covering Percy Bilton's three children, and their families, control over a third of the company. Percy Bilton lived in Virginia Water in Surrey, and left £1.8 million in his will. He left all his property to his second wife, Margherita.

Marquess of Bute   £55m

LANDOWNER   dob 27 February 1933

THE 3rd Marquess of Bute developed Cardiff into a full-scale industrial port to exploit the coal-trade in the 19th century. That built up a family fortune which still flourishes. The present 6th Marquess, a Roman Catholic, inherited the title in 1956. He was divorced and remarried in 1978. His second wife, Jennifer Percy, is the ex-wife of a Lonrho director.

He owns much of the isle of Bute and other islands off the west coast of Scotland. The family also has extensive landholdings in Spain, where they spend a good part of every year.

The family home on Bute, Mount Stuart, described as a Victorian Gothic pile, has a magnificent collection of books in its library. Some have been sold in recent years. In 1983, a collection of Bute manuscripts made over £730,000 at Sotheby's.

Lady Anne Cavendish-Bentinck £55m

LANDOWNER   dob 6 September 1916

ONE of Britain's largest landowners, Lady Anne has homes and estates in Scotland, Northumberland, Nottingham and Ireland.

The daughter of the 7th Duke of Portland (known as 'Chopper' after his exploits in Eton's carpentry workshop), Lady Anne spends much of her time at Welbeck, near Worksop. The 16,000-acre estate has a magnificent palace with miles of underground corridors and a huge ballroom created by the 5th Duke. Despite his interest in the building work, he was a recluse who stayed in his quarters, having a letter box in his bedroom door as a means of communication. The family seat, Welbeck Abbey, is now a pre-Sandhurst army training college. The Welbeck Estate Company owns the surrounding land. Lady Anne is one of three directors of the company along with her late sister's son William Parente and Commander Philip Franklin, a family friend.

Lady Anne, who has never married, does not like being called by the name of Cavendish. She has spent a large part of her life in charity work, holding numerous posts with, for example, the Royal Midland Institute for the Blind and regional branches of the National Deaf Children's Society and the NSPCC.

She is a keen huntswoman and for many years had her own private pack of hounds, the Rufford Forest Hunt, disbanded on the death of one of its leading members, Stan Worthington. She still rides most mornings and has developed an interest in horseracing. She owns four horses, trained by Jeremy Clover at Carburton, near Worksop.

She once appeared with Sir Michael Nall, Lord John Manners and Rupert Spencer in a local version of the BBC's antiques programme *Going for a Song*, staged at Welbeck Abbey.

In 1983, Lady Anne put a George III gold font commissioned by the 3rd Duke of Portland in 1797 from the master goldsmith Paul Storr up for sale at £1 million.

Tony Clegg   £55m

FORMER PROPERTY DEVELOPER
dob 8 April 1937

NORTHERN grit, determination and sheer hard work were rolled into one in the shape of Tony Clegg, an ex-property developer with the build of a Rugby League player.

Clegg, a bluff Lancastrian (born and raised in Manchester) who has defected to the other side of the Pennines, worked a reputed 18-hour day on multi-million-pound property deals for his Mountleigh company, one of the stock market stars of the 1980s. He rushed from appointment to appointment and even missed his own 50th birthday. Clegg was well known in property circles, dealing with such stars as Elliott Bernerd and Stuart Lipton (q.v.). He regularly commuted by plane from his Pudsey headquarters to his Mayfair head office and was renowned for having one of the longest lists of mobile or car telephone numbers to keep in touch with his multitude of deals.

Success brought Clegg a private plane, a Rolls-Royce Camargue with personalized number plates and a large house near Wetherby, as well as a strong following among City investors. But he has now left that life behind him and has retired to Yorkshire with some £55 million to enjoy the fruits of his 1980s dealmaking skills.

Clegg attributed his business acumen to his mother, who, left to fend for herself when her navy husband went off to the war, bought and ran a small corner shop which stayed open all hours. Later, his parents prospered and opened two restaurants. Clegg was sent to boarding school but left at 16 to become a

The Queen: £7,000m (*Camera Press*)

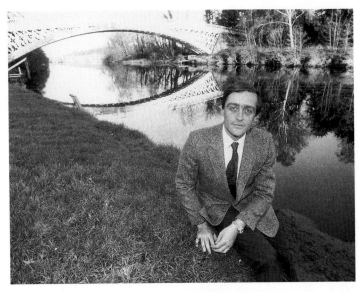

The Duke of Westminster: £3,700m (*Times Newspapers Ltd*)

Marquess of Bath: £140m (*Times Newspapers Ltd*)

Earl and Countess Spencer: £40m (*Times Newspapers Ltd*)

Paul McCartney: £380m
(*UPPA Ltd*)

Elton John: £100m
(*UPPA Ltd*)

Andrew Lloyd Webber: £80m
(Times Newspapers Ltd)

Mick Jagger: £75m
(UPPA Ltd)

Joan Collins: £30m
(Times Newspapers Ltd)

Michael Caine: £25m
(Times Newspapers Ltd)

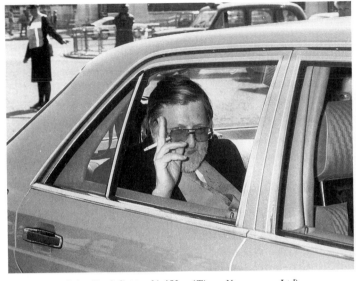

John Paul Getty: £1,450m (*Times Newspapers Ltd*)

Robert Maxwell: £1,200m (*Times Newspapers Ltd*)

Sir James Goldsmith: £750m (*Times Newspapers Ltd*)

Tiny Rowland: £190m
(*Times Newspapers Ltd*)

Lord Forte: £167m
(*Times Newspapers Ltd*)

Anita and Gordon Roddick: £103m (*Times Newspapers Ltd*)

Paul Raymond: £60m
(*Times Newspapers Ltd*)

Michael Heseltine: £40m
(*Times Newspapers Ltd*)

general dogsbody for his parents' business before the army claimed him for National Service.

In the Pay Corps, Clegg spent his time handing money over to others. But that soon changed. In 1961, he joined a Glossop textile manufacturer. By 1963, it had been taken over by Mountain Mills, a worsted suit maker based in Bradford. Ernest Hall, the Mountain boss – now a well-known developer in his own right – saw Clegg's potential and asked him to come to Bradford as his right-hand man. A strong partnership was born, and through sheer hard work Clegg and Hall built up Mountain Mills and took it to the stock market through a reverse takeover of another textile manufacturer, Leigh Mills, in 1966.

Despite the hard work, Clegg and Hall could not stave off the recession in the textile business in the 1970s. They looked around for new areas and alighted on property. It was a call from Conrad Ritblat, the top London estate agent, that made Clegg see the potential of property. Ritblat phoned to ask about buying a piece of land adjacent to one of Clegg's sites. Clegg decided to buy it himself for £24,000. He recouped the money by levelling part of the site and letting a 12,000-sq. foot building for £1 per square foot per year.

Deals followed deals through the 1970s and into the 1980s, when Clegg started to be noticed by the City. By this stage Leigh Mills had been renamed Mountleigh, and Hall had branched out on his own, leaving Clegg at the helm. In 1985 he took on Paul Bloomfield, an experienced property dealmaker with scores of contacts, as a consultant.

Clegg specialized in spotting the hidden assets in properties, snapping them up and selling them on quickly for substantial profit. In 1981, he bought 800 houses in Suffolk from the Post Office for £5.25 million. By April the following year, he had arranged a 10-year lease on them to the American government for £2 million a year. In 1986, he bought the United Real Property for £117 million and quickly sold on the individual properties it owned for a total of £140 million.

In 1987, it appeared likely that he would take over Sir Terence Conran's Storehouse group, but Clegg backed away from a hostile bid.

But the pressure of hard work took its toll. In 1988 Clegg

was found to have a brain tumour and was forced to undergo an operation and ease up on his business life. But he could not remain inactive for long and took up the reins at Mountleigh again. His stake in the business, which had been around 9 million shares in 1988, jumped to over 30 million early in 1989 as he re-established his presence in the business. This enlarged stake, which represented around 14% of the share capital, was worth nearly £60 million at the time.

The return to work proved too much for Clegg's health and within six months he had sold his shares for £70 million to two Americans and retired to his Yorkshire estate to attend to his Highland cattle, one of his main passions. He also finds time to do charitable work, sitting on the committee raising funds for Ripon Cathedral and working for the Homefarm Trust, which helps disabled and handicapped people.

The restless Clegg could not stay away from deals and in February 1991 he took a stake in a Dutch property company.

Sir Jack Hayward   £55m

FINANCIER   dob 14 June 1923

DESPITE living in the Bahamas, Hayward is intensely British. Not for nothing is he called 'Union Jack' Hayward.

He lists his recreations as promoting British endeavours and preserving the British landscape, keeping all things bright, beautiful and British. Today he is president of Wolverhampton Wanderers Football Club. He also has a home in Sussex. He served in the RAF during World War II. He has operated from the Grand Bahamas since 1956. His father, Charles Hayward, was chairman of the Firth Cleveland Group, which developed Freeport in the Bahamas. Hayward bought the Firth interests in Jamaica and the Bahamas in 1970.

Hayward has been a substantial benefactor to various causes. In 1969 he gave £150,000 to the National Trust, enabling it to buy Lundy Island with the Landmark Trust. He gave £1 million for the care of the elderly of the Falklands and also bought Brunel's ship, the *Great Eastern*, for the nation.

He frequently buys into British companies and he was a long-time backer of the Liberal Party.

Manubhai Madhvani and family £55m

INDUSTRIALIST   dob (unknown)

MANUBHAI Madhvani's father was born in India but at the age of 14 he went to Uganda, where he built up what became Uganda's largest company, employing some 15,000 people. He died in 1958, and the business was taken over by his elder sons, Jayant and Manubhai. By the time Idi Amin expelled the Ugandan Asian community, the Madhvani operations in the country provided some 10% of the GNP.

Jayant has now died and the business was divided into five worldwide units. Manubhai heads the business, called the Indeco group, with interests in property, glass, shipping and electronics, in Britain, Canada and India. The family have also re-established themselves in Uganda, where they are rehabilitating a sugar works. Manubhai oversees the Middle East from offices in London. The family are busy educating their next generation at Charterhouse, the top public school.

Mickie Most   £55m

POP MUSIC PROMOTER   dob (unknown)

EVERY day Mickie Most goes down into the basement of his £20-million dream house in the exclusive Totteridge area of London to do a series of punishing exercises. This is followed by a 4-mile run and 50 lengths of the indoor pool. 'It's one of the best things you can do with your clothes off,' he says.

He then heads off on his 1500 cc motorbike to his studios in

St John's Wood. 'I don't do any work. I oversee what is going on.' But Mickie has a lot to oversee at Rak Records, the company he founded in 1970 while working as a pop promoter. By the age of 24, he had made his first million, and between 1964 and 1984 he sold 400 million records, with 22 American number ones and 15 in Britain.

The son of a soldier and raised in north-west London, he originally planned to become an actor, but the thought of rising at 6 a.m. for filming put him off. So with rock and roll sweeping Britain, he bought a guitar and started a career as singer and guitarist in a skiffle group.

At the age of 19, at a pop concert at the Chiswick Empire, he met his wife Christina, then a 16-year-old who was on holiday from South Africa with her parents at the time. Five days later he proposed and they were married just after her 17th birthday. For four years Mickie worked in South Africa learning all about record studios and production. Then he came back home just in time for the era of the Beatles. He guided groups such as the Animals, Herman's Hermits and Hot Chocolate to success.

He discovered the Animals in Newcastle upon Tyne and financed their first top twenty hit, 'Baby Let Me Take You Home'. But it was their second, 'House of the Rising Sun', recorded in just fifteen minutes, which really put him on the road to success.

Mickie lives with Christina after some 30 years of marriage, and they have three children. His eldest, Calvin, plays in a band. His two young daughters live at the dream mansion which, he claims, is the largest private house to have been built since the war. It took seven years to build and has 33 rooms, including eight bedrooms and nine bathrooms. The swimming pool is the largest indoor/outdoor pool in Europe and has an underwater stereo system. Outside there is a five-a-side football pitch and a floodlit Astro-turfed tennis court. If he gets tired of London, the family can always move to their 11-bedroom house in Cannes, where he keeps his 36-foot boat.

Lord Palumbo   £55m

PROPERTY DEVELOPER   dob 20 July 1935

A MAN with an obsession: for nearly 20 years Old Etonian Peter Palumbo wanted to built a skyscraper on a valuable 6-acre City site built up by his father.

Although he received conditional planning permission in 1969, he could not get final approval until the 1980s, when the last of the leases covering the Mansion House site had expired. By then, the climate had changed and the City wanted to preserve the old Victorian buildings on the site.

In March 1990 the High Court upheld efforts by conservationists to stop eight listed buildings being demolished on the Mappin and Webb site opposite the Mansion House. But early in 1991, the House of Lords overturned the High Court decision, much to the annoyance of the conservation lobby.

The Prince of Wales thought the design looked like a 1930s wireless set, and this led to a rift between the two. Palumbo, the newly appointed chairman of the Arts Council, replied with a thinly veiled attack on the Prince by claiming that in the past the great patrons of architecture had been royals, but today they were entrepreneurs.

Despite these differences, Palumbo is a friend of royalty and a godfather to Princess Beatrice, elder daughter of the Duke and Duchess of York. He plays polo with Prince Charles and he lives in a manor house in Berkshire with his second wife, Hayat, who presented him with a daughter in the summer of 1989.

Peter Tom and family   £54m

QUARRIERS   dob PT 20 July 1940

T EN-year-old Peter Tom was crushed by a rail wagon at his grandfather's quarrying firm at Bardon Hill in Leicestershire. Luckily he survived the experience and up until

January 1991, he headed the Bardon group. At that point, Bardon merged with Evered, another quarrying group, in an £87 million deal.

His grandfather had started the business by quarrying in Cornwall and sold out to Amey Roadstone, using the money in 1948 to buy Bardon Hill, a 136-year-old quarry in Leicestershire. In 1958, when he died, Peter's father Greg took the helm; Peter took over in 1985.

Bardon Hill formed the core of the operation and has some of the best hardstone in Britain, ideal for motorways and runways. The quarry is also ideally situated to take advantage of the big road construction programme in the south-east. There are known reserves of about 200 million tons of high-quality Leicestershire granite at the quarry, where some £20 million is being spent over the next five years to expand capacity and improve efficiency.

Peter Tom changed a management style heavily influenced by Methodism and a paternalist approach that, in the words of *Management Today* magazine, placed 'hard work and company loyalty among employees above the quest for profits and growth'. As a result, the company only expanded very slowly.

In 1985, Peter Tom bought the Isle of Wight Vectis group for £3 million, and followed this up with the purchase of an American aggregates business for £100 million and a British wholesaler of polished marble for £8 million. The new combined group will have around 6% of the British aggregates market.

Peter Tom has a 16% stake in the business himself and lives in an old farmhouse outside Leicester, where his wife runs a fashion shop. When not working, he rides and plays tennis.

Alex Bernstein and family   £52m

TELEVISION AND ART   dob (unknown)

BROTHERS Sidney and Cecil Bernstein founded the Granada chain of cinemas. Today, Granada is one of the largest independent television companies, famous for its series such as *Coronation Street*. The business is run by Alex Bernstein, Cecil's son. The family retain around 3% of the equity, worth some £17 million. But Alex, educated at Stowe and Oxford, where he read economics, has a second fortune. He invested in an art gallery run by Leslie Waddington (q.v.) and owns half the thriving business, which would value his stake at another £35 million. Alex Bernstein started in the family business at the age of 23. His first job was running a small cinema in Clapham Junction. From that he went on to become a researcher with *University Challenge*. He then went to form the television rental company and built up a nationwide and highly profitable chain. In 1979, he became chairman of the group and changed it into a conventionally managed business. He has also expanded by buying Rediffusion from BET, and promoted some fine television programmes such as *Brideshead Revisited*.

Peter Birse   £50m

BUILDER   dob 24 November 1942

PETER Birse's first job as a contractor earned him £3,000 in 1970. It was to re-lay tarmac on a footpath at a Humberside oil refinery which a firm of contractors had bungled. He told his boss at the giant Foster Wheeler group where he was a young engineer that he could do the work better. He was awarded the contract.

Quitting his job at Foster Wheeler, Birse took three weeks to do the job and lost a stone in weight. Before long he was winning more work in the refinery and the Birse group was in business.

Today, still based in Humberside, the group is an important contractor building roads, docks, bridges and water projects. Its future looks rosy in the light of the huge spending plans by the water authorities and the road programme authorized by the government. Birse already works for seven out of ten water authorities. The group is building Felixstowe harbour's Terminal 2 in a £20 million contract.

In the first half of 1990–91 financial year Birse made over £5.6 million pre-tax profits. Five years before the figure was just £1 million. The company was floated on the stock market in 1989 and is now valued at £83 million. Prior to the flotation Peter Birse owned 93% of the shares, 15% of which were sold to his West German partner, Bilfinger & Berger, while Birse himself raised about £10 million cash from the sale. Displaying the caution and prudence which one would expect from the son of a small shopkeeper from the Scottish golfing town of Carnoustie, Birse told the *Sunday Express* that some of the money would be earmarked for charity, though his wife Helen 'would give it all away if she could. In fact, I'm giving £2 million to charity as Helen is very interested in handicapped children. For myself, I have most what I want already and I'm not a jetsetter. I have a yacht, a set of golf clubs, a lovely wife and three children. What more does a man want?'

Tony Budge   £50m

CONSTRUCTION CONTRACTOR   dob 9 August 1939

IN 1956 Tony Budge decided he did not want to be a bricklayer in his father's business, so he joined the local council highway department in Lincolnshire and became a junior engineer. After three years' apprenticeship, he went back to work for his father and built up the firm's civil engineering business. From then he never looked back, winning road contracts in the expansionist 1960s and 1970s.

Today, A. F. Budge (Contractors) is in the big league. In 1989, its after-tax profits reached £12.7 million, valuing the Budge family stake at around £50 million if the company were floated on the Stock Exchange. We have taken this rather conservative valuation because of the high borrowings of the Budge group.

Tony Budge, a member of the Turf Club, lives in Retford, where he is known for his passion for collecting old army tanks. A tank museum next to the Budge headquarters boasts 100 vehicles, including 30 Soviet tanks. Tanks line the approaches to the headquarters. An open day at the museum (in 1988) attracted a crowd of 3,000, with the funds raised going to the Army Benevolent Fund.

Tony Budge travels extensively and uses his own private aircraft based at a local airport.

Lady Butlin   £50m

TAX EXILE/WIDOW   dob (unknown)

SIR Billy Butlin, who started the holiday camp business that bears his name, arrived in Britain from Canada in 1921 with 5 cents in his pocket. Setting up as a showman running a hoopla stall, he transformed this traditional form of entertainment. He made the blocks to carry the prizes much smaller than the usual ones, which were too large to receive the hoop. He 'lost' a great deal of prizes, but was amply rewarded in the quadrupling of his takings from an eager public.

He adopted the same strategy in 1936 when the first Butlin's camp was opened at Skegness. It was an instant success and after the war the newly enriched British working class flocked in their millions to Butlins for their annual holidays. They made a fortune for Butlin, who lived on a lavish estate at Sunningdale in Surrey. He was an avid collector of art treasures, and was reckoned to have built up a collection of up to 900 paintings, some of which were dispersed round his camps.

After selling the camps to the Rank Organization, Butlin went to Jersey as a tax exile, where he was also a noted supporter of many charities. When he died in 1980, he left a fortune estimated to be around £100 million. His third wife, Sheila, who received a large part of it, still lives quietly in Jersey. After his death, she sold off Sir Billy's stake in the Miss World contest, as well as a holiday camp and hotel on the island, worth some £5 million.

Earl of Cawdor £50m

LANDOWNER   dob 6 September 1932

THERE really is a Thane of Cawdor: he is not just a character in *Macbeth*, and he does live in Cawdor Castle, where King Duncan was killed in the Shakespeare play. Historically a thane was a minor noble with certain duties to the Crown.

In 1498 the wealthy daughter of the 8th Thane was abducted by the Campbells and forced to marry a younger son of the Earl of Argyll. Fortunately the marriage worked out rather well.

The title became baron in feudal times, and later earl.

In 1976 the present Earl was forced to sell 36,000 acres in Wales to pay death duties. It was as owner of these estates that a previous Earl accepted the surrender of the last army to invade Britain – a French expeditionary force that landed in Fishguard in 1797. There are still 56,000 acres left in Cawdor hands around Nairn in Morayshire, including farms, forestry and moorland.

Cawdor Castle is being developed as a tourist attraction by the Earl's second wife, Angelika, a Hungarian countess.

Duncan and Sarah Davidson £50m

BUILDERS   dob DD 29 March 1941, SD 4 June 1942

DUNCAN Davidson had a stint as a commercial trainee with George Wimpey, the construction group, before deciding to branch out on his own. From 1965 to 1972 the urbane Scotsman ran a private building company, Ryedale, with Anthony Fawcett, a tough Yorkshireman. They then sold out to London Merchant Securities for £1 million.

Davidson and his wife Sarah immediately started up Persimmon Homes, which Fawcett joined. In 1976, the company started to move out of its Yorkshire heartland by branching out to East Anglia and the Midlands. In 1985, it came to the stock market and produced bumper profits year after year. In 1988, despite high interest rates, its profits shot up 138% to £29.5 million. In 1989, while other builders went bankrupt, Persimmon still managed to increase pre-tax profits to £32.6 million, a 10% increase which pleasantly surprised the City. But in 1990, 'it could defy the slump no longer', in the words of the *Daily Telegraph*'s Questor Column. Profits dropped to £28.8 million. But Davidson saw signs of an upturn early in 1991.

He attributes his success to building in places where people want to live, like York, Shrewsbury and other attractive market towns. His 1989 figures bear that out. The average price of the 1,796 homes he sold was £71,881, an increase of 23%. Again, in difficult 1990, the average selling price of Persimmon Homes fell to £67,000, though 2,028 were built.

Davidson, who was educated at Ampleforth, is a member of White's and the Turf Club. His mother was Lady Rachel Davidson, sister of the late Duke of Norfolk. At Ampleforth, his passion was beagling, and he was master of the college prize-winning pack. He lists country pursuits among his hobbies, and has a passionate interest in horses and racing dogs. He also sits on the boards of several companies, including the Scottish Investment Trust.

His nickname is Dynamo Dunc, reflecting one description of him as a 'cool but live wire'. Duncan and Sarah Davidson live on what has been called an 'enormous' country estate in Northumberland, south-east of Alnwick. The estate is farmed by Lilburn Estates, Davidson's private farming company.

Vivien Duffield   £50m

HEIRESS   dob *c.* 1946

DAUGHTER of the late Sir Charles Clore, the property tycoon and businessman who built up the Sears chain, Vivien is making a name for herself as a philanthropist.

In May 1989 she was named Benefactor of the Year by the trustees of the National Art-Collection Fund. In 1980 she gave

£6 million to the Tate to build the Clore gallery and in 1987 she enabled it to acquire Constable's *The Opening of Waterloo Bridge*. These gifts came from the £56 million left after the taxman had taken a record £67 million from her father's estate.

Her expenditure is not confined to charities. In 1987 she bought the Earl of Dalhousie's 18,000-acre estate near Brechin for £2.5 million. In 1986 she had chartered the *Sea Goddess*, a 4,000-ton luxury liner, to host her 40th birthday party for 110 people: the cost, £400,000. She also spent £150,000 on a birthday party in the fashionable Swiss resort of Gstaad for her long-time friend Jocelyn Stevens, the former director of Express newspapers, known as Piranha Teeth to readers of *Private Eye*. She lives in Switzerland as a tax exile, but also has a house in London.

Her success contrasts with the recent crash of her playboy brother Alan Clore, disinherited by his disapproving father. At one stage he had built up an American fortune of $150 million through corporate raiding on Wall Street. But he lost a great deal in the October 1987 stock market crash, though not all of his 300-odd thoroughbred racehorses.

Mary Foulston £50m

COMPUTERS AND PROPERTY OWNERS
dob (unknown)

MARY Foulston's husband John was killed in 1987 when his 1969 Maclaren racing car crashed at 150 m.p.h. on the Silverstone racing circuit. He was a computer engineer who had built up a huge computer leasing business, but racing his collection of 15 vintage cars was his chief passion. A year before his death, he bought Brands Hatch and two other major circuits – Oulton Park and Snetterton – for over £5.25 million.

He had married at the age of 19 – against much parental opposition on both sides. He was then earning the princely sum of £97 a month designing new computer systems. By the time he was 21, he and Mary had two daughters and life was a struggle. For nine years he toiled, making so little money that at one stage he and Mary had to use vegetable crates for chairs and the maternity allowance to cover their bills.

But Foulston joined a young American company where he discovered he had a talent for selling. He broke every sales record and within three years was UK managing director. He then decided to branch out on his own and after two failures struck gold in 1975 when, armed with a £50,000 loan from the Midland Bank, he founded Atlantic computers to lease IBM machines to British customers.

It was a huge success, coming to the stock market in 1983 with a value of around £40 million. Four years later, when he died, the value had risen to £540 million, and his own stake was worth around £90 million. His life was insured for £8 million when Atlantic was floated as a public company.

Foulston certainly relished the life of a tycoon although in the first three years of building Atlantic he never took a day off. He commuted between London and his seven-bedroom Tudor house on the Surrey/Sussex border in a £250,000 helicopter, painted in his racing colours. A private plane at Gatwick, flown by Foulston, enabled the family to go for skiing weekends or to their house in the South of France.

While Foulston ran the computer business, Mary ran the racing garage in Haslemere. She shared his passion for racing cars.

Foulston left £15 million in his will to Mary, also £10,000 to his lawyer 'in appreciation of his many tax victories on my behalf'. Today his elder daughter Nicola, in her early twenties, runs the racing circuits for her mother, who heads Brands Hatch Leisure, the parent company. In 1988 the circuits made £1 million profit.

Lord Hartwell and the Berry family   £50m

NEWSPAPER PUBLISHERS   dob 18 May 1911

THE Berry family is one of Britain's great newspaper dynasties. The first Viscount Camrose, son of a South Wales alderman, was the proprietor and editor-in-chief of the *Daily*

Telegraph. From 1915 to 1936, he was also editor-in-chief of the *Sunday Times*. He died in 1954, to be succeeded by his eldest son. But the family tradition in journalism was really carried on by a second son, Michael Berry, later Lord Hartwell.

Hartwell, who learnt his trade as editor of Glasgow's *Sunday Mail* in the depression of the 1930s and later as managing editor of the *Financial Times* from 1937 to 1939, became a world-respected editor-in-chief of the *Daily Telegraph* and later the *Sunday Telegraph*. Under his hand, the *Telegraph* became the best-selling quality paper, reaching a circulation at one time of nearly 1.5 million. But in the 1980s it was beset by financial problems. Hartwell and the Berry family had to relinquish control of the paper to Conrad Black, a Canadian businessman.

The family still have an 11% stake in the *Telegraph* group, which turned in a record profit of over £29 million in 1989 from its new Docklands home, where there is new technology and lower manning levels. But with increased competition from new quality titles such as the *Independent* and two Sunday newspapers, the *Telegraph* papers are under intense pressure. Advertising rates and volumes have also been hit, which would clip any stock market valuation of the group today. A flotation of the group would value the Berry stake at less than £50 million, though the family wealth is protected by substantial private trusts which are unaffected by the economic climate. Lord Hartwell was educated at Eton and Christ Church, Oxford. He served in the army during the war, reaching the rank of lieutenant colonel, after twice being mentioned in despatches. He lives at a country house near Aylesbury, and he has a London house. His wife, Lady Pamela, the younger daughter of the Earl of Birkenhead, was a noted society hostess. She died in 1982.

Michael Hollingbery £50m

RETAILER dob 16 April 1933

IN the 1930s, George Hollingbery founded a Hull department store, which his son Michael took over in 1958. He branched out into television rentals and later started the Comet chain of discount warehouses. Comet was finally taken over by Woolworth in 1984. The Hollingbery stake of 30% was sold for £54 million.

Comet still operates under its own name and Hollingbery still runs the business, with a seat on the Woolworth board. He lives in a picturesque village near Beverley on Humberside.

He drives an Aston Martin car with the personalized number plate MH1. He remains a private person. He has a close circle of influential business friends and maintains a keen interest in local Conservative Party activities but he remains politically and socially in the background.

His hobbies are shooting and fishing and he has a deep interest in the Round Table. He recently bought a large estate in Scotland.

Michael Hunt £50m

CAR DEALER dob (unknown)

MICHAEL Hunt is a major shareholder in one of Britain's most mysterious and profitable companies – Nissan UK. Founded by Octav Botnar, a reclusive German-born businessman, Nissan UK had the sole rights to sell all the Nissan cars sold in Britain. With thousands of Nissans coming off the production line at its Sunderland plant, the profits have risen sharply. In the year to end of July 1988, it made pre-tax profits of £132 million on a turnover of £1.2 billion.

Hunt, who has a 13.5% stake in the business in his own name and through family trusts based in Lichtenstein, worked with Botnar from the outset, and today is deputy chairman of the group, which is based in Worthing. In 1990, his stake was worth at least £160 million if sold on the stock market, given the company's profitability. But after a bitter row between the Nissan car company and Nissan UK over pricing of cars, Nissan has terminated its agreement with Botnar, and is planning to set up its own network. Botnar is fighting the move through the courts, but the row will have clipped the value of Hunt's stake.

Hunt lives with his family in an exclusive area of Hove in a luxury home. He has a huge swimming pool in the garden and all the trappings of a millionaire. In 1986, he received dividends of some £3 million from his share stake.

One of Hunt's passions is organ music and he is particularly keen to preserve pipe music. This passion led him into a bitter battle with his local council over plans to build a music room in his garden. Neighbours complained that the historic cinema organ he planned to install there would disturb the peace.

The council rejected the applications, but Hunt appealed to the Department of the Environment and an inspector ruled in his favour. A three-year battle followed over the amount of compensation the council should pay, and a figure of £7,275 was agreed – small beer for Hunt.

By then, however, Hunt had changed his mind and he built his swimming pool instead.

Viscount Leverhulme £50m

LANDOWNER   dob 1 July 1915

GRANDSON of William Lever, who founded the Lever Brothers soap company and the Port Sunlight model village, Viscount Leverhulme has shown no direct interest in the family business, now Unilever, a multi-national company. He inherited the title in 1949 and since then has devoted himself to his 10,000–15,000 acres in Cheshire and to racing.

A country lover, he took a course in estate management to prepare himself for farming. He is a former Jockey Club steward and prominent racehorse owner. Among his horses were Fascinating Forties, winner of the National Hunt Chase in 1968, and Hot Grove, runner-up in the 1977 Derby. In 1972 he bought the late Earl of Sefton's 4,200-acre Altcar estate, where the Waterloo Cup, Britain's main hare-coursing event, is run.

It was his father, known in Unilever as The Governor, who guided the company to multi-national status with 300 subsidiary companies. He was also known as a generous employer, concerned about the welfare of his staff.

Bernard and David Lewis £50m

FASHION RETAILER   dob DL 2 June 1924

BERNARD Lewis started trading out of the back of a fruit lorry after the war. With his brother David, he later progressed to open the Lewis Separates shop in Hackney, which in the 1960s became the trendy Chelsea Girl chain. Today, the Lewis Trust group still owns this well-known fashion chain and has also acquired property interests. The business has its headquarters in West London.

There are four Lewis directors on the board and the family control around 80% of the shares between them. Bernard is still the chairman, and his son Leonard deals with the marketing. In 1988, the Lewis Trust declared profits of around £8.15 million, slightly down on the previous year. The family are particularly secretive about their wealth. But they are planning a major revamp of Chelsea Girl, masterminded by Leonard. The group's 260 shops are being renamed River Island.

John and James Macdonald-Buchanan

£50m

LANDOWNERS   dob (unknown)

HEIRS to the Buchanan Black & White whisky fortune, John and James's mother left some £17 million when she died in 1987 at the age of 92. Lady Macdonald-Buchanan was a noted racehorse owner who owned the Lavington stud, founded in 1904 by her father, Lord Woolavington. Under his daughter's control, the stud produced Owen Tudor, winner of the 1941 Derby and sire of the winners of over 400 races.

Lady Macdonald-Buchanan herself had inherited what was then a huge fortune of £3 million when her father died in 1935. Following her death in February 1987, there was a considerable controversy over the way a Constable painting, *Stratford Mill*, was handed over by the family to the nation in lieu of inheritance tax of £5.5 million. The board of the Museums and Galleries Commission, which normally oversees the transfer of paintings from private to public hands, was furious at the speed with which the deal was done. It was concluded in a record three weeks as opposed to the normal six to nine months. The family wanted the deal worked out fast to prevent a hefty interest charge building up on the tax debt. The painting, then the most important Constable in private hands, was given to the National Gallery. It was valued at £10 million and formed part of a large collection built up in the 1940s and early 1950s by her husband, the late Sir Reginald Macdonald-Buchanan.

The collection included other masterpieces such as Stubbs's *Gimcrack*. *Stratford Mill* itself had been bought for £50,000 in 1951. Today, John Macdonald-Buchanan, the eldest son, lives in the family home of Cottesbrooke Hall in Northamptonshire. James lives in Scotland on the 71,100-acre Strathconan estate. The family connection with Buchanan's whisky has long ended.

Mary Mackinnon   £50m

LIQUEUR MANUFACTURER   dob (unknown)

EVERY bottle of Drambuie liqueur carries the slogan 'Prince Charles Edward's Liqueur. A link with the '45'. This refers to the personal recipe that Bonnie Prince Charlie gave to the Mackinnons of Skye to reward their services during the Scottish '45 rebellion.

The family claims the secret has remained with them ever since and, while others doubt this story, it has served the family well. The Drambuie Liqueur Company, now based in Edinburgh, remains in family hands. The link with the '45 rebellion is still kept up. One of the company conference rooms is decked out as a French frigate cabin, to commemorate the ship that took the Young Pretender into exile after the defeat at Culloden and his flight through Skye.

Today, the company is in robust health, producing £5.2 million pre-tax profits on a £36.5 million turnover in 1989, with a strong balance sheet. In 1989, Norman Mackinnon, the former chairman of the company, died and his widow Mary has now taken over. Her two sons, Calum and Duncan, are also active in the management of the company. In January 1991, the company unveiled a new strategy by taking over the Caithness glass company for £3.38 million. The aim was to achieve synergy in marketing, by selling Drambuie in decanters made of Caithness glass to the strong Japanese market.

Earl of Mansfield   £50m

LANDOWNER   dob 7 July 1930

WILLIAM Murray, the 8th Earl of Mansfield, and his family own well over 30,000 acres in Perthshire, with the 125-room Scone Palace the centrepiece of the estate. Scone was originally the capital of Scotland and the coronation place for the Scottish kings. The estate contains high quality farming land and some of the finest stretches of the Tay for fishing. There is also a fine art and porcelain collection at Scone. Mansfield, who inherited the title in 1971, served as an opposition spokesman in the Lords from 1975 to 1979 and then in the Conservative government from 1979 to 1984. His father, the 7th Earl, had handed over the estate to Mansfield some six years before his death. The present heir to the estate, Viscount Stormont, lives in London.

Stephen Morgan   £50m

PROPERTY DEVELOPER   dob 25 November 1952

DESPITE his name and his base in Clwyd, Stephen Morgan is not Welsh. He is a Scouse – a Liverpudlian – through and through and a fanatical Liverpool fan to boot. He now runs one of the biggest private building companies in Britain, Redrow, which produced £10.3 million after-tax profits on a £100 million turnover in 1989.

Morgan started his career as a labourer on a building site, earning £10 a week after he had walked out on his A-level studies. In 1974, in his early twenties, he took out a loan from his father to start a civil engineering company. He did a series of bread and butter jobs including laying new sewers and extending Manchester's Strangeways Prison.

When recession bit in the early 1980s and work dried up, he turned to house building. He built his first house in 1983 and in 1988 he completed 1,104. He aims to build 2,000 a year. A healthy reserve of building land able to provide 3,000 sites for homes has helped Redrow's developments.

At Redrow's headquarters in Alltami, outside Mold, Morgan has a workforce of 150, but nationally that figure can rise to 3,000 according to the building work on hand. From its base in Lancashire, Morgan has expanded Redrow into the Midlands and the south. In 1988 he announced plans to build a prestige office development at Ashford in Kent, the centre of operations for the Channel Tunnel. In October of that year, he also announced plans for a new 'village' for up to 8,000 people in Cheshire to be built over the next three years between Knutsford and Holmes Chapel. Redrow has bought 500 acres on a green-field site for the village and had also taken over a small Manchester construction group which had had direct experience of building a complete stand-alone community from scratch. In 1988, Redrow acquired a 5% stake in John Maunders, a quoted Manchester housebuilder. The stake was later sold.

Morgan and his wife Pamela live in Ruthin in Clwyd. Pamela plans the interior decoration of the Redrow homes.

Marquess of Northampton   £50m

LANDOWNER   dob 2 April 1946

INHERITANCE has been the controlling influence on the Marquess of Northampton's colourful life. While admirers of the British aristocracy tend to stress the concept of *noblesse oblige*, the ethos of 'do what you choose' is at least as strong. Spenny Northampton acquired from his father, the 6th Marquess, two stately homes in the Midlands, the freehold of much of Islington in London and an apparent lack of luck with his partners in marriage.

Where his passionate interest in spiritualism originated is unclear, although a mutual concern with the Other Side led him to his fourth wife, Fritzi. She was previously married to Michael Pearson, heir to the Pearson empire. Northampton's previous wives, in chronological order, were: Henriette Bentinck, the Dutch-born niece of the Thyssen steel dynasty, who gave him an heir and a daughter; Annette Smallwood and, thirdly, Rose Dawson-Damer. The third Marchioness turned out to have a head for the fashion business and created the enormously successful Northampton wellington boot. This chic mixture of canvas and rubber was seen on such high-profile calves as those of Princess Michael of Kent.

Northampton's father, universally known as Bim, was married three times. In the 1920s he lost a breach of promise case with damages of £50,000, worth over £1 million today. In 1985 the Marquess's sale of Mantegna's Renaissance masterpiece, *The Adoration of the Magi*, caused controversy. It went to the Getty Museum in California for £7.5 million amid protest from the art conservation lobby that it should stay in Britain – where it had been since its acquisition by a Northampton ancestor in the mid 19th century. The Marquess was unmoved, saying at the time, 'As far as the loss of heritage is concerned, I'm afraid I'm not very patriotic, because I believe we've got to think more globally. Art has shuffled around the world since the year dot.'

The Marquess maintained that the money was needed for the maintenance of his two homes. Castle Ashby, the grander of the pair, now operates as a superior conference centre. It is also available for commercial promotions, such as the launch of a new car. Although his Warwickshire house, Compton Wynyates, regarded as the world's finest example of Tudor architecture, is nominally the Northampton family's private home, that too is rentable if the mood takes 'Spenny'. Michael Winner used it as the location for his 1982 remake of *The Wicked Lady*. Spenny is currently trying to sell a magnificent collection of Roman silver, which Sotheby's reckon could fetch some $40 million, but legal problems have cropped up, which may delay or even prevent a sale.

Girish Patel   £50m

COMMODITY TRADING   dob (unknown)

GIRISH Patel's grandfather started a commodities trading group in Malaya in the heyday of the Empire before the last war. Today, some 60 years later, it is one of the world's largest commodity groups, dealing in palm oil, cocoa, rubber and tin. Girish Patel, who runs the business today, came to London in 1972 and was educated at the London Business School. Now permanently based in London, he is heavily involved in business deals in London, including the £12 million Atlip shopping centre at Alperton. It boasts the largest vault in

Europe, with 20,000 safety deposit boxes. His three brothers are also involved in the business in various parts of the world.

Cliff Richard £50m

POP SINGER   dob 14 October 1940

BORN Harry Webb in the Indian city of Lucknow, Cliff Richard moved to England after Indian Independence. He went to live in the London suburbs and left school at 15 with an undistinguished academic record. He first went to work in the Atlas lamp factory in Enfield, but sang in the evenings with a skiffle group. By the age of 18, with his backing group, the Drifters (soon to be called the Shadows), he appeared on television and never looked back. As Britain's answer to Elvis Presley, the hits piled up, and by the time the Beatles and Rolling Stones appeared, he was a veteran of stage and screen. For thirty years, he has stayed at the top and is as popular as ever. In 1990, his album *From a Distance* grossed £5 million, while his national tour grossed some £17.5 million in sales and merchandising. An 18-night run at the Wembley arena had every one of its 12,000 seats sold out. Still a bachelor, despite a well-publicized romance with tennis-player Sue Barker, Cliff lives in a £2.5 million Surrey mansion. He is a committed Christian and shares his house with an evangelical teacher.

Richard Tompkins £50m

GREEN SHIELD STAMP DEALER   dob 15 May 1915

IN the mid 1960s, 24 million Britons were collecting Green Shield stamps in the hope of saving enough to buy a Ford Cortina or expensive cutlery.

They made Richard Tompkins, a quiet and friendly businessman, a £50-million fortune in the process. Born and bred in

North London, Tompkins, who was once described as looking like a middle-ranking executive, left school at the age of 13, a self-confessed 'dunce'.

He went into a series of jobs including running a café and working in a laundry. On his 17th birthday he passed his driving test and within three hours he had a job as a van salesman. But the young Tompkins wanted more and took a correspondence course to become a draughtsman. As a result, he spent the war years 1939–45 in a reserved occupation.

After the war Tompkins took over a small London printing company, complete with some worn-out machines, which he managed to repair himself. In the drab post-war world he built up a thriving business based on his reputation for good delivery and reliable products.

But the big break came when he went on a holiday to Jamaica and met a Chicago businessman who told him that half the output of the American cutlery industry went to gift stamp companies. Intrigued, Tompkins went over to America and saw for himself the popularity of the stamps. Stopping on a freeway outside four gas stations, he noted that the three selling stamps were full while the fourth – without stamps – was empty.

Tompkins determined to bring stamps to Britain on a large scale (up to then there had been over 30 small-scale operations). Green Shield was born in 1958. It was tough going at first. Operating from a converted Lyons tea house in Archway, it took Tompkins seven years to put Green Shield into profit. But, offering high-quality prizes and with an expensive catalogue (the first cost £12,000 to produce), the operation eventually proved a huge success.

Typically, a supermarket with Green Shield stamps would have to add around 2% extra in costs, but in the first year turnover would be boosted by 50%. The big break came when Tesco decided to support them following the decision of rival Fine Fare to stock Pink Shield (an American venture that Tompkins was easily able to see off). Tompkins himself owned over 97% of the shares in the Green Shield company, which in its heyday employed 5,000 people.

Success transformed Tompkins's life. He moved into a flat in the exclusive Carlton Towers block in London's Belgravia and had a holiday home in the South of France. A fanatical admirer of James Bond films, he had a Rolls-Royce with the number plate 007. He also had another Rolls and a private executive jet.

In May 1968 he bought the last private residence in Belgrave Square, which he turned into a 22-room, 9-bathroom home. In 1973 his pay and dividend payments totalled £1 million.

By the late 1970s consumer interest in Green Shield stamps was waning, and in 1977 Tesco appeared to deliver a body blow to the idea by withdrawing from the scheme. Tompkins finally wound up the operation in 1980, but by then he had made £25 million from the stamps. Shrewdly, he had also anticipated the waning interest and in 1973 he set up the Argos chain of discount stores. Six years later he sold Argos to BAT for around £25 million.

Tompkins married his first wife during World War II and they had two daughters. They parted in 1962. In 1970 he married model Elizabeth Duke, a cousin of Neville Duke, the test pilot. The wedding reception at the Dorchester cost £7,000. In 1973 they had a daughter. They still live in Tompkins's Belgrave Square house. In 1978 he bought a Berkshire stud from Peter de Savary (q.v.) for £2 million. He has recently put it on the market.

Tim Jeffries, his grandson by a daughter from his first marriage, hit the headlines in 1984 when he was briefly married to Koo Stark, the former friend of Prince Andrew. They were divorced in 1989.

Sir Christopher Wates and family   £50m

BUILDING   dob 25 December 1939

WATES's progress from a small housebuilder to a large-scale developer in London was mainly the work of the late Sir Ronald Wates and his brothers Norman and Allan. The firm is still in family hands, with Sir Christopher Wates, Norman's son, running Wates Holdings.

The family floated their property business on the Stock Exchange in 1984, but they retain a 25% stake.

The Wates family have considerable bloodstock interests. Michael, Sir Ronald's son, runs the Bloodstock Breeding Company and is a successful breeder himself. Michael's brother Andrew, another director of the company, has ridden 24 winners under National Hunt Rules and is a member of the Jockey Club. He lives in Dorking.

Christopher lives in Sussex, while Michael's home is a Dorset manor house.

The Wates empire is suffering from the economic squeeze. In 1989, after-tax profits at Wates Building Group were £10 million against £23 million in 1988.

4

THE
MILLIONAIRES

£20m and more

Grant Gordon family   £48m

WHISKY DISTILLERS   dob (unknown)

IN 1887, William Grant and his nine children built the Glenfiddich distillery at Dufftown in Banffshire. Today, the family still control the Glenfiddich distillery, which turns out the quality single malt bearing that name. The distillery uses traditional equipment and distilling techniques. It is full of gleaming copper rather than modern electronics. But it works. In the late 1950s, around 500 cases of Glenfiddich were sold annually. In 1987, the figure was over 500,000. Sales rose a record 18% in 1988 and it is the best-selling wine or spirit in duty-free shops throughout the world.

The company celebrated its centenary in 1987 by flying 650 of its staff and salesmen in from round the world to the Scottish Highlands for a two-month series of Scottish country house parties.

The company is private and made £10.8 million after-tax profits in 1988. At least two family members sit on the board – Alexander and Charles. Both are great-grandsons of William Grant, the founder.

Peter Levy   £48m

PROPERTY DEVELOPER   dob (unknown)

BROTHERS Joe and David Levy went to work for Jackie Phillips, a West End property agent, in 1924. Phillips, a heavy gambler, had been asked by the Levys' bookmaking father to give them a job.

He duly obliged, and when he died Joe and David took over the business. David died in 1952, by which time Joe had bought a 'shell' company called Stock Conversion, which had links with the great railway building boom in the 19th century.

With a new partner, Scotsman Robert Clark, Joe built Stock

Conversion into one of the major London property companies in the 1960s. It was responsible for buildings such as the Euston Centre.

His son Peter Levy came into the business. But when Robert Clark died in 1984, his share of the business was sold. In 1986, Stock Conversion was taken over by P & O, the property and shipping group. The Levy shares were worth over £48 million.

Joe Levy, who died in 1990, had a home in Grosvenor Square, a villa in Antibes, a yacht and racehorses. He formed the Cystic Fibrosis foundation to research into this disease because a client's child had suffered from it. His son Peter now runs the family interest.

Richard and Henry Lumley   £48m

LLOYDS UNDERWRITING   dob RL 7 July 1923

BROTHERS Richard and Henry Lumley are the major shareholders in a highly profitable Lloyds underwriting business, Edward Lumley & Sons, founded by their father, who died in 1960. Both were educated at Eton, while Richard served in the Coldstream Guards during the war. The family have been generous supporters of charity and educational institutions. In 1969, for example, they founded the Kathleen Lumley College at the University of Adelaide in Australia, named after their late mother. Richard Lumley has close interests with Australia, and is a member of the council of the British Australia Society. Edward Lumley Holdings, based in the City, made £2.8 million after-tax profits in the year to the end of June 1989. But with healthy reserves and cash at the bank of over £57 million, the business would be worth nearly £50 million if floated on the stock market. Richard Lumley, who lists his recreations as family pursuits, walking in the country and skiing, lives in the Home Counties.

John Menzies   £46m

NEWSAGENT   dob 13 October 1926

FOUNDED in 1843 as a bookshop in Edinburgh's fashionable Princes Street, the John Menzies group is now one of the country's leading newsagents. In 1988 it made £26 million profit on sales of £672 million. Compare that to the first bookshop, which made £100 profit in its first year on sales of under £1,000. But it has had a rough time in the recent recession. In the first half of 1990–91, it made just £200,000 pre-tax profits, against £3.1 million in the previous first half.

The business remains in family hands and the current chairman, John Menzies, is a pillar of the Scottish establishment, where it is still based. He is a director of the Bank of Scotland and the Guardian Royal Exchange group.

Eton educated, Menzies served in the Grenadier Guards. He is married with four daughters. He lives on a 1,250-acre estate in Berwickshire and lists his hobbies as farming, shooting, reading and travel. He is a member of the Royal Company of Archers, the Queen's bodyguard for Scotland.

Richard Biffa   £46m

WASTE DISPOSAL ENTREPRENEUR
dob (unknown)

WHERE there's muck there's brass, as Richard Biffa has found out. Chairman of Rechem, the waste disposal firm, Biffa has made a £50 million fortune out of disposing of toxic waste materials in his highly efficient plants in Southampton and Pontypool. He has been in waste disposal for all his working life. He joined the family firm, Biffa Ltd, in 1958 and was appointed to the board in 1971 when it became a subsidiary of British Electric Traction. From 1979 to 1985 he was chairman. He was also on the board of Rechem (Reclamation and Disposal Ltd), another BET subsidiary. BET had bought Rechem in 1971 from two businessmen, Arthur Coleman and David Thomas, but sold out in 1985, disappointed with the low margins in the business. Rechem was snapped up by its management for £1.8 million and came to the stock market in 1988 with a market value of £50 million. Biffa has now over 7 million shares in the business.

Under Biffa and Malcolm Lee (q.v.), his managing director, who has 6.8 million shares, Rechem has moved up-market and is concentrating on handling and disposing of specialist toxic wastes through high-temperature incineration. For this it can charge a higher price. As a result, in the half year to the end of September 1989, Rechem's pre-tax profits rose 29% to £4.6 million. Biffa himself is regarded as a hands-on manager who likes to be involved in all aspects of the business.

Despite having Graham Searle, a founder member of Friends of the Earth, on the board, Rechem has run into severe criticism from residents around its Pontypool plant in Wales, who have voiced fears about pollution in the locality. The Torfaen Council in Wales claimed that the level of toxic waste around the plant was 88 times higher than normal. Rechem disagreed with the findings and have issued extensive reports contradicting the Torfaen conclusions. It has announced plans to improve the Pontypool facility with a new £500,000 electric hearth. It has also bought 16 acres next to the plants for expansion. Rechem also plans to spend £8 million improving efficiency at its Fawley plant.

In September 1989, Liverpool dockers refused to handle a shipment of polychlorinated biphenols from Canada which were destined for Pontypool. They were returned to Canada, leading Biffa to comment, 'Rechem firmly believes that it can and should fulfil both national and international responsibilities in the provision of a safe method for the disposal of highly toxic waste.'

Biffa owns a villa in the south of France, where he holidays at every available opportunity with his wife and three children. He is a connoisseur of wine and French cooking.

At the end of 1990, Biffa and Lee merged Rechem into another waste disposal group, Shanks & McEwan, in a £158 million deal.

Lady Eileen Joseph   £46m

INHERITANCE AND HOTELS   dob (unknown)

LADY Eileen Joseph is the widow of one of Britain's top post-war tycoons, Sir Max Joseph, who built up the Grand Metropolitan chain into a huge hotel and restaurant group. Sir Max separated from his first wife in 1953, and for twenty years Eileen lived with him, changing her name by deed poll to Joseph. In 1981, they were finally married, but Sir Max died a year later. He left some £16 million to his widow. Lady Joseph, who divides her time between London and France, has been involved in the hotel business herself. Her £16 million would be worth well over £40 million at today's prices.

John Aspinall   £45m

GAME CONSERVATIONIST AND FORMER
CASINO OWNER   dob 11 June 1926

BEFORE gaming was legalized, John Aspinall used to host floating chemmy and poker games round Belgravia for his rich chums, with the police hard on his trail. They busted him once. Hard up on one occasion in France, he won a £3,000 bet by agreeing to stand naked in the street for a minute.

Gambling has always been in his blood, and it is a way of paying for his other great obsession – saving wild animals.

He founded his first casino, the Clermont, in 1962 but sold out ten years later. This was the centre of a social set which included Lord Lucan and Sir James Goldsmith (q.v.). In 1978, he returned to casinos to support the upkeep of his two private zoos, at Canterbury and Romney Marsh, which cost up to £4,000 a day to run. Here he breeds exotic creatures such as Siberian tigers, leopards, rhinos and buffaloes.

At the end of 1987, Aspinall Holdings, the casino business he owned with Sir James Goldsmith, was sold for £90 million. He has homes in London and Kent and a £550,000 mansion outside

Cape Town. In 1991, Aspinall hit the headlines when he was the only white person to attend a huge Zulu rally in South Africa, where he praised the Zulu race and claimed that he was a 'white Zulu'.

Sir John Baring and family   £45m

BANKING   dob 2 November 1928

'THERE are six great powers in Europe,' said the Duc de Richelieu, first minister of France in 1718, 'England, France, Russia, Austria, Prussia and Baring Brothers.' Nearly three hundred years later, that power has hardly diminished.

There are five peers in the family which runs Barings, the discreet City merchant bank. In 1989, its profits surged to £69.5m against £25.9m in 1988. In 1990, the profits fell to £42 million as its formerly very successful Japanese business hit a difficult patch. The shares of the bank are now held by a charitable foundation. Much of the family wealth is tied up in large tracts of valuable land in Hampshire, around Winchester and Alresford.

The family originated in Bremen in Germany and came to the West Country in 1717 to learn about cloth-making. In the late 18th century, Francis Baring moved to London and became chairman of the East India Company, the largest trading company in the expanding British Empire. The family fortune was made.

Today, the bank manages the royal finances. Sir John Baring, the chairman, is heir to Lord Ashburton, a former Lord Lieutenant of Hampshire. His cousin, the late Earl of Cromer, was a former Governor of the Bank of England and ambassador to Washington. The earldom was created for Sir Evelyn Baring, one of the great Imperial administrators, who virtually ruled Egypt and restored its finances at the end of the last century.

Viscount Bearsted   £45m

FINANCIER/BANKER   dob 9 December 1911

THE Bearsted title conceals one of the most famous banking and industrial names from the beginning of the century. Marcus Samuel, created Viscount Bearsted in 1925, founded Shell Transport and Trading, one of the 'seven sisters' oil companies that dominated the industry, and often the politics, of whole regions in the early part of the 20th century.

Behind the oil company, however, and one explanation for its creation and growth, was the private merchant bank of M. Samuel, later to become Hill Samuel.

The bank was first floated on the Stock Exchange in 1960 and the merger with Hill took place in 1965. Apart from the bank, the Samuels owned about 14 acres of Mayfair, which had been bought by Sir Marcus Samuel in the first decade of the century. The ownership was locked into Samuels Estates Ltd, in which two other rich developers, Charles Clore (*see* Vivian Duffield) and Jack Cotton, took a half share in 1961. Most of the company, apart from the stake sold to Cotton, was held in trust for the Samuel children, and two of them became 1960s millionairesses while still at primary school.

The present Lord Bearsted succeeded to the title when his brother died in 1986. He has been a director of the family companies all his life, apart from a spell of service in the Warwickshire Yeomanry during the war, when he won a Military Cross.

Educated at Eton and New College, Oxford, he has been married three times. The first marriage ended in divorce, and the second, to a daughter of Lord Cohen, ended when his wife died in 1983. He remarried in 1984 to the widow of Michael Pocock CBE.

He maintains the family tradition of medical charity, sitting on the boards of the Royal Free Hospital, the Norwood Home for Jewish Children and the National Association for Gifted Children.

There is a small estate in Scotland and the family home is a gracious manor near Reading. In the House of Lords, Viscount Bearsted votes with the Conservatives.

Michael Bishop   £45m

AIRLINE OPERATOR   dob 10 March 1942

AIRLINE passengers on the London-to-Glasgow route can thank Michael Bishop for the improvement in the quality of service.

Before he started a rival service, meals on the shuttles were rare. Today they are standard and of high quality, such is the level of competition from British Midland, Britain's second largest airline.

Bishop, formerly with Mercury Airlines, now runs Airlines of Britain, the owner of the British Midland fleet. When he took over the airline in 1978, he could not get any financial backing in the City and went to America for the finance. With a growing demand for airline travel, profits are soaring. In the first half of 1988, the group made £7.6 million profits against just £762,000 in the previous year. The business is based in the beautiful Donington Hall, near the Castle Donington racecourse in Derbyshire.

In 1988, the capital of the group was enlarged and 25% sold to SAS, the Scandinavian airline. Early the following year, the airline suffered the loss of a Boeing 737 jet, with 44 killed as the plane tried to land and hit the M1 motorway.

Lord Bolton   £45m

LANDOWNER   dob c. 1919

ETON and Oxford educated, the 7th Lord Bolton has been described by the *Evening Standard* as 'Yorkshire Royalty'. He owns one of the largest estates in the country, the 17,000-acre Leyburn, which is famous for its grouse shooting but equally for the careful manner in which he has managed it over the years. A former Chairman of the Yorkshire Agricultural Association, one of the biggest in Britain, he has combined his landed interests with business by chairing the Waterers

Group and acting as a director of the Yorkshire General Life Company.

Twice married, first to a daughter of Lord Forester, and then to the daughter of a deputy chairman of the *Yorkshire Post* newspaper, Lord Bolton revived the family's long-dormant racing interests and runs his own stud at Park House on the estate. The present Lady Bolton, Marsha Ann, is also a keen horsewoman and runs her own string of racehorses, in her own colours, from the family seat at Leyburn Hall. The estate includes the ruins of the medieval Bolton Castle, open to the public; until 1979 it displayed Bluebird I, the boat in which Sir Malcolm Campbell won the world water speed record for Britain in 1937.

A dedicated and active Conservative, Lord Bolton was an occasional intermediary in the crisis that preceded Zimbabwe's independence.

Jonathan Clague   £45m

CASINO AND HOTEL OWNER   dob *c.* 1948

HONG Kong in the postwar period was the place to make a fortune and the late Douglas Clague was the one to make it. An ex-military man, he escaped from a Japanese prisoner of war camp and spent 18 months fighting the Japanese from behind their lines. This gave him an invaluable network of contacts who were to prove very useful after the war. In 1952 he became chairman of Hutchison, the local Hong Kong trading house, and over the next 20 years he built it into a huge international trading house to rival Jardine Matheson. Among the friends he helped were Y. K. Pao, then a local merchant. Clague helped him build his first two ships and, today, Sir Y. K. Pao is one of the top shipowners in the world.

Clague also had links with Jim Slater, the 1970s financier, and he formed a Far Eastern merchant bank with Slater Walker. A noted racehorse owner, with extensive houses in both Britain and Hong Kong, Clague owned around 10% of Hutchison's stock when he died.

Apart from his business interests, Clague was also a well-known local politician, public servant (as head of the auxiliary police) and chairman of the influential Hong Kong Jockey Club.

His son Jonathan inherited the extensive interests plus the Palace Hotel and Casino in the Isle of Man, from where he now operates. Brought up in Hong Kong, Jonathan lives quietly in a large farmhouse near Douglas with his wife and four children and is well liked locally.

His working life revolves around the Palace group, which comprises a hotel, casino, ballroom and cinema complex. There is also some land and a golf links hotel, with an 18-hole course. Clague is seeking to build a second golf course at his hotel but has run into strong opposition from local conservationists.

His extensive racehorse interests are based in Ireland, where he owns the prestigious Collinstown Stud, winner of the top breeder's award in 1984 and 1985. He also has business interests in Hong Kong and Australia. He spent much of his youth in Ireland on the family stud farm. Apart from racing, his other main interest is golf.

Lord Clinton   £45m

LANDOWNER   dob 12 July 1931

IT took an eight-year fight for Lord Clinton to establish his claim to his title. In 1957 he inherited the Devon estate of the 21st Lord Clinton, his great-grandfather, but it was not until 1965 that he became the 22nd holder of the title, after his aunt Mrs Fenella Bowes-Lyon petitioned her niece, the Queen, on his behalf.

The title had gone into abeyance on the death of his grandfather as there were no direct heirs in the next generation. But after a long and ultimately successful fight, Clinton took his seat in the Lords in 1965. He has spent the subsequent years tending the 26,000-acre estate with considerable skill, as befits a trained land agent. The estate is on the Devon coast near Exeter, and it has always been regarded as one of the most efficiently run in Britain. Under a settlement designed to minimize tax liabilities, Clinton is in effect a tenant for life on the estate, enjoying all the privileges and responsibilities of a great landowner. The estate boasts fine Italian gardens designed by Le Nôtre, who created the famous gardens at Versailles for King Louis XIV of France. The gardens were constructed by a pupil of Le Nôtre in 1735.

Clinton is well known in local farming circles, where he is a vice-president of the Devon Agricultural Association. He is also a former Justice of the Peace and Deputy Lieutenant of the county. Unsurprisingly, he lists his hobbies as shooting and fishing.

Viscount Coke   £45m

LANDOWNER   dob 6 May 1932

HEIR to the Earl of Leicester, who lives in South Africa, Viscount Coke runs one of the largest estates in England at Holkham, near Sandringham in Norfolk.

The 25,000 acres were subjected to £500,000 (equivalent to £20 million in 1990) worth of improvements in the 18th century by the great agricultural innovator, Coke of Norfolk. But he ran Holkham Hall along traditional lines. At Christmas, 18 large turkeys would be roasted on a spit in the kitchen, while it was the duty of the housemaids to sleep in all the beds in the house to give them a good airing.

Viscount Coke has had to sell paintings to meet death duties. In 1980 he sold a Leonardo da Vinci manuscript to Dr Armand Hammer for £2.2 million, which was described as a bargain price. Later, he sold a Raphael cartoon to the Washington National Gallery for £1 million. But that still leaves him with works by Rubens, Claude, Poussin, Van Dyck and Gainsborough. The furniture and sculptures at Holkham are equally impressive.

Greta Fenston and family   £45m

BUSINESSWOMAN   dob GF *c.* 1935

IN 1963, at the age of 28, Greta Borg, the daughter of an army colonel, married Felix Fenston, then one of London's richest men, who had made a fortune from buying and selling property. Fenston, the son of a theatre impresario who wanted to be a concert pianist, lost a leg and was invalided out of the Intelligence Corps during the war.

Starting with £100, he moved into property, with his first deal in Watford. Later he was to move into central London and he bought the St James's Theatre in 1957, which he turned into an office block despite the protests of the actress Vivien Leigh. He was also active abroad and pulled off what was then the biggest property deal in the Commonwealth with a large development in Montreal.

In the 1960s he gave up work and announced plans to travel and shoot big game. Within two years he was back in business but he finally relinquished his position in 1968. He died in 1970 at the age of 55, leaving one of the biggest estates for some years, worth £12.6 million gross. He also owned one of the finest houses in Mayfair, bought from the Duke of Devonshire.

Some of his funds were invested in the property and construction world; this was revealed in August 1989 when Kyle Stewart, one of the biggest private construction groups in the country, was sold to a Dutch company for around £50 million. Some 90% of the shares in the group were controlled by two trusts: one, with 30%, was controlled directly by Mrs Fenston; the other, with 60% of the shares, was another Fenston family trust, but under the trusteeship of Sidney Morris, the family solicitor.

Felix Fenston married three times. He divorced his first wife during the war and married a French woman almost immediately, in 1943. They had three children before divorcing in 1959.

Clive Hunting and family £45m

ENGINEERING AND OIL EXECUTIVE
dob (unknown)

THE Hunting family own a third of the Hunting Group, a medium-sized engineering and oil company. But their roots go back to the coal industry in the North East, where Charles Hunting, an astute Geordie, supplied equipment to the booming coal industry. He had side interests in shipping and, in 1874, set his son up as a shipowner with two sailing ships. Recognizing that oil would replace coal as the fuel of the future, the Hunting Group switched rapidly from sailing ships to oil tankers.

But it was Sir Percy Hunting, grandson of Charles, who between World Wars I and II steered the company into new fields such as aviation. He also moved down from the North East to London during the Depression. Sir Percy retired in 1960 at the age of 75; he died in 1973 after a very active life. His nephew, Clive Hunting, was chairman for many years, but now Sir Percy's grandson, Richard, is chairman. He has all the right qualifications. After schooling at Rugby, he took an engineering degree at Sheffield University and an MBA from Manchester. A sporty type, he lists his hobbies as skiing, swimming, languages, travel and choral singing.

For years Hunting was one of the most complex companies in the City, with different bits of businesses controlled by different members of the family. It was also prone to several reorganizations as it gradually shed its old businesses to move firmly into the high technology end of defence.

Finally, in 1989, all the businesses were brought together as the Hunting Group. This is now worth around £150 million on the stock market, with its headquarters in London's Knightsbridge.

Lord Margadale   £45m

LANDOWNER   dob 16 December 1906

JOHN Morrison, MP for St Ives in the 1830s, ran a thriving London drapery business. He cornered the market in black crêpe – much in demand for funerals – and left a £3 million fortune.

His great-grandson, Lord Margadale, was MP for Salisbury and rose to become chairman of the 1922 Committee of Conservative backbenchers in the early 1960s. He was reputed to be the richest MP in the Commons in those days. He inherited £500,000 on his 21st birthday, and a £15-million fortune all told.

Today, with the Islay estate on the Isle of Islay, large tracts of Wiltshire and a collection of art including Ming vases, he is worth much more.

He has three sons, two of whom are Conservative MPs, including the Hon. Peter Morrison, a junior minister and former deputy chairman of the Conservative Party, who was a strong supporter of Mrs Thatcher and served as her private secretary at the time of her resignation.

Bernard Matthews   £45m

TURKEY PRODUCER   dob 24 January 1930

BEST-KNOWN for his appearance on his own television adverts extolling the 'bootiful' virtues of his turkeys, Bernard Matthews took a long time getting into the business. He started as an auctioneer's clerk earning 30s a week and bought a job lot of turkeys and an incubator. He could not afford to feed them, changed jobs and became an insurance clerk. He bought a second batch, but the wind blew their shelter away and the birds escaped. Third time lucky. He borrowed £3,000 in 1955 and bought Great Witchingham Hall, a dilapidated Jacobean mansion near Norwich, and 35 acres. The turkeys were hatched in the dining-room, reared in the bedrooms and processed in the kitchen. Today, the hall is still the centre of his business, which has extended beyond turkeys to include boneless beef, pork and lamb roasts, which Matthews also enthusiastically promotes on television.

The business is booming even in the recession. Profits leapt 70% in 1990 to reach £15.5 million. New brands such as Golden Fishies, an up-market fishfinger, and Sea Pearls, circles of cod, are both selling well. But the 3 million turkeys in his care form the basis of the Matthews fortune.

He has a holiday home in the south of France and a stylish 157-foot yacht called *Bellissima*.

Robert Sangster £45m

HORSES AND POOLS   dob 23 May 1936

HORSES and women characterize Robert Sangster's indulgent life. He has dedicated himself to the Turf. With 1,200 horses, at first he won nearly every single classic, including the Derby and the Prix de l'Arc de Triomphe in 1977. But the uncrowned king of British racing has had a bad time on the turf in recent years. Arab sheikhs have swept all before them on the British racing circuit, leaving Sangster to pick up the odd consolation prize. His commitment to racing has been so great that it has halved the £110 million fortune he inherited from his father. Early in 1989 he was forced to put his lavish Manton stud on the market. Described as Europe's finest private training complex, the 2,050-acre farm has a price tag of around £15 million. Sangster also wants to close Phoenix Park race course in Ireland, where he is a part owner, because of heavy losses. Thrice married, Sangster is rarely out of the gossip columns. His first wife was a Lake District hotelier's daughter. His second, Susan, was the ex-wife of Australian politician Andrew Peacock. He married Sue Lilley, 20 years his junior, in 1985 after a brief romance with Jerry Hall, Mick Jagger's girlfriend. Sangster lives a luxury life in his Isle of Man home called the Nunnery. He also has a Barbados retreat.

Charanjit and Satinder Vohra   £45m

HOTELIERS   dob CV 12 February 1942, SV *c.* 1948

THE Vohra family, led by brothers Charanjit and Satinder, are rapidly building up one of the biggest hotel chains in London. They currently own some 1,500 London hotel rooms in six, mainly three- or four-star, establishments. Among the hotels run by their private Crysanta chain are the Washington in Mayfair and the Rubens in Victoria.

Ironically, the Vohras gave a big boost to their major rivals, their cousin Jasminder Singh (q.v.), who runs the Edwardian Hotel group. When Jasminder arrived in Britain from Nairobi, he sought the advice of Satinder Vohra on what career he should pursue. Vohra took him under his wing and gave him an 18-month training course in all aspects of the hotel business. They went into partnership and bought the Edwardian Hotel in London's Harrington Gardens. Eighteen months later, they sold up and bought another. But they have since parted and are now friendly rivals.

Both Charanjit and Satinder were born in Nairobi and later came to Britain to make their fortunes. Charanjit, who arrived in 1960, lists his hobbies as golf and swimming, and supports various religious, social and welfare organizations.

George Warburton and family   £45m

BAKERS   dob (unknown)

WARBURTONS, Britain's biggest privately owned bakers, was founded in Bolton in 1876. The family still control the business, which has six bakeries round the country. Its latest was opened in a former Newcastle engineering factory in 1989. In 1986, four senior members of the Warburton family resigned from the board to make way for younger staff. There are still three Warburtons on the six-man board and most of the shares are still firmly in family hands. In its latest accounts to the end of September 1989, the group made some £4.8 million after-tax profits on a £100-million turnover. The company has branched out of its traditional business, buying retail outlets and also moving into snacks and frozen foods. Warburtons is also busy increasing its sales of bread to the major supermarkets. William Warburton, one of the three family members on the board, is also a director of the famous Bolton Wanderers Football Club.

George Williams   £45m

DOUBLE GLAZING MANUFACTURER
dob (unknown)

IN the early 1960s George Williams was working as a chicken farmer in Norfolk, determining the sex of chicks for the likes of Bernard Matthews, the poultry millionaire. But in 1966, just when double glazing was becoming popular in Britain, he started work part-time in the infant double-glazing industry. Initially, with £450 capital, he had just six staff and worked from a garage at his Norfolk home, but two years later he opened his first showroom in Ipswich.

George proved to be a strong-minded boss who motivated his staff and salesmen by paying well for results. And these were achieved. Battling hard for customers in the 1970s, he built up the company, Anglian Windows, to be the second largest double-glazing firm in Britain. It had 118 showrooms and 49 branches round the country, with over 1,400 full-time employees.

In 1984, Williams sold a controlling stake in the business to the giant BET group for £25 million, which left him and his family holding the rest. He stayed on as chairman of Anglian.

In 1985 his first wife left him and their four children. In 1986 George married a Chilean girl whom he had met in a King's Road shop. They live in a Norfolk mansion set in 70 acres and have three other homes in Devon, America and the Virgin Islands. George also has a private plane and a helicopter.

Lady Willoughby de Eresby £45m

LANDOWNER   dob December 1934

LADY Jane Willoughby de Eresby is the sole surviving child of the 3rd Earl of Ancaster, who died in 1983. Twenty years earlier her brother, Lord Willoughby de Eresby, had tragically vanished while sailing from the south of France to Corsica. Regarded as a black sheep, he had been convicted of illegal gambling in 1958.

Just before his disappearance he had opened Wips, a Leicester Square nightclub. It later changed its name to Ad Lib and launched the London disco boom. He left some £400,000 in his will.

The Ancaster estates are substantial. In Lincolnshire, there are some 12,500 acres around Grimsthorpe, a beautiful 100-room castle built by Vanbrugh, the architect of Blenheim Palace. It also has a fine art collection including works by Canaletto and Holbein. There are also some 30,000 acres in Scotland surrounding Drummond Castle in Perthshire and valuable properties in Wales.

In 1978, five years before his death, Ancaster put much of the family wealth into a private charitable trust, with the aim of preserving the estates intact after his death. As a result, he left just £1.4 million in his will, and Lady Jane was able to live on at Grimsthorpe. She was a well-known member of London's Swinging Sixties set. She has never married and there are two elderly heiresses to the estate, both in their eighties. The title is likely to go to a niece, of whom there are several. Lady Jane was one of the Queen's train bearers at her 1953 Coronation.

Lord Wolfson £45m

MAIL ORDER DEALER   dob 11 November 1927

LORD Wolfson's father, Isaac Wolfson, started work in his father's furniture business in Glasgow and then built up his own larger one in Manchester, where he came into contact with Great Universal Stores, a mail order business which he subsequently joined in 1931. A consummate deal-maker, Issac Wolfson was renowned for making an offer on everything and anything.

Today, GUS is a £2.6 billion business which stretches from Burberry raincoats to furniture. In 1989, GUS profits reached £400 million. It is now moving into property and plans to develop its £1 billion portfolio with George Wimpey, the building group.

Leonard, Sir Isaac's son, was created a Conservative peer in 1985, and has been GUS chairman since 1966. He lives in Portland Place and lists history and economics as his hobbies.

Leonard is renowned as a tough businessman, but also makes large donations to medical and scientific bodies through the charitable Wolfson Foundation, which controls over £200 million-worth of GUS shares.

The family is obsessed by secrecy. Sir Isaac, who was once compared to Spencer Tracy, had a strong Glasgow accent. He once said that the secret of his success was that 'I worked with all my fingers.' He died in 1991.

His son Lord Wolfson took over from Sir John Nott as trustee of the Imperial War Museum and has strong links with the Conservative Party.

Malcolm Lee £44m

WASTE DISPOSAL ENTREPRENEUR
dob (unknown)

GRADUATING from Leeds University in 1967 with a degree in fuel science, Malcolm Lee spent ten years learning all there is to know about the disposal of toxic waste and liquids. After spells with Tarmac, developing a new waste division, he joined BET, working in their waste disposal business. In 1985, he led the management buy-out of Rechem along with Richard Biffa (q.v.).

Under Biffa and Lee, Rechem has moved upmarket and is

concentrating on high-temperature incineration of toxic wastes at its two plants situated near Southampton and at Pontypool. Graham Searle, a founder member of Friends of the Earth, sits on the Rechem board, but it still runs into ire from environmentalists, particularly over its Pontypool plant. Early in 1989 the Torfaen Council in Wales claimed that the level of toxic waste around the plant was 88 times higher than normal. Rechem took issue with the findings and has submitted its own contrary findings to the European Commission in Brussels. It had already fought a successful libel action against the BBC, which had alleged in a 1985 *Newsnight* programme that toxic waste at Pontypool had not been properly incinerated. The company and Lee were awarded a complete apology and their legal costs of £50,000 were paid by the BBC. Rechem has announced plans to expand the Pontypool facility.

But controversy surrounding the plant and toxic waste refuses to die. In September 1989, Liverpool dockers refused to handle a shipment of polychlorinated biphenols from Canada which were destined for Pontypool. They were returned to Canada. Lee accused Greenpeace, which alerted the world to the Canadian cargo, of promoting pollution. 'The only safe way to destroy this difficult waste is by high-temperature incineration. There are no alternatives,' he told the *Sunday Times*. The Pontypool plant was given a clean bill of health by the Welsh Office in November 1989.

At the end of 1990, Lee and Biffa merged Rechem into another waste disposal group, Shanks & McEwan, in a £158 million deal.

Kevin Leech   £42m

ENTREPRENEUR   dob (unknown)

KEVIN Leech started work as a chartered accountant when he left school at 15. He planned to take his articles but his father had a heart attack and Leech had to take over the running of the family garage business in Manchester. Among its various elements was a funeral business which Leech reckoned could be highly profitable. For eighteen years he concentrated on building it up, and by 1982 he was undertaking 6,000 funerals a year in the Manchester area. But a combination of the 1981 inner-city riots, fears of the return of a Labour government and a growing distaste for funerals led Leech to sell out to the Cooperative Wholesale Society for £2.3 million. He went into tax exile in Jersey where he met an inventor, Jeremiah Milner, a Liverpool chemist, who had come up with a promising alternative to kidney dialysis which did not require hours hooked up on a kidney machine. Leech backed Milner's company, ML Laboratories, to the tune of £50,000. Milner died before a new plant was opened on a technology park in Liverpool in 1990, but Leech kept faith with the project. In 1987, the company had come to the stock market, and by the beginning of 1991, with the final trials of its new glucose polymer treatment well advanced, its shares were in strong demand. Leech's stake was worth over £40 million. Apart from his business interests, Leech spends his time in Jersey sailing and fishing.

Earl of Stair £42m

LANDOWNER   dob 9 October 1906

IN the 1870s, the estates of the Earl of Stair ran to 116,000 acres and produced an annual rental of nearly £62,000. Today, the 13th Earl still owns a hefty 45,000 acres in the area around Stranraer and he has his seat at Lochinch Castle. The estate comprises farms, forestry and sporting lands.

Educated at Eton and Sandhurst, the Earl, then Viscount Dalrymple, went into the army and served in North Africa, Syria and Italy during the war. He retired in 1952 as lieutenant colonel commanding the Scots Guards.

He became a member of Wigtown County Council in 1958 and served until 1975 when the council was abolished in local government reorganization. He married Davina Katharine, daughter of Sir David Bowes-Lyon, and a cousin of the Queen, in 1960. A year later he inherited the Earldom, which dates back to 1703. They have three sons.

The royal connections are also maintained through the Earl's position as Captain General of the bodyguard for Scotland, the Royal Company of Archers. Lord Stair is now virtually retired and spends most of his spare time shooting and fishing.

Viscount Astor   £40m

LANDOWNER   dob 27 December 1951

SUCCEEDING to the title at the age of 15, William Waldorf Astor became the 4th Viscount.

Waldorf, an Astor family name, refers to the village near Heidelberg in Germany from which John Jacob Astor emigrated to America at the end of the 19th century. He later bought up land around New York. His only son, William Waldorf, was American ambassador to Italy and eventually settled in Britain, becoming Viscount Astor in 1917. The present Viscount's grandmother, Nancy Astor, was the first woman MP. The family have a long link with the *Observer* newspaper and own the old printing works and offices in the City. These are worth around £40 million at today's prices.

Viscount Astor lives in Ginge Manor, near Wantage in Oxfordshire. He is now on the board of Blakeney Hotels, which leases the old Astor family seat at Cliveden from the National Trust and uses it as a hotel. Guests are served by butlers, valets and chambermaids rigged out in Edwardian costume. Cliveden was prepared for its new role at a cost of £1 million. Viscount Astor, who lists his hobbies as fishing and shooting, lives on the income from the family trusts. His wife is a jewellery designer.

Gordon Baxter   £40m

FOOD MANUFACTURER   dob (unknown)

IN 1877, George Baxter gave up his job as gardener to the Duke of Richmond and with a borrowed £10 opened a grocery shop in the Grampian town of Fochabers. Customers who were short of cash would pay their bills with fruit and other produce from their gardens. George's wife Margaret would turn this into jam. His son William, encouraged by the Duke, later built a small factory on the banks of the Spey to make jam, and Baxter's was born.

Today those high-quality soups and jams with the well-known brand label are coveted by virtually every major food company. But the members of the Baxter family, led by Gordon Baxter, grandson of the founder, have so far resisted all overtures (150 plus so far) and can do so as they hold 96% of the shares. Though the company only makes a £2-million profit on a £22 million turnover and employs only 500 people, the brand name alone would command £40 million. Among the hopeful bidders had been Colgate-Palmolive, Campbell Soups, Heinz, Unilever and Nestlé. Gordon usually takes potential buyers fishing on the Spey and then sits them down in front of a roaring fire with a whisky before saying no.

The family feel they have a social responsibility to their staff as the area's biggest single employer. Gordon believes that any of the would-be predators would simply destroy the firm and local jobs, if successful. He joined the family firm in 1946 after doing wartime research on explosives for ICI. He was first introduced to the business when, at the age of five, he would get up at 5.30 a.m. to light the fires at home and then go out to hand over the factory keys to the manager. After school, his favourite job was to stick the labels on the jam jars. It was Gordon's mother who invented the first soup and pioneered a method of canning raspberries.

Today, his wife Ena comes up with new recipes in her own kitchen which are first tried by the family before going into production in the 50-acre factory. His three children are all either working for the business or are destined to do so. His daughter, Audrey, a former merchant banker, seems set to take over the helm when Gordon retires. Gordon himself tends his prize Highland cattle and is a prominent backer of the Scottish Conservative Party.

Edwin Boorman and family £40m

NEWSPAPER PUBLISHING   dob (unknown)

THE Boorman family own the Kent Messenger Group, publishers of local newspapers in the Garden of England. Edwin Boorman is the current chairman of the group, which made just over £4 million after-tax profits on a £19.6 million turnover in its latest accounts for 1989. Edwin's father, HR Pratt Boorman, a celebrated figure in local newspapers, had run the business for over 50 years when he retired in 1982 at the age of 82. Known as 'The Guv'nor', he had only been in journalism for six years when, in 1928, his father died and he took over the business. Edwin Boorman and the Kent Messenger Group came to public attention in 1985 when 144 members of the National Graphical Association were sacked for refusing to agree to the introduction of new technology in the firm's advertising department. At the time Boorman said: 'We are in a highly competitive situation. It is essential that we use the technology to reduce our costs.'

Tony Bramall £40m

CAR DEALER   dob 29 December 1935

CHARLES Bramall started a successful car dealership in Bradford in 1957. His son Tony, who trained as a chartered accountant, joined him in 1963 after working in a Sheffield estate agency. He later took over the reins, and the company was floated on the stock market in 1978. A period of steady growth followed, with the company holding important Ford and BL dealerships. In 1987, Bramall agreed to a £79-million takeover by Avis. The family controlled 57% of the shares and received around £45 million for them.

Bramall took up an executive directorship in Avis but resigned a few months later in June 1988. He subsequently took a 20% stake in Lyon & Lyon, a Ford main dealer based in nearby Batley. Lyon & Lyon was taken over by another group for £13.6 million. That valued the Bramall stake at £2.7 million.

Bramall is now involved with a Harrogate company, Gregory Properties, where he has been a director since 1983.

Sheffield-born Bramall now lives in the Yorkshire Dales. His wife Susan is a horse trainer and they have three daughters. Known as a hard worker, he relaxes by playing golf to an 18 handicap. He also shoots and has owned some racehorses. A very private person, he is devoted to his family.

Michael Heseltine £40m

POLITICIAN AND PUBLISHER   dob 21 March 1933

THE flowing blond locks and firm jaw helped earn him the nickname Tarzan. His impassioned oratory has made him the darling of the Conservative Party conference, though not of the party establishment since his abrupt departure from the Cabinet in 1986. Although his chances of becoming leader of the Tory party briefly improved in 1990, the prospect still looked remote.

He doesn't need the money. The son of a Swansea business-man, he went to Oxford, where he was something of a dandy (his suits and ties are still the sharpest in the Tory Party). He became president of the Union, the prestigious university debating society, and even then was tipped as a future prime minister.

In the London of the 1950s he became a property developer and was a millionaire at 26. But his political career came first and he was elected to Parliament while embarking on the road to more wealth as a publisher. He founded the Haymarket Group, which publishes glossy trade titles such as *Campaign*.

Today, Heseltine lives in a £1.5 million Belgravia house and he has a £2.5 million 18th-century estate in Oxfordshire with 400 acres, a lake, stables and a swimming pool.

Heseltine waited until 1989 to begin his public pitch for the Tory leadership. He said it would be an 'honour' to serve as leader should Mrs Thatcher go. In his book, *The Challenge of Europe*, published in May 1989, Heseltine criticized the government line, calling for Britain to embrace its European destiny. In December 1989, a Gallup poll found that he would do more than any other Tory MP to attract wavering voters back to the Conservative Party.

In November 1990, he made his bid for the leadership and challenged Margaret Thatcher. Although beaten on the first ballot, his showing on the back of his pledge to abolish the poll tax forced Mrs Thatcher to withdraw from the second ballot of Tory MPs. But in that second ballot, Heseltine was beaten by John Major. However, he agreed to serve in the Major government as secretary of state for the environment, with the task of devising an alternative for the poll tax. A modified form of property tax was unveiled in March 1991.

Sir Anthony Jacobs   £40m

INDUSTRIALIST   dob 13 November 1931

THOUSANDS of Britain's learner drivers have a link with Sir Anthony Jacobs, though few will actually know it. Jacobs, a prominent supporter of the Liberal Party and latterly of the Liberal Democrats, owned the British School of Motoring group until April 1990, when he sold the business for £40 million.

Born in London, Sir Anthony was educated at Clifton College and London University, where he took a degree in commerce. He is a chartered accountant by profession but in 1961, after six years' practice, he started his own fashion business, called Tricoville.

Twelve years later he became chairman of BSM and, in 1978, with a group of associates, he took over the business for £3.5 million. Founded 80 years ago, the BSM has a strong brand image, and the Jacobs family retains £5 million worth of shares in the business, which was sold to its management.

Apart from his business career, Sir Anthony (knighted in 1988) lists his hobbies as golf, theatre, riding, opera and travel. He stood as Liberal candidate for Watford in the two 1974 elections. He was a prominent fund-raiser for the party, appealing to industry for support at party conferences. BSM gave £188,000 to the Liberals in 1983 and £20,000 in 1987.

Peter Jones   £40m

BUILDER   dob (unknown)

PETER Jones, a former bricklayer, set up as a housebuilder in Cheshire in 1959. 'PE', as he is always known, had a reputation for taking risks which netted him big rewards, and he showed this flair early on. Buying a waterlogged site in the exclusive village of Alderley Edge for a very low price, he was able to drain it, build some houses and make a considerable profit.

He followed this success in the 1970s and early 1980s by buying up as much land as he could in the then unpopular South Manchester area, where there is now great demand for land. His latest venture is an office park on the outskirts of Moss Side, a site rejected by many other developers.

His main company, Emerson Holdings, is called after his second name – the E in PE. The various subsidiaries operate in housebuilding, construction and office development. In the year to the end of April 1987, Emerson Holdings made £2.6 million after-tax profits on sales of £25 million. The company, which is owned by Jones and his family trusts, has a property portfolio with a value of up to £50 million.

Recently, the group has also expanded into the south with projects around Heathrow, and it also has property interests in Portugal and America.

Now in his fifties, Jones lives in a £1 million mansion in Alderley Edge which he built himself. He drives a Rolls-Royce and is a fanatical snooker follower, having started a snooker league with some of Manchester's leading developers. Matches are generally played in his purpose-built snooker room.

He is regarded as a tough businessman and is a perfectionist, personally negotiating all the business development plans and agreements himself.

Brian Morrison and family   £40m

WHISKY DISTILLERS   dob (unknown)

THE Morrison family company, Morrison Bowmore, is one of Scotland's leading whisky producers, with fine malts such as Bowmore, Glen Garioch and Auchentoshan. It is also one of the most profitable, with £3 million after-tax profits on a £23-million turnover in 1988.

The business was founded in 1951 by Stanley Morrison, who teamed up with a young accountant, James Howat. Morrison had done an apprenticeship with a Glasgow engineering firm, which took him out to the Far East. On his return in the early 1920s, he joined a whisky broking firm, where he learnt the business.

In the 1950s, Stanley Morrison acted as a conventional broker. But in 1963, hearing that the Bowmore distillery on Islay was for sale, he managed to buy it. In 1970 he bought the Glen Garioch distillery, which had lain empty for two years because of its poor water supplies. By tapping into new water sources, he managed to increase capacity sixfold on its previously dormant period. In 1971 Stanley Morrison died and his son Brian took over. He followed his father's expansion and acquired the third distillery at Auchentoshan in 1984.

In 1989 he relaunched the company as Morrison Bowmore and brought the Japanese group Suntory in as a partner. The aim is to give the three malt brands a much higher prominence, rather than relying on selling bulk malt to overseas markets, particularly Japan. Many Scots regard that as simply selling Scotland's birthright. Morrison also has a brother, Stanley, in the business. They both live in Ayrshire. The company has a reputation for clever conservation, and at the Glen Garioch distillery there are 2 acres of greenhouses, fed by waste heat from the whisky plant and fertilized by surplus carbon dioxide from the distilling process, which aids photosynthesis. In 1989 the company harvested 40 tons of tomatoes, and from 1990 onwards there were plans to increase this to 600 tons.

Christopher Needler   £40m

QUARRYING INDUSTRIALIST
dob 4 September 1944

CHRISTOPHER Needler's late father, Harold, was one of the major figures in postwar British construction. He built up his Hull-based Hoveringham Group to be one of the biggest sand and gravel companies in the country. It was floated on the stock market in 1963, but in 1981 the family sold out to Tarmac for £21 million.

They decided to keep their substantial Canadian gravel and quarrying interests, acquired in 1956. The Canadian interests operate under the name TCG Materials (TCG itself stands for Telephone City Gravel: Telephone City was the home of Alexander Graham Bell, inventor of the telephone). In 1988, these interests were floated on the British Unlisted Securities Market as the Needler Group. Christopher Needler owns around 10.5 million shares, worth £10 million. The group supplies much of the Canadian industrial heartland with aggregates and has some 75 million tonnes of reserves in its 3,000 acres of land.

Needler also raised some £1 million by selling his Lloyds insurance broking business. He commutes between his London home and Canada to run the business.

Needler was educated at Repton before becoming an articled clerk for six years in 1962, ultimately qualifying as a chartered accountant. He went to Trinity College, Cambridge, in 1968, at the relatively late age of 24. Graduating in 1971, he immediately became a director of Hoveringham and was made chairman in 1975. He followed his father to become chairman of Hull City. Though no longer chairman today, he remains a director. His hobby is golf.

Earl of Pembroke   £40m

LANDOWNER AND FILM-MAKER
dob 19 May 1939

WILTON House outside Salisbury is regarded as one of the finest English country houses. It has been home to the Earls of Pembroke since the days of Henry VIII. Today, the 17th Earl is best known for his work as a film director. He has his fully paid-up ACTT union card and has made several films under the name Henry Herbert. These include *Emily*, starring Koo Stark, and the BBC series *By the Sword Divided*, about the Civil War.

The Pembroke estates cover 16,000 acres. But the family's real wealth is the art collection, which includes works by Van Dyck, Claude, Rembrandt, Lorenzo Lotto, Andrea del Sarto and Reynolds.

In 1984, the Earl turned down a bid for some of his art treasures from the Getty Museum in California. One painting, *The Card Player* by Lucas van Leyden, was estimated to be worth £3 million on its own. In 1964, the Earl married Claire Pelley, daughter of the former High Sheriff of Essex. They had four children, but she left him to live with a neighbouring landowner. They were divorced in 1987, and the Earl remarried a London kindergarten owner in 1988.

Viscount Petersham   £40m

LANDOWNER   dob 20 July 1945

HEIR to the Earl of Harrington, Viscount Petersham was briefly a tax exile in Ireland in the 1970s. His father still lives there, but the Viscount now has a Chelsea home and a Wiltshire estate.

His father moved to Ireland in 1963 when he sold Elvaston Castle and 4500 acres in Derbyshire for over £1 million. He is a noted bloodstock agent.

Petersham is a keen sportsman, listing sailing, hunting, shooting, skiing and fishing as his hobbies. He spent two years circumnavigating the globe on the yacht *Surama*. He is married to Anita Robsham, formerly the wife of the Earl of Suffolk. It is his second marriage.

The family fortune derives from their ownership of a large chunk of London's fashionable South Kensington and Gloucester Road.

Duke of Richmond   £40m

LANDOWNER   dob 19 September 1929

CHARLES Lennox, the 1st Duke of Richmond, was the bastard son of Charles II and Louise de Kéroualle. He acquired Goodwood in Sussex in 1695, but it was the 3rd Duke who built it up into a full-scale ducal estate.

Today the 10th Duke, who inherited the title in 1989, presides over a 12,000-acre estate. He has been able to make considerable sums of money by selling estate properties. In 1984, 11 cottages fetched £472,000. There are 200 left on the estate.

Goodwood has a long association with horse and car racing, through the racecourse above the house. The 'Glorious' Goodwood race meetings are held there. The Duke is also busy trying to turn the Goodwood estate into a more commercial operation.

The Duke's art treasures include four Canalettos, together

with portraits by Reynolds, Lely, Kellner, Hoppner and Law-rence. There is also some magnificent French furniture, tape-stries and porcelain acquired by the 3rd Duke when he was ambassador to the court of Louis XV of France.

Duke of Rutland   £40m

LANDOWNER   dob 28 May 1919

THE Duke came to public notice in 1977 when he threatened to lie in front of a bulldozer if British Coal started trying to exploit the coal reserves under the Vale of Belvoir in the North of England. He owns 18,000 acres of the vale and, claim-ing the mineral rights, said he did not want any pits dug there. But it was a campaign doomed to failure, and British Coal is currently developing a super-pit in the area, to produce low-cost high-grade coal for the 1990s and beyond.

Lady Teresa Manners, his youngest daughter, has also hit the headlines. She was once discovered passionately embracing a man while driving along a motorway. She was a lead singer in a pop group made up of aristocrats, including the heir to the Duke of Beaufort.

Belvoir Castle, the Rutland home, is built on the foundations of a Norman stronghold. A fire necessitated rebuilding in 1816. The art collection includes works by Van de Velde, Gains-borough, the younger Teniers, Holbein, five Poussins and a Murillo.

Earl Spencer   £40m

LANDOWNER   dob 24 January 1924

EARL Spencer is best remembered for his dignified presence at the wedding of his daughter, Diana, to the Prince of Wales in 1981.

The 8th Earl lives on the 15,000-acre Althorp estate in North-amptonshire. It has been home to the Spencers since 1508 and contains some of the finest collections of paintings, furniture and porcelain in Europe. There are 700 paintings, acquired since the end of the 17th century. Some have been sold off in recent years to meet the cost of Althorp's upkeep and death duties. In 1977 four Van Dyck works were sold, breaking up one of the finest collections in the country.

Recently Earl Spencer was given permission by the Department of the Environment to develop some land for housing. He is married to Raine, the daughter of Barbara Cartland (q.v.), the romantic novelist. His first wife, Princess Diana's mother, is now Mrs Shand Kydd. His heir, Viscount Althorp, was married in 1989 in what was called the society wedding of the year. He worked for American television until early 1991.

Michael Stone £40m

COMMODITY BROKING   dob 10 May 1936

STONE runs one of the City's least-known yet most profitable trading companies, the Man Group. His company has been in business since 1763 and supplied ultra-potent rum to the Admiralty until the navy's grog ration was discontinued in 1970. Its principal business remains international trade – sugar, coffee, cocoa and money. Stone, who joined Man in 1957, changed it in the 1960s from a highly regarded if small produce broker into a major force in the international raw materials world.

He will be remembered in the City for his secret deal with the Russian government in 1972 to buy enough sugar to supply the whole of Russia for a year. The western world remained unaware of the operation until it was finished. In 1985 Suchard, the Swiss confectionery giant, acquired 45% of his company for a sum thought to be around $385 million, including an option to acquire the balance in 1990. Stone's personal stake in the company was believed to be around 20%, and the Suchard deal valued it at over $170 million. He is married and lives on a farm in Surrey. He lists his hobbies as shooting, fishing, farming, skiing and gardening.

In 1987, Man gave £138,000 to the Conservative Party, making it one of the biggest business contributors to party funds.

Richard Walduck and family   £40m

HOTELIER   dob (unknown)

THE Walduck family first entered the London hotel trade in the 19th century. In the Edwardian period at the turn of the century, the Imperial Hotel in Bloomsbury was built by a Harold Walduck. Designed by Sir Charles Fitzroy-Doll, the hotel resembled a Bavarian Schloss. But it was in the postwar period that the Walduck family's Imperial chain really developed under the control of Harold's two sons, Stanley and Norman Walduck. Their five hotels in central London epitomized the heady expansionist and optimistic 1950s and 1960s, with names such as the President and the Royal National. The family prospered, and the two brothers lived close to each other and farmed near Hatfield in Hertfordshire, where they were active in Conservative politics. Today the business is run by Stanley's three sons, Richard, Tom and Stephen Walduck. In its latest accounts to the end of April 1989, the group made £4.8 million after-tax profits on a £30.9 million turnover. With £24.3 million shareholders' funds, the group is in a strong position to weather recessionary storms.

Sir Mark Weinberg   £40m

FINANCIER   dob 9 August 1931

WEINBERG qualified and practised as a barrister in South Africa before moving to Britain in 1961 to set up his own life assurance business, Abbey Life, with a £50,000 loan. It was remarkably successful because he paid high commissions to brokers. He sold the business in 1970 and promptly started again with Hambro Life. In 1985 that business was sold for £664 million to BAT, the tobacco giant.

Sir Mark is now a poacher turned gamekeeper as deputy chairman of the Securities and Investment Board, policing the pension industry.

His other claim is his second marriage to the beautiful Australian actress and budding millionairess in her own right, Anouska Hempel. His first wife, Sandra, was her best friend until her death in 1978. Out of a run-down Earls Court boarding house, Anouska Hempel created Blake's Hotel, one of London's most fashionable hotels. She also runs a boutique in Fulham Road. The Weinbergs live in Holland Park and have a country house in Wiltshire.

James Wood   £40m

INDUSTRIALIST   dob (unknown)

JIM Wood was born a Geordie but has made his fortune thousands of miles away from the Tyne as one of America's top food retailers. The son of a building contractor, he had retailing in his blood. At 14, he became a grocer's apprentice, stacking shelves at a Co-op corner store in Newcastle; later he worked his way up the Co-op before making the move which transformed his career. In 1965, he saw an anonymous advert for a retail director in the *Financial Times*. He landed the job and discovered he was working for Sir James Goldsmith (q.v.).

For the next 15 years, he was a vital part of Goldsmith's operations. When the financier bought a new company he would hand over the day-to-day running to Wood. Wood helped him buy, turn round and sell a dozen retailers and several real estate properties.

By 1980 Wood was becoming restless. For 6 of the 15 years, he had been making Goldsmith a fortune running the Grand Union supermarket chain in America. He felt that he should have an equity stake in the business, but nothing materialized.

It took another billionaire to make Wood rich, although he was wary of the initial approach from Erivan Haub, owner of the Tengelmann chain, who wanted him to run his American business, Great Atlantic & Pacific Tea. 'I said no way in the bloody world would I be interested in another one of these rich guys who wants you to do something for him,' Wood told *Business Week*.

But, unlike Goldsmith, Haub offered Wood what added up to a 10% stake in A & P. This immediately attracted him. 'I stayed up in bed and smoked cigars all night. The next morning I called Jimmy in London and said: "You know who you're talking to? The chairman of A & P."'

At A & P, Wood bought up £600-million worth of new businesses, often poorly run family firms where he introduced strong financial discipline. Initially on a 10-year contract, Wood has signed on for another 5 years beyond the 1990 expiry date. He is described by colleagues as a quiet, serious man, not a joiner. Yet he has a reputation for being tough and un-compromising in dealing with trade unions.

In 1989 he backed an unsuccessful attempt by the manage-ment of the Gateway supermarket chain to mount a buy-out of the group, which was facing a rival takeover bid.

Marquess of Salisbury   £37m

LANDOWNER   dob 24 October 1916

THE Cecil family have long had a distinguished record of public service. In the late 16th century they were ministers to Elizabeth I. Later, the family acquired the title of Marquess of Salisbury. The 3rd Marquess was prime minister in the 19th century, and more recently the Salisbury family have played a decisive role in the Conservative Party.

The family own 13,000 acres in Dorset and two homes: the Manor House at Cranborne and the magnificent Hatfield House in Hertfordshire. Completed in 1612, this house contains numer-ous treasures, including paintings by Dahl, Mytems, Wissing,

Reynolds, Romney and Lawrence. Portraits of Elizabeth I by Nicholas Hilliard have pride of place in the collection.

Much of the family wealth has been held in a nominee company, Gascoyne Holdings, based in London's Charing Cross Road. This enabled the estate to avoid crippling duties when the last Marquess died in 1972.

The present Marquess was seriously injured in an aircraft accident during the war but recovered sufficiently to fight the 1945 election as a Conservative. He lost, but he won the Bournemouth West seat in 1950, giving up in 1954 due to ill health. He was a long-time president of the Conservative Party Monday Club and a prominent supporter of the Smith regime in Rhodesia. One of his sons was killed in the Rhodesian insurgency while reporting on the fighting for the *Daily Telegraph*.

Lady Salisbury took an HGV licence in 1982 to enable her to drive relief supplies to Poland during the period of martial law and food shortages. She is also a highly respected gardener and helped Prince Charles design his gardens at Highgrove House in 1982.

Ronald Diggens   £37m

PROPERTY OWNER   dob 26 November 1911

STARTING after World War I as a £1-a-week surveyor's lad with the property magnate Major Alfred Allnat, Ronald Diggens took over the business when his boss retired. He then served in the army as a bridge-building engineer during World War II, reaching the rank of lieutenant colonel.

After the war, he shrewdly built up two property groups which owned large numbers of factories in north and west London. He was noted as a generous employer and many of his staff had shares in the companies. He is now a large shareholder in the Slough Estates property group, which runs the famous Slough trading estate.

He lives comfortably in Northwood in the north of London, and he has a cottage in Cornwall. A shy bachelor, he took up flying at the age of 48 and sails a dinghy for relaxation.

Duke of Wellington £37m

LANDOWNER dob 2 July 1915

THE hero of Waterloo was given a £200,000 grant by the nation to build a Waterloo Palace, similar to the Duke of Marlborough's Blenheim. But there was not enough money, so the Iron Duke made do with Stratfield Saye in Hampshire instead.

It is now the home of the 8th Duke. As well as this 7,000-acre estate, the family also has 2,300 acres in Spain, a reward for the Iron Duke's role in clearing Spain of Napoleon's troops. The house is filled with the treasures from the Iron Duke's military triumphs and major art works given to him by grateful European monarchs. The family also own Apsley House in London, though they only occupy a flat there today as the rest is a museum.

The Duke was educated at Eton and Oxford. Later he joined the army, rising to the rank of brigadier. Among his many service appointments was that of military attaché in Spain, where he is also the Duke of Vittoria. The eldest of his four sons, the Marquess of Douro, was a member of the European Parliament, and Lady Jane Wellesley, his daughter, was romantically linked with Prince Charles in the late 1970s.

Viscount Allendale £36m

LANDOWNER dob 12 September 1922

A LIFELONG friend of the Royal family who played with the Queen and Princess Margaret as a child, Viscount Allendale is one of the great landowners of the north of England. He has a 20,000-acre estate in Northumberland and two large houses, Allenheads and Bywell Hall. There is a large art collection at Bywell with works by Rembrandt, Turner and Gainsborough.

His early childhood was dogged by accidents. In 1927 he was

rescued from a fire. In 1936 he was nearly electrocuted in the bath and a year later he was injured in a shooting accident. He was an RAF pilot in the war. He was shot down in 1942 and imprisoned in Stalag Luft III.

In 1948 his wedding to Sarah Ismay, daughter of the former Chief of the General Staff, was attended by the Queen, Princess Margaret and Clement Attlee, then prime minister. But he was divorced in 1986. He was a steward of the Jockey Club from 1963 to 1965.

He inherited the title from his father in 1956, and saved the main family estates by selling a large Yorkshire property. In 1986 he indicated that he was preparing to marry a divorcee, but family pressure forced him to cancel the wedding plans.

Lord Barnard £36m

LANDOWNER   dob 21 September 1923

THE 53,000-acre Raby estate in Durham forms the basis of Lord Barnard's wealth. It is centred on two homes: Raby Castle and Selaby Hall.

Harry John Neville Vane is the 11th Lord Barnard. Educated at Eton and later at Durham University, he married Lady Davina Cecil, daughter of the Marquess of Exeter, in 1952. He is a former joint master of the Zetland Hunt, with which Prince Charles has ridden. His daughter married a labourer in 1982.

The Vane family has owned Raby since 1626. In 1714, the entire contents of the castle were sold by the 1st Lord Barnard, because he disapproved strongly of his son's choice of bride. But an extensive art collection was built up after that date. This has portraits by Van Dyck, Reynolds and Batoni.

The estate includes some grouse moors with good shooting and up to 14 miles of fishing. At one time, the estate boasted its own full-time mole catcher, who was paid 2d an acre by Raby tenants.

Sting   £36m

SINGER AND ACTOR   dob 2 October 1951

POP star turned actor turned campaigner to save the Amazon rain forest, Gordon Sumner, alias Sting, started life as a primary school teacher in his native Newcastle upon Tyne after dropping out of Warwick University. The son of a milkman, his name comes from the wasp-striped T-shirts he wore in early stage appearances as a struggling rock musician.

His first big break came in 1976 – not on the stage but when he married Frances Tomelty, the Irish actress. The marriage seemed to release a flood of creative energy in Sting and a string of hits with his band, Police, followed, culminating in the album *Synchronicity*, which sold over 7 million copies.

Sting later left his wife for Trudie Styler, a young actress, and they live in a 17th-century Highgate house which formerly belonged to Sir Yehudi Menuhin. Sting has four children, two by each of the women in his life. Early in 1989, he splashed out £3 million for a luxury apartment overlooking New York's Central Park.

Sting has moved into acting, though he has no formal training. He has appeared in films such as *Quadrophenia*, *Plenty*, *Dune* and *Brimstone and Treacle*. He has also helped his friend Bruce Springsteen by taking part in a world tour on behalf of Amnesty International.

But today, much of Sting's energy is taken up with the fight to save the rain forests in the Amazon basin. After some highly successful concerts in Brazil which culminated in a show before 200,000 people at Rio's Maracana Stadium, he met Chief Raoni of the Kayapo tribe, who inhabit an area of Brazil the size of Italy. The Kayapo are fighting deforestation and Sting joined them in their crusade.

Sting arranged a two-month world tour for the Chief to highlight the plight of his tribe (best known for the large wooden plates inserted in their lower lips) and he has set up the Brazilian-based Rainforest Foundation. So famous has the Chief become that he even appeared on BBC television's *Wogan*. Sting's girlfriend Trudie is vice-president of the Foundation.

He denies that his ambitions will turn to politics: 'I'm a dreamer, a Utopian. I would be no good at full-time politics. And it's exhausting. We've got to do this for the Indians. My feeling is that once they are destroyed then we all are in time,' he recently told *The Times*.

Sir John Barlow and family   £35m

FINANCIERS   dob JB 22 April 1934

WHEN the British Empire was at its most powerful, and the world map was largely coloured red, the Manchester trading firm of Thomas Barlow and Brother was a major beneficiary. Barlow owned huge rubber and tea estates in the Far East with offices in Calcutta, Shanghai and Singapore. At the turn of the century, the head of the family, John Emmott Barlow, was a senior partner in the firm, as well as an active Liberal and MP for Frome in Somerset from 1892 to 1918. He was created a baronet in 1907. When he died in 1932, he was succeeded in the baronetcy by his son John Denman Barlow, who was first a Liberal National MP, and later a Conservative MP until the 1966 General Election.

During his time as an MP, Sir John continued to play a part in the family firm. He was also chairman of the Tory Party Trade and Industry Committee. In 1958, while on a visit to Singapore, he made an offer to buy the City Council's mace, in recognition of the 100 years in which the Barlow family firm had been linked to Singapore. His last major action came during the Falklands war in 1982, when he published a letter he had received in 1968 from Denis Healey, the then Labour defence minister, arguing that the small marine garrison in Port Stanley was big enough to deter aggression. Barlow had been chairman of a Falkland Islands emergency committee set up in 1968.

In 1986, Sir John died, to be succeeded by his eldest son, John Kemp Barlow. The new Sir John Barlow does not sit in Parliament, concentrating instead on running the family businesses. In 1982, the Malaysian government took over many of the

Barlow plantations, and Sir John reinvested the compensation funds in property and other areas. He also streamlined the business into one company, Majedie Investments, with three Barlows on the board. Apart from Sir John, his younger brother Mark is an executive director, while his cousin Henry is a non-executive director. Between them, they have over 14 million shares in the company.

Sir John lives in Cheshire, and lists his hobbies as steeple-chasing, hunting and shooting. He is a steward of the Jockey Club and has four sons. He was a High Sheriff of Cheshire in 1979.

Topham Brinton and family £35m

CARPETS   dob 10 September 1939

IN 1783, a William Brinton established his carpet company in Kidderminster. Topham Brinton is the seventh Brinton to occupy the chairman's seat in the company, still firmly controlled by the family. He is happy to admit that paternalism is alive and well, flourishing in the Victorian factory next to the town hall. But few could dispute the benefits of a paternalist approach that allows the company pensioners to enjoy a subsidized lunch and bingo session every Friday in the social club. 'It helps loyalty. We have 64 people working here who have done over 40 years,' Brinton recently told the *Daily Telegraph*. But the company is no slouch when it comes to new investment. In the next five years it is planning to spend £40 million, to add to the £28 million spent since 1985. In its latest 1989 results, the company produced some £4.9 million after-tax profits on a £74.8 million turnover. Topham Brinton was educated at Eton and Brown University in America. He holds important posts in the British carpet industry governing and advisory bodies, and lists his hobbies as shooting and squash.

Sir Adrian Cadbury and family   £35m

CONFECTIONERY   dob 15 April 1929

IN 1824, a John Cadbury started selling tea and coffee in Birmingham's Bull Street. Seven years later, he opened a small factory to produce cocoa and drinking chocolate. His sons Richard and George expanded the family business, moving to Bournville, still the centre of the group operations. The famous Dairy Milk chocolate was introduced in 1905. Merging first with Fry (in 1919) and later with Schweppes in 1969, the combined group Cadbury Schweppes is now one of the largest confectionery groups in the world, worth £2.2 billion on the stock market at the start of the year.

The Cadbury family are still closely associated with the business. Until 1989, Sir Adrian Cadbury, great-grandson of George Cadbury, was chairman of the group. His younger brother, Dominic, is a brilliant chief executive and credited with piloting the company on a burst of growth, which has enabled it to see off overseas predators in the last few years.

Although when the *Sunday Times* first started looking at the richest people in Britain two years ago, we rejected the Cadbury family as candidates as the family members on the board had under 0.5% of the shares, we have now concluded that the extended family actually has slightly under 4% of the shares, though much of the wealth is in charitable trusts supporting a wide range of deserving causes.

A realistic value for the direct family wealth, taking into account assets such as houses and land, would be around £35 million. The wealth of the individual family members may be gauged from the will of Jocelyn Cadbury, the Conservative MP and younger brother of Adrian, who died in 1982. He left an estate of over £810,000.

George Harrison   £35m

MUSICIAN AND FILM PRODUCER
dob 25 February 1943

EX-BEATLE George was the youngest member of 'the Fab Four'. He later graduated to Indian sitar music and to films as a successful independent producer.

An ardent supporter of the Green movement, George grows his own organic vegetables on his £3 million estate near Henley-on-Thames. Built in 1889 by the millionaire Sir Frank Crisp, Friar Park had formerly been a religious retreat. George rescued and lovingly restored it. The house boasts an Alpine rock garden complete with 20,000 tons of Yorkshire rock, hauled to the site by train.

With his second wife Olivia (his first, the celebrated 1960s model Patti Boyd, went off with Eric Clapton, his best friend), George takes his Green commitment seriously. The couple avoid chlorine-bleached paper and also use the local bottle bank for their empties. They even have a shredder to convert newspapers into garden fertilizer.

Handmade Films, the production company he founded, uses predominantly British casts, crews and studios to produce low-budget but usually highly popular films. Successes have included *The Life of Brian*, *The Long Good Friday*, *Mona Lisa* and *A Private Function*. The only failure was *Shanghai Surprise*, starring Madonna.

George still keeps up his interest in music. When the Beatles split, he topped the charts with his own work 'My Sweet Lord' in 1971, and has since worked with a galaxy of famous stars. His most recent musical venture was to form the Travelling Wilburys – a group which embraced Bob Dylan and the late Roy Orbison. It was set up – in part – as a protest against computerized music.

George's relations with the other ex-Beatles are not always cordial. He refused to join Paul McCartney and Ringo Starr in a reunion for the Live Aid concert. He had been overshadowed by John and Paul, who wrote and sang most of the Beatles hits. He also lacks the royalties that have made Paul (a fellow Green supporter) even richer. But George enjoys considerable wealth. His house includes a recording studio and private cinema. He also has holiday homes in Hawaii and on Australia's Great Barrier Reef. As a treat for his eleven-year-old son, he recently splashed out £10,000 to bring a top American skateboarding team over to Britain.

Nicholas van Hoogstraten £35m

PROPERTY OWNER   dob (unknown)

NICHOLAS van Hoogstraten was once described by a judge as 'a sort of self-imagined devil'. The judge, sentencing Hoogstraten at the time to a four-year sentence for a grenade attack on a synagogue, went on, 'He thinks that he is an emissary of Beelzebub.'

It is an image that Hoogstraten has done nothing to dispel. Indeed, he relishes it: anyone who crosses him 'will come well unstuck but I do not want it traced back to me. It is all well down the line,' he told the *Independent*.

The aura of violence which surrounds the black-suited Hoogstraten has been good for his business as one of Britain's largest residential landlords. His tenants have frequently complained of a reign of terror – including forcible entry to remove their belongings and even the removal of a staircase for one unfortunate tenant. He is on record as saying that his tenants are 'absolute filth', and after one operation when he and a gang entered a tenant's house and hurled the furniture into the road, he said, 'It's the best bit of fun we've had for some time.'

Although Hoogstraten's violence has resulted in a string of convictions and brushes with the law, they have not hindered his money-making skills. The son of a Sussex shipping agent, he made his first fortune through stamps: by the age of 15, his collection was worth £30,000. At 16, he went into the navy for a year, during which he bought land cheaply in the Bahamas. At 17 he entered the property business by buying up four houses in Brighton. All were tenanted, but he managed to sell three with vacant possession at a huge profit and was on the way to his millions. At 22, he was described as Britain's youngest millionaire, with 350 properties in Brighton and Hove alone.

Today there are about 450 properties, of which a third are in west London. He has a £4.5 million mansion in Sussex, built on the site of an old people's home where – predictably – the last old residents were persuaded to leave. The water and electricity were cut off and eventually the old people were removed by the social services department.

At the time, Hoogstraten was living in Liechtenstein for tax reasons, having just paid £5 million, the biggest ever tax bill, to the Inland Revenue.

Apart from the house, Hoogstraten also owns the finest collection of French antiques in Britain, two Turners and a Holbein, and he has extensive overseas property interests.

He is very much a loner. His parents hardly have anything to do with him. He has never married, preferring the company of four mistresses who can't get their hands on his fortune, as he sees it. He has two children by different women. Few people ever visit him at his home or get close to him. One close associate, Rodney Markworth, who met Hoogstraten in prison, became his strong-arm man. But Markworth, who had a long reputation for violence, owed Hoogstraten nearly £9,000 in 1979 and simply disappeared. Hoogstraten was quoted in the press at the time as saying of his former associate: 'He wasn't the cleverest of blokes. I think he stepped out of line and was dealt with.'

Simon Howard   £35m

LANDOWNER   dob 26 January 1956

CASTLE Howard, the setting for the television series *Brideshead Revisited*, is the magnificent home of the Howard family. It was designed by Sir John Vanbrugh at the beginning of the 18th century for John Howard, the 3rd Earl of Carlisle, to replace a partially burnt castle on his Yorkshire estate.

Today, Simon Howard, the third son of the late Lord Howard

of Henderskelfe, runs the 10,000-acre estate which he inherited when his father, chairman of the BBC, died in 1984. His two elder brothers did not want the responsibility. Simon went to Eton and then did an estate management course. In 1983, he married Annette, Countess Compton, the former wife of the Marquess of Northampton. He lists his hobbies as photography, wine and country sports.

Castle Howard is filled with art treasures. There are works by Rubens, Holbein, Van Dyck, Lely, Murillo, Reynolds, Vermeer and Gainsborough. Priceless porcelain, furniture and sculptures complement the paintings. Recently, a bust by Bernini was sold to raise £3 million for death duties.

Simon Howard's forebears include the formidable Rosalind, Countess of Carlisle, in the 19th century. She made her daughters walk barefoot outside in the Yorkshire winter. She was also accused of taking her obsession with temperance too far and pouring wine and beer from the Howard cellars into a lake. She dismissed all the menservants and replaced them with burly parlourmaids when the footmen were too drunk to rescue an equally drunken guest who had slid under the table at dinner.

Sir William Lithgow £35m

INDUSTRIALIST dob 10 May 1934

THE Clyde used to be the cradle of Britain's heavy industry, and the ships built on its banks were proud advertisements for its engineering and shipbuilding expertise. Lithgows, based at Greenock at the river mouth, were regarded as one of the best shipbuilders under the careful management of Sir James Lithgow, the 1st Baronet. In 1908 he had joined the shipbuilding business, Russell and Co. of Port Glasgow, of which his father was one of the three founding partners. Later it became Lithgows, and Sir James, at the age of 29, was chairman of the Clyde Shipbuilders Association.

He continued to play a prominent role in shipbuilding in both world wars right up to his death in 1952. His son William, then a 17-year-old schoolboy at Winchester, inherited the title and an estate valued then at £1.9 million. Sir James had been preparing for the handover for some years. In 1937, at the age of three, William was left a quarter share in the Lithgow group with his two elder sisters. By 1950 some two-thirds of the business and two large estates were in trust for him.

On his father's death, Sir William continued his education at Winchester while his mother ran the family empire. He intended to take a degree at Glasgow University, but his studies were interrupted by illness and he went up to Oxford instead to read engineering. He had to leave the university to do national service, but when an army medical board rejected him, he started work in the shipyard as a 35-shilling-a-week apprentice. In 1956, at the age of 21, he was made a director of the company and three years later he took over from his mother as chairman.

During the halcyon years of the 1950s and 1960s he transformed the yard into one of the most modern shipbuilding facilities in Europe. But the rise of Far East competitors from Japan and then Korea hit the British and European yards heavily in the 1970s. In 1978 the yard was nationalized by the Labour government and Sir William ended a family association that had lasted 100 years.

For years after the takeover, Lithgow fought a campaign right up to the European courts over the £3.5 million compensation given for the loss of the yard. But this was rejected. Despite building up a new and thriving business in farming, marine engineering and electronics, which in its last accounts produced £2.29 million after-tax profits, Sir William never forgot the way he had been treated. In the latest accounts of Lithgow Holdings, he said: 'We could have done without the present government's oppressive behaviour in minimizing the amount of our capital returned to us following the expropriation of the Scott Lithgow companies. I regret the ends the government has gone to in justifying their part in this sorry affair.'

Sir William, who earns a salary of £554,000 as chairman of Lithgow Holdings, lives on the 14,400-acre Ormsary estate, famous for its herd of Highland cattle. A keen shot and amateur photographer, he is anxious to promote viable employment projects in the Kintyre peninsula. He suffered a personal tragedy in 1964, when his first wife died within a few months of their marriage. He remarried three years later and has two sons and a daughter.

Duke of Marlborough   £35m

LANDOWNER   dob 13 April 1926

JOHN Churchill, the 1st Duke of Marlborough, named his new palace after his great victory at the battle of Blenheim. Work started on the palace in 1705, though it was not completed until 1720. He was awarded a £5,000-a-year pension by a grateful nation to add to his army salary of £10,000.

Today, the 11th Duke occupies the only non-royal palace in the country and owns the surrounding 11,500 acres. He has turned the estate into a thriving business enterprise, with a conference centre and accommodation for paying guests.

For much of the 18th and 19th centuries, the Marlborough family lacked the resources to maintain Blenheim properly. The 8th Duke sold off many art treasures, though his son, the 9th Duke, did much to restore the family fortunes. In 1895, he married Consuelo Vanderbilt, daughter of the American industrialist, giving the Blenheim estates access to huge new reserves of capital. The paintings which escaped the 8th Duke's sales included works by Van Dyck, Kneller, Reynolds and Romney.

Sir Winston Churchill was directly related to the Marlborough family. His father, Lord Randolph Spencer-Churchill, was the third son of the 7th Duke.

Peter Savill   £35m

PUBLISHER   dob (unknown)

THIS tough, self-made man comes from the Yorkshire resort town of Scarborough. He went from there to study law at Cambridge. He later worked with John Bentley, the financier, who made his name with what were termed asset-stripping deals in the early 1970s.

Today, Savill's business interests span publishing and real estate in Grand Cayman and the United States. His main American company is International Voyager, which publishes tourism guides and company magazines for cruise ships. His other companies include P & D International, based in Cayman, and Biscayne Holdings. He employs some 70 people, mainly in America.

Savill has three homes: in Cayman, Miami and London's Battersea. Though single, his live-in companion is an air hostess with Eastern Airlines. A devoted fan of the Miami Dolphins American football team, he will travel anywhere to watch them. A loner, his other main passions are gambling and the turf. He is reputed to bet $10,000 a game on the Dolphins. He also loves to play the stock market.

Though very secretive and shy of any publicity, he is best known in the UK for his vast racing interests. He has a remarkable ability to buy likely winners very cheaply. His best-known horse is Chaplins Club, a prolific winner over sprint distances. In 1985 it won a record nine races. Savill paid just 8,000 guineas for the horse as a three-year-old at the Ascot sales. His other good horses included Wiki Wiki Wheels and Time To Go Home.

Ian Skipper   £35m

BUSINESSMAN   dob 28 November 1931

VISITORS to the Jorvik Viking Centre in York can see a reconstruction of a 10th-century village as they travel on an electric trolley, accompanied by a commentary from Magnus Magnusson.

This is a new type of museum and much of the inspiration for it came from Ian Skipper, a local businessman and entrepreneur. Skipper ran a Ford dealership before selling up in the early 1970s to invest in high-technology companies which made his fortune.

He now runs Heritage Projects: the Jorvik Centre was his first one. Others have been developed in Canterbury and Oxford. So successful has the Jorvik Centre been that all its bank loans were paid off in 1990.

Skipper's talents in tourism development have not escaped the notice of the government and he is now a member of the English Tourist Board.

Ivan Twigden   £35m

BUILDER   dob 10 January 1938

RUNNING a housebuilding firm in East Anglia, where house prices were soaring by over 50% a year in the 1980s, proved to be a profitable business for Ivan Twigden. His building firm, Twigden PLC, increased its after-tax profits from £3.9 million to £8.7 million between 1987 and 1988.

But the collapse of house prices and the recession took their toll on Twigden in 1990. After-tax profits in 1989 had reached £9.8 million, but in 1990, they fell to £5.2 million. With 85% of the shares, Twigden's stake would have fallen from £60 million to around £35 million in value.

Twigden lives on a farm in Kimbolton in Cambridge and lists his hobbies as tennis, golf and bridge. He is a former county squash men's singles winner and he played tennis for Bedfordshire. He also owns racehorses, trained by Josh Gifford and Geoffrey Huffer. His best horses have been called, appropriately, Show Home and Showhouse.

Leslie Waddington   £35m

ART DEALER   dob (unknown)

IN 1957, Leslie Waddington started in business as an art dealer with his father Victor Waddington. In 1966, Victor withdrew to a small gallery in Mayfair, leaving his son to run their original gallery. Badly needing capital, Leslie turned to Alex Bernstein, now the chairman of Granada Television. Within seconds, Bernstein agreed to back Waddington, and today still has a half stake in the business. Waddington prospered, and in 1976, he merged with Arthur Tooth & Son to form one of the top modern art dealers in Europe. Today, it has four galleries in Cork Street, Mayfair and another round the corner. In its latest accounts for 1989, Waddington Galleries produced sparkling after-tax profits of £14.4 million on a £74 million turnover. Waddington is highly critical of Britain's lack of interest in art compared with France. In 1990, he hit the headlines by attacking the 'greed and stupidity' of the auction houses for causing a downturn in the art market.

Frederick and Michael Evans   £34m

PROPERTY DEVELOPERS   dob (unknown)

THE son of a Leeds tailor, Frederick Evans decided early in life that he did not like sewing and stitching. So he went into transport work around Leeds with one or two lorries. From there he went on to develop a small-scale housebuilding business. Later, he moved into building tower blocks, including a 16-storey building which at the time was the highest in Leeds.

Evans, who once said he had no hobbies other than work, is still chief executive of the group though he is now in his nineties. In his mid eighties he came into the office every day. His son Michael is deputy chairman. In 1962, they sold some businesses to a London property group, Estates Property Investment Company, for £1.4 million worth of shares.

Today, Evans of Leeds is one of Yorkshire's biggest property developers, with a number of major developments in the Leeds area. It came to the stock market in 1971 and is worth around £67 million today. Half the shares are owned by Frederick and Michael Evans.

In the mid-1980s, Evans switched from industrial property to offices and shops, neatly catching the boom in retailing and the service economy. One of the company's latest developments is a new £100-million shopping centre, planned with Yorkshire Water in south Leeds on the site of an old sewage works.

Michael and David Green £34m

VIDEO AND TELEVISION PRODUCTION
dob DG 14 February 1946, MG 2 December 1947

FOR a boy who left school half-way through his A-level economics course because it was too boring, Michael Green has not done too badly.

Born into a comfortable north London family, with a textile business which he did not join, he had his own photographic and printing operation by the time he was 20. Today, his Carlton Communications is worth nearly £750 million on the stock market and he bought Technicolor, the world-famous American film processing business.

Green, an unassuming man, is determined to build Carlton into one of the world's major television and entertainment businesses for the 1990s. He has the right connections. He used to play poker regularly with one of the Saatchi brothers (q.v.), plays bridge with the financier Jim Slater (q.v.), and was married to a daughter of Lord Wolfson (q.v.), the stores magnate, although they are now separated. (Lord Young, the former Secretary of State for Industry, is a cousin of the Wolfsons.) He lives in a comfortable Mayfair flat, drives a Mercedes and has a mill house in the country.

David, his elder brother, is still on the Carlton board but devotes more of his energies to Colefax & Fowler, the upmarket wallpaper and home furnishings group, in which he has a 40% stake.

Carlton's position as the major force in servicing British television companies was confirmed in 1989 when Michael Green took over the rival UEI group in a friendly bid worth £513 million. In view of the deregulation of television, he could make an even bigger mark on the broadcasting scene in the 1990s.

In 1990, the shares of Carlton Communications were under pressure, though its financial position is very strong, with no borrowings.

Nurdin Jivraj   £34m

HOTELIER   dob 13 January 1933

NURDIN Jivraj first set up in business as a 19-year-old in the Tanzanian capital of Dar-es-Salaam. That was in 1959 and it was the start of his first business empire. Wisely he invested in Britain in the 1960s, so that when his private assets were nationalized in Tanzania in 1967 he had the resources to start again when he arrived in Britain in 1971.

He acquired hotels in the Kensington area of London and then moved into residential property. By 1984, Nurdin had bought the London Park Hotels group for £13 million and his son Nick had also joined the business.

Since then, companies and stakes in them have been regularly bought and sold for a profit. In January 1989 father and son took over Leisuretime International from the Beaverbrook family. They have turned round Leisuretime from loss to profit and renamed it Buckingham International. In 1989–90, Buckingham's pre-tax profits reached £5.9 million, against £5.41 million in the previous year.

Nurdin and Nick Jivraj have not been slow to look for new opportunities, acquiring a Portuguese property group and later a new hotel in Lisbon. The hotel cost them some £14.7 million in cash. They have also moved into the British retirement home business by buying a 5% stake in Anglia Secure Homes.

Thomas and Gordon Black £32m

INDUSTRIALISTS
dob TB 17 November 1938, GB 2 March 1943

ONE of the finest private collections of old cars in the country – worth at least £8 million – sits in an anonymous warehouse in Keighley, West Yorkshire. Among the 200 cars on display is an 1894 German Benz, one of only 67 produced. The collection was started by Peter Black, who arrived in Britain as a 25-year-old in 1933 to escape Nazi persecution of the Jews. His first job was in London working for an uncle who built cars on a small scale under the name Sabella.

On the outbreak of war, Black moved to Keighley to join a company making webbing for the armed forces. When peace came, Black bought out the Keighley branch and shrewdly started making shopping bags out of the army surplus material. Peter Black died in 1977, leaving his two sons, Thomas and Gordon, who are joint chairmen, to run the flourishing business. It has some 3,500 employees in 17 companies making footwear, ceramics, toiletries and furniture. It is a major supplier to Marks & Spencer, producing pre-tax profits of £5.3 million in the first half of 1990.

The car collection was started in 1960 when Peter Black was laid up with a slipped disc, and his family doctor, a vintage car enthusiast himself, suggested that he started the same sort of hobby. He did and was hooked, reading all the books on vintage cars, visiting auctions and, dressed in old gardening clothes, supervising the restoration of his first car, a 1922 Rolls-Royce Silver Ghost. He had found it in a Scarborough orchard with a tree growing through the bonnet; the price was £30, with another £40 spent on getting it back to Keighley. Today, the collection costs around £1,500 a month to maintain, and the Black brothers are keen that it should pay its way. As a result, a number of the cars have been exhibited to raise funds. The brothers regularly take part in the London to Brighton race and hire out the cars for films such as *Those Magnificent Men in Their Flying Machines*.

Robin Lodge £32m

COMPUTER ENTREPRENEUR   dob (unknown)

ROBIN Lodge started his business career as general manager of a computer timeshare business in 1968. That was sold in 1975 to an American company and two years later he branched out into software, founding Metier to market Artimus, a package used for project planning. By 1985 his was a highly successful company, with sales of over £70 million in some 36 countries worldwide. He sold the business that year to Lockheed, the American aerospace giant, for £75 million.

Two years later, on the day of the stock market crash in October 1987, he resurfaced by taking a stake with a fellow entrepreneur, Brooke Johns, in a small quoted shell company called Nesco Investments, which used to supply electricity to Nigeria. They used Baytree Investments, a Cayman Islands company they controlled, to make their move. Nesco is now moving into the computer business after two acquisitions.

In 1976 Lodge married Mary Groves, daughter of Sir Charles Groves, conductor with the Royal Philharmonic Orchestra. They have three daughters. He lives on a farm in West Sussex, and lists his hobbies as music, vintage cars, country pursuits and farming.

Viscount Mountgarret £32m

LANDOWNER   dob 8 November 1936

THE present Lord Mountgarret has a penchant for minor controversy. In the mid-1980s he was accused of blazing away with his gun at a hot air balloon which had disturbed his grouse shooting. In 1987 he exercised aristocratic privilege by having a vicar removed from a parish church within the family estate. He accused the priest, the Rev. John Steggall, of looking like the character Compo from the Yorkshire TV series: he had turned up for Sunday service having forgotten to change into his Sunday best. The Bishop of Ripon acceded to Mountgarret's request and the Rev. Mr Steggall went to a small fishing parish near Edinburgh.

Mountgarret had a classic aristocratic education, moving from Eton to the Royal Military Academy, Sandhurst and retiring from the Irish Guards as a captain. The Mountgarret title is originally Irish, going back to the 16th century. The family name is Butler, and one of Mountgarret's ancestors was the Butler Earl of Ormond, who led the Irish rebellion against Elizabeth I as general of all the Irish forces.

The rebellion was unsuccessful and led to the Flight of the Earls, in which the majority of the Irish Catholic aristocracy fled to the Continent. This deprived Ireland of a native-born leadership for almost 300 years. In 1660 the family were pardoned and by the late 18th century had established links with Yorkshire. Mountgarret sits in the House of Lords as a Conservative with the title of Baron Mountgarret.

He has been married three times, his second and third wives being the daughters of army officers. He is a member of White's and Pratt's, and enjoys shooting and fishing on his 20,000-acre estate near Harrogate.

Earl of Seafield £32m

LANDOWNER   dob 20 March 1939

THE Earl of Seafield's mother was reputed to be the wealthiest woman in Britain after the Queen. At one stage she owned 800 square miles of prime Scottish land, including grouse moors, salmon rivers, forestry and farms. She was able to stave off some of the death duties on the estate by transferring much of the land to her son. He inherited the title in 1969.

Since then, he has sold off some of his inheritance. In 1972, he raised £1 million by selling a 21,000-acre estate. In 1975, he sold the entire contents of Cullen House, the family seat, for £300,000. He gave a major armoury of antique weapons to the nation in 1976. But he still retains property in the Bahamas.

The Earl, known as Ginger, was educated at Eton. He has

been married twice. His first wife, a City stockbroker's daughter, gave him two sons. They were divorced in 1971, and in the same year he married again. He survived a serious air crash in 1958.

Leslie Silver £31m

PAINTS   dob 22 January 1925

BORN in London, where his family were involved in the East End rag trade, Leslie Silver was an early supporter of Arsenal. He went to his first football match in 1934 at the age of 9, taken by an uncle to see legendary players such as Alex James. 'They mesmerized me,' he told the *Sunday Times* football correspondent in 1990. Today, Silver is chairman of Leeds United, his adopted city. He has masterminded the football club's return to its position as one of the country's top clubs, a status it enjoyed under the late Don Revie in the 1960s and early 1970s.

But aside from his love of football, Silver's other passion is his paint business, Kalon Paints, based in West Yorkshire. It was founded in 1947, after Silver came out of the RAF, where he had served from 1943 to 1946, rising to be a warrant officer. With his wartime gratuity and loans, he raised £1,000 to start the business. By 1991, it was so highly regarded on the stock market that when Silver sold 18.5% of the shares, he had no trouble finding buyers. The sale netted him nearly £12 million, but still left his family interests with over £19 million worth of shares. He was awarded an OBE in 1982.

Bill Benyon £30m

LANDOWNER, MP   dob 17 January 1930

BILL Benyon, the Conservative MP for Milton Keynes, is one of the few rich men to have been educated at the Royal Naval College, Dartmouth. He is even more unusual in being a very major landowner in a prime south-east county, Berkshire.

In 1956, he left the navy after nine years' service and joined Courtaulds to pursue a commercial career. This plan went awry in 1964 when a cousin died without an heir and left him one of the finest houses and estates in the Home Counties.

This was Englefield House and estate near Newbury, acquired by his ancestors in the 18th century; in 1880 it stood at 16,007 acres spread across Berkshire, Essex and Hampshire. When Benyon inherited it, it totalled 14,000 acres, concentrated at Englefield. The house is not open to the public although it is large and contains many fascinating artefacts. It is used by the local people for school parties and events, and forms the centre of a community, linked to the local village but with the estate and its tenants at its heart.

In a revealing interview given to *The Times* in 1985, Benyon described how he had saved the local post office and store, kept the developers at bay and commuters out, and revived the local school through a merger. 'But we must get away from the old paternalism,' he told *The Times*.

In the House of Commons he has had what might be called a 'quiet' career. He was a parliamentary private secretary to the minister of housing in 1972–4 and a Conservative whip from 1974 to 1976. Normally this sort of progress should have led to a ministerial post, however junior, in the current government. But it has not, largely because Bill Benyon allied himself very firmly with the 'wets' and was a prominent member of Francis Pym's Centre Forward group, which sought to reorient the party away from Thatcherite policies.

His favourite story, told to *The Times*, concerns the media mogul and Labour supporter Robert Maxwell (q.v.), whom he beat in the 1970 election. He tells how when they met years later, 'Captain Bob' Maxwell put his arm around Benyon's shoulder and said: 'Bill, that's one of the best things you ever did for me.'

He is a Deputy Lord Lieutenant for the county of Berkshire and a local Justice of the Peace, and belongs to Boodles, the same club as did his ancestor in the 1880s.

Aldo and Frank Berni   £30m

EX-RESTAURATEURS   dob (unknown)

IN the 1920s, Louis Berni and his two sons, Frank and Aldo, moved from South Wales to Exeter looking for a better living. Louis bought an ice-cream factory, while his two sons used a legacy of £200 each to open a café in 1930. By the outbreak of war, they had some half dozen cafés in the South-West, but in the Luftwaffe's terror raids in 1942, two were destroyed and the brothers moved to Bristol to run their surviving businesses. After the war, they expanded by buying a restaurant in Bristol, followed by the 15th-century New Inn in Gloucester. They soon realized that the British public hungered for beef and steak in the period of postwar austerity. When meat rationing was lifted, their steak houses became enormously popular, with set meals and prices. Between 1954 and 1969, they opened over 200 Berni Inns in converted pubs. In 1970, the business was sold to Grand Metropolitan for some £15 million. Some £7 million of that money was put in trust for the Berni brothers' daughters. Frank Berni now lives in retirement in Jersey, while Aldo still lives in the West Country.

Alan Brazier   £30m

VACUUM CLEANERS   dob (unknown)

IN 1973, Alan Brazier was a mixed farmer who ran his own contract cleaning firm as a sideline. But after an awful experience trying to clean the carpets at Newport Pagnell service station – which resulted in his machines breaking down and some 30 hours of cleaning by hand – Brazier determined to design his own cleaner. In his farm workshop, he used a milk churn to come up with a prototype for a new and highly efficient machine named the Invader, which enabled Brazier to capture 70% of the industrial cleaning market. He took the plunge and gave up farming, selling his 500-acre farm and racehorses. In 1977, he came up with the three-in-one VAX machine for the domestic market, which cleans up spills as well as vacuuming and washing the carpet. It proved a huge success, so much so that VAX now ranks second in the British vacuum-cleaning market behind mighty Hoover. In its latest annual results to the end of March 1989, Brazier's holding company, Quillgold Ltd, produced some £5.7 million after-tax profits on a £57.7 million turnover. Most of the shares are held by Brazier and his family. The company is based at a new £10 million factory in the Worcestershire town of Droitwich. It has also opened factories in Australia and America.

Alan Bristow   £30m

HELICOPTERS AND TRANSPORT
ENTREPRENEUR   dob 3 September 1923

THE term bulldog breed could have been coined for Alan Bristow, a tough businessman who made his name building the largest helicopter operation in the world.

A wartime sailor who joined the Fleet Air Arm in 1943, Bristow once described himself as 'red, white and blue to the core'. His pugnacious style was evident when he was chief test pilot for Westland after the war for three years. He quit in spectacular style by punching his boss on the nose and storming out to join the French Foreign Legion as a mercenary. For two years he flew missions for the French in Indo-China, earning a Croix de Guerre and enough money to start his own helicopter company.

Air Whaling, founded in 1953, specialized in guiding whaling ships in Antarctica. Bristow developed a technique for firing the harpoons at the whales from helicopters, but it was so deadly that the Whaling Commission banned all whaling from the air in 1954. But Bristow by that stage had sold the invention to a Dutch company and moved on to other helicopter work.

The oil industry proved to be fertile ground for Bristow, who was introduced to Shell by an old friend, the late Sir Douglas

Bader. Bristow built up a large fleet of 140 helicopters supporting the oil industry round the world, particularly in the North Sea. He found time off to run British United Airlines in the late 1960s, leading the company in an industrial dispute with its pilots. In 1977 he had another dispute with his helicopter crews, resulting in a public inquiry. Lord McDonald, who headed it, said of Bristow: 'He has a turn of phrase more suited to the barrack room than the boardroom.' By the early 1980s he had reduced his stake in the helicopter business, selling the equity to British & Commonwealth Holdings, an early backer. In 1983 the sale of a 7% stake netted Bristow £10 million, leaving him with 13%, valued at £17 million.

In 1985 Bristow led an abortive bid to take over Westland, where he had first worked. But the £89 million bid (into which Bristow had put £8 million of his own money) was eventually withdrawn. Later, during the 1985–6 Westland crisis, he claimed that he had been offered a knighthood in return for supporting an American takeover for the ailing helicopter group. But he vigorously opposed the US bid.

Today Bristow lives on his 1,400-acre Cranleigh estate in Surrey, working on a new project. He has sunk an estimated £10 million into designing a revolutionary rubber-wheeled tram and has a working model hurtling round the grounds of the estate. With a strong team of high-powered professionals he developed his prototype in just 16 months. His reward: a potential £40-million contract to build a system in Southampton.

In 1977 Bristow was refused planning permission to knock down the Elizabethan manor house on his Baynards Park estate, which had been built by Sir George More, cousin of Sir Thomas More. The cost of refurbishment would have been £750,000. Less than two years later the house was burnt down while Bristow was abroad, and in 1980 he was given permission to build his dream home. By 1988 he had spent £1 million on house improvements, including a helicopter landing pad. As well as owning a six-seater plane, Bristow also has *Twirlybird*, a £1 million yacht, and a £300,000 Mediterranean penthouse and marina berth.

Peter Cameron-Webb   £30m

FORMER UNDERWRITER   dob (unknown)

THERE are a lot of people in Britain who would like to meet Peter Cameron-Webb again, preferably on British soil and in a court of law. A former star underwriter on the Lloyds insurance market, Cameron-Webb and his partner, Peter Dixon, fled to America in 1982 with over £130 million of their clients' money. The list of clients reads like *Who's Who*, and includes the Duchess of Kent, Lord Portman, the Duchess of Marlborough and Virginia Wade, the former tennis star.

Over a number of years, Cameron-Webb and Dixon simply siphoned off the money from various Lloyds syndicates, known as the PCW syndicates after Cameron-Webb's initials. This money went into offshore tax havens, disguised as reinsurance contracts. But when the scandal was uncovered, Cameron-Webb and Dixon fled to America. It took years for the British authorities to unravel the complex case, by which time it was too late for the pair to be extradited to Britain to face justice. Although both have reached a settlement with Lloyds involving hefty fines, they continue to be out of reach of the long arm of British law.

Stanley Clarke   £30m

PROPERTY DEVELOPER   dob 7 June 1932

IN 1954 Stan Clarke, a Staffordshire plumber who had had ambitions to be a farmer, started his own village plumbing business with capital of £100. He later moved into housebuilding and some 33 years later sold the business to the giant BICC group for £51 million. Clarke himself owned 80% of the shares in his Clarke Securities, which by then was one of Britain's largest private housebuilders. In 1986 it sold more than 600 homes at an average price of £52,000 under the name 'Clarke Quality Homes'.

Clarke moved out of housebuilding but kept the property development side of his business, called St Modwen Properties (after the patron saint of beer). Through St Modwen he is actively developing sites as far apart as Plymouth, Sheffield, London and Manchester. But he is particularly active on his home patch in Staffordshire and in 1987 he pulled off his biggest coup in beating off a fierce challenge from rival developers to win control of the former National Garden Exhibition site in Stoke for over £7 million.

In 1988 work started on a £100 million redevelopment of the site, which included a huge Toys 'R' US store. Clarke took the controls of the first excavator on site, promising that over 2,000 jobs would be created on what had been a derelict area before the garden festival.

He was educated at the Burton-on-Trent technical high school and lists his hobbies as farming, horses and building heritage. He chairs the appeal for the restoration of Lichfield Cathedral. At a meeting of leading industrialists to raise the £1.25 million funds needed, he said: 'Sweat, blood and tears built the cathedral. We are the captains of industry and it is part of our responsibility to help sustain this building in the most substantial way.'

Reflecting his interest in training point-to-point racehorses, Clarke took over Uttoxeter racecourse in early 1989, saying: 'Uttoxeter's future as a jumping course is secure. We have no high-falutin plans for flat or all-weather tracks – just to improve the racing and the course and make it better for owners, trainers and jockeys as well as the public.' As he was buying the course, his wife Hilda's horse, Honest Word, had just given jockey Martin Pipe his 107th win of the season.

Joan and Jackie Collins £30m

ACTRESS AND AUTHORESS
dob Joan 23 May 1933, Jackie 4 October 1937

THE two daughters of a show-business agent have become richer and more famous than even their late father could have hoped. Joan, the eldest, was still a stunning beauty as she approached retirement age. She was a *Playboy* centrefold at the age of 50. After three years playing super-bitch Alexis in the soap series, *Dynasty*, she is now branching out on a new career in novels and film production. She has already had one best-seller with her first novel, *Prime Time*, and has finished a second.

Jackie, her younger sister, tried acting but found her talent lay in writing steamy novels such as *The World is Full of Married Men* and *Hollywood Husbands*. Her total sales to date have been 100 million, and in 1989 she received a world record advance of £10 million for three books.

Joan started out as a Rank starlet, appearing in best-forgotten films such as *The Girl in the Red Velvet Swing*. Along the way, she acquired husbands. To date she has had four: the actor Anthony Newley was number two. Her fourth marriage, to former Swedish pop star Peter Holm, lasted barely a year. He was 14 years her junior. Her career really took off in the 1970s when she appeared in explicit films of Jackie's novels, *The Bitch* and *The Stud*. But it is her role as Alexis that made her an international star and allowed her to make some lucrative commercials, such as the Cinzano advert with the late Leonard Rossiter.

She has a Los Angeles mansion and a £2 million home in the south of France. She gave another south of France villa to Peter Holm after a bitter divorce battle.

Jackie lives in Beverly Hills with her husband Oscar Lerner, owner of the Tramp disco. Until the early 1980s they lived in London, but then decided to pack up and leave for California. Many of the characters in her novels are based on real-life figures she knows from the film world, but she refuses to reveal who for fear of precipitating huge libel claims.

Though her novels are full of sexual antics, Jackie herself leads a quiet life and drives a battered Cadillac. She once told Jean Rook of the *Daily Express*: 'People dash up to me at parties to tell me the strangest things.... What goes on in Tinseltown makes my books read like nursery school.'

Timothy Colman and family £30m

NEWSPAPERS AND INHERITANCE
dob 19 September 1929

EARLY in the 19th century, a Jeremiah Colman took over a water mill in East Anglia and in 1814 announced in an advert in the *Norfolk Chronicle* 'that he will continue the manufacturing of mustard, and he takes leave to assure those who may be pleased to favour him with their orders that they shall be supplied in such a manner as cannot fail to secure their approbation'. The business prospered and moved to Norwich in 1856, where it had a steam-driven mill. At the same time, the number of employees rose from 200 to 1500. In the late 19th century, Colmans expanded overseas and started to come into direct competition with a Hull-based company, Reckitt & Sons. The competition nearly killed both companies and, in 1913, they decided to pool their talents and established a joint trading company to handle their business in South America. In 1938, they merged all their activities and became Reckitt & Colman. Today, Reckitt & Colman is a major force in the British health and household products market. But the Colman family no longer play a major role in the business, which is in the hands of professional managers, and largely owned by City institutions. There is one Colman on the board as chairman, Sir Michael Jeremiah Colman. But he has a tiny stake in the business.

Much of the family wealth today is tied up in the local newspaper group, Eastern Counties Newspapers, which in its latest accounts for 1989, produced £12.2 million after-tax profits on a £96.5 million turnover. Timothy Colman, the current chairman of the group, is well-connected with Norfolk and East Anglia society, and married to Lady Mary Bowes-Lyon, a cousin of the Queen Mother.

Martin Dawes   £30m

COMMUNICATIONS ENTREPRENEUR
dob (unknown)

MARTIN Dawes was born into the communications industry. The son of a television and radio engineer, he
started his business career in the 1960s by opening his own
television rental shop in Stockport. By a combination of aggressive advertising and good highstreet sites, the business has
prospered despite the general decline of the television rental
market. Today, there are 22 outlets with a turnover of nearly
£20 million.

But Dawes's great strength is his expanding mobile communications business. He claims to have been one of the first
people to spot the potential of the mobile phone and Martin
Dawes Communications, based in Warrington, is one of the
largest independent retailers in Britain. It has also recently
expanded into Germany and France, while it is signing up new
subscribers at the rate of 1,000 a week. Dawes aims to gain up
to 15% of the European market. In 1989, the Racal telecommunications group paid £7 million for a 20% stake in the
business, leaving Dawes and his family with the rest, then worth
£28 million. He is planning a stock market flotation of the business.

The opportunities for growth seemed limitless, as *Business*
magazine noted: 'Martin Dawes recently installed a computerized billing system that can handled 200,000 subscribers,
six times its present customer base. If it and the other service
providers can tap successfully into the corporate market, their
licence to print money could run and run.' But the 1991 Budget,
which taxed car phones and mobile phones as a business perk,
is likely to limit future growth.

Dawes is a popular man with the Manchester financial community. A fervent Northerner, he believes that businesses in the
South have it easy when getting backing from the City of
London. He is also renowned for his willingness to try out new
ideas and is said to have a strong sense of humour.

He lives in considerable style in mid-Cheshire with his family of two children. He expects them to carry on the family business.

Sheena Easton   £30m

SINGER   dob *c.* 1959

THE first singer ever to have had hits in all five of the American *Billboard* magazine's charts was born in a Lanarkshire council house outside Glasgow. Sheena Easton was the youngest of six children, whose father died when she was ten. Raised by her mother, who worked in a factory to support the family, Sheena showed academic ability and became a drama student, graduating from Glasgow University in 1979.

Prompted by her then husband – a folk-singer called Sandi Easton – whom she married at 19, she entered *The Big Time*, a BBC television talent-spotting show hosted by Esther Rantzen. The experts on the show said she would never make the big time, but she proved them wrong. A string of hits followed, including the 1981 Bond theme, 'For Your Eyes Only'. She became the first girl to have two hits in the British top ten at the same time.

It was in America, where she went in 1982, that Sheena's career took off. She topped the charts with what was dubbed the secretaries' anthem, '9 to 5'. She became equally popular in Japan, and the money soon piled up.

She bought a huge 1930s Hollywood house set in 2 acres and, divorced from her first husband, married again. But that marriage, to Hollywood agent Rob Light, lasted just 13 months.

Her career has been helped by her association with the top singer, Prince. In 1987 they had a big worldwide hit called 'U Got the Look'. She has also turned to acting and appeared in the popular television series, *Miami Vice*, as the wife of Sonny Crockett, a detective played by Hollywood heart-throb Don Johnson.

Regarded as a shrewd businesswoman in her own right, Sheena has bought a home for her hard-working mother by the

English seaside as a thank you for all the years of struggle. She told one interviewer that her mother is her 'role model', adding: 'Being brought up the way I was in Scotland, I saw hardship throughout my early life. My mother was left to raise six of us by herself. I was a selfish little teenager, going, "I've got to have a new dress and a pair of high heels for the school dance or everyone will laugh at me," but she always pulled through. Maybe the Christmas dress wouldn't be paid off until August, but she never fell apart.'

Dave Gilmour and Nick Mason £30m

POP STARS   dob (unknown)

DAVE Gilmour and Nick Mason are two of the original members of the hugely successful 1960s group, Pink Floyd, which made an amazing come-back in the 1980s. In the two years of 1988 and 1989, Pink Floyd's income reached over £35 million, making them the seventh highest-paid performers in the world. They have also had huge success in the record field. In May 1988, their album *Dark Side of the Moon* finally dropped out of the American Billboard Top 100 chart after an unbroken 725 weeks. All told, by the end of the 1980s they had sold around 60 million albums, and the entire production of a German compact disc factory is now devoted to Pink Floyd CDs.

Pink Floyd were formed in 1967 under the leadership of Roger Waters, an only child who had been raised in Cambridge by his widowed mother. Through the 1960s, they were at the centre of the psychedelic culture associated with the drug LSD. In the 1970s, their live performances were dominated by sophisticated light shows, fireworks, crashing planes and inflatable pigs.

In 1983, Waters left the band after a public row with Dave Gilmour, Pink Floyd's guitarist. Gilmour and drummer Nick Mason were rejoined by Rick Wright, who had retired from the band some years previously. Despite efforts by Waters to prevent them using the name Pink Floyd, they continued to do so and made a fortune on their spectacular tours. In 1984, Waters took them to court over the issue and a protracted legal battle followed, with no result in sight, though there have been reports that an out-of-court settlement has been reached.

Despite the legal wrangles, Pink Floyd have continued to play before thousands of fans. At Versailles in 1988 they performed before 80,000 people, putting on a show with £1 million-worth of lasers sweeping the sky. In the summer of 1989, they held a controversial concert in Venice before 200,000 fans that left a trail of rubbish and excrement in the city.

Gilmour and Mason have done well out of the tours and record sales. In 1989 Mason bought a 17th-century house near Hampstead Heath in London for £2.5 million, beating Dave Stewart (q.v.) of the Eurythmics to the property.

Everard Goodman   £30m

PROPERTY DEVELOPER   dob 24 February 1932

EVERARD Goodman is the publicity-shy founder of a profitable property company known as TOPS Estates, originally called Trust of Property Shares Ltd. During the 1980s the company specialized in shop-related assets, prospering through the boom in the retail sector that was a hallmark of the early Thatcher years. Goodman's roots go back to shops, when he built up the Collingwood group, which incorporated County Jewellers. He sold this group in 1971/2 following a bad car smash, and stayed out of the market for a few years.

Sensing the coming boom at the end of the 1970s, he began a series of unspectacular but key purchases, first of Crawley Town Centre, then Basildon Town Centre, Dewsbury Town Centre and Corby Town Centre. Crawley benefited enormously from the boom at Gatwick, and Corby became one of the real success stories of the Midlands.

Despite the downturn at the end of the 1980s, none of these four key sites looks at all vulnerable. Goodman's approach to development is described by the trade as 'ultra-conservative', and TOPS has very low borrowings. He is described by associates as someone who treats short-term income as irrelevant and goes for maximizing rents on prime central sites while simultaneously maximizing asset value.

He has never indulged in publicity on the grounds that it does not earn money for the shareholder. One of his sons is a stockbroker in London. Goodman was born in Leeds. His wealth derives from his 20 million shares in his businesses.

Duke of Grafton   £30m

LANDOWNER   dob 3 April 1919

THE dukedom was one of four created for the bastard sons of Charles II. The 1st Duke, Henry Fitzroy, was the son of Barbara Villiers, royal favourite and Duchess of Cleveland. The 11th Duke, who now bears the title, lives at the family seat, Euston Hall in Suffolk. The family used to own land around Euston in London but that has now gone. Their holdings are comparatively small today, consisting of just 10,500 acres.

But Euston Hall has a unique collection of late 17th-century portraits. These include works by Van Dyck, Lely, Van Somer and Mytens. A famous Stubbs, *Mares and Foals*, hangs in the entrance to the hall.

The Duke, educated at Eton and Cambridge, served in the Grenadier Guards. He is a godfather to the Duke of York, while his wife, Ann, is Mistress of the Robes to the Queen. The Earl of Euston, his heir, is married to a daughter of the Marquess of Lothian and is a director of several large City institutions.

The Duke is a fervent conservationist and is chairman of numerous preservation bodies, including the Society for the Protection of Ancient Buildings. His father pulled down two-thirds of Euston Hall, owing to the high cost of maintenance.

Eric Grove   £30m

PROPERTY DEVELOPER   dob 30 April 1930

A MIDLANDS builder, Eric Grove started his own company, Canberra, in 1968 after working for a Stourport, Worcestershire company. He built high-quality middle-price homes along the M1 corridor to Milton Keynes, along the M5 to Bristol and in the Southampton area.

Based in Solihull, Grove expanded Canberra to the point where it made £8.3 million pre-tax profits on a turnover of £51 million in 1988. In November that year, Grove and his family sold 60% of the company to Alfred McAlpine and there are plans to float the group on the stock market, where it is likely to be valued at £100 million. Under the terms of the deal, Grove and his family were paid special dividends of £3 million per year for two years, with more to come when the group is floated.

Bobby McAlpine (q.v.), the chairman of the group, said at the time of the purchase, 'We have had our eye on Canberra for some considerable time and we have followed them with admiration. Of all the companies we have followed, they have made the shrewdest purchases of land.'

Under the takeover, Grove is responsible for all the land deals in the combined operation. He lives in the Lapworth area of Birmingham.

Paul Judge   £30m

FOOD MANUFACTURER   dob (unknown)

P AUL Judge's formidable intellect was evident at an early age. He won an open scholarship to Trinity College, Cambridge, in 1968, graduating in 1971 with a BA in natural sciences. He then won a Thouron scholarship to the prestigious Wharton Business School at the University of Pennsylvania, where he graduated with an MBA in 1973.

He joined the British food and drinks group, Cadbury Schweppes, as a financial analyst and quickly impressed the management with his skills. Early in 1974, he was made group planning director and later, while still in his twenties, became deputy finance director. Spells in Kenya and America broadened his career, and in 1982 he was appointed managing director of Cadbury Typhoo, best known for its famous tea and the chimpanzee television adverts.

In 1984, Dominic Cadbury, the new chief executive of the food group, asked Judge to become group planning director, his first task being to sell off unwanted businesses. He had no problem in selling some of the businesses, such as Jeyes, to existing managers, but despite a dozen inquiries from large companies he could not get the right terms for the food manufacturing business, which made products such as Marvel, Smash and Hartley's jam.

By Christmas 1985 Judge was feeling disappointed with the results and went to ask Dominic Cadbury if he could mount a buy-out of the food businesses. Cadbury gave him eight days to present proposals to a board meeting. Using a business school contact, he managed to raise the necessary £97 million funding and support from eight other directors. After some protracted bargaining – with other foods groups showing interest in snatching the prize from Judge and his team – they finally took over the food business early in 1986. It was renamed Premier Brands and appeared to have a tricky future loaded down with debt. But Judge was able to slash overheads and costs, and he won over the staff completely by giving them shares in the business. Using the 1984 Finance Act, which granted executives share options in a company, Judge promptly treated his staff as executives and devised a share scheme for all 5,000 of them.

Within two years, trading profits had quadrupled and the group was planning a stock market flotation in 1989. But in March that year, the board of Premier decided to put the group up for sale to the highest bidder. Judge disagreed with that decision and resigned as chairman, though he still remained on the board. In May, the group was taken over by Hillsdown Holdings for £215 million. Judge received Hillsdown shares worth over £36 million and agreed to sell them only on a phased basis until the end of 1991. He took a sabbatical to consider his future after his decision to leave Premier.

He is a Freeman of the City of London and Fellow of the Royal Society of Arts. He lives on a farm near Droitwich in Worcestershire. A modest man who drives a battered old car, Judge has already spent £8 million funding a new Management School at Cambridge. He has also backed a new magazine, *Management Week*, aimed at British managers.

Tim Kilroe   £30m

BUILDING AND AVIATION CONTRACTOR
dob (unknown)

WHEN the young Tim Kilroe arrived from Ireland in the late 1950s, he went to Manchester to seek his fortune. He had little money but huge ambition and was regarded as 'a wonderful worker who was obviously going somewhere', according to one former employer.

He quickly made his mark in the North-West. Instead of doing a traditional labouring job, he hired his own equipment and became a sub-contractor. In the 1950s and 1960s building boom, Kilroe expanded his business through regular work on small civil engineering projects around Manchester.

Today his Kilroe Group, covering all areas of building and civil engineering, employs around 1,000 staff. With a £45 million turnover, it has worked on many of the North-West's largest projects.

Tim Kilroe has a number of other businesses, including two charter airlines (Air Kilroe and Air Arran) which are based at Manchester airport. He also owns hotels in Cumbria and Cheshire, including the Four Seasons, regarded as the North's most expensive.

Air Kilroe is doing very well and has five aircraft. In 1989, it became the first airline to order a Jetstream Super 31, British Aerospace's new 19-seater feeder aircraft. A favourite with pop groups, media stars and sports teams, it is used by the likes of Bryan Robson, Barry McGuigan and Def Leppard.

Kilroe lives in a £900,000 home in exclusive Alderley Edge, one of Cheshire's most expensive areas. But wealth has not gone to his head. A devout Catholic, he sent all his five children to local Catholic schools. A man of modest tastes and very shy, he is happiest visiting Manchester's Irish folk clubs to indulge his passion for that kind of music.

His main extravagance is the turf. He travels around the British racing circuit to follow his own runners and regularly goes to bloodstock sales. His greatest triumph came in 1985 when his horse Forgive 'n' Forget won the Cheltenham Gold Cup, an appropriate victory for an Irish owner. A picture of Kilroe receiving the trophy from the Queen Mother takes pride of place in the Four Seasons.

Kilroe has his own helicopter for getting around the North-West quickly. He also drives a Mercedes; the family Rolls-Royce is mainly used by domestic staff for errands.

Lord King   £30m

INDUSTRIALIST   dob 29 August 1916

BORN in Essex, the son of an army sergeant, just as World War I was at its height, John King grew up in Surrey. His father, on surviving the war, became postman in the leafy village of Dunsfold. After a fairly uneventful schooling, King went to work for local engineering companies in the Guildford area. When World War II broke out he was only 23 and recently married, working in his father-in-law's engineering and motor business. He displayed a genius for getting engineering contracts to help the war effort and was also able to acquire modern American machine tools. After the war, he moved his machine tools to a large site in Yorkshire and built up what was to become the third largest ball-bearing manufacturer in Britain. Through dint of sheer hard work, with the devoted backing of his wife and an ability to satisfy customers, King prospered to the extent that when a Labour-government-inspired merger of ball-bearing manufacturers took place in 1969, he walked away with over £10 million. His wife's death in 1969 hit King hard. But, in 1970, he married Isabel Monckton, the youngest daughter of Viscount Galway. In the 1970s, he was heavily involved in the British engineering industry as chairman of Babcock & Wilcox, and later at Dennis, the Guildford bus and fire-engine maker.

Knighted in 1979, he really hit the headlines in 1981 when Margaret Thatcher made him chairman of British Airways. He was largely credited with BA's turnround into the world's favourite and most profitable airline. He received his life peerage in 1983, and apart from his business work he is a keen country gentleman and farmer, with the 2,000-acre Wartnaby estate in Leicestershire. He is a formidable huntsman as chairman of the Belvoir hunt and was a passionate supporter of Margaret Thatcher and her policies.

Paul and Robin Leach   £30m

BUILDERS   dob (unknown)

HUBERT Leach, a World War I veteran, started his own building company near London in 1933 after participating in several speculative building projects in previous years. He started modestly with shops and houses in Enfield, before moving on to building a housing estate at Waltham Cross.

During the war, when housebuilding virtually stopped, Leach built army camps for both the British and American forces. In 1949, his son Paul joined the business after two years' national service and became a site clerk. After working in all the company's operations, he joined the board in 1952.

A year later, the company was hit by financial problems when building licences, which strictly controlled development, were hard to come by. But it survived with the help of its bank and prospered. Hubert died in 1968 at the age of 68, leaving the business in the hands of Paul and his other son Robin, who had joined in 1962.

The company now carries out work all over North London, Bedfordshire and Hertfordshire. It is particularly strong in the Lea Valley, building office blocks, factories and shopping centres as well as housing developments.

In 1976 an Acton company, Lewis & Lewis, was acquired. Today, the Hubert C. Leach group has some ten subsidiaries, and in the year to the end of December 1988 it made after-tax profits of over £5.1 million.

The company headquarters is Hamels Mansion, a large 400-year-old house in Hertfordshire, which was extensively restored by Hubert C. Leach from 1977 to 1979. The third generation of the family is now involved in running the business. Julian Leach, Paul's son, is a director of a subsidiary. Paul and Robin Leach live in large homes in Buntingford and Bishop's Stortford respectively.

Jim and Bob McNeil   £30m

BLIND MANUFACTURERS   dob (unknown)

THE first sign of entrepreneurial spirit from the two McNeil brothers came when as boys they sold mice they had bred to local hospitals. Breeding animals was something they had learnt from their father. He first bred mink at the back of his Scotstoun tenement in Glasgow before moving to Aberdeen and becoming the country's top mink farmer. Though the business eventually folded, it helped nurture the same enterprising spirit in his sons.

Later the pair went their own ways for a while. Bob worked in a Fort William pulp mill, while Jim, after initially working in an Aberdeen insurance office as an executive, moved to London to work for a mail order company. One of their product lines was blinds and Jim noticed how many of the orders came from north of the border, where there were no significant manufacturers. Risking everything, he teamed up with Bob in Fort William, using the garage of a local transport company. They soon moved to a small factory at Hillington in Glasgow and within nine months their company, Apollo, had built up a turnover of £250,000.

Their first shop was in Glasgow's Union Street. Before long they had hit on the idea of franchising, to remove the risk of disappointing potential customers. They reasoned that a shop manager would be more motivated if he had a stake in the business. The idea came to them when 'one of our self-employed salesmen said he would like to have a shop and would like to run it himself', Apollo's franchise director said recently.

The franchisee, who is accepted by Apollo after a battery of interviews and aptitude tests (only one in four passes), invests some £20,000 in the business. As this business expands, it develops into its own manufacturing capability, with Apollo providing the tooling, fabrics and fittings.

By 1989, Apollo had 25% of the British blind market, worth around £150 million a year and projected to grow to £500 million by 1992. The group also sells to 15 countries, from Bangladesh to Australia.

In May 1989, they sold the company to the London-based Ashley group (though staying on as executives) for a sum that will eventually reach £54 million, provided they can generate £10 million pre-tax profits by 1992. Even before the sale, the two brothers were doing well. In 1988, they received £3.75 million dividends and sold some investment properties for over £6 million.

Marquess of Normanby   £30m

LANDOWNER   dob 29 July 1912

IN 1876 the Governor of New Zealand, the Rt Hon. the Marquess of Normanby, had what was by the standards of the time a small spread of just 6,800 acres in the North Riding of Yorkshire. The present Marquess, who still lives in the same home as his ancestor, Mulgrave Castle, is understood to be the master of something closer to 50,000 acres, a considerable increase on the ancestral landholdings: a trend not much evident among the great landowners of Britain in the 20th century.

Unlike his ancestors, who were cabinet ministers and important colonial governors, the present Marquess, who was educated at Eton and Christ Church, Oxford, has confined himself to activities closer to home and to Yorkshire.

During the war he was wounded and taken prisoner in France. He was awarded the military and civil MBEs in 1943 and, at the end of the war, he was parliamentary private secretary to the Secretary of State for Dominion Affairs, PPS to the Lord President of the Council and then a lord-in-waiting. Since the war he has occupied all the customary roles of a Marquess. He is the chairman of the National Art Collection Fund, High Steward of York Minster, Lord Lieutenant of North Yorkshire and its *Custos Rutulorum* (custodian of the land rolls).

In 1951 the Marquess married Grania Guinness, the daughter of Lord Moyne, who was assassinated in Cairo in the 1940s. What should have been a quiet wedding was interrupted when an alternative claimant to the title appeared at the ceremony in the church at Lythe in Yorkshire, and objected to the nuptials proceeding. The claimant, an engineer from Newcastle called T. A. Trueman, who had four different meetings with Queen Mary in the 1930s, was later sent to prison for a month for threatening to kill Lord Normanby. He died without succeeding in his lonely cause.

The couple have seven children but one of their sons-in-law, Adam Sedgwick, was shot dead by armed robbers in Fulham in 1982. Adam Sedgwick was separated from his wife at the time.

In the late Seventies the Marquess made the headlines when he sacked a farm manager on his estate for having an affair with another estate employee's wife. Politically, the Marquess moved from the Conservative side before the war to Labour in the late 1940s before resigning in 1950 to sit as an independent on the crossbenches.

Pradyuman Patel £30m

PHARMACEUTICALS AND PROPERTY
dob (unknown)

UNIVERSALLY known as PR Patel, he came to Britain from Uganda. Today he owns Latap Pharmaceuticals and Regent Laboratories. He also has a link with a Copenhagen pharmaceutical group. With Dadubhai Patel (q.v.) he has been involved in the takeover of a large British taxi group. He recently acquired an interest in seven passenger aircraft, which he is leasing to international airlines.

Lord Roborough £30m

LANDOWNER   dob 4 October 1903

THE Roboroughs have been associated with the county of Devon since the end of the 18th century, when the founder of the dynasty, Manasseh Massey Lopes, sat as MP for South Molton. By the 19th century, the family had amassed over 12,000 acres of prime agricultural land and married into three of the great Devon landowning families: the Churstons, the Bullers and the Edgecombes.

The title was created in January 1938 and the present Lord Roborough succeeded his father a mere four months later. On the outbreak of war, Massey Henry Lopes joined the Royal Armoured Corps and was wounded twice on active service. Earlier he had served as ADC to the Governor General of South Africa, following a traditional education at Eton and Christ Church, Oxford.

After the war he returned to running the family acres, which are believed to have remained as large as they were in the late 1800s, and to the usual duties of the landed county aristocrat. These included the Lord Lieutenancy of the county, guardianship of its land rolls (*Custos Rutulorum*) and the High Stewardship of Barnstaple. Unlike some of the landed gentry,

Roborough has also taken part in a whole raft of social duties, all connected with the smooth running of the upper end of the county. These include the governorship of private schools such as Kelly College and Exeter School. He is also a long-standing member of the Council of Exeter University.

The Hon. Henry Lopes, his eldest son and heir, was educated at Eton, followed by a spell in the Coldstream Guards. He lives and works in Devon. His younger son is married to a daughter of Lord Astor of Hever.

William Rooney £30m

KITCHEN AND BATHROOM MANUFACTURER
dob 22 November 1940

BILL Rooney started his working life as a graduate trainee with the Milk Marketing Board before joining the Hygena furniture business. He rose to become general sales manager and boosted Hygena's turnover from £6.5 million to £24 million in two years. His business acumen attracted the attention of Gower Flatpack, a Yorkshire kitchen company. Rooney arrived as marketing director and stayed for eight years, ending up as chairman. When the business was sold, Rooney and partner Robert Murray (q.v.) went to work for the new company but became so disenchanted that they decided to branch out on their own. That was in 1979, the first year of Conservative government, and their company Spring Ram (the Ram stands for Rooney and Murray) was very much a child of the Thatcherite years. Foreseeing a huge leap in home ownership and home improvements, they went into the bathroom fittings market, and later branched out into kitchens. Pooling £250,000, and with the support of their bank, they bought a derelict blanket mill in Sowerby Bridge, near Halifax. The business took off, and in four years the original team of five had grown to 240 people in some five factories. The company came to the stock market that year, making Rooney and Murray millionaires several times over. Growing at 50% a year, Spring Ram opened a brand new £12 million factory in Scunthorpe in 1988.

The onset of higher interest rates and the slowdown in consumer spending of the last two years have not really affected Spring Ram. Pre-tax profits for 1990 rose by 25% to £30 million. Its investment programme runs to £85 million over the next three years, while the workforce will expand from 1,650 to 3,100. The use of new technology has enabled Rooney to keep prices down, while an all-out effort to give the best service possible has helped overcome the cowboy image of the kitchen industry. In June 1991, Rooney sold 22 million of his shares in Spring Ram, raising some £23 million. He had been advised by financial advisers that too high a proportion of his family wealth was tied up in one place.

Lady Samuel £30m

PROPERTY DEVELOPER   dob (unknown)

HAROLD Samuel, later Lord Samuel, began his career as an estate agent, but by the mid-1930s he had devoted himself to central London property development.

During the war he acquired various central London properties, and in 1944 he bought Land Securities, a small company, for £20,000. When he died in 1987 it was the world's biggest property company, with assets of more than £3 billion.

Samuel came from a comfortable middle-class background in north London and was educated at Mill Hill. In 1936 he married Edna, daughter of Harry Nedas. They lived in London near Regent's Park and on a large Sussex estate, where Lord Samuel collected Dutch paintings and grew flowers. They had three daughters, Jacqueline, Carole and Marion.

Lord Samuel was a noted benefactor, donating £250,000 to Cambridge and a similar sum to London University. His own brush with controversy came in 1953, when an attempt to gain control of the Savoy Hotel Group ended in débâcle.

He left an estate of £26 million. His collection of paintings was left to Lady Samuel for her life, but was to be passed on to the City of London. In December 1987 she gave them to the City to go on permanent display, saying: 'I have had the pleasure of them for 35 years. This is what my husband wanted, that the collection should remain together and be on display at the Mansion House.'

Sir John Smith   £30m

LANDOWNER AND FINANCIER   dob 3 April 1923

FRIEND of Prince Philip and former Conservative MP for Westminster, Sir John Smith owns large tracts of Regent Street and other lucrative London acreages. He was recently knighted for his service to charity, notably his £5 million gift to restore HMS *Warrior*, the navy's first proper ironclad ship, to full working condition.

Sir John, a director of Coutts Bank and a keen historic buildings enthusiast, loves the sound of church bells, and has personally funded the restoration of bells at 80 churches around the country. He lives on a large Berkshire estate and was once Lord Lieutenant of the county.

Countess of Sutherland   £30m

LANDOWNER   dob 30 March 1921

THE Sutherland estates used to stretch over 1.3 million acres of the Scottish Highlands. Today, they have shrunk to 100,000 acres.

The Dukes of Sutherland are often remembered for the Highland Clearances. In 1805, the then Duke ordered 5,000 crofters off his land to make way for more profitable tenants – sheep.

The Sutherlands have never been very successful with money. The 3rd Duke lost money on railways. The 4th Duke sold some

Van Dyck paintings to buy land in Canada. It appeared to contain water so he promptly sold it but vast oil reserves were then uncovered there.

The Countess inherited the title Clan Chief of the Sutherlands in 1963.

Her uncle had spent prodigiously and the Countess has been carefully trying to restore the estates ever since. They contain extensive forestry, fishing and grouse moors. In 1981, she sold a 1,000-acre estate in Stoke on Trent for £4 million.

Stephen Tucker £30m

CAR PARKS   dob (unknown)

RAISED in Manchester, Stephen Tucker was a multi-millionaire before he had reached the age of 30. His money came in the unlikely area of car parks, where his Europarks company became the principal competitor to the National Car Parks group run by Sir Donald Gosling (q.v.) and Ronald Hobson (q.v.). Tucker's big break came in 1985 when he moved down to London, and a year later won the contract for car parking at Heathrow, much to the fury of the NCP, which regarded Tucker as a major threat on their home territory. In 1990, the extent of this outrage was apparent when the *Sunday Times* Insight team reported on a case of industrial espionage conducted by the NCP against Europarks. The surveillance on Tucker revealed him to be a very tough and shrewd business-man, describing him as 'an extremely dynamic, self-assured man. He expects to be successful and knows exactly what he wants.' Since then the two sides have buried their hatchets, and Tucker sold his stake in Europarks to the NCP group for some £30 million. He has a place on the NCP board as a consultant. He lives in Chelsea and his wife runs a car valet service out of Heath-row.

Viscount Wimborne £30m

LANDOWNER AND HEIR   dob 2 December 1939

DESCENDED from the Guest steel family (of Guest, Keen & Nettlefolds – GKN), Viscount Wimborne divides his life between London and Paris.

The family estates, built up by his father, a Lloyds underwriter, at one time extended to 32,000 acres. These included valuable property with development potential on the outskirts of Poole. In 1972 this was worth some £26 million. In 1976 the Viscount sold a Northampton estate he owned to the British Airways pension scheme for around £2 million.

In 1983 Viscount Wimborne married his second wife, Mrs Venetia Barker, eldest daughter of Lady Mancroft and former wife of Captain Fred Barker, a racehorse breeder and heir to the Singer sewing-machine fortune.

He became involved in controversy in 1986 over the sale of Goya's painting, *The Marquesa of Santa Cruz*, which he had acquired in 1983. Spain claimed the picture had been smuggled out of the country, a charge the Viscount vigorously denied. He claimed to have bought it in good faith. Eventually the Spanish government paid him £4.1 million for it. In 1988 he planned to set up a fighting bull farm in Bilbao, in northern Spain.

Ian Wood £30m

INDUSTRIALIST   dob (unknown)

A FIRST class honours degree in psychology from Aberdeen University may not seem the obvious training for running one of Britain's most successful companies in the hard and tough world of North Sea oil exploration. But Ian Wood, a tall, powerful ex-rugby player with distinctive mutton-chop whiskers, has turned his family fishing-boat business into the leading British offshore oil service company.

He very nearly did not go into the business at all. When his father's health was failing, he asked Ian to help out in the family business for a couple of years, after which he could leave if he did not like it. Ian did enjoy it, and quickly learned the ropes by teaching himself accountancy.

In 1964, the Wood Group had just 100 employees. Today, there are over 2,000, and the group, which is still family-controlled, has expanded into the Middle East, the Far East and North America.

Although it has suffered sharp peaks and troughs according to the prevailing oil price and the consequent level of exploration activity, the Wood Group reported a surge in its profits to £4.5 million on a turnover of £82 million in 1988. Recent events in the Gulf will have helped Wood's exploration activities.

Known for his passionate commitment to Aberdeen, Wood is a considerable force in local politics. He sits on the board of the Scottish Development Agency and is bidding to head the Grampian Local Enterprise Company. He was named Scottish Young Businessman of the Year in 1979. He lives in an exclusive part of Aberdeen.

David Crossland £29m

PACKAGE HOLIDAYS   dob (unknown)

IN the 1960s, David Crossland was a penniless clerk working in a Lancashire travel agency business. Today, he is Britain's third biggest package holiday operator, and rapidly heading to the top with his company, Airtours.

Getting to the top has been a hard slog. First, Crossland and his brother-in-law opened a small travel agency business in the mill town of Pendle. By 1980, they had nine outlets. In 1982, he decided that there was more money to be made from arranging his own package holidays, and he bought out a small business. Airtours, from an elderly Lancashire couple. In 1986, he sold the chain of shops – 21 strong by then – to Hogg Robinson for £2.75 million and never looked back. A stock market float followed in 1987, and by 1990, Airtours was able to turn in profits of £6.3 million on a £183 million turnover.

But it was the collapse of arch-rival Harry Goodman's Intasun business early in 1991 that really helped Airtours to take off. Within a week, Airtours had taken 90,000 bookings, and Crossland claimed that bookings were up 'by a factor of ten'. He sent his sales teams out to the Mediterranean to buy up beds from hoteliers stranded by the Intasun collapse. Airtours shares soared from 138p to 341p, enabling Crossland to tap the City for a further £16 million in cash to help finance the surge in bookings. At that time, his stake in the business was worth some £29 million.

Crossland is still firmly wedded to his Lancashire roots. Airtours headquarters is in Rossendale, though Crossland now lives in the smart Cheshire commuter belt. He works a 14-hour day, and eschews many of the luxury items associated with the super-rich, though he recently traded in a Mercedes for a Jaguar XJR sports car, telling *Business* magazine: 'It matched my ego.'

John Delaney   £29m

BUSINESSMAN   dob (unknown)

IN 1966, John Delaney married Mrs Denise Pigott, the daughter of Denys Erskine and niece of Keith Erskine. Mrs Pigott, who had previously married a partner in a firm of London tea merchants, was heiress to the Securicor fortune, controlling nearly half the voting shares in the group.

Denys Erskine was originally a hotelier, and his brother Keith was a solicitor. In the 1950s, the hotel business, Associated Hotels, ran up to five hotels including the original Eccleston Hotel in Victoria, bought by their father. Securicor, which was started in 1935, was acquired from one of Keith's clients and the brothers decided to move out of hotels into what they saw as a lucrative market. By 1979, the business had 1,800 armoured vans carrying £38 billion of cash round the country.

Denise Delaney had trained as a shorthand typist. She

planned the décor in the hotels and sat on the Securicor board, commuting to meetings from her Sussex farm. When she died in 1980, leaving some £3.4 million net in her will, her husband, John Delaney, who also sat on the Securicor board, took over the role of watching the family interests in the firm.

These became much more valuable in the 1980s when Securicor, in association with British Telecom, won the licence to operate a mobile phone service in Britain. Their service – known as Cellnet – became immensely profitable and had an impact on Securicor's share price, lifting it to around £8 or more a share. With over 4 million shares in the business, John Delaney's fortune now stands at over £29 million.

Ronald and Derek Frost   £29m

INDUSTRIALISTS   dob (unknown)

BROTHERS Ronald and Derek Frost ran a company, Farmhouse Securities, which was taken over by the long-established Hays Group in 1981. Two years later, Ronald Frost became chief executive of Hays, which was then owned by the Kuwait Investment Office. He led the £225 million management buy-out of Hays from the KIO just one day after the stock market crash on Black Monday in October 1987. Two years later, Hays was floated on the stock market, and the Frost brothers' stake was valued at nearly £30 million. Though the flotation had been received with only lukewarm support from the City, Hays prospered. In its half-year profits to the end of December 1990, it unveiled a marginal improvement to £27 million, no mean feat in a difficult recessionary period. The business, with headquarters in Surrey, is involved in transport and distribution and temporary staff agencies. Ronald Frost described 1990 as 'bloody difficult' when unveiling the profit figures. He lives in Surrey and lists his hobbies as game shooting and sailing.

Kevin McDonald   £29m

PLASTIC PIPE MANUFACTURER
dob 20 October 1933

KEVIN McDonald started early in the plastics business and founded a small company, Bartol Plastics, which was taken over by Hepworth Ceramics. McDonald became managing director of the plastics division but, by the late 1970s, he was convinced that he could undercut the major companies in this field by as much as 50%.

So, in 1979, he teamed up with Geoffrey Harrison and Brian Leesing to start a new business, pooling their different expertise. McDonald knew all about running a plastics business, Harrison was the technical and engineering expert, while Leesing handled the finances. The business was called Polypipe.

The three took a 125-year lease for £25,000 on land owned by Doncaster Council. They put their own money and funds borrowed from the bank into building a brand-new 5,000-square-foot factory, complete with the best tools and moulding machines.

The aim was simple. Polypipe was to grab as large a share of the market as possible by undercutting its bigger rivals on price by cutting out all the frills. Within two years, they had expanded the factory to 25,000 square feet and a year later it doubled again to 50,000 square feet.

In 1985, the company came to the stock market, and then embarked on a series of acquisitions to expand into different parts of the country. The strategy paid off. In March 1991 the half-year results rose by 3.7% to £5.27 million and McDonald tapped his shareholders for £13.6 million to fund further acquisitions.

In March 1987, McDonald had sold 4 million shares, netting him £9 million. That still left him with 37% of the shares.

David McMurtry   £29m

INDUSTRIALIST   dob 15 March 1940

AT the age of 18, David McMurtry ran away from his
Dublin home to become an aerospace apprentice at Bristol
Siddeley Engines factory. Over the years he climbed the hierarchy, eventually becoming deputy chief designer and assistant
chief of engine design for all engines made at the Filton works
(by then owned by Rolls-Royce). In 17 years he created some
17 patented inventions, one of which was crucial for the development of Concorde's engines. The fuel pipes needed to be fitted
with extreme precision and McMurtry came up with a 4-inch
probe that measured them with great accuracy.

Rolls, though pleased with the work, which meant that Concorde could fly, was not prepared to market the device. So, in
1973, McMurtry set up his own company with John Deer, a
colleague at Rolls. For the first three years, McMurtry still
worked at Rolls, while Deer built up the business from a spare
bedroom in his home. At night McMurtry provided the technical input needed. 'My main task was convincing Dave that
there would be enough to occupy his technical mind,' Deer later
recalled.

He succeeded and in 1976, with McMurtry on the board, the
company moved operations to a disused ice-cream factory at
Wootton under Edge in the Bristol commuter belt. At that
time, the company had five employees and sales of £200,000.
Six years later, it employed 150 staff, with sales of £3 million,
85% of which went overseas.

In 1983, the company came to the stock market to an enthusiastic reception, and it has been growing ever since. It has
moved into robots and has set up a large research and development arm. McMurtry has 39% of the shares and Deer 19%,
making a takeover impossible. The group leads the way in front
of the Japanese in this market.

Lord Burton   £28m

LANDOWNER   dob 27 June 1924

LORD Burton is a direct descendant of the Bass family, the Derbyshire brewers. Today, Bass is Britain's biggest brewer, though the family has long ceased to have any say in the running of the company.

The 3rd Baron Burton – named after the Burton brewing town – is a major Scottish landowner with over 58,000 acres in Inverness. He is noted for his abrupt manner: it was once said of him by a Scottish Procurator-Fiscal that he had 'a temper which seems to me at times very easily aroused and at other times ungoverned'.

The Burton fortune enabled the family to build up an extensive art collection, including works by Gainsborough and Reynolds, which were on display at the City of Birmingham Art Gallery. The gallery bought a Gainsborough from Lord Burton in 1983 for £100,000.

Lord Burton inherited the title in 1962 from his grandmother, as his father was killed on active service in the war. His grandmother was regarded as one of the richest heiresses in the country in the late 1890s and on her marriage in 1894 she received a diamond tiara for every day of the week. Lord Burton's mother was a daughter of the Duke of Devonshire and a sister of Lady Dorothy Macmillan, wife of the late Earl of Stockton, Harold Macmillan.

Twice married, Burton has often been involved in controversial issues. In 1983, he tried to block access to a marina development near his Dochfour estate, claiming that the £1 million scheme was unnecessary and would take trade away from a local shop. He also sought permission to shoot a marauding golden eagle, a protected species, which had been carrying off local lambs, but the request was turned down by the Nature Conservancy Council.

Described by one paper as an 'eccentric baron' because of such incidents, Burton has resorted to shipping lion's dung from an Essex zoo to spread over his fields in a bid to scare off herds of red deer.

Ron Jacques   £28m

FOOD   dob (unknown)

UNTIL the end of April 1991, Ron Jacques and his family owned a 79% stake in a little-known food wholesaler, called Amalgamated Foods, based in Coventry. At that point, Jacques decided to consummate a long-running courtship with Watson & Philip, a Dundee-based stores group, in an agreed takeover. The deal netted the Jacques family some £28 million in shares and cash. This marriage to Watson & Philip was a perfect geographic fit, with their respective strengths in different areas of Britain.

Amalgamated had been transformed by Jacques from a loss-making operation in the early 1980s to a group producing healthy profits of £5.4 million in 1990. It had found a profitable niche to exploit: small supermarkets which were based in prosperous towns over the South of England, and which stayed open for long hours. To emphasize their convenience to the customer, they operated under labels such as Allday or Spar Eight Till Late.

Robert Murray   £28m

KITCHENS AND BATHROOMS   dob 3 August 1946

IN 1979 Bob Murray and partner Bill Rooney (q.v.) invested £200,000 of their money into their own bathroom fittings company called Spring Ram (the Ram stood for Rooney and Murray). They acquired a derelict cotton mill on a 10-acre site at Sowerby Bridge in West Yorkshire. It was an immediate success, coming to the stock market in 1983. Through the Eighties, Spring Ram had the fastest growth rate of any firm in Britain. Even in the depths of the recession in 1990, it was still able to push its half-year profits up by 27% to £13 million. With highly advanced and efficient manufacturing, a healthy balance-sheet, and very careful market research, Spring Ram's shares soared, making Rooney and Murray very rich. But in June 1990, Murray, then deputy chairman, announced that he was leaving the company 'to seek a new challenge'. A month later he sold 12.5 million of his shares, netting £15 million. In June 1991 Murray sold his remaining shares in Spring Ram, raising a further £13 million. He is chairman of Sunderland Football Club.

Earl of Shelburne   £28m

LANDOWNER   dob 21 February 1941

HEIR to the Marquess of Lansdowne, Charlie Shelburne lives on a stately 5,000-acre estate in Wiltshire. His father now lives in comfortable retirement at another family estate of 10,000 acres at Melkour in Perthshire.

Shelburne, who was formerly married for 21 years to the Earl of St German's daughter, remarried in 1987. His name had been linked to the Duke of Westminster's sister, Lady Leonora Lichfield, the former wife of Lord Lichfield. But in the event, he married Fiona Merritt, a long-standing friend.

As deputy president of the Historic Houses Association, he is regarded as the coming man of the heritage movement and has turned his estate, Bowood, into a booming tourist attraction. He contested Coventry North East for the Conservatives in the 1979 election and lists country pursuits as his hobby.

Earl of Yarborough   £28m

LANDOWNER   dob 5 November 1963

IN 1794, Charles Anderson-Pelham, MP for Lincolnshire, was created baron Yarborough. Today, his direct heir, the 8th Earl, holds the title and also runs the 28,000-acre Brocklesby estate in largely agrarian Lincolnshire. The Earl inherited the title from his father, who died in March 1991 at the age of 70. A publicity-shy peer, the 7th earl had the traditional aristocratic pedigree. After Eton, Trinity College, Cambridge, and wartime service with the Grenadier Guards, he was a former Lord Lieutenant of Lincolnshire, as well as a member of Boodle's and the Cavalry & Guards Club. He spent much of his life running his estates efficiently. The new Earl is noted for being a convert to Islam, and will be the only Muslim earl in the Lords, according to the *Daily Telegraph*'s Peterborough column.

John Zochonis and family   £28m

SOAP AND OVERSEAS TRADERS
dob 2 October 1929

CUSSONS Imperial Leather, the quintessential British soap, is actually made by Paterson-Zochonis, a family-controlled company with Greek origins, based in Manchester. It is run by chairman John Zochonis.

As well as making soap and toiletries, it trades with Nigeria. This was very profitable when the Nigerian economy was flush with oil revenues, but as a big debtor nation it now has little room for trade. Every time there is a coup in Nigeria, the Paterson share price immediately drops.

Manchester-born John Zochonis is the grandson of the Greek entrepreneur who co-founded Paterson-Zochonis, the West Africa-based merchants, in 1884. He was educated at Rugby School, where he excelled at cricket, and he studied law at Corpus Christi College, Oxford. He completed two years' National Service in 1950, gaining the rank of second lieutenant.

In 1953 he joined Paterson-Zochonis as a junior executive, working in West Africa and England. Four years later he was appointed a director and in 1970 he became chairman. In 1975 he masterminded the takeover of Cussons, then valued at £8.6 million.

Zochonis, whose father is now dead, has never married and lives in Altrincham, Cheshire. He is a member of the Travellers'

Club and the Marylebone Cricket Club. He chairs the Council of Manchester University and is president of the Greater Manchester Youth Association. He is also a liveryman of the Tallow Chandlers Company and a Freeman of the City of London. His hobbies are cricket and horse-racing and he owns at least one racehorse.

Sir Owen Aisher and family £27m

BUILDING SUPPLIER   dob OA 28 May 1900

THERE can hardly be a British handyman or DIY enthusiast who has not used Marley tiles or other bits of Marley equipment in their time. Marley was founded by Sir Owen Aisher in 1934 and the family still control around 10% of the shares. Though president of the company, Sir Owen has now retired from day-to-day control, devoting himself to his passion for sailing. He was president of the Royal Yachting Association from 1970 to 1975. In 1958, he was named Yachtsman of the Year.

He lives in Surrey and when not sailing, he is fishing or shooting. He regularly attends Cowes week, and in 1989 Prince Philip borrowed his boat *Yeoman XXVIII* to race.

Lord Ashcombe £27m

LANDOWNER   dob 31 March 1924

THE thrice-married 4th Lord Ashcombe, already wealthy as heir to the Cubitt family fortune and an active director of the company, acquired, along with his third wife, one of the most elegant castles in England. The third Lady Ashcombe was the widow of an old family friend, Mark Dent Brocklehurst, whose family owned Sudeley Castle near the Gloucestershire village of Winchcombe.

The castle was the home of Henry VIII's sixth wife Catherine Parr, who died there. Elisabeth Dent Brocklehurst had already opened the castle to the public before she married Ashcombe in 1979. He lists himself as director of Sudeley Castle Ltd.

Eton-educated and described in the gossip columns as 'Mad Harry', Lord Ashcombe was the first member of the family to chair Cubitts for four generations. He served in the RAF during World War II and worked at the building company for several years before he took over the top post.

His first marriage in 1955 was to a former American TV hostess. His second marriage in 1973 was to a daughter of Lord Carrington, the former minister of defence and NATO secretary general, but this marriage, reported in trouble as early as 1977, was dissolved in 1979. There are no children by any of the three marriages and the title may pass to a cousin in Ireland.

The present Lady Ashcombe has two children by her first marriage, but they cannot inherit her husband's title. They are, however, the beneficiaries of one of the wealthiest and least-known trusts in the UK, the Walter Morrison Family Trust. During the 1980s the trust sold a Poussin, a Turner, a Rembrandt and several other Old Masters to various galleries and museums, raising over £2 million in the process.

The Times described the founding of the Cubitt title and fortune in the following terms in 1961: 'Thomas Cubitt was the prodigious builder (1788–1855) whose massive achievements, including most of Belgravia, Bloomsbury and Pimlico, made him the "spec" builder par excellence and a millionaire in those far-off Victorian pounds.'

Lord Egremont £27m

LANDOWNER   dob 21 April 1948

CRIPPLING death duties have hit the Egremonts three times since 1952, but they still have large estates and art treasures.

The present Lord Egremont, who succeeded in 1972, lives at Petworth House in Sussex and owns a 12,000-acre estate there. The house itself is owned by the National Trust, as are a third of the art treasures inside. But the family still own paintings by Van Dyck, Gainsborough and Reynolds and a famous collection by Turner, who stayed at the house and painted many pictures there. They also own a 4,000-acre estate in Cumbria and Cockermouth Castle, where Lord Egremont's widowed mother lives.

His late father was private secretary to Harold Macmillan when he was Prime Minister. Lord Egremont was present with his father in Macmillan's office during part of the crisis following the Profumo scandal. He later went to work as a publisher's rep in Scotland. He was working for an American senator during the Watergate crisis.

Lord Egremont is married to the former Caroline Nelson, a publishing heiress. He is also a noted author and has written four books under the name Max Wyndham. These include *The Cousins*, *The Ladies' Man* and *Dear Shadows*.

Ron Jelley and family   £27m

BUILDERS   dob (unknown)

IN 1889 a builder called Jelley started his own firm in Leicester. It was taken over by his son Herbert Jelley in the early 1920s, when it developed into a local housebuilders with a reputation for good-quality work. In the 1960s and 1970s, the company built nearly 20,000 homes for local councils and the private sector. Today, it is still very much a quality firm, building everything from starter homes to £250,000 executive houses. It has also built many commercial and industrial buildings over the years in the East Midlands.

In its latest accounts for 1989 the business (now called Jelson Ltd) produced healthy after-tax profits of £5.1 million on a turnover of £37.6 million. With large cash reserves and relatively small borrowings, the firm would fetch around £27 million on the stock market. Most of the shares are very tightly held by the Jelley family.

Ronald Jelley, grandson of the founder, is chairman of the business, and his two sons are now working in the firm. One, Robert, is managing director.

Ronald Jelley lives in a large house with 40 acres of woodland in Leicestershire. He also farms locally and is known for his generous support for local causes. In 1969 he financed a new £12,000 village hall in a Leicester village, saying, 'I hope this will make the village tick.'

Sir Tatton Sykes £27m

LANDOWNER   dob 24 December 1943

THE Sykes family has been prominent in East Yorkshire since the end of the 18th century. The present baronet, Sir Tatton, is the eighth holder of the title and lives at the family seat and stud farm near Driffield. A previous Sykes gave his name to the Sykes-Picot treaty signed in 1916, which put Lebanon and Syria in the sphere of French influence. Sir Tatton's fame comes from his racing interests: the Tatton Sykes colours of orange with purple sleeves are well known on northern racecourses, and winners have included Siegfried, Mirnaya and Exact.

In the 19th century the Sykes lands ran to over 30,000 acres. They are believed to be still largely intact. Sir Tatton was educated at Ampleforth, the prominent Catholic private school, and then went on to the University d'Aix near Marseilles, before completing the traditional land owner's preparation for running his estates by attending the Royal Agricultural College at Cirencester.

Lord Tollemache   £27m

BREWER AND LANDOWNER   dob 13 December 1939

LIKE a number of other titled families (see Daresbury), the
Tollemache fortune is based on alcohol, in this case the
Tollemache Cobbold brewing empire, originally based in Ips-
wich.

The brewing interests were backed by enormous personal
wealth. At the end of the last century the Tollemache lands
consisted of the original family home, Helmingham Hall in
Suffolk, with around 7,000 acres, and Peckforton Castle in
Cheshire with 28,561 acres. There were also homes in fashionable parts of London. The latest indications are that the Helmingham estate is still over 7,000 acres but that at Peckforton is
down to about 6,000 acres. Both estates have land worth at
least £30 million all told. The present Lord Tollemache had the
traditional Eton education followed by a spell in the Coldstream
Guards. When he came of age, he gave no less than six parties,
all for his father's staff and tenants. He left the Guards after
three years' service to train in estate management under the
Queen's manager on the royal estate at Sandringham. And he
struck up a close personal friendship with Prince Charles, who
is godfather to his eldest son and heir. He married the daughter
of a leading Staffordshire landowner, who is related to the Earl
of Halifax. In 1977, they started accepting American tourists as
visitors to Helmingham Hall.

He was quoted in the *Daily Mail* as saying, 'We're not out to
make a profit. We're just trying to keep the roof on.' He told
the first group of visitors that during the Civil War one of the
Tollemache women was rumoured to be Cromwell's mistress,
while the rest of the household were plotting to restore the
monarchy. The *Mail* reported that the Americans loved it.

Recently the Tollemache Cobbold breweries have been
through several changes of ownership. In the early 1980s they
belonged to Ellermans, who retained Lord Tollemache on their
board. By 1989 the company had been bought by the Brent
Walker group. Lord Tollemache did not follow the company
and, in the middle of 1989, brewing ceased at the Tollemache

Cobbold site in Ipswich, breaking a link that was more than 260 years old.

Jeremy Agace £26m

FORMER ESTATE AGENT   dob 15 May 1940

SELLING houses in London and the South-East proved to be a goldmine for Jeremy Agace. He followed his father to become chairman of Mann & Co., a leading estate agency based in the Surrey commuter town of Woking and founded in 1891.

In 1985, at the height of the property boom, Mann was the third largest agency in the country. Agace floated the group on the stock market, and it was initially valued at around £31 million, with Agace owning 46% of the equity. A year later, with house prices rising by 20% or more, every large financial institution was scrambling to acquire an agency.

Mann joined with Hambros and another agency to form Hambro Countrywide, with Agace as chief executive. In April 1988 he resigned from the board with his right-hand man, Paul Locke. A month later, they bought two small employment bureaux. Agace, who has since retired abroad, must be feeling thankful that he moved out of estate agency work at the right time. In 1990, scores of estate agents' offices closed, with the housing market in the doldrums.

Robert Gavron £26m

PUBLISHER AND PRINTER   dob 13 September 1930

ALTHOUGH he originally intended to go to the Bar, Bob Gavron now runs Britain's second largest printing company. Only Robert Maxwell's (q.v.) is larger. The company, St Ives, was in the news in 1988 when it sued the Department of

Trade and Industry for libel over a damaging advert in the DTI's Enterprise Initiative campaign.

Gavron's family originally hailed from South Africa and they were appalled at the thought of their son going into industry. But the young Gavron was lured there by the late Geoffrey Crowther, the editor of the *Economist*.

He went into printing and, with the help of some City backers, bought the St Ives printing group. After years of building up the company, he floated it on the Stock Exchange in 1985. It was a huge success and Gavron immediately embarked on a hectic takeover spree, gobbling up smaller printing companies, who were happy to sell up. The shares were badly hit by the October 1987 stock market crash, though the company's performance has not been affected.

Gavron owns a Georgian house in Highgate with 2 acres of garden and superb views of London. He plays tennis or swims for an hour before going to work, and he has several outside charitable interests, including helping handicapped children. He also served on the literary panel of the Arts Council from 1979 to 1983. He is a close friend of publisher Paul Hamlyn (q.v.).

Ralph Oppenheimer   £26m

STEEL   dob (unknown)

RALPH Oppenheimer and his family own a large stake in one of Britain's largest steel stockholding companies, ASD. The company had been one of the star performers on the stock market after it was floated on the Unlisted Securities Market in 1985. In 1985, pre-tax profits stood at some £2.6 million, rising to £7 million in 1990. Oppenheimer and his management team pursued a rapid expansion policy on the back of healthy demand. In 1989, ASD acquired a Newcastle plastic pipeline company, and also quadrupled its number of outlets. But the onset of the recession hit ASD hard, and in 1990, its losses were estimated to have reached £1.5 million. Oppenheimer responded by allowing the French steel group,

Usinor Sacilor, to take a controlling stake in ASD. The bid valued the whole of ASD at £34.9 million, and netted Oppenheimer and his family some £10 million.

Peter Prowting   £26m

PROPERTY DEVELOPER   dob 19 December 1924

IN 1912, Peter Prowting's father founded a construction company in the London suburb of Ruislip. He died in 1977 and Peter took over. He had moved the company out of contracting and into housebuilding. Its first large-scale development took place in the Northwood area of Middlesex in 1953, using a modern interpretation of a Tudor design. Working mainly in the South-East, Prowting built upmarket homes and managed to make twice as much as his rivals on every house he sold. The company was floated on the stock market in 1988, when it also expanded out of its traditional southern base. It was declared Housebuilder of the Year in that year.

Peter Prowting also has a big shareholding in Estates & General, another property group. He lists his hobbies as golf, gardening and jazz. Married twice, he has a daughter by his first marriage.

In 1966, he was in the news when he angered residents of Praa Sands, a Cornish beauty spot between Lizard and Penzance, by building a concrete cliff-top balcony in the garden of his large holiday home. The local council and then minister of local government both condemned the balcony as unsightly. Prowting lived in Buckinghamshire at the time.

Though he remains chairman, day-to-day running of the company is in the hands of Terry Roydon, his managing director.

Shami Ahmad   £25m

FASHIONS   dob (unknown)

EVEN as a schoolboy, Shami Ahmad was determined to get into the fashion business. He would leave school in Burnley and take a 90-minute bus ride to Manchester to help his father, Nizam, in his Manchester clothes shop. His father had originally started a market stall in 1963 on his arrival in Britain from Pakistan. He later moved into the wholesale jeans business, but had rows with other jeans suppliers, who objected to his policy of undercutting them. The family then went into the retail trade and have never looked back.

Shami Ahmad left school at 17 and joined the business, but four years ago branched out on his own and launched the Legendary Joe Bloggs Jeans Company, a name he chose because it was 'common sounding and truly British'.

Today, it is one of the fastest-growing fashion chains in Britain, and Ahmad is still only 28. In 1989, the company was primarily a northern operation. Since then, it has gone nationwide, and Ahmad has plans to launch the jeans in America, Europe and Australia. It makes some 1.5m pairs of jeans a year, selling for up to £50 a pair.

The secret of Ahmad's success is the speed with which he reacts to the market. Within weeks of new fashions appearing in northern clubs, Ahmad has them manufactured and in the shops. He recently likened his approach to McDonalds, noting that teenagers were getting their fast fashions from Joe Bloggs.

The family enjoy the trappings of wealth: luxury Cheshire commuter-belt homes and cars that include a Ferrari, Bentley and Rolls-Royce. Ahmad is not modest about his achievements, boasting to *The Times* recently: 'We make the widest flares in England at 25 inches. There's two things in Manchester: one is Strangeways, the other is us.'

Kenneth and William Alexander £25m

CHEMICALS PRODUCERS
dob KA 21 November 1928

THE Alexander family, led by brothers Kenneth and William, owns nearly 37% of the shares in one of Britain's most profitable yet secretive companies, Tennants Consolidated. The group, which makes chemicals for gardeners and for many other specialized purposes, produced £7.5 million after-tax profits on a turnover of £149 million in 1989. With total assets of £74 million and small borrowings, the group could be valued at well over £80 million on the stock market.

The business was originally started by a Glasgow chemist, Charles Tennant, at the end of the 18th century. The Tennant family, now led by Lord Glenconner (q.v.), the fun-loving friend of Princess Margaret, no longer have any involvement in the business. They sold the firm in 1960.

The Alexander brothers' involvement with the industry started with their father, Sir William Alexander, who died in 1954. A brilliant industrialist, he was made director of administration at the National Explosive Factories in 1916, at a time when the British Army was experiencing a critical shortage of shells. A year later, he became Controller of Aircraft Supply and Production. After World War I, he became a Conservative MP for Glasgow Central, and served in Parliament for 22 years until 1945. He retired to Jersey, where he died in 1954.

His son Kenneth, after education at Winchester and Cambridge and army service in the Royal Tank Regiment, joined the Tennants group, where he became chairman and chief executive in 1972. His brother, Dr William Alexander, is also a director of the group. He is a retired doctor, having qualified during the war. He was head of the neurology department at the Middlesex Hospital in London for a period and now lives in Surrey.

Kenneth Alexander, who lives on a farm in Berkshire, lists his recreations as music and shooting. He married in 1957 and has a son and three daughters.

In August 1990, the group sold a subsidiary, Pan Britannica Industries, to the Japanese Sumitomo group for £30 million.

Jeffrey Archer   £25m

AUTHOR   dob 15 April 1940

JEFFREY Archer's life could come straight out of one of his blockbusting novels that have earned him a £25 million fortune. The son of an army sergeant, he won a scholarship to school and went to Oxford to study education. He distinguished himself on the sports field, gaining blues for athletics and gymnastics. He also persuaded the Beatles to give a charity concert for Oxfam which raised £1 million. He married Mary Weeden, one of the cleverest undergraduates at the university, who was later to become a Cambridge fellow. After leaving university, Archer embarked on a career as a professional fund-raiser for charity and became a Conservative councillor on the Greater London Council at the age of 26. In 1969, he won a parliamentary by-election and at the age of 29 was the youngest MP, representing Louth in Lincolnshire. His ambition was soon evident. Asked whether he wanted to be prime minister, he replied damned right he did. But it was not to be. Seeking to amass the fortune which would enable him to live comfortably in his Boltons house in South Kensington and concentrate on politics, he invested in a Canadian cement company and found he had been the victim of an elaborate sting. As a result, Archer faced ruin, with debts of £427,000, and he resigned his seat and sold his house, Rolls-Royce and art collection.

But Archer had not earned the nickname Jumping-bean at Oxford for nothing. He determined to repay his debts and went to stay at a friend's house, where he wrote a novel, *Not a Penny More, Not a Penny Less*, which turned out to be a best-seller. His debts were repaid in full and a string of novels followed, all of which were hugely successful. Archer's fortune was restored and he made a return to politics as deputy chairman of the Conservative Party. But he resigned in 1986 after the *News of the World* published false allegations against him. In a libel action that followed, he won damages of £550,000, which he donated to charity. Archer continues to write prolifically from his flat on the Victoria Embankment, returning to his Grantchester home in Cambridge for the weekends. In the summer of 1990, he negotiated royalties of $25 million for the world rights to his next three novels.

A genius for self-publicity, Archer assiduously promotes his books and himself in the media with an easy confidence. Apart from his books, his one remaining ambition is to open the batting for England and Somerset at cricket, but even that will now be beyond Archer.

Earl of Bathurst £25m

LANDOWNER   dob 1 May 1927

A FORMER lord-in-waiting to the Queen and junior Conservative minister, Lord Bathurst owns the 15,000-acre Cirencester Park estate in Gloucestershire, which includes some of Britain's best farmland.

The Earl was a keen polo player and former Master of the White Horse Hunt until 1966. He only took government office in 1957 on condition that he could always hunt on Tuesdays. He resigned from the government in 1962. Once an escort to Princess Margaret, he married a Gloucestershire woman in 1959. In 1966, his wife Judith opened a boutique in Cirencester, which was sold in 1969. In 1975, the Earl and his wife were separated and they divorced a year later. He later remarried. Lord Apsley, the Earl's eldest son, is heir to the title.

Earl of Bradford   £25m

LANDOWNER   dob 3 October 1947

WHEN Richard Orlando Bridgeman, 7th Earl of Bradford, inherited the title in 1981, he also inherited death duties of £8 million. But the Earl, who had a reputation as a deb's delight and a trencherman of some renown, settled down to pay off the duties while saving the family estates.

He opened Weston Park, the family pile, to the public through Weston Park Enterprises. Art treasures worth £5.5 million were sold and the family estates reduced by 1,000 acres to 13,000.

But the Earl is still left with paintings worth over £15 million at today's prices, including works by Van Dyck, Reynolds, Holbein, Stubbs and Gainsborough. He no longer lives in the 17th-century house, but instead uses an eight-bedroom home on the estate. In his youth the Earl could call on a full-time staff of 15 in the house; today, this has been reduced to two nannies, a gardener and some daily help.

John Brotherton-Ratcliffe and family   £25m

PROPERTY OWNERS AND DEVELOPERS
dob (unknown)

BORN in the London suburb of Ealing and later moving to Purley, John Brotherton-Ratcliffe went to Oxford University before the war, in which he served as an airman in the university air squadron. He was commissioned in the RAF Volunteer Reserve in 1939, serving in South Africa and the Middle East. In August 1944, by then a squadron leader, he was awarded the DSO for displaying 'outstanding determination to complete his missions regardless alike of enemy opposition or adverse weather'. In December 1943, the citation continued: 'Squadron Leader Brotherton-Ratcliffe was forced to leave his aircraft by parachute and, early in this year, he was involved in a very serious crash. Despite these harassing experiences, his keenness for operational flying is undiminished and by his skill, courage and devotion to duty this officer has set an inspiring example to all.'

After the war, he founded Croudace, a small family building company. Today, it is one of the largest builders and developers in the country still in private hands. In 1989 it reported after-tax profits of over £4.8 million, a huge drop from the £15 million in 1988. All the shares in the company are now owned by Brotherton-Ratcliffe or his four children, who are now all grown up. If the company was floated on the stock market, it would be worth around £25 million. In the early 1960s, he moved from South Godstone to a large Sussex mansion, which was completely gutted by fire in 1977 and has since been re-built.

The company is based in the Surrey town of Caterham and undertakes housebuilding, construction work and property development mainly in the London and Home Counties area. In the year to the end of September 1988, Croudace built 1,062 homes and was planning a major shopping centre in Sutton. But the group could not avoid the effect of high interest rates on housebuilding. Brotherton-Ratcliffe warned in his annual report: 'Because of changes in market conditions, we expect the margins on sales to be reduced from the 26% level to more normal levels.' But he also saw a boost to general construction work, which 'is looking more promising than it has for several years, so we are now planning to expand in that area, building upon a current 18-months' workload'.

Michael Caine   £25m

ACTOR   dob 14 March 1933

SON of a Billingsgate fish porter and a charlady, Michael Caine (born Maurice Micklewhite) was born and raised in two rooms in London's Elephant and Castle. He was an evacuee during the war. When he was just six he stayed with a policeman's wife, who beat him until his ears bled and locked him in a cupboard. But he was rescued by the NSPCC and sent with other evacuees to a big country house.

He first became interested in acting as a 16-year-old pupil at Wilson's Grammar School, Peckham. He peered into a drama class to gain a closer look at a girl he rather liked and fell through the door. The teacher, who was short of boys in the class, immediately enrolled him. His interest in acting was further heightened by regular visits to the cinema.

A series of dead-end jobs followed – mixing cement, making pies and working with a pneumatic drill – before he did his National Service. He saw action in Korea and was later one of the British army's best marksmen before wangling his first job as a tea-boy on a film set. In 1953 he became a general dogsbody for a Sussex repertory company. In 1955 he came to London to work under Joan Littlewood, the leading theatre director of the day, learning new acting skills all the time.

After ten years in parts on stage and television, his first starring role in films came in *Zulu*, where he played an upper-class officer, a role far removed from his Cockney background. He had changed his name to Caine after seeing the film, *The Caine Mutiny*. His big break came when he starred as Harry Palmer, the Cockney agent and womanizer, in the 1965 film of Len Deighton's book *The Ipcress File*. Later, his role in *Alfie*, also as a Cockney womanizer, made him a star.

Throughout the swinging sixties, he lived in London, enjoying flings with starlets and revelling in his reputation as a ladies' man.

In 1979, he moved to Hollywood, complaining he could not exist under a Labour government that had taxed his earnings at 98%. He bought a £10 million Beverly Hills mansion but returned to Britain in 1987 as he missed his old haunts and he wanted his daughter to be educated at an English boarding school. He bought a £2 million house at Henley, overlooking the Thames, where he settled with his second wife, Shakira Baksh, a Guyanese beauty queen.

Caine has made over 60 films and while some were savaged by the critics, there have been memorable ones such as *Educating Rita* and *The Fourth Protocol*. In 1986, he won an Oscar for

Hannah and her Sisters. He can now command well over £1 million a film and two films in 1987 earned him £3.5 million. He also made £1 million for his part in the television serialization, *Jack the Ripper*.

Apart from his films, Caine also owns a third of Langan's Brasserie, founded by the late Peter Langan. In 1976, he put £25,000 into the venture. He is also developing multi-screen cinemas in Britain, and has a flourishing wine business. In America, he has invested in shopping malls and bowling alleys.

Robert Carter   £25m

BUILDER AND CONTRACTOR   dob (unknown)

ROBERT Carter is the third generation of the Carter family to take the helm of the fast-expanding family firm, RG Carter Holdings.

The company prides itself on being called 'East Anglia's construction company with the national reputation'. With 2,000 employees and a turnover of over £104 million, it is also one of the largest private construction groups in Britain. With no borrowings, a cash surplus and healthy after-tax profits of £4.1 million, the Carter group would be worth some £25 million if floated on the stock market today.

It was Carter's grandfather, Robert George Carter, who founded the company in 1921 in a tiny office in the Drayton district of Norwich. It is still based there though in a much larger building.

Robert Carter began by taking on simple repairs and renovations of buildings before winning larger contracts from private and public clients. In 1989, in Norwich alone, the company built new headquarters for the Norwich Union insurance company and a new Sainsbury's superstore.

In recent years the company has built banks, building societies, hotels, office blocks, shops and a television studio development for Anglia TV in Norwich. Contracts from the public sector have included building Wayland Prison in Norfolk over

70 acres, and the main ward block at the Norfolk and Norwich Hospital. Smaller developments include a church and a swimming pool. The group has not forgotten its roots and still tackles small jobs in people's homes despite its size today.

The company grew by acquiring other family-run businesses in East Anglia and now has some 25 subsidiaries, ranging from large construction firms in Ipswich, Colchester, Norwich and Grimsby to a small interior design company in Norfolk's North Walsham.

The original Bob Carter was joined by his son, R.E. (Bob) Carter, in 1938 and they worked together at the head of the organization for the next 25 years. When Robert Carter, the founder, died in 1966, his son took over as managing director and chairman. But he died in 1974 and so the third Robert Carter rose to prominence.

Sir Ivar Colquhoun (of Luss)   £25m

LANDOWNER   dob (unknown)

THE present Laird of Luss is the 8th Baronet and the chief of Clan Colquhoun. The family were once among the largest landowners in Dumbartonshire with over 40,000 acres. The Colquhouns are related to the Seafields (q.v.), who are still the fourth largest landowners in modern Britain. More recently Sir Ivar's daughter married the Marquess of Lorne, now the Duke of Argyll. But the family have not been without their share of controversy and tragedy.

As a boy Sir Ivar was said to wander the estates around Loch Lomond, barefooted and in a kilt. Later he was educated at Eton and then joined the Scots Guards. Before World War II, he was the lightweight boxing champion of the army. During the war he led units of his regiment in bayonet charges and raids. After the war he took part in a polar expedition.

In 1963 tragedy struck when the heir to the title, Torquil Iain, was found dead in bed at the age of 19. Torquil's brother, Malcolm, was once prosecuted by his father for allegedly stealing £300,000 worth of family heirlooms. Like his father, Malcolm was educated at Eton, and like many old Etonians, provides plenty of fodder for the gossip columnists.

In 1974 the Laird was beset by yet other problems, this time in the form of an American claimant to the title. Bill Colquhoun, a former American naval officer, said that he was a direct descendant of a Colquhoun brother who fled the battle of Culloden, at which the English defeated Scots rebels in 1746. The American provided the *News of the World* with some racy copy, to which Sir Ivar did not respond.

Sir Ivar won a legal victory when, after five years' wrangling, the courts recognized his claim to 300 yards of foreshore at Finnart where BP had built a large oil terminal.

Roger De Haan and family   £25m

HOLIDAY COMPANY OPERATOR   dob (unknown)

WHEN Roger De Haan's father, Sidney, was running the 36-room family hotel in Folkestone after the war, he began to fill the rooms off-season with elderly visitors. So popular was the idea that he founded a holiday company which was specifically designed for the over-60s. Today that company, Saga, caters for 250,000 elderly holidaymakers each year. As we are living longer and becoming more affluent and numerous, Saga's prospects are also improving year by year. Already it has noted that its clients are getting more adventurous, so it organizes walking tours around the foothills of Everest or canoeing up the Amazon.

The group has had only one hiccup since it came to the stock market in 1978. In 1982, it tried to diversify into general holidays by buying Laker Air Travel from the wreckage of Sir Freddie Laker's business. After losing £2 million, Saga decided to close it down. In 1984, Sidney De Haan retired to his Somerset cottage with his wife, saying he planned to play a full role in his local community. The business is now run by his son Roger as chairman. Two other De Haans are also on the Saga board.

One of Roger's first acts as chairman was to sell five Saga hotels, including the original Burlington in Folkestone for £4 million. The money was used to expand the retirement holiday business. In 1989, the company announced plans to diversify into retirement homes.

The family still control around 63% of the equity and, to avoid the risk of takeover, are determined that this should never fall below 50%. At the end of 1989, they announced plans to buy the 37% of the shares they did not own and take the group private again. The unwillingness to issue more shares and so to dilute their stake had made it difficult for the De Haans to expand the business by acquisition. Roger De Haan also criticized the City's short-term approach, which is geared to making bigger profits and dividends in the immediate future rather than investing for the long term.

John Joseph Gallagher and family   £25m

BUILDERS   dob (unknown)

JOHN Joseph Gallagher runs J. J. Gallagher, a very private building and plant hire firm in the West Midlands. The shares of the group are all owned by members of his family or family trusts which he has established. He has no shares in his own name.

In the late 1980s, the company enjoyed rapid growth, with after-tax profits rising from £274,000 in 1985 to just under £4.4 million in 1988. Turnover has similarly risen from £3 million to £37 million, while there are large cash reserves of £20 million. If the Gallaghers floated the company on the stock market or sold it privately, they could get at least £25 million for it.

Its latest scheme, to develop 64 acres of the old Park Lane site near junction 9 of the M6, in conjunction with the Triplex Lloyd group, should bring even more rewards to Gallagher. The site is being turned into a business park, and Ikea, the Swedish furniture group, has bought 15 acres for a superstore.

John Joseph Gallagher lives in the exclusive Solihull area of Birmingham. Though he hates publicity, he did make the news when he took over Wolverhampton Wanderers Football Club in 1986 as part of an eleventh-hour rescue package. Wolves had collapsed with debts of £1.75 million. Gallagher now owns the team while the Wolverhampton Council owns the ground. Tony Gallagher, John Joseph's son, is known to be a close friend of Ken Wheldon, the former chairman of Birmingham City Football Club.

Peter Jarrold and family   £25m

PRINTERS   dob (unknown)

IN the 1820s the Jarrold printing firm was established in Norwich. Today it is still family-controlled, and still printing in the city though its activities have now expanded to include department stores and publishing.

The business is run by Peter Jarrold, the chairman, who took over when his father died in 1978. Peter, who was educated at Cambridge and trained as a printer, joined the family firm over 30 years ago. He was appointed general manager within a few weeks of joining. His two brothers also work with him: Richard and Anthony run the retail and publishing sides of the business.

Its latest accounts show that Jarrold & Sons is a healthy business, reporting £5 million pre-tax profits. Since 1984 it has invested £10 million in new plant and machinery. It employs over 10,000 people, and the various members of the Jarrold family hold over half the shares between them. If floated on the stock market, it could easily command a £40 million price tag, valuing the family stake at around £25 million.

Peter has a keen interest in modern art and is active in the cultural life of Norwich. He regularly attends productions at the Theatre Royal and Maddermarket Theatre in the city. His wife Juliet is a former actress. His interest in the theatre is wide ranging and he is on the board of trustees of the tiny Norwich Puppet Theatre, one of the few in the country dedicated to that form of dramatic art. A keen sailor, he keeps his 9½m Swedish yacht at Woodbridge in Suffolk, where the family were originally based. He has an ambition to sail round the world and if he can't realize that he will settle for the Atlantic. He also enjoys other sports, going skiing in the winter and playing golf and tennis.

He has said that he wouldn't mind taking up painting when he retires and enjoys reading when on holiday. He lives in a former pub just outside Norwich. It is not yet known whether his own children will be entering the family business, although it seems likely. His daughter works for another publisher and his son works for Granada Television.

Gulu Lalvani   £25m

ELECTRONICS   dob (unknown)

BORN in Karachi, but raised in Bombay after the partition of India, Gulu Lalvani arrived in Leeds as a student at the age of 17, accompanied by his elder brother Partap. He entered the pearl business and was soon making a fortune by the standards of the 1950s. In the 1960s, he moved into the pocket transistor radio business, with cheap imports from Hong Kong. Sales took off when *Which?* magazine named one of his radios as a best buy. Today, the company has sales of £55 million. Lalvani is always looking for new markets and in July 1990, bought Dialatron, one of Britain's largest suppliers of telephones, from the receiver. He is planning a major assault on the European market. Partap now runs the operation in India. Gulu recently moved from exclusive Bishops Avenue in London's Hampstead to equally prestigious Hyde Park. He drives a Rolls-Royce, complete with personalized number-plate.

John Lelliott   £25m

BUILDER   dob 3 April 1935

BORN in Teddington, south-west London, John Lelliott went to school locally and to the nearby technical college before being called up for National Service. After two years in the Royal Engineers, he came back to 'civvy street' and went into the building industry, working in a small works department of a private firm. His crucial move came in 1963, when he joined a company called Winter & King as manager of their small works department. When the parent company went into liquidation in 1964, he bought the business and changed its name to John Lelliott. It has grown to become one of London's leading building contractors, with an annual turnover of £250 million.

After a disastrous foray into property development in the early 1980s, the company recovered to build a solid reputation, particularly for its refurbishment work. It aborted a stock market float at the time of the October 1987 crash, but could go for one again soon, if the property market picks up.

Lelliott has been married for over 30 years, and is a keen supporter of Wimbledon Football Club, where he is vice-chairman. In the mid-1980s, he was involved in a project to build a new stadium for Wimbledon in south London, but difficulties with raising the £20 million finance have held it up.

Despite the recession in the building industry, particularly in the south-east, Lelliott managed to secure some £42 million worth of orders in December 1989, including work on stands at Lords cricket ground. The group has plush headquarters in exclusive South Audley Street, Mayfair.

Paul, John and Michael Madeley

£25m

EX-DIY BUSINESSMEN   dob (unknown)

PAUL Madeley was best known as the Leeds United and England footballer who made his name in the late 1960s and early 1970s. He played in every position for Leeds except in goal, helping them to two league titles, the FA Cup, the Football League Cup and, twice, the UEFA Cup.

The late Don Revie described Madeley as his gilt-edged security, saying, 'Wherever I ask him to play, he just nods his head and says "Right." We don't get much conversation out of Paul. He comes in, says "Good morning," stays at the forefront of training and goes home as quietly as he came.'

Madeley, who signed from Farsley Celtic in 1962, made a record 708 appearances for Leeds before retiring in 1981. He also won 24 England caps, despite telling Sir Alf Ramsey, the then England manager, that he did not wish to play in the 1970 World Cup.

On retirement he began helping his two brothers in the family wallpaper business. The Madeley brothers started their chain in 1969 with a single store in Otley, just when Paul was making his name as a footballer. By 1987, they had built it up to 27 stores, mainly in Yorkshire, but with a strong presence in Wales and the West Country. In 1984, it made the transition to out-of-town superstores and the business grew fast. By 1987, the brothers had built up a £30 million annual turnover and £2.4 million profits. They planned to sell the chain to their managers for around £25 million, but Philip Birch, then the boss of the Ward White group, pipped them at the post by offering £27 million for the Madeley business.

The deal left Paul Madeley with his own sports shop in Leeds, which he had opened in 1980 with his wife Ann. They live quietly in a four-bedroom detached house on the outskirts of the city with their two sons.

Lord Matthews   £25m

TAX EXILE   dob 5 December 1919

BORN in Islington after World War I, Victor Matthews went to the local elementary school. His father died of wounds received in the trenches. Matthews was raised by his mother, who ran a small credit business long before the days of hire purchase. The Thirties was a tough time for Matthews and he was unemployed for a year. During the war, he served in the Navy, rising from ordinary to able seaman. After the war, Matthews went to work for the Trollope & Colls building group, mainly concerned with repairing war damage.

He taught himself quantity-surveying through a postal course. Impatient to get to the top, and seeing the way that sub-contractors were making a lot of money, Matthews joined a sub-contractor in 1955. The business soared under his guidance and when he left in 1960, his boss encouraged and backed him. Matthews bought into a small building company called Bridge Walker. In four years, he raised the turnover tenfold. But it was in 1964, when Matthews went to do some contract work for Trafalgar House, that he really started on the path to fame and fortune. He hit it off with Nigel Broackes, the Trafalgar boss (q.v.). Despite their widely differing social backgrounds, they eventually joined forces in 1967, when Trafalgar took over Matthews' business. Matthews went on to the Trafalgar board and actually ran the company, leaving Broackes to dream up new ideas and deals. In 1968, they took over Trollope & Colls, where Matthews had first worked. They also added Cunard and the *Express* newspapers to their stable. In the early 1980s, the partnership was dissolved when Matthews went his own way to run the newspapers. For three years, he enjoyed the role of press baron until, in 1985, the business was taken over by a rival group, United Newspapers, after a bitter takeover battle. Matthews decided to cash in his shares and retired from his north London home to tax exile in Jersey, selling his string of racehorses along the way. His son, Ian, joined him in Jersey and runs a local bakery.

Lord Middleton   £25m

LANDOWNER   dob 1 May 1921

IN a country with more than its fair share of wealthy land-owners, few come more distinguished than the 12th Lord Middleton. Based at Malton in North Yorkshire, and educated at Eton, Middleton distinguished himself in World War II. He won a Military Cross as a major in the Coldstream Guards, was mentioned in despatches and won the coveted French Croix de Guerre. His brother, a professional soldier, retired as colonel of the regiment.

Many of his cousins and relatives were soldiers or sailors and the web of family connection spans the British aristocracy, including links to the De l'Isles and the Earls of Cromer. One notable relative was his great-uncle, Sir Alexander Penrose Gordon Cumming, who founded MI6.

In the 1870s the Middleton lands ran to 99,576 acres, scattered across Ross in Scotland, Yorkshire and the Midlands. Their holdings put them among the top 50 landowners in the United Kingdom at the time. While the precise current acreage is unknown, the huge Ross estate, covering 63,000 acres, has been sold to the Wills tobacco dynasty. Most of the Yorkshire lands, and some of those in Nottingham, Lincoln and Warwick, are still believed to be in the hands of the Middleton family.

Middleton has been president of the Yorkshire Agricultural Society, Britain's largest, and went on to head the Country Landowners' Association, which claims to represent the owners of over 85% of the agricultural land of the country. He sat as a County Councillor for North Yorkshire, is a Justice of the Peace for the East Riding and is the Deputy Lord Lieutenant of North Yorkshire.

He married in 1947, and his wife Janet is the daughter of an army general. She formed and chaired the influential city organization known as the Lloyds External Names Association, representing those non-professional members of Lloyds insurance whose unlimited commitment of their assets is the foundation stone of the market. She did this in response to the scandals that swept Lloyds in the early 1980s, figuring Peter Cameron

Webb (q.v.). Two of their three sons went to Eton and joined the Coldstream Guards. The third broke with tradition and went to Harrow, and from there to Manchester University, where he took an MSc.

Swraj Paul   £25m

INDUSTRIALIST   dob 18 February 1931

A DEGREE from the Massachusetts Institute of Technology and a spell at the Harvard Business School have helped Swraj Paul build one of Britain's most successful industrial groups.

Paul, who was born in the Punjab, worked in his family's steel, shipping and hotels business from 1953 until 1966, when he came to Britain. He came originally to seek treatment, unsuccessfully, for a daughter who died of cancer. Paul recovered from the tragedy by concentrating wholly on work. He bought a small steel-making firm in Huntingdon and then established a steel tube-manufacturing plant in Wales, which was to be the start of his Caparo empire. For most of the 1980s he specialized in buying up old and apparently dying British companies or doomed factories and turning them into highly profitable concerns. Old steel mills, Midland metal bashers and the like have all responded to the Paul touch. He still retains his links with India and he was a firm friend and biographer of the late Mrs Gandhi. She in turn saw him as someone capable of modernizing the creaking Indian economy and its bureaucracy.

As well as Caparo, Paul has substantial property and hotel interests in Britain and he owns Indian tea plantations.

Today, he employs 5,000 people, and Caparo has a £400 million turnover. Like many other tycoons he hires the best British management experts available for huge salaries. 'God,' Paul, a devout Hindu, is fond of saying, 'has been good to me.' He insists that for Asians the most important business value is 'integrity'.

Paul is now looking beyond the confines of Britain to Europe,

America, Australia and other countries. His twin sons, Ambar and Akash, also play a key role in the business today. He sent them to The Hall, a preparatory school in north London, and then to Harrow. This was topped with spells doing business studies in the United States. His youngest son, Angad, who was also at Harrow, will join the family business after finishing his studies in the United States. Like many Asian tycoons, Paul believes an American education gives children an extra edge over others.

Paul gives his sons considerable independence to run their bits of the business (the turnover of the 'bits' total £100 million each for Ambar and Akash).

Ambar, for example, persuaded his father to let him run Clydesdale Engineering, a firm based in Dudley in the Midlands, which was about to be sold. Within three years, Ambar had increased a £30,000 profit on a turnover of £1.7 million to a £500,000 profit on a turnover of £4.1 million. 'My father leaves me to myself. He likes to be informed and I use him as an adviser,' Ambar comments.

Akash is based at Scunthorpe, supervising United Marchant Bar, a joint steel-rolling venture with British Steel. 'Dad,' he says, 'is in charge of America and strategic planning.' Board meetings are conveniently held on Friday or Monday, so that the boys and their families can be with their parents for the whole weekend.

Roy Sandhu £25m

INDUSTRIALIST, PROPERTY DEVELOPER
dob (unknown)

ROY Sandhu left Delhi in 1962 as a 14-year-old and settled in the East End of London. The crowded, tenemented area still contained the working docks which provided much of the community with a livelihood, either directly or indirectly.

In the 1970s, when the docks were in decline, Sandhu began his own textile manufacturing business, following a family tradition. He also began to acquire property and with it a taste for development.

His timing was excellent. The vast new Dockland development scheme, including the Wapping site of News International and the 850-foot tower at Canary Wharf, had begun to take shape, just as his first really big project, Aliffe House on the corner of Mansell Street in London E1, was opened by the Trade and Industry Secretary, Lord Young, in 1988.

In 1986 Sandhu had made a formal application to Tower Hamlets Council for permission to create a 60-storey, 1.4m-square-foot project on the corner of Whitechapel High Street and Commercial Road, also in E1. He received a mixed reception. Some Labour and Liberal councillors wanted to abolish the planning committee so that he could be given the go-ahead for the project, which would bring valuable new jobs and a new look to a very run-down area. The Royal Fine Arts Commission, whose acquaintance with E1 must be thought to be slight, said that the case for such a large development 'had not been proven'. Sandhu, now with his entire family over from India and working in the company, instead built 73 flats a little further east, at Narrow Street and Shoulder of Mutton Alley.

In an interview with the *Estate Times* in 1989, when he revived and restarted his plan for the big project, though with the height scaled down to 40 storeys, he said that 'success in a building lies in how you design the outer skin'. His buildings are both decorative and imaginative, with echoes of Indian Moghul architecture.

His Roy Properties group made £7.2 million after-tax profits up to the end of December 1987. There are three Sandhus on the board.

James Sherwood   £25m

SHIPPING AND HOTEL OWNER   dob 8 August 1933

JIM Sherwood may be the Yale-educated son of a Kentucky attorney, but he is a confirmed anglophile. He lives and works in London, and has run the Sea Containers shipping business since he founded it in 1965.

While doing his military service with the US Naval Reserve he was one of the first people to spot the potential of container traffic. Today Sea Containers is one of the largest container leasing businesses in the world. But Sherwood, who lives in the exclusive Boltons area of South Kensington in London and in an Oxfordshire mansion, has built up an impressive array of luxury businesses. He revitalized the Orient-Express, turning it into a de luxe service between London and Venice. There is an Orient-Express hotel chain, including the Cipriani in Venice and the Villa San Michele in Florence.

He also took over the Sealink ferry business from British Rail and fought a long campaign against the Channel tunnel, which is expected to hit the ferries in 1993. But he will be looking for new opportunities in 1990, having sold virtually all of Sea Containers' assets to two rival groups for $1.1 billion. The two companies, Tiphook and Stena, had been trying to take over Sea Containers for several months against fierce resistance from Sherwood, who finally agreed to the takeover only when the terms were increased. Sherwood plans to use the proceeds of the sale to buy more hotels and start another luxury train service in the Far East. The takeover bid helped increase the value of Sherwood's 7% stake in the business by £10 million to £55 million, though it is worth around £25 million today.

Charles and Edward St George   £25m

LLOYDS UNDERWRITERS
dob CSG 21 June 1925, ESG 6 March 1928

WHEN Lester Piggott, the jockey, was seeking to raise £1 million for his bail after being arrested on tax evasion charges, one of his great friends, Charles St George, came to his rescue and chipped in £25,000. For St George, an ex-Coldstream Guards officer, the money was small beer. Together with his younger brother, Edward, he owns a majority of shares in

Oakley Vaughan, a leading Lloyds underwriter, where he is also chairman.

The two men have the cash to indulge all their passions. In 1980 Charles bought Fort Belvedere, the Berkshire castle where King Edward VIII signed his abdication, for £650,000. Within six months he had sold it for £850,000. Edward lives as a tax exile in the Bahamas, where he serves as chairman of the Grand Bahama Port Authority.

Both have substantial racing interests. In 1975 Charles, nicknamed Lucky, paid $92,000 for a leading American horse. Many of his horses are trained by Henry Cecil, the top trainer; he also has horses under training in America. He is reputed to be an astute gambler, like many involved with the Turf, and, on the eve of his 50th birthday in 1975, he won £69,600 from a £275 bet. He lives in a Mayfair house and also owns a large spread at Newmarket, in the heart of racing country.

Rod Stewart   £25m

POP STAR   dob 9 September 1945

'DO ya think I'm sexy?' Rod Stewart asks as he belts out the repertoire on stage that has earned him a £25 million fortune since his first top ten hit 'Stay with Me' in 1970. Several of the world's most glamorous women may have the answer, including Joanna Lumley, Britt Eklund, Alana Hamilton and top American model Kelly Emberg.

Stewart's love life has made him a natural target for the tabloid press and the gossip columns. But the brash Londoner, a fanatical supporter of the Scottish national football team, started life in very different circumstances.

Though his father bought Stewart a guitar as a birthday present, his first job was as a gravedigger. But as the guitarist with the Hoochie Coochie Men, who backed Long John Baldry, Stewart's pop career was born. He later became a lead singer with The Faces, and was with them when they made their breakthrough.

'Maggie May', his first solo hit in 1971, established Stewart as an international star, and from then on he was rarely out of the news. He was banned from British Airways flights after smashing up a plane in a drunken brawl. Heavy drinking, he felt, was part of the image of the hell-raising pop star. In 1981, after taking a special cure in Barbados, he managed to kick the habit, and today rarely drinks more than a glass of wine. 'I don't think I live a rock 'n' roll lifestyle any more. I don't smoke, don't take drugs, don't drink a lot. I don't even go out much,' he told the *Sunday Express*.

The old Stewart loved partying through the night, so much so that he exhausted Alana Hamilton, his first wife. She suffered from a debilitating fatigue syndrome, but Stewart dragged her out to parties even when she was pregnant. They separated in 1983 after just four years of marriage. They had two children, Kimberley and Sean, who live with Alana in California. Stewart lives there too but says he misses England enormously.

In recent years he has also tried to change his image as a womanizer. 'I don't want to be a sex symbol any more. I've proved that and it's so silly really. If George Michael wants to take over the sex symbol crown he can. I've given up all that.' He is now married again to Rachel Hunter, some twenty years his junior.

Nigel Wray   £25m

FINANCIER   dob 9 April 1948

SINGER & Friedlander is a very traditional merchant bank in the City. 'My main reaction was that it was a very weird name but I thought merchant banking had a nice sound to it,' recalls Nigel Wray. Eighteen years ago he joined the bank as a trainee. Bored with the conventions of that world, Wray left after four years only to rejoin in 1987 as deputy chairman and part owner.

In between he made his fortune several times over, having what he terms 'an eye for an opportunity'. Wray's big 'punt' was to take over the *Fleet Street Letter*, an ailing tip sheet, for £6,500 in 1975. Although his family had owned a small North London printing company, Wray showed no talent for publishing. 'The whole of 1976 was a minor disaster. Things were going nowhere and I had £98 in the bank,' he says.

Among the lessons he learnt the hard way were to double the price and send the *FSL* out fortnightly instead of weekly. More for less, in other words.

The *FSL* came to the Unlisted Securities Market in 1981 and in 1983 Wray merged it with the phenomenally successful Carlton Communications, founded by Michael Green (q.v.).

'I just met Green at a party and we got on well,' explains Wray. 'I'm good at assessing opportunities but I would never describe myself as someone with a vision like Michael. All I can do is add up and spot downside risk at a considerable distance.'

Wray's next coup was to spot the potential of a sleepy property company, Gilbert House. He bought control for £3 million and eventually, through a series of deals, got back into banking. On lending he is now a conservative – although he has borrowed plenty in his time and was 'underwater' in the 1974 property crash.

'Once you get creative in banking – like pouring money into Mexico because "a country can't go bust" – it all goes wrong. The big trend of the moment is always a disaster a few years down the track,' he says firmly.

Wray lives modestly with his wife and child, deploring yachts and racehorses. 'Having a lot of money means I can drive a decent car, go on holiday occasionally and go to the theatre without saving up ... Tycoonery is anathema to me. I don't know many, thank goodness.'

His convictions are strong. 'I have very strong views on how to run a company. I don't think directors should have perks. There should be no corporate donations to politics or charity. If you feel *that* strongly, spend your own money.'

Don Lewin   £23m

RETAILER   dob (unknown)

AFTER he left the armed forces, Don Lewin worked in a variety of jobs, including one as a Kleen-eze brush salesman, knocking on countless front doors. He answered an advert offering an agency to sell greetings cards for a firm in Leeds, and he went to work with enthusiasm, finding a ready market in newsagents and chain stores. He even expanded and employed some sub-agents. But he believed that there was a market for shops selling a wider range of better-quality cards and hit on the idea of specialist shops. He borrowed £100 from his father to open a bank account and establish his credentials.

In 1968 he opened his first shop in Essex, selling American Hallmark cards. Named after his son Clinton (who was christened after the 1960s cowboy star Clint Walker), the group began to expand and soon there were seven shops, requiring Lewin to work 18 hours a day for seven days a week. He sold up on his 40th birthday, intending to take life easy.

But he soon became bored and before his next birthday was in business again with a new venture called Clinton Card Shops. When it came to the stock market in 1988, there were 72 shops and some 7 million customers, mainly in Essex and London.

The British market for cards is worth £600 million annually, with large numbers sent every Christmas and St Valentine's Day. In 1990 Clinton Card profits rose by 46% while the number of shops had risen to 225. Valued at around £30 million, Lewin and his family hold 75% of the shares, worth £22.5 million. Married for almost 40 years, he drives a Rolls-Royce.

Lawrie Lewis £23m

EXHIBITIONER ORGANIZER   dob (unknown)

IT was a case of rags to riches – quite literally – for Lawrie Lewis, former deputy chairman of the Blenheim Exhibitions Group, which, as its name implies, specializes in organizing exhibitions.

Trained initially in garment production, Lewis was a sales director for a fashion company from 1970 to 1974, marketing the output of such well-known designers as Ossie Clark and Sheridan Barnett. In 1975 he branched out on his own, setting up a design company. He knew the ups and downs of the business. Three companies he was associated with in the early 1980s went into voluntary liquidation, though all the creditors were paid in full and no blame was attached to Lewis.

Through the 1970s, he had attended some 150 exhibitions as an exhibitor. This experience convinced him that there was a market for organizing exhibitions and in 1979 he set up Blenheim Dresswell, which specialized in organizing fashion fairs and shows for the clothes sector. By 1982, it was becoming what *Acquisitions Monthly* magazine called 'a serious business' and Lewis called in Neville Buch, a City investment consultant, as chairman – initially for one day a week, but soon it was a full-time job.

In 1982, Blenheim organized five exhibitions. By 1986, when it came to the Unlisted Securities Market, that figure had risen to 36, including one for the chilled food industry. As a quoted company, Blenheim has been in the news for its hectic pace of acquisitions, particularly in Europe. It was also named a USM company of the year by the USM magazine.

The shares, which were floated at 95p, rose to over 900p within three years. Lewis is one of the few company founders who had not sold any shares when his business was floated on the stock market.

In May 1991, Lewis decided to sell his entire stake in Blenheim to an American publisher, raising some £28 million from the sale.

Three times married, he told the *Sunday Telegraph*: 'I lost my third wife because she was away on business for six months of the year and my second because I was.'

Lewis works a 75-hour week. He lives in London's fashionable Holland Park during the week, commuting to his Wiltshire home in his American sports car on Friday evenings. He is noted for his bright bow-ties.

David Parker   £23m

CLOTHING WHOLESALER   dob 18 May 1939

DAVID Parker's Sherwood group is one of Britain's largest bra makers and the main rival to the giant Courtaulds. Sherwood was established in 1947: it makes exotic ladies' lingerie and nightdresses. Worn by glamorous models, all these products are advertised in the annual report, making it almost a collector's item in the City.

Sherwood numbers the Burton Group, Asda, Littlewoods and British Home Stores among its clients. Parker was a former management trainee with Boots who moved into the textile industry. In 1968 he branched out on his own and took over Sherwood (then named Debfor) for £12,100 with the backing of a sleeping partner who has since sold out. In those days, the group made golfing clothes as well as bras, but Parker abandoned them to concentrate on underwear.

Through the 1970s, Parker expanded the business from its Nottingham base and in 1986 he took the group to the stock market. Since then it has made sizeable acquisitions, including a Dutch company. He holds just under 60% of the shares, worth around £23 million.

His strategy appears to be working. In the year to the end of December 1989, Sherwood reported pre-tax profits of over £8 million, against £6.5 million in the previous year. Turnover rose from £47.6 million to £74.3 million in the same period.

Sir Harry Solomon   £23m

FOOD DISTRIBUTOR   dob 20 March 1937

THE chickens, bacon, eggs and vegetables bought off supermarket shelves may have the supermarket's own brand
label attached, but the chances are that they have been produced
by Hillsdown Holdings, a company hardly heard of in 1980.
Today, it is one of Britain's largest companies.

Hillsdown was the brainchild of two men, David Thompson
(q.v.) and Harry Solomon. They met through their wives' chance
encounter in 1964 at an ante-natal clinic in Hadley Wood, a
North London suburb. Talking before their appointments,
Judith Solomon discovered that Patricia Thompson's husband
David was a butcher by trade but a wheeler-dealer at heart,
who bought businesses and assets almost on whim. He needed a
lawyer, and Judith Solomon mentioned that her husband was a
newly qualified solicitor.

Thompson became his client and increasingly took a larger
and larger share of his time. Solomon was quite happy with
this, since the rest of his business seemed increasingly mundane,
and Thompson's work was 'like a breath of fresh air', according
to one recent study of Hillsdown.

In 1975, they formed a company to bring some order to
Thompson's scattered interests, and called it Hillsdown after his
North London house. In 1980, Solomon resigned from his law
firm to work full-time for Hillsdown and the buying of new
companies began in earnest. They came at a bewildering speed.
In 10 years, the duo bought 284 new businesses and borrowed
£600 million to fund the purchases.

Some of their most successful purchases were from the receiver. They found nothing wrong with the businesses, just the
way they had been managed. A new streamlined management
system with speedy decision-making was installed, while Thompson and Solomon visited the factories frequently. This hands-on
management worked wonders, and in the ten years from 1977
to 1987 profits rose from £116,000 to £110 million.

Thompson, who had always been the ideas man, leaving
Solomon to run the business, stepped down from Hillsdown in

April 1987, selling half his shares. He recently sold the rest and no longer has any connection with the business. Solomon, a workaholic, who keeps fit by jogging and careful dieting, now runs Hillsdown as chairman.

The Stewart-Liberty family £23m

RETAILERS   dob (unknown)

THE Liberty shop in London's Regent Street is one of the West End's better known and loved landmarks. It stands on the site where Arthur Lasenby Liberty opened his first store over 115 years ago, and it is one of the very few stores of any size still to have a significant family involvement. Two Stewart-Liberty brothers head major divisions of the company, which is publicly quoted, and Arthur Stewart-Liberty, son of the founder, sat on the main board as a non-executive director until his death in July 1990. The presence of the two brothers, Richard and Oliver, should ensure continuity of the Liberty family talent at the firm.

Generally, the family have kept a very low public profile, in sharp contrast with the store itself, which regularly promotes special offers in conjunction with papers like *The Times*. In the late 1960s and early 1970s Arthur's only daughter, Francesca, had a brief fling with the gossip columns, who followed her long-legged, miniskirted moves through various other stores with intense interest. They had very mild things to report, especially after she was fired from Harrods after just five weeks because so many of her friends came to visit. She hung around for a brief period with the jet set, cruising on the Mediterranean on a huge yacht hired by Michael Pearson, heir to the Cowdray title and the Pearson fortune. She did not pursue her interest in stores and is not on the board of the company.

The store, with 21 branches all over the UK and one in New York, is noted for its distinctive clothes and for the wide range of its merchandise. Long before green issues became popular, Liberty was practising an early form of Third-World awareness by selling goods from the poorer or more remote parts of the globe. They removed all golliwogs and related merchandise from the store after a single complaint.

Earl of Wemyss and March £23m

LANDOWNER   dob 19 January 1912

WHEN the two earldoms of Wemyss and March were created in the 17th century, the Wemyss family were already great landowners in Scotland. The 1st Earl built the harbour at Methil with his own money. By the late 19th century the lands ran to 57,000 acres in Gloucester and Worcester. Most of those lands are now held in a trust in the Wemyss and March Estate Management Co. Ltd, of which the present Earl is a director. He sits in the House of Lords as a Conservative.

A nephew of the Duke of Rutland, Francis David Charteris succeeded to the title in 1937. Educated at Eton and Oxford, he served as a major in the Middle East during World War II with troops from Basutoland, where he had been a colonial administrator. After the war he took up his position as a leading Scottish aristocrat, serving as a Justice of the Peace and as Lord Lieutenant of East Lothian. A strongly religious man, he is a Lord High Commissioner of the Church of Scotland and was for a time the president of the National Bible Society of Scotland. His other activities include membership of the Queen's bodyguard in Scotland, the Royal Company of Archers, and acting as the Lord Clerk Register of Scotland and Keeper of HM Signet for Scotland.

In 1954 tragedy struck the Earl's family when his first son, aged eight, was killed in a car crash on the Croshill Dailly road in Ayrshire.

His son and heir, Lord Neidpath, was page of honour to the Queen Mother and is married to a Guinness heiress. He is extremely bright, with a doctorate from St Anthony's College, Oxford.

Earl of Airlie £22m

LANDOWNER   dob 17 May 1926

THE Lord Chamberlain and a leading Scottish peer, the
13th Earl of Airlie enjoyed a conventional upper-class education – Eton and wartime service in the Scots Guards. He
stayed in the army until 1950, when he went to the Royal
Agricultural College at Cirencester to learn estate management.
It was a wise move: the Airlie estates cover 69,000 acres in the
rich farming county of Angus. He has two large stately homes
on the estate: Cortachy Castle and Airlie Castle. He also has a
home in London's fashionable Chelsea.

A riding accident in 1952 soon after his marriage to Virginia
Ryan, the daughter of an American multi-millionaire, put paid
to his career of running the estates. He took up merchant
banking, saying 'We all have to make a living now.' He joined
J. Henry Schroder in 1953, and became a director in 1961 and
chairman 12 years later. He inherited the title from his father in
1968. Wisely, most of the family property had been passed on
years previously: as a result, his father's estate was valued at
only £97,110. His father had also been Lord Chamberlain to
the Queen Mother when she was queen.

In 1977, Airlie became chairman of the ultimate holding company, Schroder PLC. In 1984, he had to give up the £168,000-
a-year job to take up his royal duties.

In the early 1950s Airlie had been tipped as a suitor for
Princess Margaret, but in the event it was his younger brother,
Angus Ogilvy, who married into royalty. He married Princess
Alexandra of Kent. Family relations with the British monarchy
have not always been as close. The 4th and 5th Earls forfeited
their lands for joining the 1715 and 1745 Jacobite rebellions
against the Hanoverian monarchy. But they were later pardoned
and had the lands restored.

Airlie has six children. His heir, Lord Ogilvy, married Lord
Rothermere's daughter Camilla in 1981. His eldest daughter
married Hereward Wake, the heir of another Scottish landowner. As Lord Chamberlain, he cares for the royal residences,
the royal art treasures and crown jewels. He also advises on royal

warrants and titles. But the only really controversial role of the Lord Chamberlain – censorship of the theatre – was dropped in 1969 to avoid embarrassment over the musical *Hair*.

Phil Collins   £22m

POP STAR   dob 31 January 1951

RAISED in the London suburb of Hounslow in a classic three-bedroom semi with bay windows, Phil Collins has a £1 million mansion in the Sussex village of Loxwood, complete with a £50,000 garden pond. Known locally as the Squire, he is extremely popular with the villagers, often nipping down to the local pub for a pint. His fortune is based on his role as drummer and singer in the group Genesis, which has sold over 50 million records in 15 years.

Acting and performing have always been in Collins' blood. His mother jointly runs the Barbara Speake Stage School, while his sister runs her own theatrical agency.

He started as a drummer with his own drum set at the age of three. Later his mother paid £3 an hour for him to have lessons. An aunt taught him to play the piano. His first professional role came when he was a child actor in Lionel Bart's musical *Oliver*, playing the Artful Dodger. After Chiswick Grammar School, he was in a band called Flaming Youth and later joined Genesis as its only non-private school member.

In 1981 he developed a solo career – first as a singer with hits like 'You Can't Hurry Love' and 'No Jacket Required'. The latter won three Grammie awards in Los Angeles in 1987.

His acting career has also been successful, starting with a guest appearance in the American television series, *Miami Vice*. His feature-film debut was in *Buster*, where he played the great train robber of that name.

Despite his superstar image, Collins admits that he is 'no Don Johnson [the star of *Miami Vice*]. I think fans can relate to me rather than having someone just to admire because they're fantastic-looking.'

He is close to his family, particularly his elder brother Clive, who is a renowned cartoonist, winning the Cartoonist of the Year award in 1984, 1985 and 1987.

Known as a workaholic, Collins split up from his first wife, childhood sweetheart Andrea, which greatly depressed him. She lives in Vancouver with their two children, Joley and Simon. Collins has since remarried. His second wife, Jill, is an American and they have had a daughter, Lily.

David Gestetner and family £22m

OFFICE EQUIPMENT SUPPLIERS   dob 1 June 1937

IN 1881, David Gestetner produced the first stencil by applying wax coating to some special long-grained paper he found on a Japanese toy kite. Thus was born the Gestetner duplicator and a business that grew to employ some 17,000 people in 1,300 offices worldwide in its heyday in the 1970s.

The first David Gestetner ran the business until the 1920s, when he was succeeded by his son Sigmund. By then an ex-employee had set up the rival Roneo company, but Gestetner still prospered. Sigmund died in 1956, while his son David was doing National Service. David took a history degree at Oxford before joining the business.

It was not until 1972 that David and his younger brother Jonathan became joint chairmen. By then, David had worked his way round the business, starting on the shop floor in the firm's Tottenham factory; he later worked for the American sales operation in 1963. He joined the board in 1967 and became export director.

Gestetner's profits peaked at £30 million in 1977. Five years later, the company was reporting a loss of around £3 million and was struggling to find new products in an age when photocopiers were replacing duplicators. It suffered a severe blow in 1981 when a deal with the British Technology Group to market its Nexos word processor fell through.

In 1986, an Australian group took over the running of Gestetner in an agreed deal with the Gestetner family, which owned around 28% of the shares. In return for injecting badly needed capital, the Australians undertook some severe cutbacks. The 14-acre Tottenham site was closed, sold and replaced by a new streamlined head office. New products were brought in and by 1988 profits were back up to nearly £28 million. David Gestetner remains a director of the company.

David Samworth £22m

FOOD PRODUCTION   dob 26 June 1935

DAVID Samworth and his brothers are the third generation of his family to enter the pig trade. His father and grandfather used to run a stall in the Birmingham meat market, selling pork wholesale to butchers. During the war, Samworth's father managed a company making pork pies and sausages. He continued in this trade after the war, buying an old family company with three butcher's shops. After his army service in the Sudan and Cyprus, David Samworth joined his father and brothers in the business in 1956. In 1960, the family bought a brand-new factory to make pork pies and their fortunes prospered. In 1967, David Samworth went to the Harvard Business School and came back to take over the business as chairman and managing director. One of his first moves was to buy a long-time rival firm, Pork Farms, from Garfield Weston (q.v.). In 1971, Samworth took his enlarged business to the stock market. Within a year, the shares had doubled. Eventually the business was taken over by Northern Foods and Samworth went on the Northern board. From 1980 to 1984, Samworth represented the industry as chairman of the Meat and Livestock Commission. In 1984, he went back into business with his two brothers in a high-quality food-manufacturing group called Samworth Brothers.

The family own all the shares in the business, which made £2.5 million after-tax profits on a £38.5 million turnover in 1989. With healthy reserves, the business would easily be worth

£22 million if floated on the stock market. David Samworth is a keen hunter as joint master of the Cottesmore hunt. He was also appointed as deputy to the Lord Lieutenant of Leicestershire in 1984. He lives, appropriately, in Melton Mowbray, the centre of the British pork pie industry.

Sir Nicholas Bacon, Bt £21m

LAWYER AND LANDOWNER   dob 17 May 1953

THE premier baronet of England, Sir Nicholas Bacon is a qualified barrister. He has a degree from Dundee University, where he went after Eton. A close friend of the Royal family, he was page of honour to the Queen in the late 1960s. His father was the noted soldier and agriculturist Sir Edmund Bacon, and all four of his sisters have married into distinguished aristocratic families, including that of the Earl of Selborne.

One of the two titles he holds, that of Baronet of Redgrave, was the first baronetcy created in England and denoted with the letters Bt. The title was given to the eldest son of Sir Nicholas Bacon, Lord Keeper of the Great Seal to Elizabeth I, and father of Sir Francis Bacon, the great scientist.

The family seat and estates are situated near Norwich, and Sir Nicholas lives there with his wife and daughter. The estates run to some 14,000 acres.

Sir Neville and Trevor Bowman-Shaw

£21m

INDUSTRIALISTS   dob 4 October 1930

EDUCATED by a private tutor and with a commission in the 5th Royal Inniskillin Dragoon Guards, the young Neville Bowman-Shaw appeared to be the perfect example of the 1950s upper-class playboy. He had joined the cavalry because he did not know what else to do. However, while in the army and working on farms, he acquired a taste for machinery, which took him into the infant British mechanical handling industry in the early 1950s. But initially there was a clash of cultures. In two years, he went through three jobs. He was either sacked or left of his own accord after pointing out how the companies could be improved.

He then decided to put his theory into practice and set up his own forklift truck operation with his brother Trevor. Called Lancer Boss, a name which harked back to his cavalry days, it started in a small room in Tite Street near the Chelsea Hospital in 1957. Initially the brothers acted as agents for a Dutch forklift company. But when they had sold their entire allocation of vehicles very quickly 'we started looking around and suddenly realized we could buy the components and make them ourselves for less than we were paying the Dutch', Neville Bowman-Shaw told the *Sunday Times* in 1966.

So, armed with a £20,000 loan raised on an uncle's security, they spent the autumn of 1958 building their first machine. This was sold to Montague L. Meyer, a timber importer, and was delivered to his Manchester operation as soon as the agreement with the Dutch ended on 1 January 1959. 'It worked, Meyer paid us on the 20th and on the 21st the front axle fell off. But we screwed it on again and it's working in Manchester to this day,' he was able to boast eight years later. Meyer came back for another five machines.

In 1960, Sir Neville moved Lancer Boss to Leighton Buzzard, where the group is still based. By 1969, the business was booming and they were making 200 vehicles a month. He paid well for good managers, but insisted on a tight financial control with budgets thrashed out monthly. 'We're a provincial Weinstock organization when it comes to that,' he later said.

In the 1960s Neville Bowman-Shaw realized that the fragmented industry would have to expand. He approached Sir Emmanuel Kaye of Lansing Bagnall suggesting collaboration, but he met with a lukewarm response.

Though the business flourished, it was not until 1983 that he was able to find his partner. He took over an ailing German company, and applied distinctly British or even Thatcherite medicine to revive it. Financial controls were tightened and the workforce pruned. Within seven months it was back in profit.

Today, following the takeover of Kaye's business by another German company, Boss, as it is now called, is the largest British-owned forklift truck company. Sir Neville Bowman-Shaw (knighted in 1984) remains at the helm with Trevor. He lives in a large manor house in Toddington, near the M1 motorway, and is known to be a fervent admirer of Mrs Thatcher.

Tom Clarke   £21m

BEDDING MANUFACTURER   dob 2 June 1919

MILLIONS of Britons owe a good night's sleep to Tom Clarke's mother-in-law. In 1945, on his demob from the navy, Tom Clarke had a £170 gratuity but no job and a wife to support. His mother-in-law gave him the idea. 'Look, lad,' she said, 'what about opening up shop as a mattress repairer? War may be over but you can't get new ones for love nor brass. Most folk are making do with ones fit for nowt.'

Clarke and his wife Joan, who had once been an upholsterer, took her advice and never looked back. He rented a small lock-up in Skipton, bought his first machine and carried it home on his back. With materials in short supply, he was forced to improvise. Soon Clarke was able to repair anything, from covers to springs. In 1948, he started making his own divans. A year later, at Christmas 1949, when business was slack, the nine employees and Clarke sat down to think of a company name.

They came up with the appropriately festive Silentnight. Silentnight beds were soon extremely popular with the British, who were shrugging off wartime shortages in the boom years of the 1950s. Today, it is the largest bed manufacturer in Europe, making over £8 million profit in 1987. More recently, it has been hit by the recession.

Though Clarke had a reputation as 'a boss in a million', he was badly shaken by a bitter strike which began in 1985. He sacked 346 workers who struck over a pay dispute. The strike had been called because the workforce felt Clarke had reneged on an earlier promise not to declare redundancies in return for a wage freeze at a time when the recession was hurting the business. The strike lasted nearly two years before petering out in defeat for the strikers.

Clarke was appalled at the way the strike had started. He felt contact had been lost between management and workforce, and determined on changes. 'We learnt a very bitter lesson about staying close to the people who work for you. I learnt it in the Royal Navy in the war. As soon as we passed the Liverpool bar the captain always told us everything. It made all the difference to the way we behaved and fought. It is a basic principle of management. People here forgot,' he said afterwards.

Clarke stood down from day-to-day management in 1987 although he still owns over half the shares through family trusts. He has received an OBE for his political and business services. He now lives in a large redbrick house in Skipton. Until the early 1970s, he had lived in a small cottage in the town. His two sons, Peter and John, are directors of Silentnight, though Peter also runs a Ford car dealership.

Lord Home of the Hirsel £21m

LANDOWNER AND POLITICIAN dob 2 July 1903

WHEN Sir Alec Douglas Home lost the 1964 General Election to Harold Wilson, few people realized that he had been the last true Conservative aristocrat and grandee to occupy 10 Downing Street.

He had pipped R. A. Butler to the post of prime minister in 1963. But even within the party the manner of his selection, by appointment rather by an election, set in motion a process that led to the election by Conservative MPs first of Ted Heath and later of Margaret Thatcher.

Despite losing the election and later resigning as leader of the opposition in 1965, Home returned to high office as foreign secretary in the Heath government in 1970. When Ted Heath lost the 1974 election, Sir Alec resigned, and for the second time became a full member of the House of Lords. He had resigned his earldom in 1963 so that he could become prime minister, and in 1974 he was created a life peer as Lord Home of the Hirsel.

Born the son of the 13th Earl of Home, Alec Douglas Home was heir not only to a title but to vast Scottish estates. In the late 19th century the Home acreage, 106,550 acres scattered across six counties, made the family the 40th largest landowners in the UK. Today there are about 20,000 acres, much of it prime farming land.

At Eton, Home was noted more for his enthusiastic cricket than his brains. He went up to Oxford, continuing his cricket career. Conservative MP for Lanark from 1931 to 1945, he had the unfortunate task, as a joint Under-Secretary of State for Foreign Affairs, of accompanying Neville Chamberlain to sign the Munich pact with Hitler in 1938. He was always more interested in foreign affairs than in domestic politics.

Allen Lloyd   £21m

CHEMIST   dob 9 May 1949

A S a Coventry schoolboy, Allen Lloyd was good at science and had a passion for cars. But lacking the cash to run his Mini Cooper, he sought a career that would earn him enough to fund his hobby.

A Boots chemist at a school careers meeting convinced him that he should become a pharmacist. Having worked in his mother's newsagent's shop at weekends, he reckoned he knew a thing or two about retailing.

Initially Lloyd worked in Boots on Saturdays and in his holidays while he qualified as a pharmacist at Leicester Polytechnic. In his first year after graduating (the pre-registration year) he bought a house with the help of a £500 loan from his father. After 18 months he sold it, making an £8,000 profit. With money from his family and a Nat West bank loan, he bought his first shop. This was at Polsworth, near Warwick, and it opened on 4 February 1973. His wife Marilyn (they had met while he was a scout and she a guide) did the books. Today, she is data-processing controller for the group.

'The early years were a struggle, although I had support from my family. I had to sell everything to get enough money – my car, my home, everything. I worked and worked and luckily everything began to take off from there,' he told the *Sunday Mercury*.

By 1986, there were over 100 shops. They offered self-service but, unlike some other cut-price drug stores, all had a pharmacist attached. The group is based mainly in the West Midlands, but after coming to the stock market in 1986, it has pursued an aggressive takeover policy, expanding its range to around 1,000 shops, making it second only to Boots in the British market.

Peter Lloyd, Allen's younger brother, works in the group as development director. Allen Lloyd, an earnest chap, continues to indulge his passion for cars and drives a vintage Jaguar. He still has the original Mini Cooper whose upkeep propelled him into a career as a chemist.

Stephen Merrett   £21m

LLOYD'S UNDERWRITER   dob 30 May 1939

STEPHEN Merrett's father Roy was considered to be one of the great figures of the Lloyd's insurance market. He brought young Stephen into the market. In 1962 his father sold his underwriting agency for £500,000, though Stephen bought it back in 1976 for £3 million. Stephen has turned Merrett Holdings into the second largest underwriting agency at Lloyd's and he has over half the equity, which is worth well over £20 million.

As a young man in his father's agency, Stephen Merrett was often overshadowed by another rising star, Dick Outhwaite. Outhwaite broke away to establish his own business and a deadly rivalry ensued. It has lasted until the present day, with both running their own businesses, though Outhwaite has encountered problems over huge losses incurred by his syndicates from the early 1980s.

Merrett has become a specialist insurer of satellites in space. Ex-President Reagan decorated him for organizing and financing the rescue of a stray American satellite.

Oxford-educated, Merrett is a member of the Lloyd's ruling council. He is married to Helen Fearnley, a vivacious journalist, who works for *Financial Weekly*. They first met when she went to interview him, and she later became Mrs Merrett the second.

In its accounts for 1989, Merrett Holdings made £9.8 million pre-tax profits on a turnover of over £23 million. It is quoted on what is called the over-the-counter market, though Stephen Merrett has indicated that he would like to go for a full stock market quotation.

Tony Travis   £21m

TIMBER MERCHANT   dob 18 May 1943

IN 1899, a timber-importing company called Travis & Arnold was founded. Today, Tony Travis, a Harrow-educated barrister, runs the business, which has expanded to become a builders' merchant.

In 1989 it merged with Sandell Perkins, another builders' merchant, after a bitter takeover battle. The merger was nearly spoilt by the intervention of another group, Meyer International,

tional, which offered a much higher price for Travis & Arnold shares. But in the end, the support of the Travis family, holding 38% of the Travis & Arnold shares, proved decisive, and the Sandell merger went through.

Tony Travis is now chairman of the enlarged group, which is based in Northampton. Married three times, he lives in Fulham, London. His first wife was the daughter of Lord Pritchard, and his third is a daughter of Sir Peter Foster.

Peter Yuill and family   £21m

BUILDING   dob 16 May 1949

PETER Yuill trained as a civil engineer with Laings after a public school and university education. It served him well when he took over his father's building company, Cecil M. Yuill Investments. Today he is chairman and vice-chairman of the group, which made £3.7 million after-tax profits on a £33.9 million turnover in the year to the beginning of April 1989. Based in Hartlepool, the company is active in house-building in the North-East. Cecil Yuill made the news in 1980 when the Law Lords unanimously allowed his appeal through, reducing an inland revenue tax assessment from £1,095,853 to £1,417. Peter Yuill, who is on the board of several local companies, is a pillar of the local community as magistrate and school governor. He lists his hobbies as squash, golf, snooker and bridge.

Yaqub Ali   £20m

RETAILER   dob (unknown)

YAQUB Ali fled Pakistan soon after the partition of India and arrived in Glasgow in 1952, with just £4 10s in his pocket. He started work as a door-to-door salesman. Today, with his brother Taj, he owns Europe's largest wholesale ware-house, in the notorious Gorbals. It is called, appropriately, Castle. They also have an off-licence chain.

Despite being awarded the title of Scotland's most successful Asian immigrant by the *Scottish Business Insider* magazine, Ali lives a simple life with his Scots wife, apart from his one indulgence, a Jaguar. In 1989, his business made a £1.9 million profit on a £90 million turnover. A strong supporter of Mrs Thatcher, Ali organized a dinner for her on one of her visits north of the border. He also reckons the British economy would benefit from an influx of Hong Kong Chinese: 'New people work harder and new blood is good for business,' he said.

Georgina Andrews   £20m

DEPARTMENT STORES   dob (unknown)

IN 1894, a Simeon Simpson established his own clothiers' business in London's Piccadilly. His eldest son, Alexander, took over the running of the family-controlled business, but he died of leukaemia in 1937 and the running of the business was taken over by his younger brother, Leonard. By then, Leonard was a brilliant doctor, having taken a first class honours degree at Cambridge in natural sciences. A leading expert on hormone disorders, he kept up his medical research as well as running his family firm, which expanded enormously under his direction. Its most famous product were the DAKS self-supporting trousers (hence the group's later name DAKS Simpson). DAKS was an amalgam of dad and slacks, and proved to be a winner. Until the age of 70, Dr Simpson continued to practise in his Harley Street surgery and was still chairman of the family business on his death in 1983.

His only daughter, Georgina, trained as an actress at the Bristol Old Vic. She later married the actor, Anthony Andrews, best known for his role as Sebastian in *Brideshead Revisited*. Georgina was a director of the family firm, which was sold to the Japanese Sankyo Seiko group for £65 million in February

The sale netted Georgina just under £20 million. She remains a board member under the new owners.

Raffaello Bacci £20m

VAN HIRE ENTREPRENEUR dob *c.* 1938

IN 1951 Raffaello Bacci, a 13-year-old working-class Italian boy, left the small Tuscan town of Lucca to come to England for a holiday. But he stayed to help in his grandfather's lamp-making business.

The business was highly seasonal and every Christmas a boom in orders would carry them through the next year. Hiring transport to distribute the Christmas orders proved progressively difficult, giving young Bacci an idea for a new company. In 1965, together with a cousin, he bought 4 vans and went into business for himself. Within three years he had 56 vehicles. Today the company, Salford Van Hire, has over 5,000 vehicles at depots in Manchester and Leeds. It is also involved in car hire.

It is now one of the largest commercial vehicle hire firms in Britain, with its latest accounts for 1988 showing after-tax profits of over £2 million. The firm is wholly owned by the Bacci family, giving them a net worth of some £20 million.

Success means Bacci no longer needs to work a 16-hour day, though he still arrives at his Salford headquarters at 8 a.m. and works until 6 p.m. six days a week.

'Perhaps it's the immigrant thing, that we have to work harder than everybody else just to prove ourselves,' he says in his deep Mancunian accent.

His children, two daughters and a son, have all been privately educated in England and are involved in the family business. His youngest daughter Patrizia, in her early twenties, is now managing the company's latest venture in Florence.

Despite his wealth, Bacci lives modestly. His lifestyle is that of a fairly successful stockbroker. There is a Rolls-Royce, but he is most often seen in a Mercedes and home is a modest detached in the middle-class Manchester suburb of Whitefield.

'I suppose I could afford a bigger house in a better area, but where we are suits us. Anyway, what would I do with a yacht?' At the age of 52 Bacci admitted that he had often contemplated selling up or heading for the stock market, but the prospect of losing control always stopped him. 'I don't think I could work for somebody else. Even if I retained majority control I'd still be responsible to other shareholders and I wouldn't like that. I enjoy what I do and hopefully I can keep on doing it.'

Trevor Baines   £20m

ENTREPRENEUR   dob (unknown)

TREVOR Baines has an unusual background. His father owned a mine in Wales, while his mother was one of the first white women traders in Africa. After education at Stowe, he went to Liverpool Tech to do his O-levels. He took time off to go to America for a couple of years, selling clothes and acting as caretaker on Errol Flynn's yacht in Jamaica.

At 21 he joined the family's African trading business – selling beads and the like – and was made a director at 25. In 1969 the business moved from Britain to the Isle of Man. Trendy Trev, as he is known, inherited £3 million from his father in 1972 and has been involved in several property deals on and off the island. In 1982 he also made a cheeky bid worth some £56 million for the exclusive Beverly Wilshire hotel in Los Angeles, but nothing came of it. He was also part of a consortium that at one stage owned the Miss World competition, but he sold out, complaining that television had spoiled it.

Baines lives for much of the year on the Isle of Man with his wife Wendy, one of three sisters who make up the Brazil pop group, now called Press the Flesh. They have been married since 1979 and Trevor is heavily involved with the business, going to concerts and even enduring a 13-hour flight to the Falklands when they went to entertain the British garrison. His wife, formerly Condessa Wendy Nicolau de Almeida Reid, is also a Portuguese port heiress.

A thirst for adventure and travel has led Trevor to ride the Cresta sleigh run every winter since the mid-1970s. He has also been made a Fellow of the Royal Geographical Society for his inspired travel. He took a camel-racing team to the middle of Arabian desert on one occasion.

Known in the island for his charity work, he helps deprived Manx children with special treats such as visits to Disneyland. He celebrated his 50th birthday with a weekend of 1940s-style celebrations, culminating in the world's largest birthday party, for 10,000 people.

Margaret Barbour and family   £20m

BARBOUR JACKETS   dob (unknown)

THE waxed Barbour jackets so beloved of the Sloane Ranger or city type were invented by John Barbour in 1909. For years, the jackets were the staple wet weather clothing of farmers and sportsmen. But in the Eighties, they were 'discovered' and the business took off. Today, J. Barbour & Sons, based in South Shields, is a multi-million pound business, with sales of £23.2 million and £3.59 million after-tax profits in its latest accounts for 1988. Until the early 1970s, the business was run by another John Barbour, but when he died at the age of 30, his widow, Margaret took over the reins. Trained as a home economics teacher, she worked her way up through the various departments before becoming chairman. The company, under her guidance, was very careful to expand gradually and keep a tight rein on costs, though the loyal workforce is well paid and highly productive, using the latest computer-controlled equipment. In the late 1980s, demand for old and worn Barbour jackets was so great that thieves broke into the factory to steal old jackets awaiting repair.

Lord Beaverbrook   £20m

BANKER AND FINANCIER   dob 29 December 1951

THE *Sun* newspaper was characteristically blunt when Max Aitken, having revived his grandfather's peerage in 1985, was given a government job: 'Beaverbrook is not a chip off the old press baron, who created a newspaper.'

Whether stung by what the *Sun* said, or through natural reserve, Max Aitken no longer appears amongst the junior ranks of the Thatcher government. Educated at Charterhouse and Pembroke College, Cambridge, he is married to a niece of Lady Cowdray, whose husband heads the Pearson family.

They have three children and he is the head of a small, successful venture capital company and chairman of the Beaverbrook Foundation. He is a member of White's club and the Royal Yacht Squadron.

The original Beaverbrook fortune was created by William Maxwell Aitken, the son of a Canadian Presbyterian minister. He made his money in Canada and came to Britain in 1910, determined to enter politics. When hostilities broke out in 1914, he became the Canadian government representative at the front. By end of World War I, he was Chancellor of the Duchy of Lancaster and Minister for Information. He later founded the Express Group of newspapers, which made him yet another fortune. In the inter-war years, as his British papers made him richer, he moved in the most exalted establishment circles while, according to his daughter, involving himself in endless love affairs with a variety of women. During World War II he was, successively, Minister of Aircraft Production, Minister of State and Minister of Supply, member of the war cabinet and finally Lord Privy Seal. He had been made a peer in 1917. He married his second wife in 1963, a year before he died. She is one of Britain's top racehorse owners.

Beaverbrook's son disclaimed the peerage but used the Baronetcy which had preceded it. Sir Max, who spent his life at his father's newspapers, was one of the air aces of World War II. He had enlisted in the Air Reserve in 1935 and when war broke out in 1939 he was already a pilot in the crack 601 Squadron.

He finished the war as a group captain, having downed 16 enemy planes, and won both a DSC and a DSO. He was not a success as a newspaper proprietor and ownership of the Express Group passed to Victor Matthews. Sir Max died in 1985.

Major John Berkeley   £20m

LANDOWNER   dob 24 July 1931

THE Berkeley family, now headed by Major John Berkeley, own two of the largest estates in the West of England, both of which have survived intact despite severe estate duty problems in the late 1960s.

The first is the Spetchley Park estate of over 4,500 acres in Worcestershire. The other is the Berkeley estate in Gloucester. The latter contains Berkeley Castle, where the Berkeley family live. It is described as the oldest inhabited fortress in Britain and was first opened to the public in 1956. It was the scene of the murder of King Edward II on 21 September 1327. The occupant, Lord Thomas Berkeley, who was the King's custodian, was charged with the murder but acquitted. At one time or another the Berkeley family have held the titles of Viscount, Earl and Marquess. The earldom became extinct in 1942 and silver sold in 1960 to meet death duties on the Earl's estate made a world auction record of £207,000 at Sotheby's. A cousin of the Berkeleys sits in the House of Lords as Baroness Berkeley, one of only 20 hereditary female titles.

The army title sported by the present occupant of Berkeley Castle derives from his position as a company commander in the Queen's Own Warwicks and Worcester yeomanry. His professional military experience was as a lieutenant in the 10th Royal Hussars. He was educated at the Oratory, a Catholic private school, and then went to Magdalen College, Oxford. He is the Deputy Lord Lieutenant of Hereford, Worcester and Gloucester, and was High Sheriff of Worcester in 1967 and of Gloucester in 1982. He still runs one of the very few private foxhound packs in the country, first started in the 12th century to hunt deer on the estates. He married the daughter of a landowner from Scotland in 1967 and they have two sons. As well as the two estates, the castle contains a magnificent art collection and many other priceless treasures.

David Bowie   £20m

POP STAR   dob 8 January 1947

BORN David Jones in the tough inner London district of Brixton, David Bowie's early life was as exotic as his pop career. His father ran a Soho wrestling club, while his mother was a cinema usherette. He learnt the saxophone and began playing with local groups while working in a West End advertising agency as a copy clerk. He moved out of his parents' tiny Bromley house into digs to pursue his musical career, but with little success.

Keen to hit the big time, Bowie wrote to David Bloom, the washing-machine magnate, seeking financial backing. Bloom, who later went bust in spectacular fashion, booked Bowie for his wedding anniversary party. But after two numbers, he told Bowie to clear off, complaining that the party was being ruined.

Undaunted, in 1969, after five flops, Bowie achieved his first hit with 'Space Oddity'. By then he had met Angie, the American model who was to become his wife. He was also playing every Sunday night at the Three Tuns pub in Beckenham, where he had a huge cult following. He changed his appearance, cutting his hair short and spiky and dying it orange, to create the character Ziggy Stardust.

The tabloid press was full of minute details of his sex life and drug-taking in the late 1970s. He parted from Angie and became a recluse, living in Berlin's Turkish quarter. He became the first pop star to admit publicly to being bisexual.

Turning to acting helped to rescue his career and life. He has appeared in a number of films including *The Man Who Fell to Earth*, *Just a Gigolo* and *The Hunger*. But it was his role in the 1980 Broadway production of *The Elephant Man* which really won him critical acclaim.

Today, Bowie is linked in the gossip columns to Melissa Hurley, a ballet dancer. His relationship with his former wife Angie is bitter. They have both used the media to castigate each other and Bowie charges that she has no interest in their son Joe, who, at Bowie's insistence, was educated at Gordonstoun.

In the late 1960s and early 1970s, Bowie's 19 albums sold 19 million copies, while one tour in 1987 grossed £3 million. He has a £3 million Swiss château, where he lives as a tax exile, and a £1 million apartment in Japan. He now lives a much healthier life, having kicked drugs and drinking to excess.

Barbara Taylor Bradford   £20m

AUTHOR   dob (unknown)

A REAL Yorkshire lass born in the Leeds suburb of Armley, Barbara Taylor Bradford is one of the world's highest-paid living authors. Before she even began to write her last three books she had received a $9 million advance from her three English publishers. Her books are described as 'romantic fiction' and have sold over 50 million copies worldwide, in 32 languages. Her first book, which she wrote when she was in her forties, was called *A Woman of Substance*, and dealt with the rags-to-riches story of a young Yorkshire girl at the turn of the century. In many of the regular interviews she has given, both here and in the USA, where she lives, she has emphatically denied any connection between her own life and the life of the leading character in that first book.

She was the only daughter of middle-class parents who enrolled her in Armley library when she had read most of Dickens by the age of 12, and then bought her a typewriter. She earned her first pay cheque, 10/6d, at the age of 12 for a children's short story. Her formal education ended early and she was working in the typing pool at the *Yorkshire Post* by the age of 15. However, a year later she was a cub reporter and at 20 had become the women's editor of the paper. She then moved to London, where she was first fashion editor of

Woman's Own, and then worked on the *London Evening News*, *Today* magazine and finally the *London American*.

On Christmas Eve 1963 she married the American film producer Robert Bradford in London. They had been introduced by the press officer at the Savoy Hotel. Early the following year she left with him for New York, where she has lived ever since. She was always a working wife and initially wrote books on interior design. In an interview with Linda Lee Potter for the *Daily Mail* in 1984, she said, 'I kept starting novels but never getting past chapter five.' Then she gives a very important clue about her writing: she told Potter that she read an interview with Graham Greene in which he said 'character is plot'. Her books are based on very strong personalities.

Beginning with *A Woman of Substance*, all her books have been made into TV mini-series, which have been sold and shown worldwide. Her parents died in 1981, a traumatic event for her, but she still visits Yorkshire and her interviews are littered with references to her roots and the importance they hold for her.

Marquess of Bristol £20m

LANDOWNER   dob 15 September 1954

'JOHNNIE' to his chums, the 7th Marquess of Bristol is one of the more colourful members of the British aristocracy, and one of the few in modern times to have had their collars felt by the long arm of the law.

In September 1989 he was fined £3,000 on drugs charges at a court in Bury St Edmunds, after admitting that he had a habit costing him £1,500 a week. Five months earlier he had been released from prison in Jersey after serving seven months of a twelve-month sentence imposed for smuggling cocaine. While in La Moye prison, Bristol loved to lord it up, according to a fellow prisoner, even to the extent of having a personal monogram on his uniform. More practically, the Marquess claimed to have made £4 million in property deals while a guest of Her Majesty. He was visited regularly in prison by his business manager.

Bristol has known wealth all his life. His Suffolk home, Ickworth House, is one of the finest mansions in the country. Though it is managed by the National Trust, Bristol lives in one luxury wing, surrounded by servants. He also has 4,500 acres surrounding the house. Shrewd investments in the early 1970s in oil speculation, money broking and sheep farming in Australia (where he has a 59,000-acre farm) helped increase his fortune from the £4 million he inherited to around £20 million today.

He was estranged from his late father, who disapproved of his fast and extravagant lifestyle, which included stunts such as flying to London by helicopter for a haircut. In the late 1970s, he lived in Monaco as a tax exile. He married a property magnate's daughter in 1984, and they celebrated their wedding with a £100,000 reception. Francesca, his wife, had been married to an American rock musician and was a former Oxford Street shop assistant. But the marriage ended after two years when she ran off with a Brazilian house-guest.

His business manager said of Bristol once: 'John needs a close family unit and wants children so that he can pass on Ickworth.'

He once told the *Daily Mail*: 'I am scared to death of going broke. I am petrified at the thought of ever being poor and think about it every morning when I wake up.'

Controversy has never been far from Bristol. In 1986, a house-guest at an Italian villa he had rented was found dead in his bed. The Italian police were called to investigate but the guest had died from a brain haemorrhage after a fall.

Sir Nigel Broackes £20m

PROPERTY AND SHIPPING   dob 21 July 1934

THE son of a lawyer who was killed in the war, Nigel Broackes went to Stowe public school, his education paid for by his wealthy grandparents. After National Service in the 3rd Hussars, Broackes then went into property development in the 1950s. His initial forays were a disaster and he lost nearly all the proceeds of a £30,000 inheritance by the time he was 23. He put his last remaining asset, a block of flats, into the tiny Trafalgar House property group, and never looked back. Within a year he was managing director and four years later, he became a millionaire. In 1963, Trafalgar was floated on the stock market, but it was in 1964, when Broackes first met Victor Matthews (q.v.), that the business really took off. Matthews, who was running his own building company, took on a contract for Trafalgar. The pair hit it off, and Broackes took a stake in Matthews' business. Three years later, the companies merged and Matthews joined the Trafalgar board. One of the most famous partnerships in British business was born. They branched out first into shipping by buying the famous Cunard line and later moved into Fleet Street by taking over Beaverbrook newspapers. Matthews ran the business while Broackes came up with the ideas and looked to the long term as a brilliant strategic thinker.

In the early 1980s, the partnership dissolved when Matthews went his own way to run the newspapers. But Broackes continued to look for new Trafalgar business. He pushed a combined bridge-tunnel to cross the English Channel, which was rejected in favour of the Channel Tunnel. He oversaw the development of London's derelict docklands during a five-year stint as chairman of the London Docklands Development Corporation.

Broackes enjoys his wealth, which includes a palatial Oxfordshire mansion, a yacht and a villa in the South of France and a fine townhouse in London. His boredeom threshold is regarded as extremely low, and his main hobby, outside dealmaking and work, is working with silver as an accomplished silversmith. His wife, Joyce, is a former model.

Earl of Carnarvon £20m

LANDOWNER, RACING MANAGER
dob 19 January 1924

THE Carnarvon family are rich and aristocratic: the present Earl, the 7th, is said to be one of the closest family friends of the Queen and Prince Philip. He is also the Queen's racing manager, a post he has held since 1970. The Carnarvon title was originally created for a grandson of the Earl of Pembroke and its first holder had equine links with the Royal family even then, as the Master of the King's Horse. In the 1880s the family had land in six English counties, totalling over 35,000 acres. The family seat, Highclere, is one of the few castles in the country not regularly open to the public. The current estates, including land in Somerset, are thought to be around 10,000 acres.

The royal connection has made the present Earl a deal more discreet than his father, who turned self-parody into a minor art form. *The Times* obituary did him generous justice with one of the most colourful and indiscreet pieces that it ever printed. It variously described him as 'a most uncompromisingly direct ladies' man', and 'an inveterate stage-door johnny'. Predictably his first two marriages, the second to the Viennese dancer and singer Tilly Losch, ended in divorce. He was widowed in 1985. *The Times* said of his routine in London that 'he held court at White's (which excluded women) and played bridge at the Portland Club, but his metropolitan base was the Ritz Hotel in Piccadilly. At the hotel the canny Carnarvon's chief concern was to find a suite, not so much overlooking the Park as overlooking the rent.'

The telegram he sent to Sir Jock Delves Broughton when he was acquitted of the murder of the 22nd Earl of Errol in Kenya in 1941 (on which the film *White Mischief* is based) is framed in White's and reads, 'Hearty congratulations on winning a neck cleverly.'

In his later years, the 6th Earl wrote two books of racy memoirs, *No Regrets* and *Ermine Tales*, and he became an outrageous chat-show celebrity.

His father, the 5th Earl of Carnarvon, is best remembered as one of the people directly responsible for the discovery of the tomb of the Egyptian god-king Tutankhamun. His sudden death gave rise to the legend of the 'Curse of Tutankhamun', which certainly did not affect his son, who lived to the ripe old age of 88.

The present Earl has come in for some pointed comment in the gossip columns over the performance of the Queen's horses, but not apparently from his employer. Yet it is said that one of the Queen's real regrets is that she has never had a Derby winner.

Sean Connery   £20m

ACTOR   dob 25 August 1930

IF the ship that was supposed to be evacuating Sean Connery to Australia in 1940 had not been sunk, he might have gone there, stayed and become a clerk or waiter. Instead, he is one of the world's best-loved actors – and one of the richest – thanks largely to the part of James Bond in the series of films based on Ian Fleming's books. At one stage in the 1960s, he was earning the princely sum £1,000 an hour, 24 hours a day.

But his roots were far from the upper-class world portrayed by Bond. He left school at 13 during the war and took a series of temporary jobs on building sites, before learning a trade as a French polisher, working for an undertaker polishing coffins.

After three years' service in the Navy he was invalided out because of ulcers, but the experience left him with an abiding hatred of the snobbery and prejudice of officers. A spell of body-building led him to London to win a bronze medal in the Mr Universe contest. He was captivated by the bright lights and stayed.

He made it into the infant British television industry, winning parts in *Dixon of Dock Green* before making his début in films in 1956. But it was not until 1962, at the age of 32, that he was cast as Bond in *Dr No*. The film was an instant hit and the Bond legend grew. The third Bond film, *Goldfinger*, took $10 million in 14 weeks, a cinema record up to then.

After he tired of Bond, he went through a lean spell in the 1970s, but has re-emerged as a big star in the 1980s, winning his first Oscar for best supporting actor in *The Untouchables* and having a major role in the latest *Indiana Jones* blockbuster.

Cautious with his money, Connery lives in Marbella as a tax exile. He was careful always to claim his overtime on the Bond set and, in his last Bond film, *Diamonds are Forever*, he demanded, and got, 12.5% of the profits. He has also been astute in developing outside business interests, including his own private bank, Dunbar & Co., based in Pall Mall.

After his first marriage to the actress Diane Cilento broke up in 1973, he married his second wife, Micheline, a year later.

Ramesh Dewan £20m

PROPERTY AND PUBLISHING   dob (unknown)

A DIRECTOR of 37 companies spanning the property and publishing world, Ramesh Dewan's real wealth derives from his frenetic building work in the English regions. His Trans-Britannia properties group has put up 200 medium and small factories in the North of England, Plymouth and Wales, over an eight-year period. Like many of the Asian rich, Dewan lives quietly and discreetly in the affluent London suburb of Harrow.

Terry Ellis £20m

MUSIC PROMOTER   dob (unknown)

TERRY Ellis's fortune derives from his highly successful partnership with Chris Wright in the Chrysalis record company. Educated at Welwyn Garden Grammar School, he took an honours degree in maths and metallurgy at Newcastle University, before converting his part-time work as college social secretary into a full-time occupation in 1967. That was the year he got together with Chris Wright, who was also running an artists' booking agency. They quickly converted the Ellis Wright Agency into Chrysalis and signed up pop groups such as the Sex Pistols and Blondie and many of the key artists of the 1970s.

Ellis' original job with the company took him to America for six years and he signed up many of the best American groups. Establishing a reputation as a dealmaker, he was elected chairman of the Record Industry Association of America in 1981, the only foreigner ever to hold the post. By the mid-1970s both Wright and Ellis were millionaires and in 1984 Wright bought out Ellis for £17.4 million before taking the company public the following year, making himself a multimillionaire in the process.

After splitting with Wright he set up his own Ellis Corporation. Chrysalis moved into a period of very erratic results, often disappointing the City; but Ellis moved on to greater things, running Ellis Corp. as an investment rather than entertainment company.

In May 1989 he was elected chairman of British Phonographic Industries, the representative body for the whole UK record business. The post is an important one, as Ellis now has to face increasing demands for a reduction in the price of compact discs, where market growth has been artificially constrained by high prices. He must also manage the vital relationship between BPI and the Prince's Trust, for which it is a major and significant fundraiser.

Tom Farmer £20m

TYRE FITTER   dob 10 July 1940

THE youngest of seven children from a staunchly Catholic family, and raised in a three-room tenement, Tom Farmer had his first job cleaning cookers while he was at school in Leith, Edinburgh's run-down port area. When he left school he started work in the stores of a local tyre depot. He graduated to collecting old tyres and finally became a tyre salesman.

He left in 1964, at the age of 23, and he started his own tyre and car accessory business in an old grocer's shop in Edinburgh with an initial investment of £200. He opened the shop seven days a week and, in the era of strict resale price maintenance, started a discount operation. It was an immediate success and by the time he was 29 he was a millionaire.

Retiring to San Francisco to enjoy life with his family, Farmer soon became homesick and bored. Within three months he was back in Edinburgh, recruiting his old fitters and starting two new tyre and exhaust centres, which he called Kwik-Fit. He had been impressed by California muffler shops which fitted new exhausts while the driver waited, and he determined to try the same in Britain. Within 10 years he had 52 branches, and today there are over 600, which he oversees with an eagle eye.

Kwik-Fit, which came to the stock market in 1982, now employs 2,200 people and services 175,000 cars a month.

In 1990, Kwik-Fit's profits roared ahead by 62% to £24.4 million and sales rose by 22% to £217 million. Farmer extricated the group from a loss-making French venture, selling it in March 1991 for £5.6 million.

Lord Glenconner £20m

LANDOWNER dob 1 December 1926

THE Tennant family fortune goes back to the end of the 18th century when a Glasgow chemist, Charles Tennant, invented a new bleach which revolutionized the industry. He became a powerful industrialist and was later a Liberal MP and baronet.

Today, the family have no interest in the business but are well-known Scottish landowners, with 9,000 prime farming acres in Peebles, owned by Charles Tennant, 3rd Lord Glenconner. There are also extensive land holdings in Australia and Glenconner used to own the exclusive West Indies island of Mustique, which he developed into a millionaire's paradise. He sold it in 1977 and went on to spend £3 million building another exclusive resort on an old plantation in nearby St Lucia. The Glenconners also have one of the most desirable properties in Kensington.

In 1986, he organized a 60th birthday party in the West Indies which cost a reputed £500,000. Among the guests were

Princess Margaret, a long-time friend of Glenconner, Mick Jagger, Jerry Hall and Raquel Welch. In 1960, Glenconner had given the newly married Anthony Armstrong-Jones and Princess Margaret a 10-acre plot on Mustique, which helped raise its profile as an exclusive resort.

Glenconner married the daughter of the Earl of Leicester, who is a lady-in-waiting to Princess Margaret. But despite their 30-year marriage, their children have caused enormous problems. Eldest son Charlie was a heroin addict and their middle son Henry dropped out to teach transcendental meditation. He died of Aids, while their youngest, Chris, suffered horrific head injuries when he was in a motorbike crash in central America. Expected to die, he was in a coma for four months.

Despite his lifestyle, Glenconner has a good business brain and has managed to protect his fortune by shrewd property deals. The family frequently appear in the gossip columns of the tabloid press.

Edward Harrison £20m

CAR DEALER   dob (unknown)

THOMAS Cuthbert Harrison was in at the start of the motor age. After World War I he started work in Sheffield as an apprentice motor mechanic at the age of 14. In 1931, at the height of the Depression, he took the bold step of starting on his own with £500 capital, and soon afterwards he had a Ford dealership at his modest garage in the city's Abbeydale Road. It was tough going in the Depression and war years. But with the great expansion of car ownership in the 1950s, the T. C. Harrison Group really took off.

In 1968 Harrison decided to finance further expansion by taking the group on to the stock market. New branches were established in Sheffield, Rotherham, Derby and Peterborough. The group also began distributing Ford trucks and JCB diggers.

Thomas Harrison died in 1981 and his son Edward took over

as chairman. A year later the group won the coveted Ford National Gold Award. In 1984 Edward decided to take the group private again and, using the family's 37% stake in the business, bought out the other shareholders at a hefty 26p premium on the existing share price of 48p. The move valued the company at £16.6 million.

Today the group has its headquarters in London Road, Sheffield. It produced £2.5 million post-tax profits in 1988 on a £162 million turnover. With negligible borrowings and large cash reserves, the group could now fetch £20 million if floated on the stock market.

Edward Harrison lives in an old manorial hall in Derbyshire's beautiful Peak District.

Maurice Hatter   £20m

INDUSTRIALIST   dob (unknown)

IN 1948, Maurice Hatter left the Army's Royal Signals regiment, where he had worked as a radio mechanic, with just £100 in his pocket. 'I had a lot of ideas about electronics. I got a few off the ground and started a nice little electronics company,' he recalls. Ten years later, he sold that nice little company for £30,000. Two years later, he founded IMO Precision Controls, based in North London, which markets electronic components for leading companies. In 1989, it made £4.3 million post-tax profits on sales of over £32 million. In the same year, the Growth Companies Register singled out IMO Precision as a company with great potential. Hatter himself made the news in 1988 because his salary was over £1 million.

Hatter lives for his work and claims that 'money is a by-product'. He starts work soon after getting up at 7 a.m. After reading documents, he usually has a working breakfast with colleagues at 8 a.m. before driving to his factory off the North Circular Road at 9.30 a.m. He keeps going until 8.30 p.m. He lives in Regent's Park, London, and drives an Aston Martin. A father of four, Hatter is divorced. He supports charities, giving away £100,000 a year.

Peter Jones and family   £20m

INDUSTRIALISTS   dob PJ 5 August 1936

JONES Stroud Holdings is one of those small companies
that has been the backbone of the British economy for the
last 20 years. With a majority of the shares held by the Jones
family, this Nottingham company is in textiles and electrical
insulation, making accessories and material for both industries.
Originally a textile company founded in 1923, it started making
parachute cords during the war. This side of the business was
later adapted to the electrical industry and now it is the same
size as the textile business.

With family trusts and their own interests, the Jones family
have around 12 million of the 15 million shares in the group.
With the group being quoted on the stock market, this stake is
worth around £20 million. There are three Joneses on the board:
Philip, David and Peter. They are all in their fifties.

In its results for the year ending 31 January 1990, the group
made £6 million pre-tax profits on a £60.3 million turnover.
The family maintain a very low profile.

Christos Lazari   £20m

FASHIONWEAR AND PROPERTY   dob (unknown)

IN the early 1970s, Christos Lazari, a Greek-Cypriot immigrant from the small village of Dhora near Limassol, moved
to Britain and began working in the London fashion industry.
After several years gaining experience of different jobs, he set
up his own ladieswear and wholesale company in London. In
1978, the group, known as Christy Dresses, started to diversify
into property through a company called Lazaris Property Investments Ltd. Today, it is a large property player in central and
north London. Despite the problems with the London property
market, gross rentals of the property arm increased by 51% in
1990-91. Lazari's success in writing export markets for his fash-

ions to Eastern Europe was recognized when the Princess Royal visited his north London headquarters in May 1989. The business, with £51 million of assets, is totally owned by Lazari and his wife.

Anthony and Nicholas Marmont and family £20

DRINK MANUFACTURERS   dob (unknown)

IN the 1920s, the Marmont family bought out a Leicestershire drinks company called Carters, which had been established way back in 1894. Today, the Marmonts still control most of the shares in the flourishing business, which makes its own drinks, bottles and vending machines. Its drinks are sold under a variety of labels, including Lemontime, Diet Lemontime, Zzipp, English Royal and Sunspel, as well as the Carters name.

The group has enjoyed good growth in recent years. In 1986, it reported after-tax profits of £1.1 million on a £26.3 million turnover. This rose to £2.5 million profits in 1989 on a £45.6 million turnover. The number of employees also rose from around 420 to around 600, spread over three sites in the East Midlands. Two of the sites are modern complexes, including a new packaging plant at Long Eaton, near Nottingham.

The Marmont family still keep a close eye on the running of the company. Anthony Marmont is president; his son Nicholas, as chairman, is responsible for day-to-day operations. Other members of the Marmont family, including Anthony's wife Angela, are also large shareholders in the business.

The Marmonts are a proud family, proud of their success in business and of their Leicestershire roots. They live within a few miles of their plants in Loughborough.

The McLean family   £20m

PROPERTY HEIRS   dob (unknown)

THE former chairman and chief executive of CSE Aviation, Murray McLean, made his fortune running his own business in his native South Africa. He left the country in 1976 after the breakup of his first marriage and went to France with his new wife, gaining a degree at the Paris School of Economics.

He spent a year working for a charity in Cambodia during the aftermath of the Pol Pot regime and then came to England, settling in a manor house at Begbroke, Oxfordshire.

In 1981 he gained control of the plastics company Robert Moss Ltd, of Kidlington, Oxfordshire, with a bid which valued it at £3.2 million. In four years the company's value rose to £26 million and McLean made £4.5 million when he sold his shares to the Bunzl group in 1986.

In 1985 he became a non-executive director of CSE Aviation, which, with its air training school at Kidlington, is the largest general aviation organization in Europe. The following year he became its chairman and chief executive in a boardroom shake-up. In 1988 a new holding company, Oxford Airport Holdings, was formed to control all the issued share capital of its principal subsidiary, CSE Aviation.

McLean devoted a lot of his time to charity work, spending one day a week helping the trading side of Oxfam's operation. He died aged 54, never having recovered from a heart attack in 1988 shortly after marrying his third wife, Sophie. Control of the company was left to a family trust. In February 1990, the trust members decided to sell after reaching the conclusion that their future did not lie with aviation. The airport is valued at some £20 million. In 1990, it was finally sold to a Swedish aviation group keen to expand into Europe.

Richard Northcott   £20m

BUSINESSMAN AND FILM MAKER
dob 24 September 1947

CHARGED with sorting out his father's ailing paint and
wallpaper shops in Scotland, Richard Northcott visited
America in 1973. He came back with plans for Dodge City, a
chain of cut-price DIY shops. They were to be out of town,
with parking, refreshments, late-night shopping, as well as
Sunday opening. In all, he built 32 stores and, in 1980, he
doubled the size of the business by building 500,000 square feet
of space – more than any other UK retailer.

'Not bad when you consider I never invested a penny myself.
It was all borrowing from the bank, very low profit margins
and high stock turnover,' he later recalled. In 1981 he sold the
business to Woolworth, pocketing £17 million.

Educated at Blundell's, the West Country private school,
Northcott later trained as an accountant and worked as a financial investigator before his Dodge City experience. But even
after he had sold up, he was not finished with retailing. A year
later he started a new chain, Brown Bear, selling home furnishings and kitchens. He sold that in 1984 to Gerald Ronson's
(q.v.) Heron group for £5.5 million, only to see Ronson sell it
on within an hour to Sir Phil Harris (q.v.), the carpet tycoon.

He then tried his hand as a farmer and lotus-eater. 'I thought
it would be wonderful. I could relax and look at the farm. But I
was just bored,' he told the *Sunday Times*. He decided on a new
career as a Hollywood film producer, with Lord Anthony
Rufus-Isaacs, the Marquess of Reading's brother. Their biggest
success was the controversial film $9\frac{1}{2}$ *Weeks*, starring Kim Bas-
inger.

Northcott has been frequently spotted at fashionable parties
and often graces the gossip columns. He was a long-time friend
of Davina Phillips, a prominent London hostess and property
tycoon in her own right. She sold him her London house, worth
some £1.25 million. In 1985 he married Kirsten Lund, a Canadian model, whose sister married Lord Anthony Rufus-Isaacs.
Northcott lives in a £3 million white mansion overlooking Los

Angeles and, apart from his London house, he also owns a 900-acre Sussex farm.

Charles Patel   £20m

NEWSAGENTS AND ENERGY   dob (unknown)

BASED in north London, Chandrakant Babau (popularly known as Charles) Patel came to Britain from Fiji in 1958. He started his own retail operation in 1975 and today runs the Capital Newsagent chain via his holding company, Vapgate. Though there are nearly 300 shops in the chain, it has suffered in the 1990–91 downturn in retail sales. Patel is cushioned by a lucrative deal, selling land in Texas which turned out to have natural gas. He also owns substantial property interests in Australia and Britain. Patel enjoys a close relationship with the boards of top clearing banks. He has been involved in the campaign to draw attention to the plight of Fiji's Indian community following the army coup on the island. An active supporter of the Variety Club of Great Britain, Patel is married with two sons. He lives in some style in north London and drives a Rolls-Royce.

Dadu Patel   £20m

PROPERTY   dob (unknown)

BY the age of 21, Dadu Patel was already a veteran of the British business world. In 1963, he arrived from Kenya, at 19, to study for the bar at Lincoln's Inn. Two years later, he had already purchased his first commercial property. Today, aged 47, his property empire embraces pharmacy shops, a cash and carry, a stake in the five-star St James Court Hotel near Buckingham Palace and a string of clubs and shopping centres. He lives, surrounded by an extended family, in a large Surrey manor house. In a 1988 interview with the *Sunday Times* magazine, he attributed the success of Patels in business thus: 'If each household has six members earning £200 a week, that brings in £1200. Allow £400 for mortgage and general expenses and that leaves £800 to save. In five years the family has £200,000 without scrimping, and then you can really start to build a firm business base. The banks know that if they lend to one Patel, the whole family is involved, and so have been exceedingly good to us.'

Anwar Pervez   £20m

RETAILER   dob *c.* 1934

THE big name in cash and carry is Anwar Pervez, head of Bestway, which he started in 1976. Group turnover in the year to the end of June 1989 was £340 million (18% increase on the previous year), giving a profit of £7.2 million (16% increase on the previous year). This has been increasing at the rate of 20% a year. He has contributed £140,000 recently to the fund set up by Prince Charles to regenerate industry. His first shop was in the Park Royal area of west London. His operation is now highly computerized. He drives a Mercedes.

Robin Phillips   £20m

INDUSTRIALIST   dob 4 April 1933

ROBIN Phillips's fortune is built on the hand dryers found in virtually every public lavatory. His company, Warner Howard, in which he is the largest shareholder, rents out hand dryers by the thousand and makes a fortune as a result.

In the early 1960s, Phillips worked in Canada for a local company which owned a British offshoot, Coinamatic. In 1964, Phillips (Kidderminster Grammar School, first class honours in Economics from the London School of Economics and a qualified chartered accountant) was sent to become managing director of Coinamatic in London. The company then specialized in renting coin-operated washing machines.

By 1980, the Canadian parent was losing interest in the business, and a management buy-out was launched, backed by a venture capitalist. A year later, the Warner Howard hand-drying business was bought and the combined group was renamed after it. In 1987, the group came to the stock market, and today Robin Phillips has over 11 million shares. The company produced record profits of £2.3 million in the first half of 1989.

Though ill-health has forced him to take a back seat, he is still involved in strategic decision-making. He lists his hobbies as cricket and swimming.

Lionel Pickering   £20m

EX-JOURNALIST AND PUBLISHER   dob (unknown)

THE manor house in Derbyshire complete with tennis court and 50 acres is a far cry from Lionel Pickering's early days as a junior reporter on the *Burton Chronicle*. But this ex-journalist established one of the largest chains of free newspapers in the country, the Trader group, which he sold to the Thomson group for £25 million in the summer of 1989.

Starting as a junior reporter in 1957 after his National Service, Pickering later became a sports reporter and subeditor with the *Derby Evening Telegraph* before emigrating to Australia. He worked first with a news agency; then he moved from job to job, including a spell working for Rupert Murdoch, developing his skills.

Fed up with the rat-race in Australia, Pickering came back to Derby in 1966, bringing his Australian wife with him and moving into a terraced house bought for him by his parents. Having seen the success of free newspapers in Australia (82 in the Sydney area alone), he decided to try his luck in the East Midlands. For Christmas 1966, he started a free eight-page paper in Derby. 'I did the lot – sold the advertising, wrote the copy, did the layout and headlines and even delivered the bloody thing,' he later recalled.

It was a struggle at first. Despite his living on just £5 a week, the paper was consuming his £800 savings and a lot of money from his parents. But in the end he survived and prospered by ploughing the profits into the business and expanding into other areas. In 1974, he opened a purpose-built factory to produce the papers. Learning about management from reading teach-yourself books, Pickering eventually turned the group into a thriving business and the offers started coming in. He did not want to sell but in the end, he says, 'I thought of a number, doubled it and added 50% and Thomson said okay. My bluff was called.' In 1988, the Trader group made profits of £1.4 million on its 10 titles.

Though he planned to stay on for a year to help Thomson with the takeover, Pickering says he has no intention of going back into free papers, but will look around at new business opportunities.

Rajan Pillai   £20m

FOODS   dob (unknown)

RAJAN Pillai is head of the Singapore-based biscuit and snack empire, Britannia Industries. Although most of his business interests are in South and South-East Asia, 44-year-old Pillai spends most of his time in London on the look-out for potential acquisitions. He inherited his father's business, selling out in 1974 to a company that was eventually taken over by RJR Nabisco. In the past three years, Pillai has turned the tables and has busily been buying up Nabisco's biscuit and snack interests in India, Pakistan, New Zealand, Australia and South-East Asia. A close friend and business partner of Indian tennis star, Vijay Amritraj, Pillai intends starting an air taxi service in India with a Swiss firm. He is in a joint venture with a French biscuit company.

Alan Prince £20m

IN 1971, Alan Prince, a pharmacist based in Southampton, was fed up with managing shops for Boots or Westons. 'I wasn't prepared to sit there and count the days to my retirement.' So he and his wife Sylvia, a legal secretary, sold a plot in their back garden for £3,000 and opened their own chemist shop in the Bitterne area of Southampton.

Prince had seen how cut-price chemist shops worked while on a trip to America. He determined to try the same in Britain, cutting out the wholesaler and having self-service in the stores. It was an immediate success. By 1980, he had 25 shops, and by 1984 there were 50. That year, Sharedrug, as his group was called, came to the stock market and was well received by investors. A year later, with profits rising strongly, there were 74 stores. The business also began to expand out of its Solent heartland into the Midlands and the West Country. Early in 1988, Prince decided to accept an offer from Woolworth for the chain, which was 145-strong by this time. The £32 million price resulted in Prince and his wife netting some £20 million. At that point he announced that he was retiring at the age of 44.

William Salomon and family £20m

WILLIAM Salomon, a City banker, inherited a fortune when his father, the legendary banker, Sir Walter Salomon, died in 1987. Sir Walter was born in 1906 in Hamburg, where his family had been bankers for several hundred years. Through the 1920s, he saw the terrible inflation of the Weimar Republic and the rise of the Nazis. When their persecution reached its height in the late 1930s, Sir Walter came to Britain with £2,000 in his pocket, though he had access to considerable interests in Canada. In 1937, he set himself up as a merchant banker, but his real success came after the war when, in 1950, he bought the respected City bank, Rea Brothers. For the next thirty-four years, he built up a business empire, embracing shipping, banking and trading. He admired Mrs Thatcher, who knighted him and dubbed him 'sergeant major of the awkward squad' for his strong monetarist views and passionate belief in sound money.

Salomon relished difficult takeover battles, winning some and losing others. But at the end of his career, Rea Brothers was nearly wiped out after a disastrous purchase of a stake in a Dutch bank resulted in Rea's inner reserves almost being lost. After he died in 1987, his son William has been trying to reorganize and simplify the web of complex companies.

John Seddon and family   £20m

CONSTRUCTION CONTRACTORS AND
DEVELOPERS   dob (unknown)

GEORGE and John Seddon were two Lancashire bricklayers who formed their own company, G & J Seddon, at Worsley, near Bolton, in 1897.

Until the building boom after World War II, the company was a relatively small-scale operation. Today it is one of the ten largest privately owned contractors in the country. All the shares in the group are still held by the Seddon family, which is now in its third generation of running the business.

The company has spread out of contracting into property development, housebuilding and managing country and golf clubs. But it specializes in the medium-sized contracts, rather than huge but risky multimillion-pound contracts. It was responsible for the award-winning Wigan Pier development.

With some 1,600 employees in its nine subsidiary companies, the Seddon group had a £76.3 million turnover in 1989 and after-tax profits of £2.46 million. If the family were to sell today, the company could fetch around £20 million.

Apart from its strong profit performance, the Seddon group

is rich in assets. It owns the Tytherington Links estate in exclusive Cheshire, centred on a health and country club and golf course.

John Seddon, a third-generation member, is chairman of the business, with Christopher, another third-generation Seddon, also on the board. The fourth generation are now beginning to make their mark on the management of the firm.

Notoriously publicity-shy, the Seddons are also very downbeat in displaying their wealth. Large houses or luxury cars are rare and the family still live in the Manchester area – albeit in the Cheshire stockbroker belt. They are known to be strong supporters of local charities.

Eddie Shah £20m

PUBLISHER   dob 20 January 1944

EDDIE Shah's roots gave few clues to his later role as architect of a British industrial revolution. The son of a prominent international lawyer who married the daughter of a well-known Cambridge boat-building family, Eddie spent several years of his childhood in India, before embarking on a thoroughly English middle-class education, which he did not take to at all. He was 'suspended' from Gordonstoun, and then went to a Reigate grammar school before finally ending up at a Haywards Heath secondary modern school. He led a self-confessed 'wild' life, and left school without O-levels. His real love was sport and at Gordonstoun he held nine athletics records.

After his education, Shah worked as an assistant stage manager in a theatre and had a small walk-on part in one play. This character was called Eddie, and the name has stuck with him ever since, replacing his real name, Selim Jehane. He went on to become floor manager on *Coronation Street*, the hugely popular soap opera.

After a spell working as a space salesman on a free newspaper published by the *Manchester Evening News*, he decided in March 1974 to start on his own. With £3,000 raised by mortgaging his home and a further £6,000 invested by two friends, he launched the *Sale and Altrincham Messenger*. In the first year, he lost £10,000, but built up a 35,000 circulation and went from strength to strength. By 1983, he had built up profits of £600,000 on a £5 million turnover, and enjoyed the fruits of success such as a large BMW car and his own private plane – registration mark G-BOSS. A golf addict, he collects antique clubs and at one time played off a handicap of three.

But in 1983 he rose to national prominence when he had a huge battle with the then all-powerful National Graphical Association over union recognition at his Stockport works. Thousands of pickets attempted to besiege his plant, while he was subject to a number of death threats. Coffins were even delivered to his home for his family. In the end, he won the battle and determined to break the grip of the print unions nationally by opening a new non-union national newspaper called *Today*. Despite its brave campaigning style and a bold use of colour, it was a financial disaster and had to be taken over by Lonrho. Eventually, Lonrho sold *Today* to Rupert Murdoch.

Shah then retreated back to the north, and continued to run the Messenger group. But in 1988 he decided to enter television production, sensing that the television industry was about to undergo the same transformation as newspapers. He also had another go at launching a paper, but the *Post*, a tabloid without sleaze, was not a success and folded after just 33 issues. The experience seems to have left a scar on Shah, who at the same time sold the by then 20-strong Messenger chain to Reed International for £25 million. He has retained the Messenger assets, valued at around £7 million, and has said he intends to concentrate on television production, property development and providing seed-corn capital for small businesses.

Ian Skelly   £20m

FORMER CAR DEALER   dob (unknown)

MOTHERWELL-BORN and bred, Ian Skelly worked
with his two brothers, Billy and Sherwood, in their
father's Ford dealership, which they expanded enormously until
a bitter dispute in 1974. Ian set up on his own and on American
Independence Day, July 4 1976, he opened the Ian Skelly group
in derelict premises in Glasgow's Rutherglen district.

It was at the height of a recession and a fuel crisis, but Skelly
reckoned that high-technology, fuel-efficient German cars
would prove winners in Scotland. He used an impressive sales
technique developed from numerous visits to America, and he
expected all his staff, from top to bottom, to wear the blue
company pullovers, blazers and overalls. He fitted coffee bars,
television rooms and children's play areas to keep his customers
happy during a sales pitch. In 1981, he had expanded into
Liverpool and, in May 1989, a £5 million centre opened in Manchester.

By then, he had Europe's highest volume VW-Audi network,
with annual sales of nearly £100 million. At this point Skelly
decided to sell up, and netted £18.3 million from the Leeds-
based Appleyard group. He chose Appleyard because they
promised to look after his 490 staff.

Skelly sold because he had been working seven days a week
on the business, rarely relaxing apart from playing tennis at his
luxury Carluke home. The death of his father hastened his
decision, as did the fact that he had no son to take over. 'I
reckoned we had become too big for me to give that personal
touch,' he told the *Glasgow Herald*.

Skelly and his wife Rita owned all the shares in the business.
They are regarded as generous supporters of charity. He is also
a large shareholder and sponsor of Motherwell, the Scottish
Football club.

With the money in his pocket from the sale, Skelly said, 'I
don't know what I shall do in the future but right now I am
going to have a rest. I want to travel and do what I want to do
before I am too old. One thing is sure – I'll remain in Scotland.

I have never considered becoming a tax exile. I'm happy to stay and pay my taxes and enjoy my football, despite the weather.'

Bob Sperring £20m

RETAILER   dob (unknown)

STARTING out in his father's newsagent's shop in a suburb of Southampton in 1965, Bob Sperring built up a chain of convenience stores open for 12 hours a day, 7 days a week. By his early 30s, Sperring was a millionaire, and Sperrings, as the chain was called, was a big success. At the age of 42 he decided to sell the business and pocketed nearly £20 million to add to his considerable fortune. But the company's growth had nearly cost him his health and he suffered a heart attack from the huge strain of work.

Today, Sperring lives in a luxury house in Southampton, and lists his hobbies as property consultancy, travel, skiing, tennis and shooting. He has also supported the Solent Stars, the highly rated local basketball team. He is also a director of the local radio station.

Dave Stewart £20m

POP MUSICIAN   dob 9 September 1952

BORN in Sunderland of 'respectable lower middle-class' parents, who separated when he was 14, Dave Stewart left home at 17 to make his fortune in London.

He formed his first band, Longdancer, which signed the first ever record contract with Elton John's Rocket label in 1973. It was not a success and Stewart moved into a Crouch End flat, parted from his wife and got caught up in the pop drug scene, abandoning hope of a music career.

But a chance meeting with a waitress in a North London

restaurant in 1977 changed his life for ever. It was love at first sight for Stewart and Annie Lennox, a drop-out from the Royal College of Music. They formed their own band, The Tourists, which achieved a number-one hit with a new version of 'I Only Want To Be With You'. A year later The Tourists disbanded, but the duo kept together and in 1981 achieved a hit as The Eurythmics with 'Love is a Stranger'. Though the pair ceased to be lovers in 1980, The Eurythmics survived and prospered. Some 16 million LPs have been sold.

Stewart has also moved into record production and set up his own recording studio in an old Crouch End church. Superstars such as Bob Dylan, Mick Jagger and George Harrison have had records produced by Stewart, making him one of the world's top producers.

In 1987, he set up his own record label, called Anxious. He recorded a song by his old chauffeur, but that was a flop.

Today Stewart has abandoned drugs for a healthier life and he has large homes in London and Los Angeles. He enjoys the company of other pop stars such as Mick Jagger and has been linked with a string of girl friends, the last of whom was Siobhan Fahey of Bananarama. 'I rang her up and said: "I can't get you off my mind and that's the top and bottom of it. What are we going to do about it?"' They are now married and have a baby.

John Sunley   £20m

PROPERTY DEALER   dob (unknown)

BERNARD Sunley started work at 14, 'muck-shifting', but later became a prominent Mayfair property developer and builder in the 1950s and early 1960s. He also ran a thriving plant hire business based in Northamptonshire. His son John took over the business in 1964 on his father's premature death, and has found himself a regular in the gossip as well as the financial pages of the national media. In 1960, at the age of 24, Sunley broke off his engagement to an ex-debutante, Judith Lund. At the time he was working for his father and he was also a rally car driver. Six months later, he was engaged again and was described in the press as 'young sporting Mr Sunley – he is keen on cricket, golf, and shooting – [who] is regarded as one of the up-and-coming powers in the building and property worlds'. He married and had 4 children but 13 years later the couple were divorced. John Sunley married again. But his second marriage also ended, with his ex-wife Anne receiving a £1 million divorce settlement. Sunley is a keen golfer and friend of Dennis Thatcher. He lives in a large country house overlooking Sandwich golf course. He also has a town house in Belgravia. In recent years, he has become embroiled in the bitter battle between Tiny Rowland (q.v.), the head of Lonrho, and the Al-Fayed brothers over the ownership of the House of Fraser Group. At one time he supported the Al Fayed brothers when they tried to become UK citizens, an attempt that they subsequently abandoned.

John Sunley's business affairs prospered in the late 1970s. The Sunley group won a £53 million contract in Dubai and John Sunley enjoyed close contacts with the oil-rich sheikhs. In 1977 he bought Heath House, London's highest house, near Hampstead Heath, for £450,000. But in little over a year he had sold it for £625,000 to a Saudi buyer. In that time, Sunley never lived there. Just 20 days later, the Arab put it on the market for £2 million, an increase in price of £68,750 per day. The Bernard Sunley group was also making a reputation in the late 1970s and early 1980s for its astute buying and selling of large blocks of London flats which were left in the hands of the financial institutions after the 1973–4 property crash. In 1977, Sunley bought many blocks from Sun Alliance, and bought 20 blocks from Legal & General for £27 million. Most were sold within a few weeks at a substantial profit.

Rashmi Thakrar   £20m

FOODS   dob (unknown)

THE Thakrar family were expelled from Uganda in 1972 by Idi Amin. Like many Ugandan Asians, they prospered in Britain and today they own Tilda Rice Ltd, one of the biggest rice suppliers in the country. Based in Rainham in Essex, the business was started by Narsibhai Thakrar but his son Rashmi now runs it. He buys rice from India, Pakistan, Italy, America and Surinam. The family also own a private dock to import the rice and a mill to prepare it. Thakrar claims the title 'Britain's rice-king', with some 52% of the retail trade.

Value Index

VALUE INDEX / 399

Name Index

FOR THE BEST IN PAPERBACKS, LOOK FOR THE 🐧

In every corner of the world, on every subject under the sun, Penguin represents quality and variety – the very best in publishing today.

For complete information about books available from Penguin – including Puffins, Penguin Classics and Arkana – and how to order them, write to us at the appropriate address below. Please note that for copyright reasons the selection of books varies from country to country.

In the United Kingdom: Please write to *Dept E.P., Penguin Books Ltd, Harmondsworth, Middlesex, UB7 0DA.*

If you have any difficulty in obtaining a title, please send your order with the correct money, plus ten per cent for postage and packaging, to *PO Box No 11, West Drayton, Middlesex*

In the United States: Please write to *Dept BA, Penguin, 299 Murray Hill Parkway, East Rutherford, New Jersey 07073*

In Canada: Please write to *Penguin Books Canada Ltd, 2801 John Street, Markham, Ontario L3R 1B4*

In Australia: Please write to the *Marketing Department, Penguin Books Australia Ltd, P.O. Box 257, Ringwood, Victoria 3134*

In New Zealand: Please write to the *Marketing Department, Penguin Books (NZ) Ltd, Private Bag, Takapuna, Auckland 9*

In India: Please write to *Penguin Overseas Ltd, 706 Eros Apartments, 56 Nehru Place, New Delhi, 110019*

In the Netherlands: Please write to *Penguin Books Netherlands B.V., Postbus 195, NL–1380AD Weesp*

In West Germany: Please write to *Penguin Books Ltd, Friedrichstrasse 10–12, D–6000 Frankfurt/Main 1*

In Spain: Please write to *Alhambra Longman S.A., Fernandez de la Hoz 9, E–28010 Madrid*

In Italy: Please write to *Penguin Italia s.r.l., Via Como 4, I-20096 Pioltello (Milano)*

In France: Please write to *Penguin Books Ltd, 39 Rue de Montmorency, F-75003 Paris*

In Japan: Please write to *Longman Penguin Japan Co Ltd, Yamaguchi Building, 2–12–9 Kanda Jimbocho, Chiyoda-Ku, Tokyo 101*